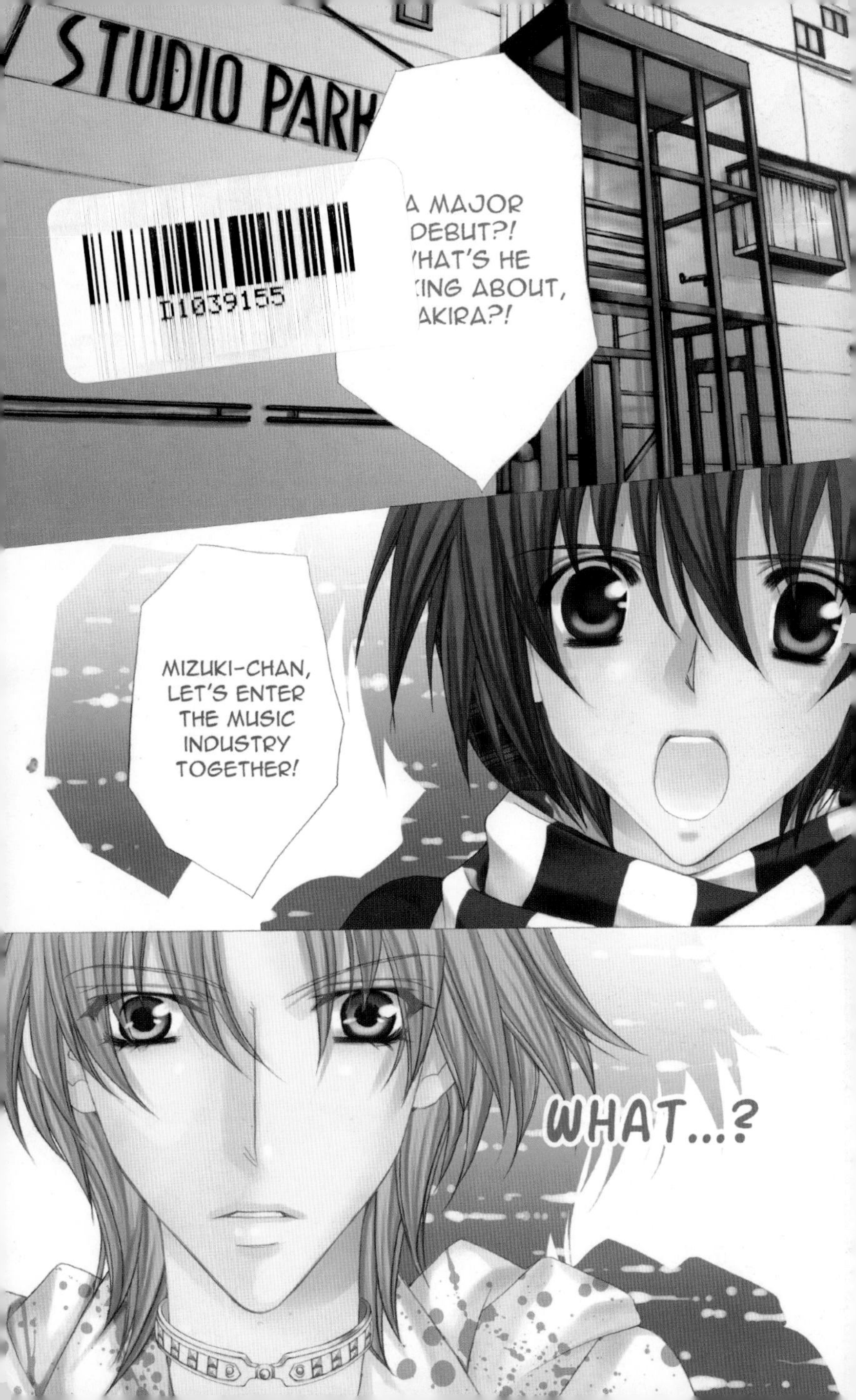
STUDIO PARK
A MAJOR DEBUT?! HAT'S HE KING ABOUT, AKIRA?!
MIZUKI-CHAN, LET'S ENTER THE MUSIC INDUSTRY TOGETHER!
WHAT...?

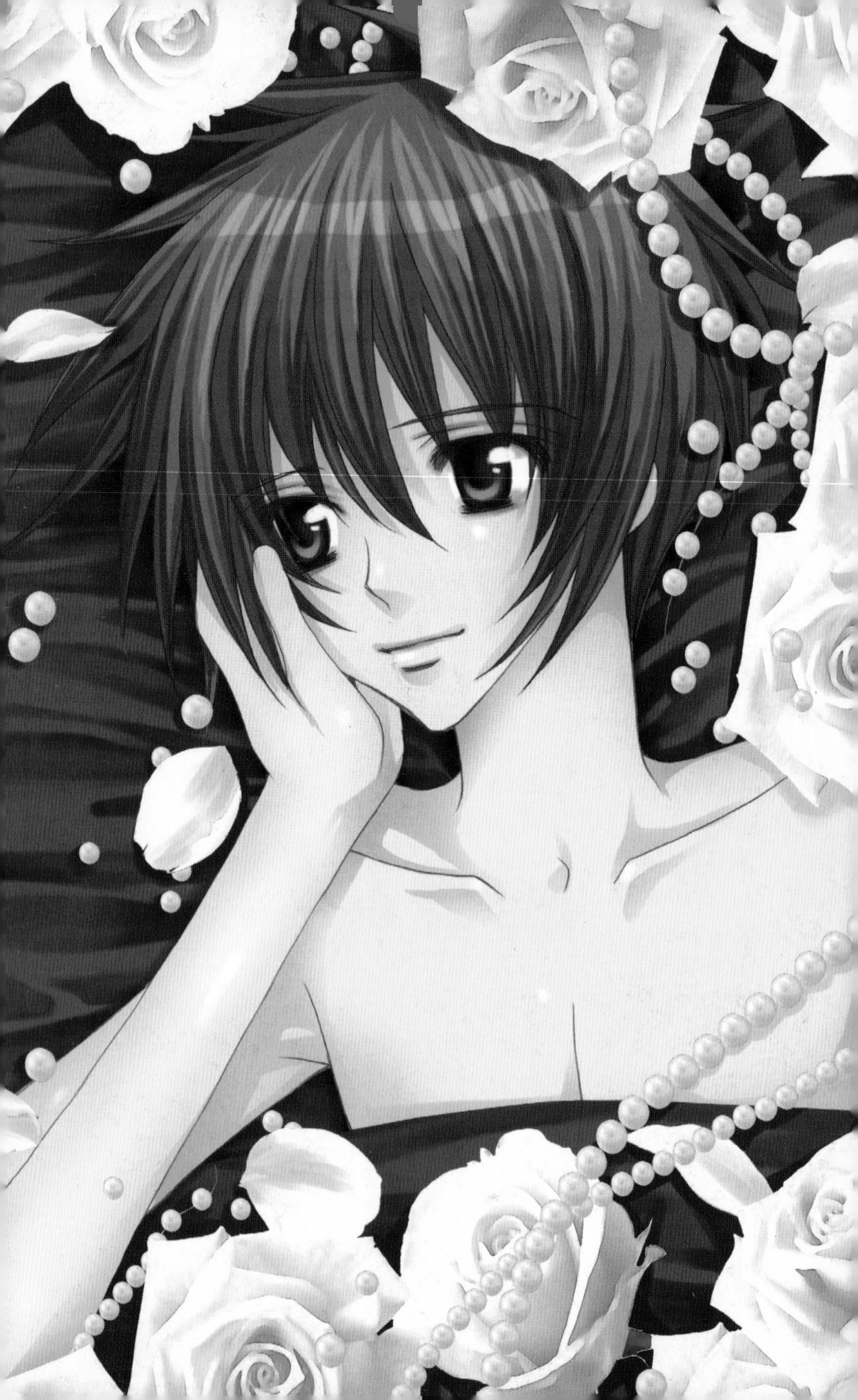

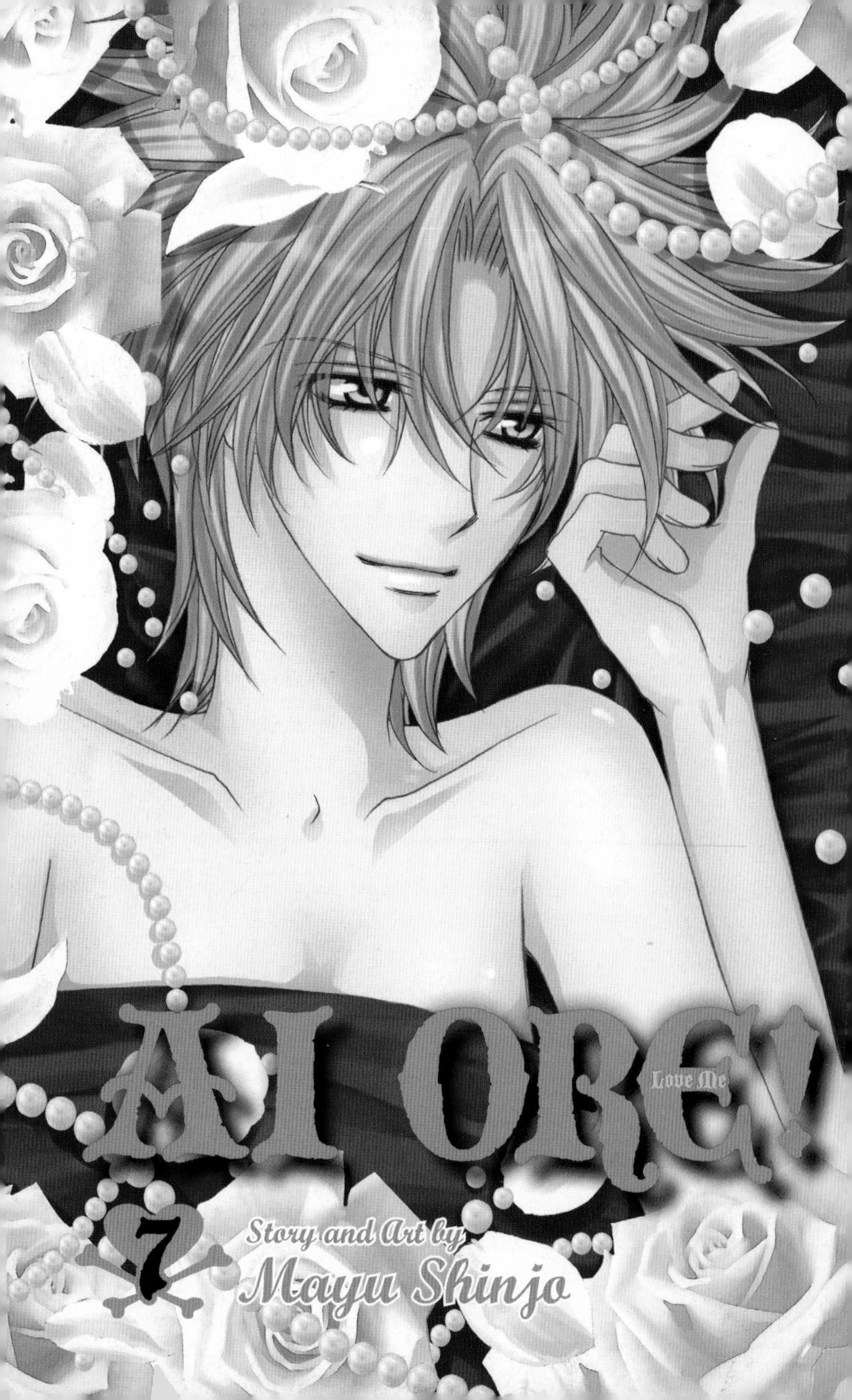
AI ORE!
Love Me
7
Story and Art by
Mayu Shinjo

AI ORE!
Love Me

7

Story Thus Far

❦ Mizuki, the "prince" of St. Nobara Academy, an elite all-girls school, is dating Akira, the "princess" of Dankaisan, an infamous all-boys school next door. The two are members of Blaue Rosen, a girl band.

❦ Blaue Rosen are back after the summer vacation, and their former lead singer, Kaoru, returns from New York for a while! All the band members are overjoyed at Kaoru's return except Akira, who has mixed feelings…

❦ As the band is practicing for their upcoming show at St. Nobara's school festival, a man from a talent agency appears. Akira has struck a deal with the agency, agreeing to sign with them as long as Blaue Rosen has a major debut with him as the lead singer. But he didn't tell Mizuki or the others about it…?!

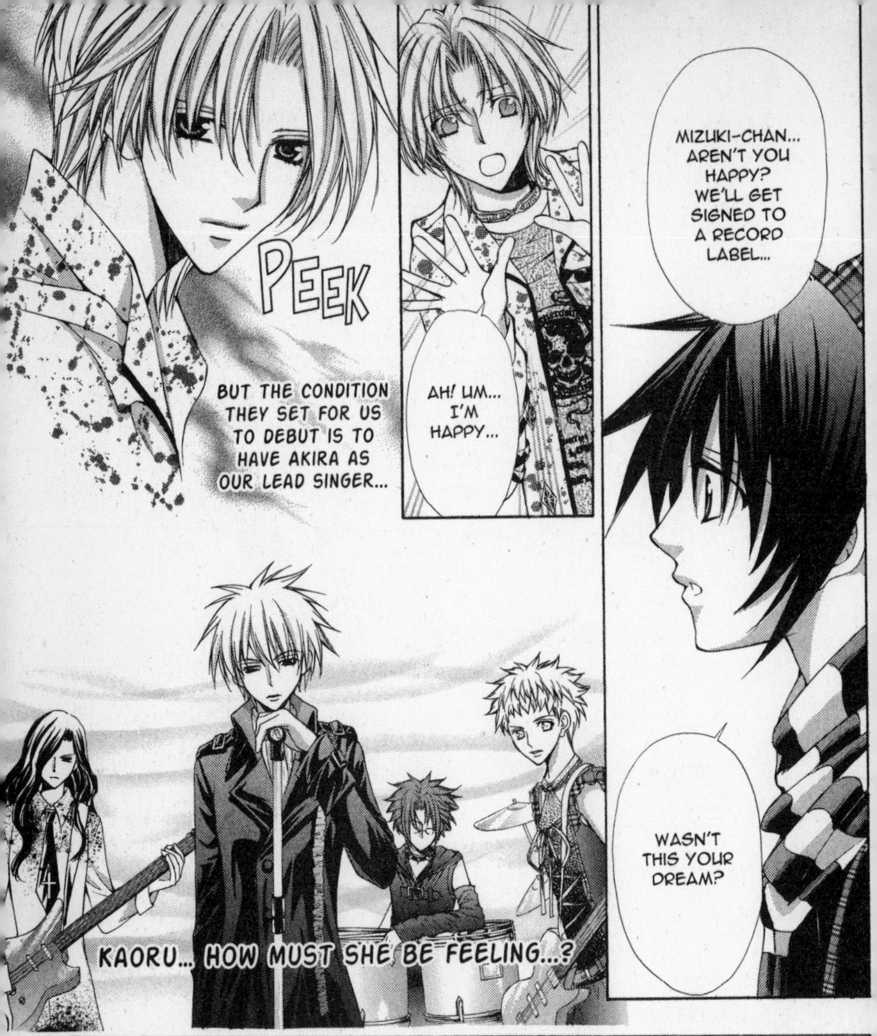
MIZUKI-CHAN... AREN'T YOU HAPPY? WE'LL GET SIGNED TO A RECORD LABEL...
WASN'T THIS YOUR DREAM?
AH! UM... I'M HAPPY...
PEEK
BUT THE CONDITION THEY SET FOR US TO DEBUT IS TO HAVE AKIRA AS OUR LEAD SINGER...
KAORU... HOW MUST SHE BE FEELING...?

Ai Ore! volume 7!!

I don't think anyone reading this is new to the series now. I'm sorry I made you wait for such a long time, but I've finally been able to release this volume!! And to top it off, the first part of this series, which I had created during my Shogakukan days, will be rereleased in Japan by Kadokawa Shoten! For those who started reading this series later on and never read the first volumes, please check it out. And I did a new cover illustration for the "I've read it before!" people too. It has a really nice design, so please pick up a set for home or to hand out to your friends. Thank you very much!

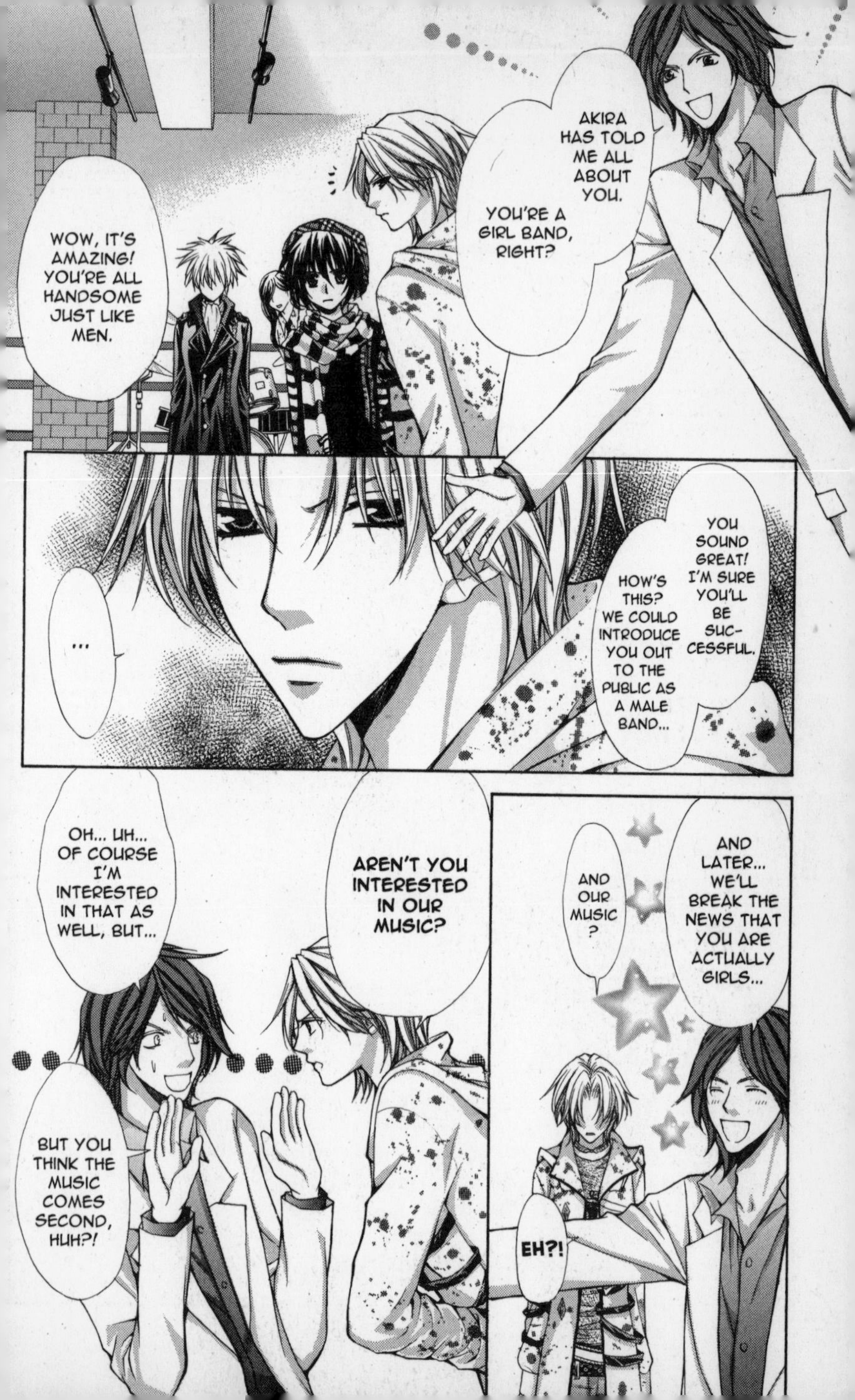
AKIRA HAS TOLD ME ALL ABOUT YOU.
YOU'RE A GIRL BAND, RIGHT?
WOW, IT'S AMAZING! YOU'RE ALL HANDSOME JUST LIKE MEN.
YOU SOUND GREAT! I'M SURE YOU'LL BE SUC-CESSFUL.
HOW'S THIS? WE COULD INTRODUCE YOU OUT TO THE PUBLIC AS A MALE BAND...
...
AND LATER... WE'LL BREAK THE NEWS THAT YOU ARE ACTUALLY GIRLS...
AND OUR MUSIC?
EH?!
AREN'T YOU INTERESTED IN OUR MUSIC?
OH... UH... OF COURSE I'M INTERESTED IN THAT AS WELL, BUT...
BUT YOU THINK THE MUSIC COMES SECOND, HUH?!

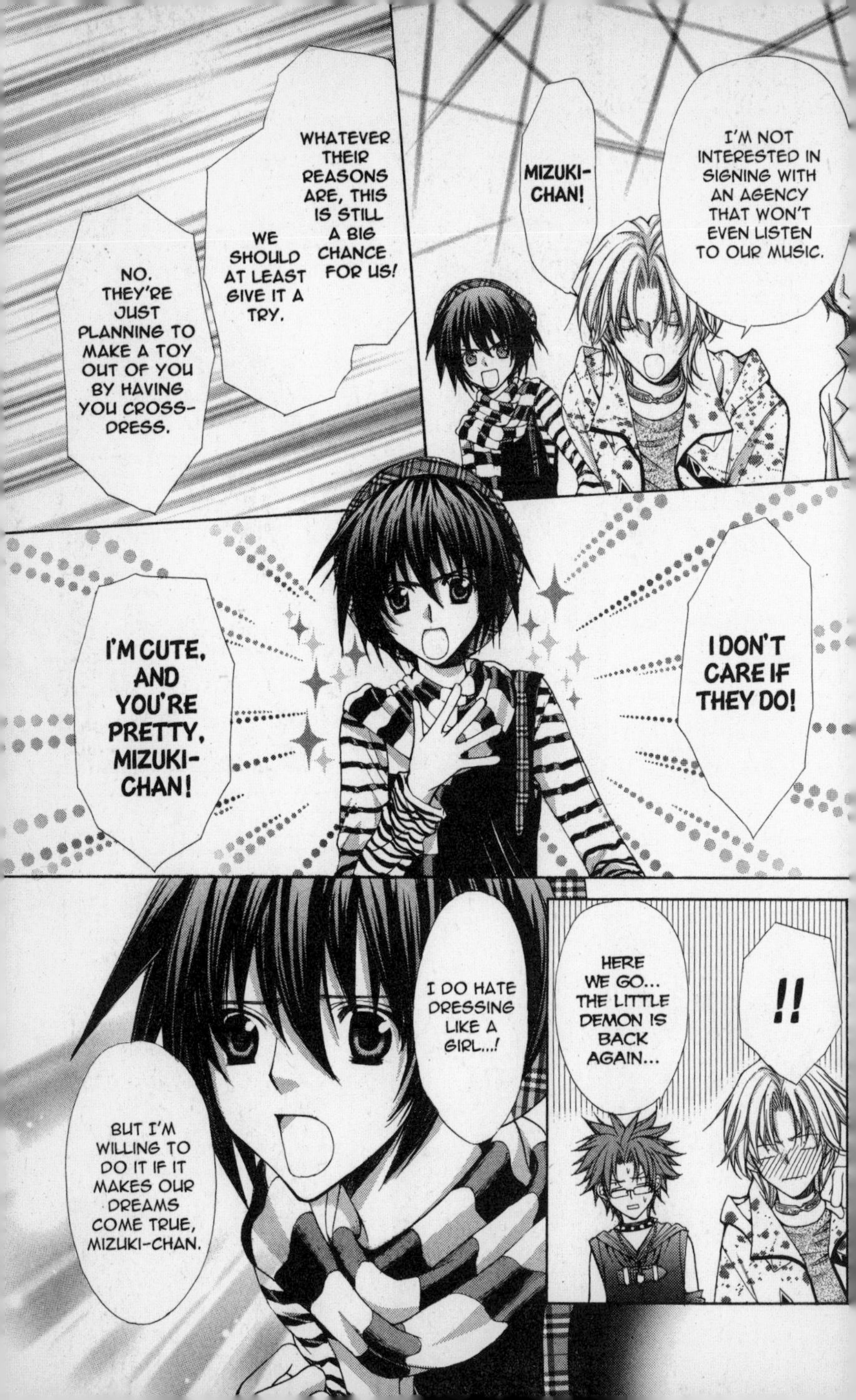
I'M NOT INTERESTED IN SIGNING WITH AN AGENCY THAT WON'T EVEN LISTEN TO OUR MUSIC.
MIZUKI-CHAN!
WHATEVER THEIR REASONS ARE, THIS IS STILL A BIG CHANCE FOR US!
WE SHOULD AT LEAST GIVE IT A TRY.
NO. THEY'RE JUST PLANNING TO MAKE A TOY OUT OF YOU BY HAVING YOU CROSS-DRESS.
I DON'T CARE IF THEY DO!
I'M CUTE, AND YOU'RE PRETTY, MIZUKI-CHAN!
I DO HATE DRESSING LIKE A GIRL...!
BUT I'M WILLING TO DO IT IF IT MAKES OUR DREAMS COME TRUE, MIZUKI-CHAN.
!!
HERE WE GO... THE LITTLE DEMON IS BACK AGAIN...

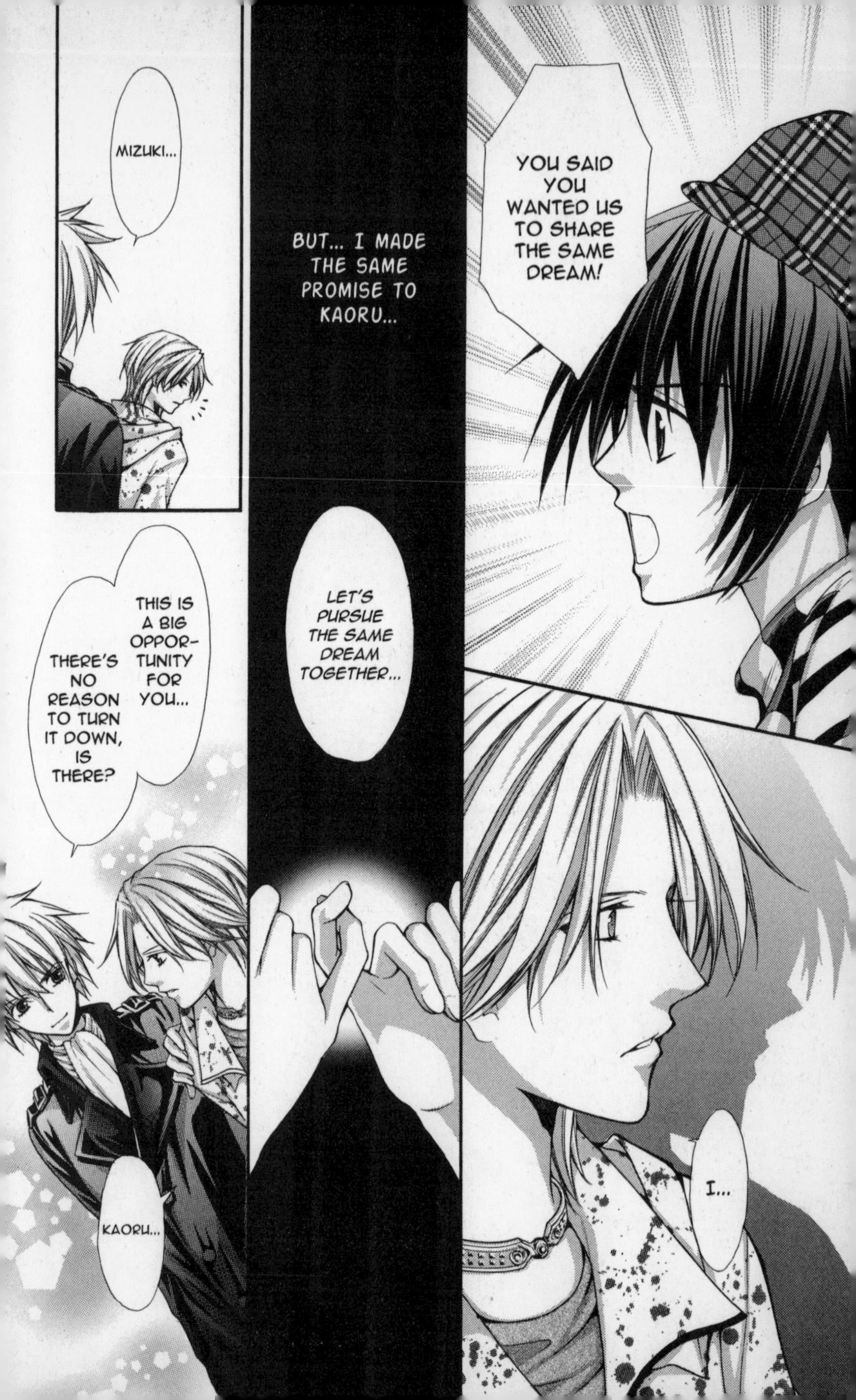
YOU SAID YOU WANTED US TO SHARE THE SAME DREAM!
I...
BUT... I MADE THE SAME PROMISE TO KAORU...
LET'S PURSUE THE SAME DREAM TOGETHER...
MIZUKI...
THIS IS A BIG OPPOR-TUNITY FOR YOU...
THERE'S NO REASON TO TURN IT DOWN, IS THERE?
KAORU...

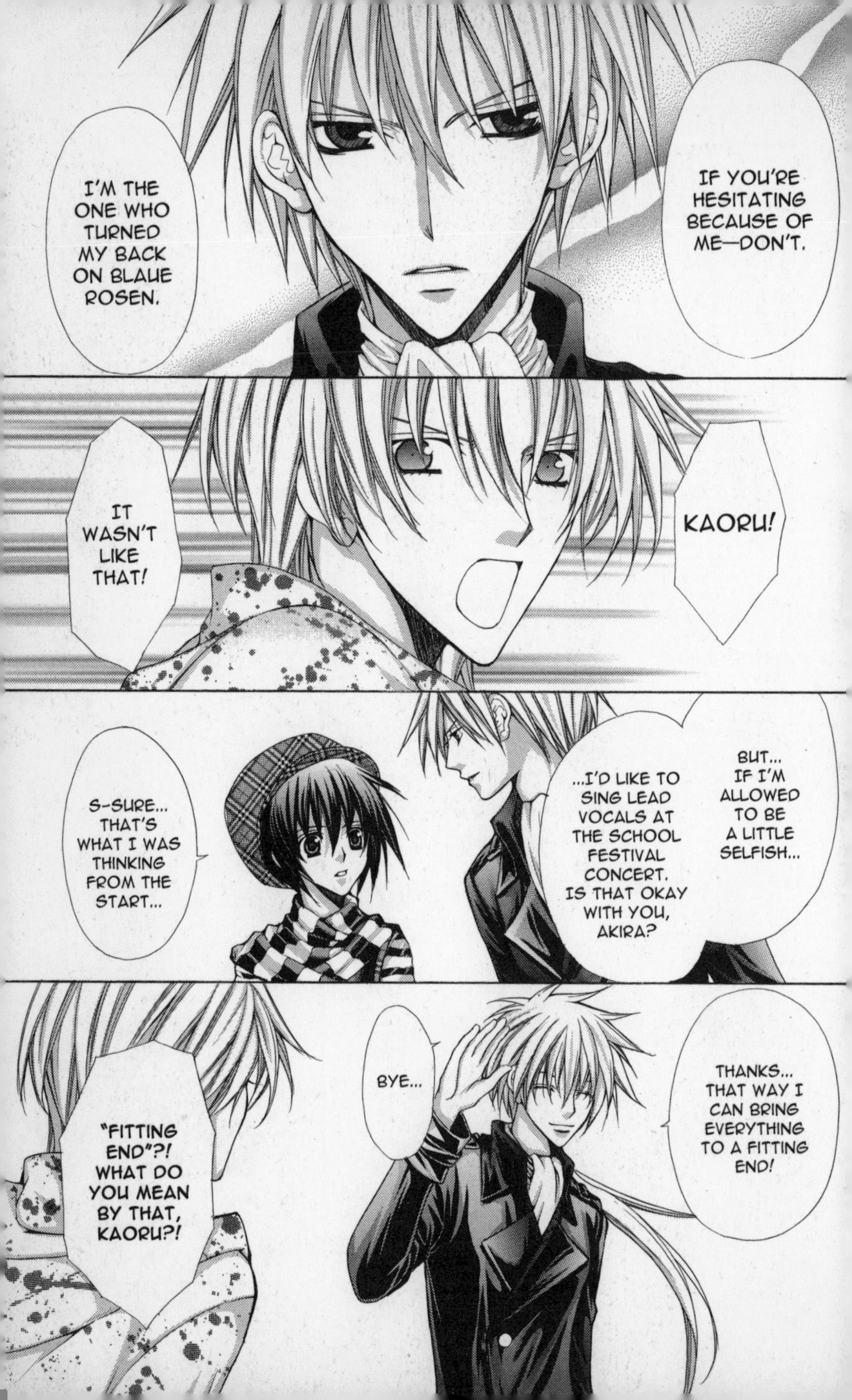
IF YOU'RE HESITATING BECAUSE OF ME—DON'T.
I'M THE ONE WHO TURNED MY BACK ON BLAUE ROSEN.
KAORU!
IT WASN'T LIKE THAT!
BUT... IF I'M ALLOWED TO BE A LITTLE SELFISH...
...I'D LIKE TO SING LEAD VOCALS AT THE SCHOOL FESTIVAL CONCERT. IS THAT OKAY WITH YOU, AKIRA?
S-SURE... THAT'S WHAT I WAS THINKING FROM THE START...
THANKS... THAT WAY I CAN BRING EVERYTHING TO A FITTING END!
BYE...
"FITTING END"?! WHAT DO YOU MEAN BY THAT, KAORU?!

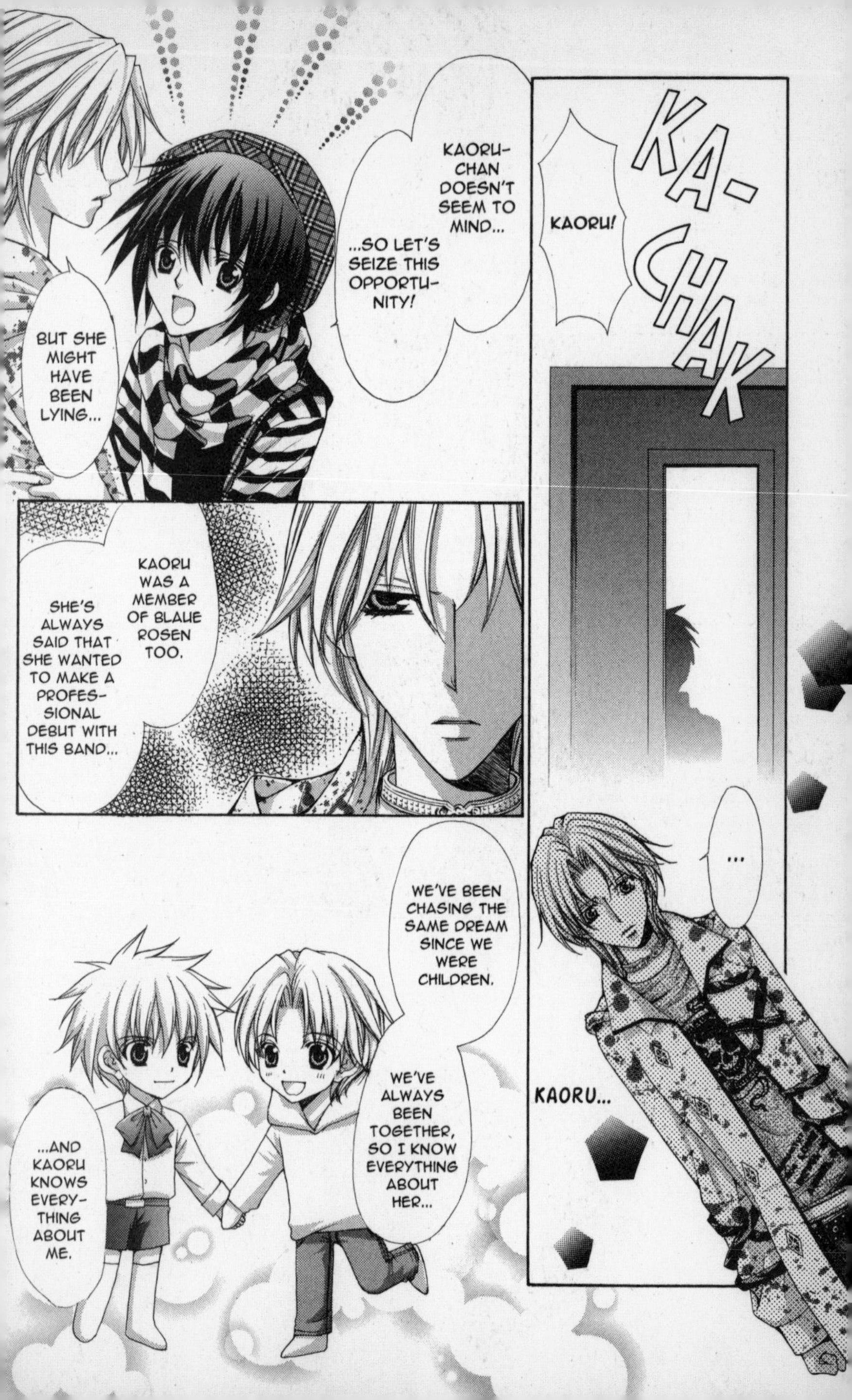
KA-CHAK
KAORU!
...
KAORU...
KAORU-CHAN DOESN'T SEEM TO MIND...
...SO LET'S SEIZE THIS OPPORTUNITY!
BUT SHE MIGHT HAVE BEEN LYING...
KAORU WAS A MEMBER OF BLAUE ROSEN TOO.
SHE'S ALWAYS SAID THAT SHE WANTED TO MAKE A PROFESSIONAL DEBUT WITH THIS BAND...
WE'VE BEEN CHASING THE SAME DREAM SINCE WE WERE CHILDREN.
WE'VE ALWAYS BEEN TOGETHER, SO I KNOW EVERYTHING ABOUT HER...
...AND KAORU KNOWS EVERYTHING ABOUT ME.

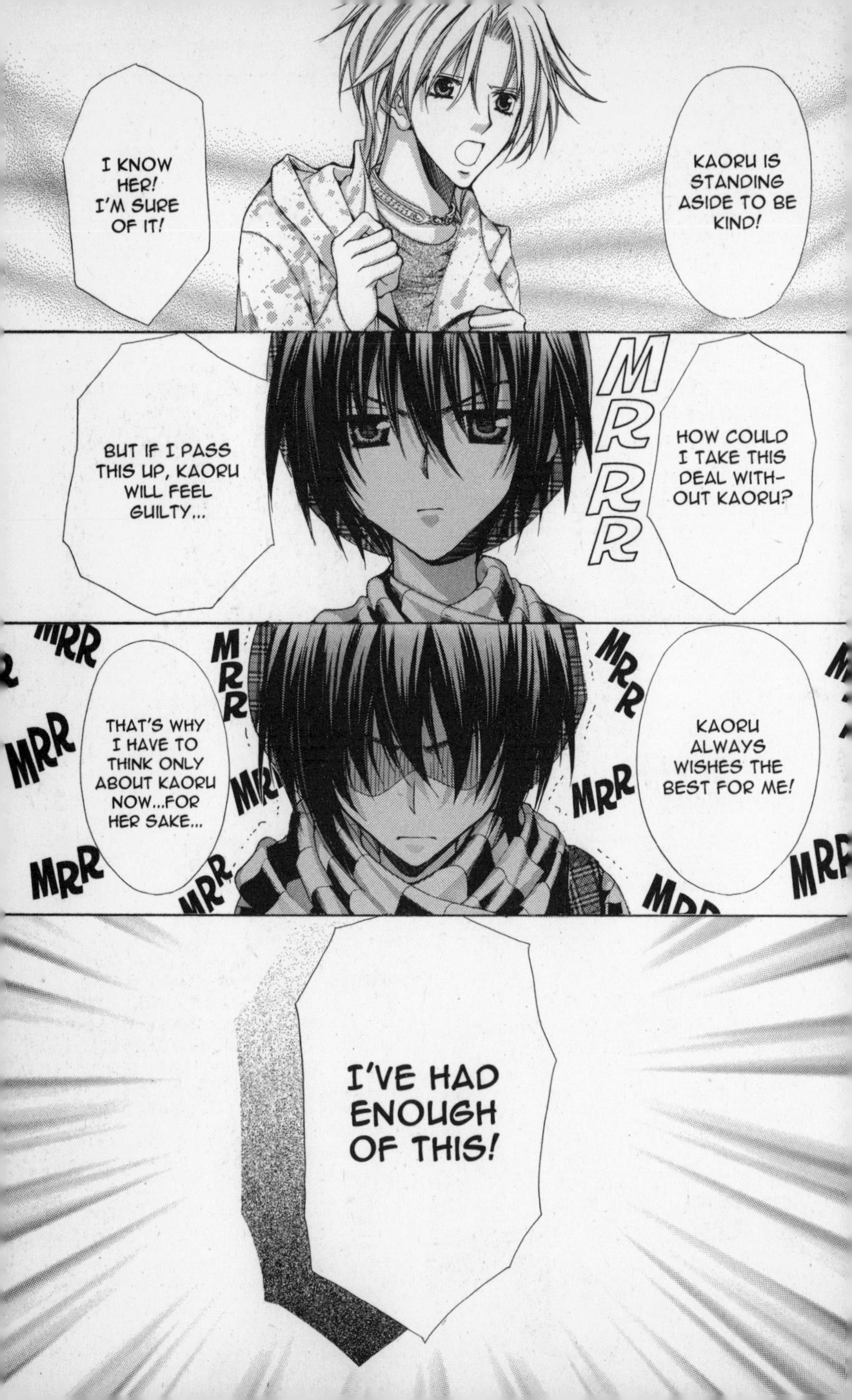
KAORU IS STANDING ASIDE TO BE KIND!
I KNOW HER! I'M SURE OF IT!
MRRR
HOW COULD I TAKE THIS DEAL WITH-OUT KAORU?
BUT IF I PASS THIS UP, KAORU WILL FEEL GUILTY...
MRR
MRR
MRR
KAORU ALWAYS WISHES THE BEST FOR ME!
MRR
MRR
THAT'S WHY I HAVE TO THINK ONLY ABOUT KAORU NOW...FOR HER SAKE...
MRR
MRR
MRR
I'VE HAD ENOUGH OF THIS!

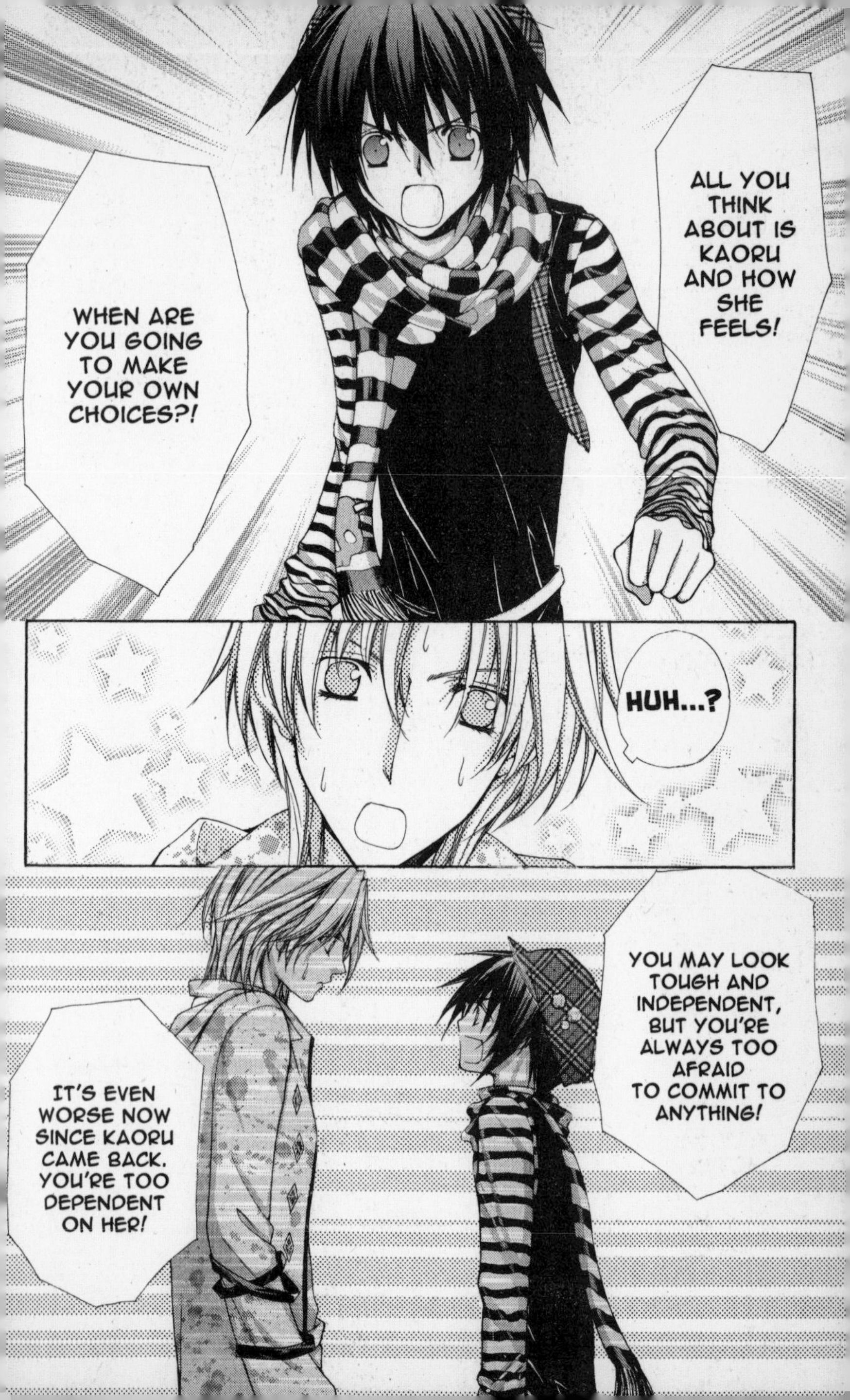
ALL YOU THINK ABOUT IS KAORU AND HOW SHE FEELS!
WHEN ARE YOU GOING TO MAKE YOUR OWN CHOICES?!
HUH...?
YOU MAY LOOK TOUGH AND INDEPENDENT, BUT YOU'RE ALWAYS TOO AFRAID TO COMMIT TO ANYTHING!
IT'S EVEN WORSE NOW SINCE KAORU CAME BACK. YOU'RE TOO DEPENDENT ON HER!

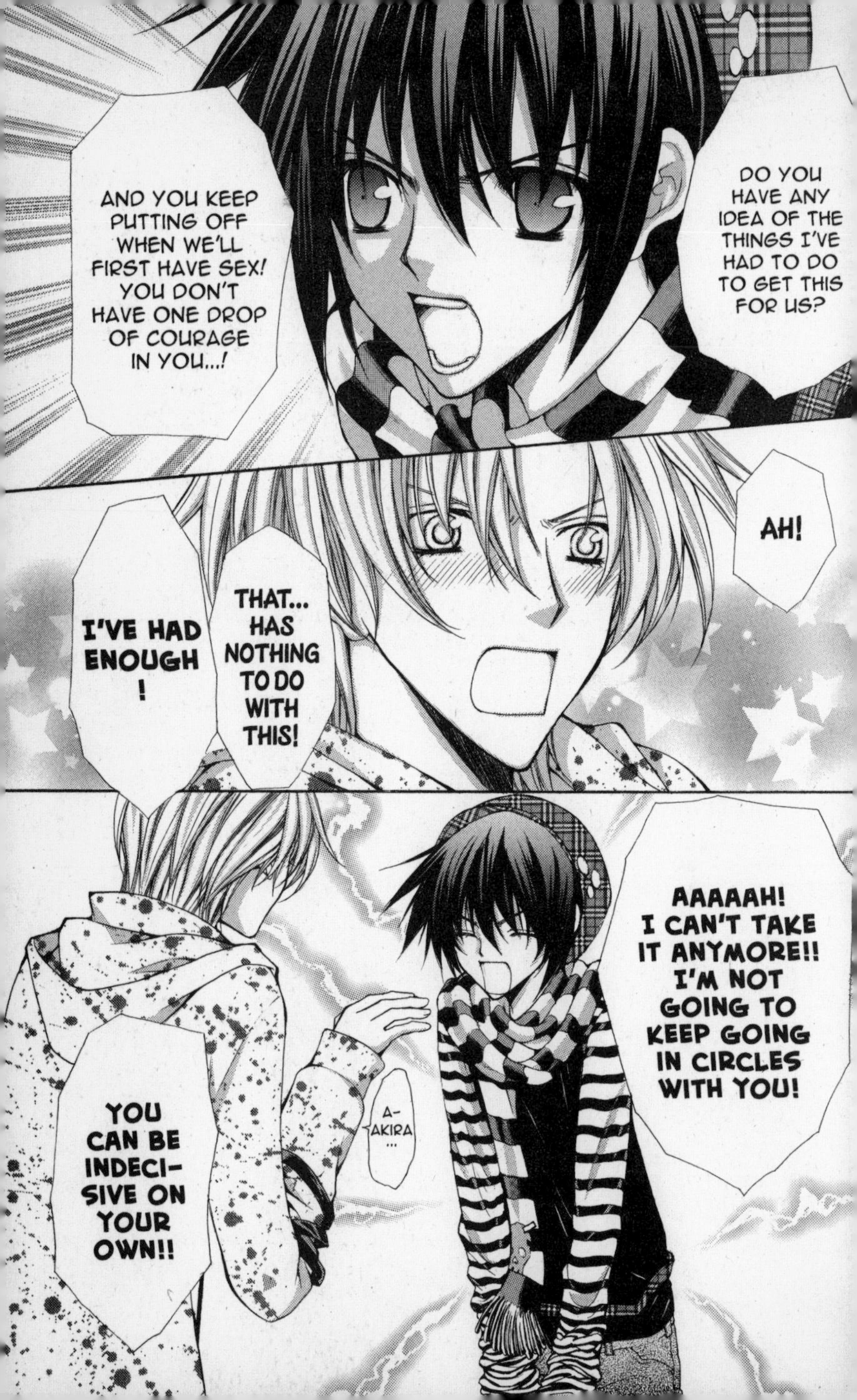
DO YOU HAVE ANY IDEA OF THE THINGS I'VE HAD TO DO TO GET THIS FOR US?
AND YOU KEEP PUTTING OFF WHEN WE'LL FIRST HAVE SEX! YOU DON'T HAVE ONE DROP OF COURAGE IN YOU...!
AH!
THAT... HAS NOTHING TO DO WITH THIS!
I'VE HAD ENOUGH!
AAAAAH! I CAN'T TAKE IT ANYMORE!! I'M NOT GOING TO KEEP GOING IN CIRCLES WITH YOU!
A-AKIRA...
YOU CAN BE INDECISIVE ON YOUR OWN!!

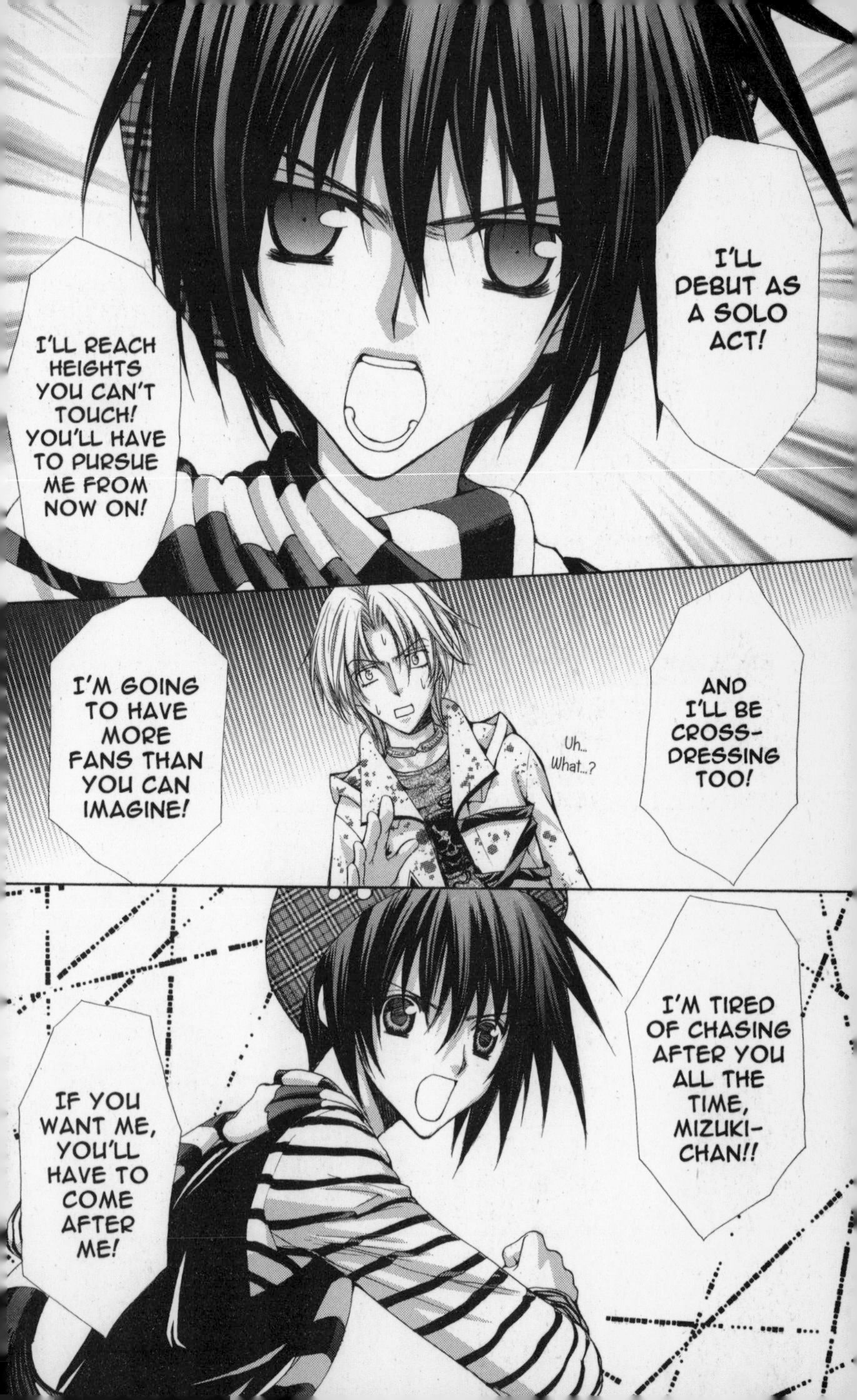
I'LL DEBUT AS A SOLO ACT!
I'LL REACH HEIGHTS YOU CAN'T TOUCH! YOU'LL HAVE TO PURSUE ME FROM NOW ON!
AND I'LL BE CROSS-DRESSING TOO!
Uh... What...?
I'M GOING TO HAVE MORE FANS THAN YOU CAN IMAGINE!
I'M TIRED OF CHASING AFTER YOU ALL THE TIME, MIZUKI-CHAN!!
IF YOU WANT ME, YOU'LL HAVE TO COME AFTER ME!

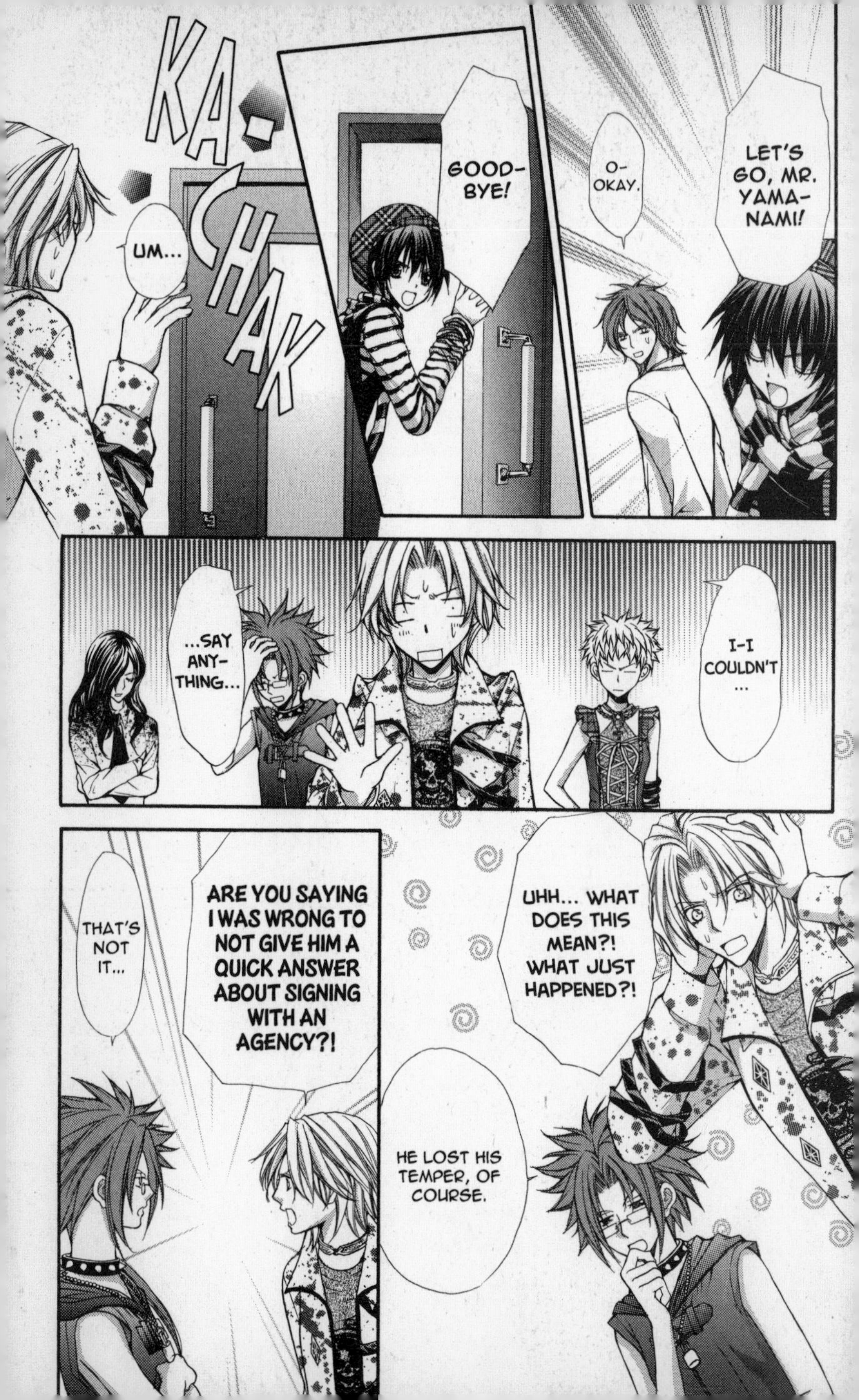
LET'S GO, MR. YAMANAMI!
O-OKAY.
GOOD-BYE!
KA-CHAK
UM...
I-I COULDN'T ...
...SAY ANYTHING...
UHH... WHAT DOES THIS MEAN?! WHAT JUST HAPPENED?!
HE LOST HIS TEMPER, OF COURSE.
ARE YOU SAYING I WAS WRONG TO NOT GIVE HIM A QUICK ANSWER ABOUT SIGNING WITH AN AGENCY?!
THAT'S NOT IT...

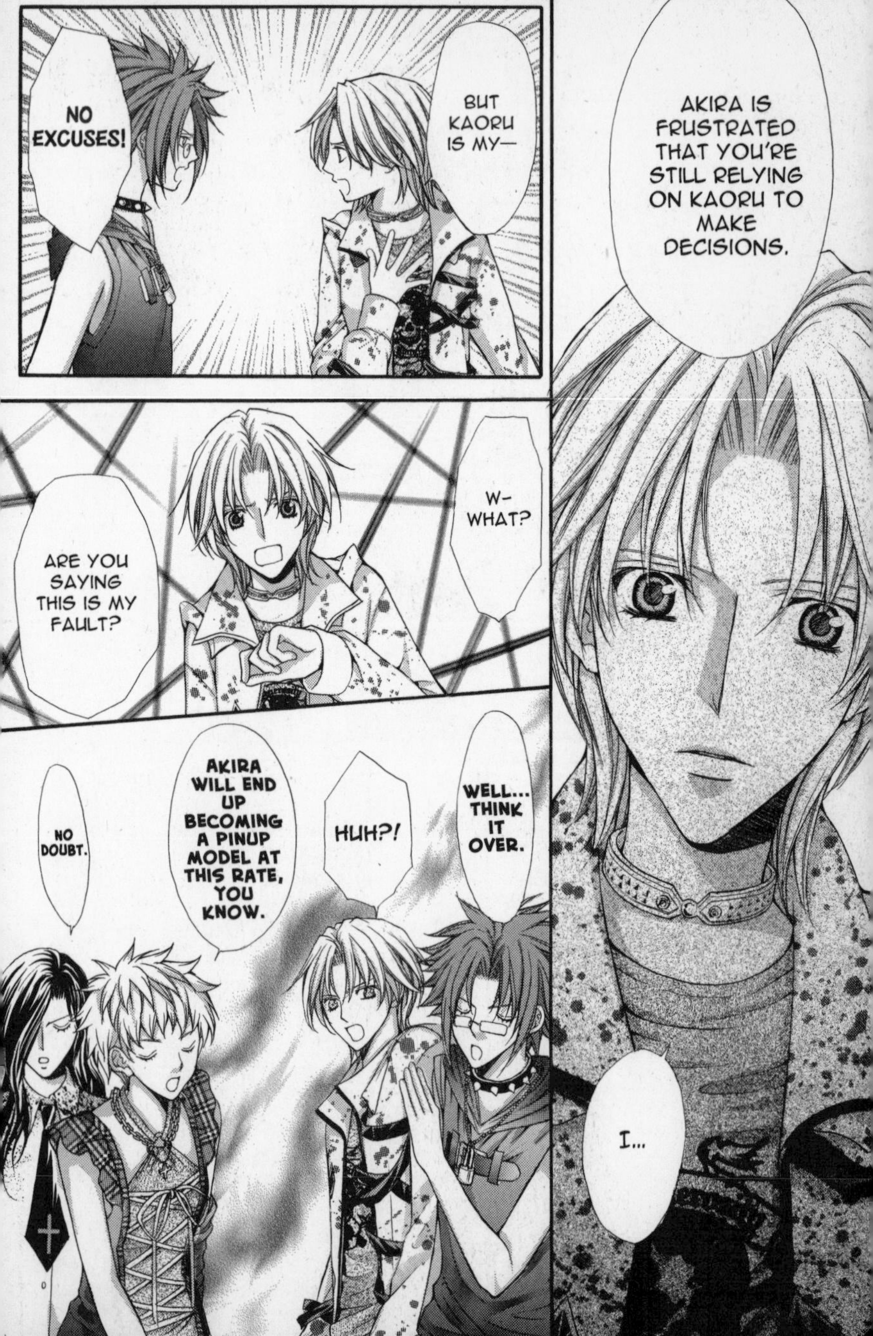
AKIRA IS FRUSTRATED THAT YOU'RE STILL RELYING ON KAORU TO MAKE DECISIONS.
I...
BUT KAORU IS MY—
NO EXCUSES!
W- WHAT?
ARE YOU SAYING THIS IS MY FAULT?
WELL... THINK IT OVER.
HUH?!
AKIRA WILL END UP BECOMING A PINUP MODEL AT THIS RATE, YOU KNOW.
NO DOUBT.

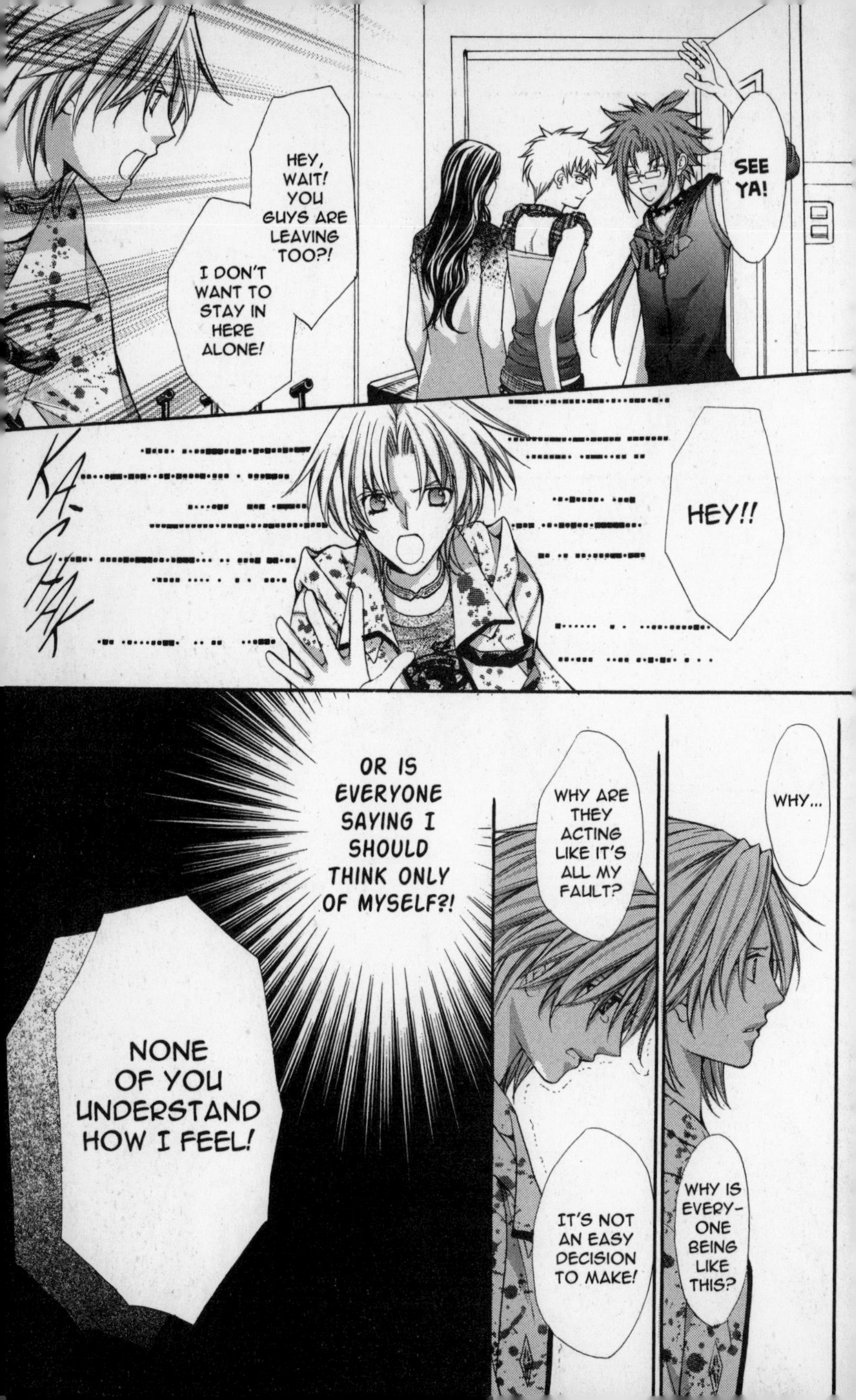
SEE YA!
HEY, WAIT! YOU GUYS ARE LEAVING TOO?!
I DON'T WANT TO STAY IN HERE ALONE!
HEY!!
KA-CHAK
WHY...
WHY IS EVERY-ONE BEING LIKE THIS?
WHY ARE THEY ACTING LIKE IT'S ALL MY FAULT?
IT'S NOT AN EASY DECISION TO MAKE!
OR IS EVERYONE SAYING I SHOULD THINK ONLY OF MYSELF?!
NONE OF YOU UNDERSTAND HOW I FEEL!

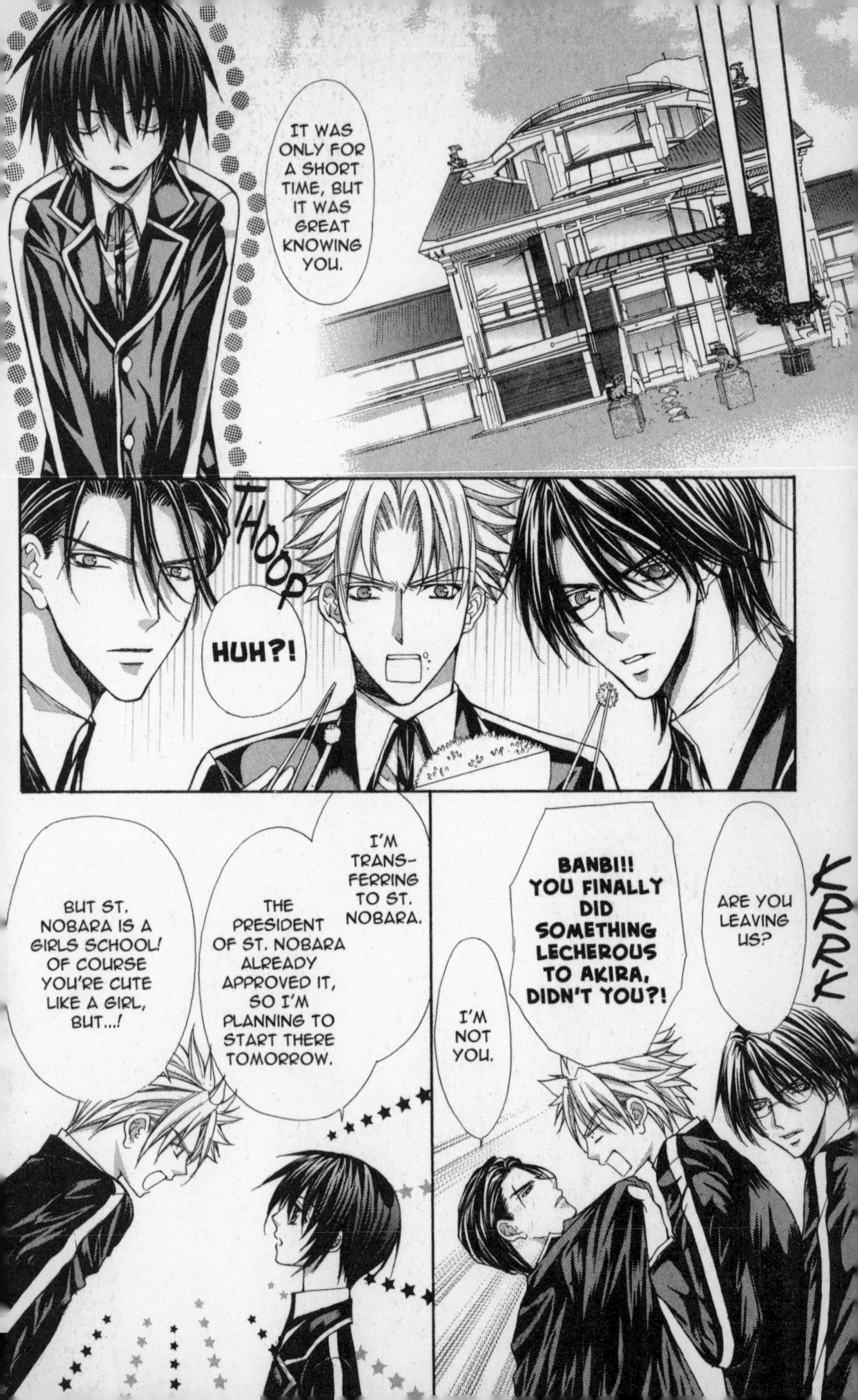
IT WAS ONLY FOR A SHORT TIME, BUT IT WAS GREAT KNOWING YOU.
THOOP
HUH?!
KRRK
ARE YOU LEAVING US?
BANBI!!! YOU FINALLY DID SOMETHING LECHEROUS TO AKIRA, DIDN'T YOU?!
I'M NOT YOU.
I'M TRANS-FERRING TO ST. NOBARA.
THE PRESIDENT OF ST. NOBARA ALREADY APPROVED IT, SO I'M PLANNING TO START THERE TOMORROW.
BUT ST. NOBARA IS A GIRLS SCHOOL! OF COURSE YOU'RE CUTE LIKE A GIRL, BUT...!

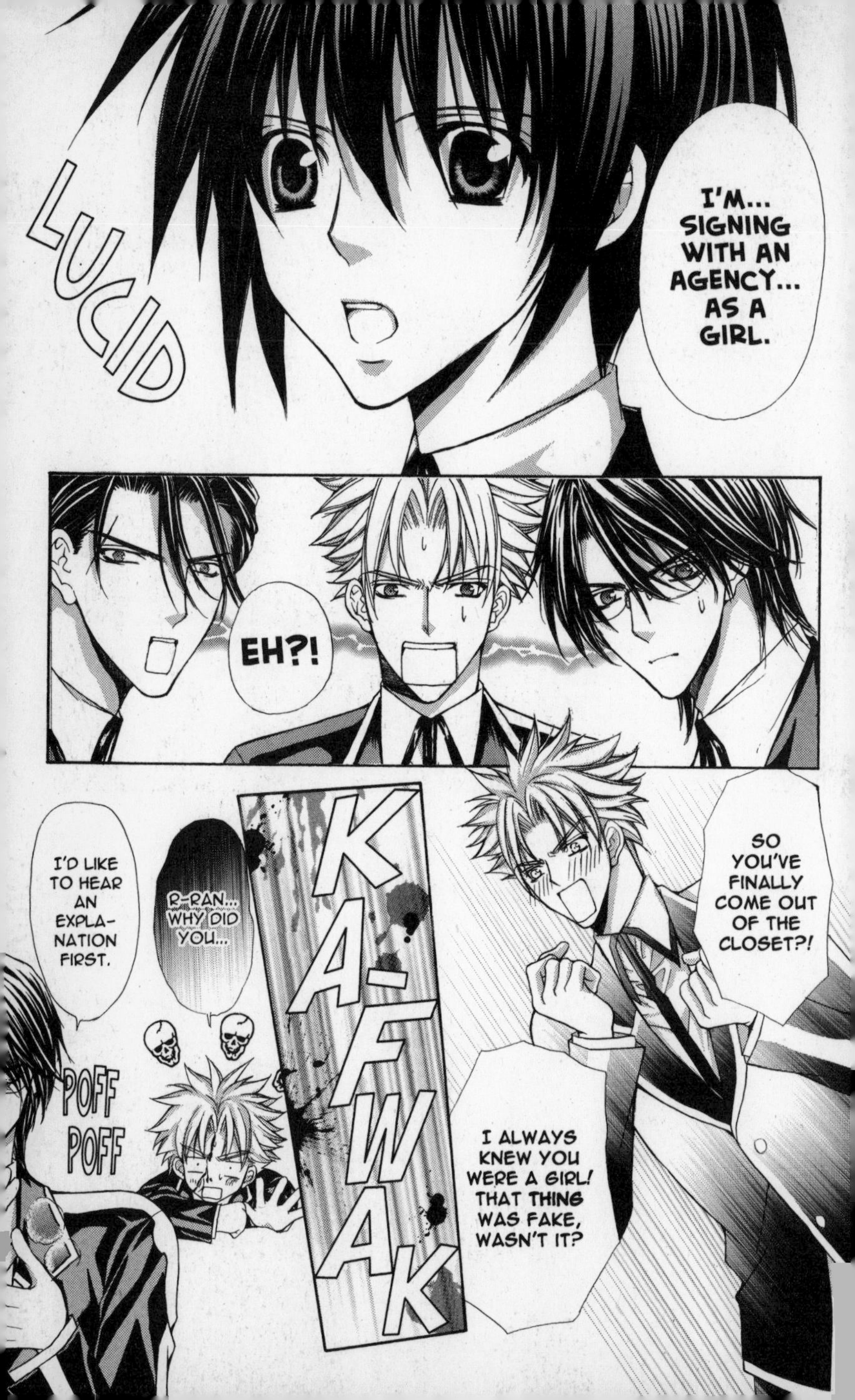
I'M... SIGNING WITH AN AGENCY... AS A GIRL.
LUCID
EH?!
SO YOU'VE FINALLY COME OUT OF THE CLOSET?!
I ALWAYS KNEW YOU WERE A GIRL! THAT THING WAS FAKE, WASN'T IT?
KA-FWAK
R-RAN... WHY DID YOU...
I'D LIKE TO HEAR AN EXPLA-NATION FIRST.
POFF POFF

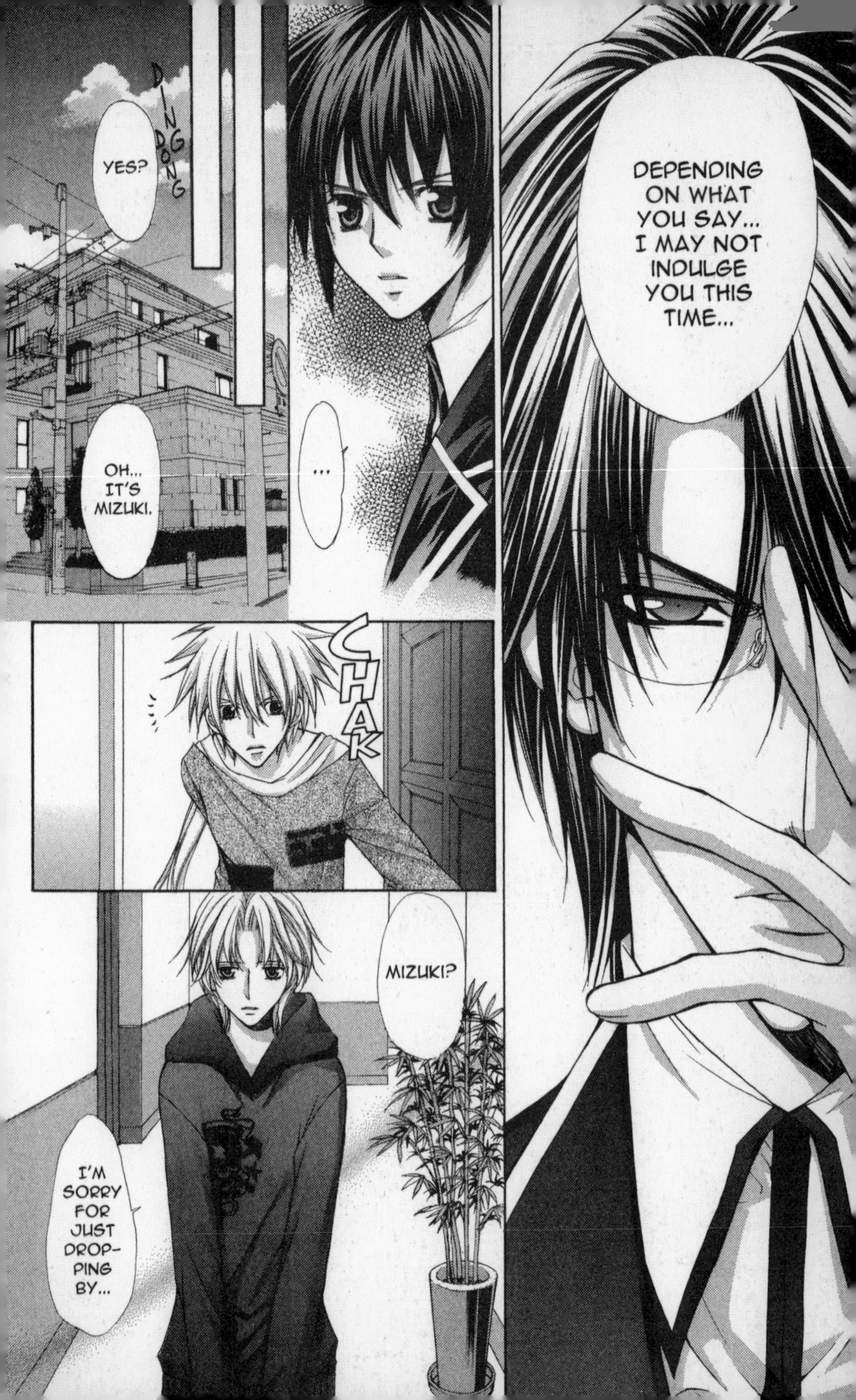
DEPENDING ON WHAT YOU SAY... I MAY NOT INDULGE YOU THIS TIME...
...
DING DONG
YES?
OH... IT'S MIZUKI.
CHAK
MIZUKI?
I'M SORRY FOR JUST DROPPING BY...

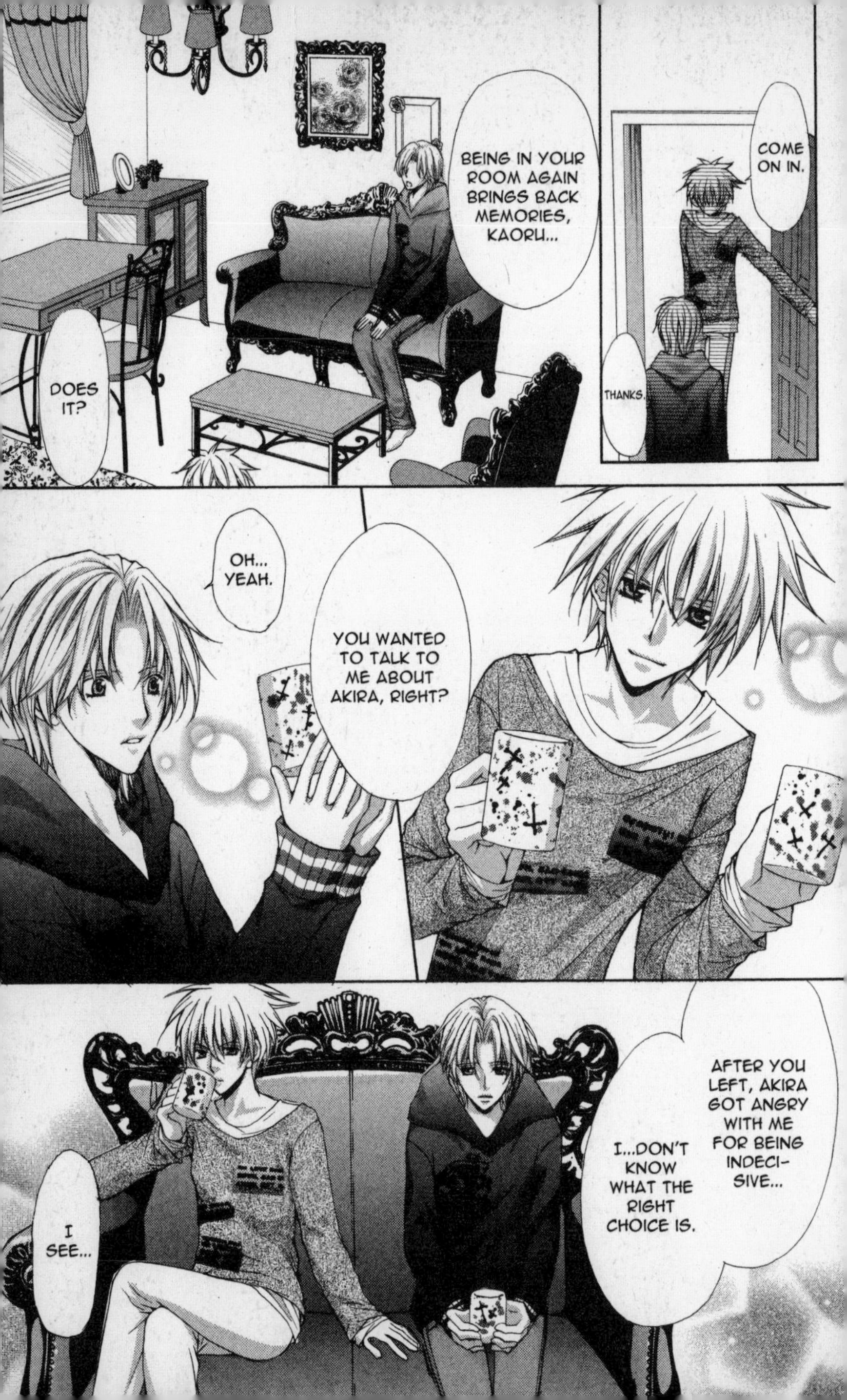
COME ON IN.
THANKS.
BEING IN YOUR ROOM AGAIN BRINGS BACK MEMORIES, KAORU...
DOES IT?
YOU WANTED TO TALK TO ME ABOUT AKIRA, RIGHT?
OH... YEAH.
AFTER YOU LEFT, AKIRA GOT ANGRY WITH ME FOR BEING INDECI-SIVE...
I...DON'T KNOW WHAT THE RIGHT CHOICE IS.
I SEE...

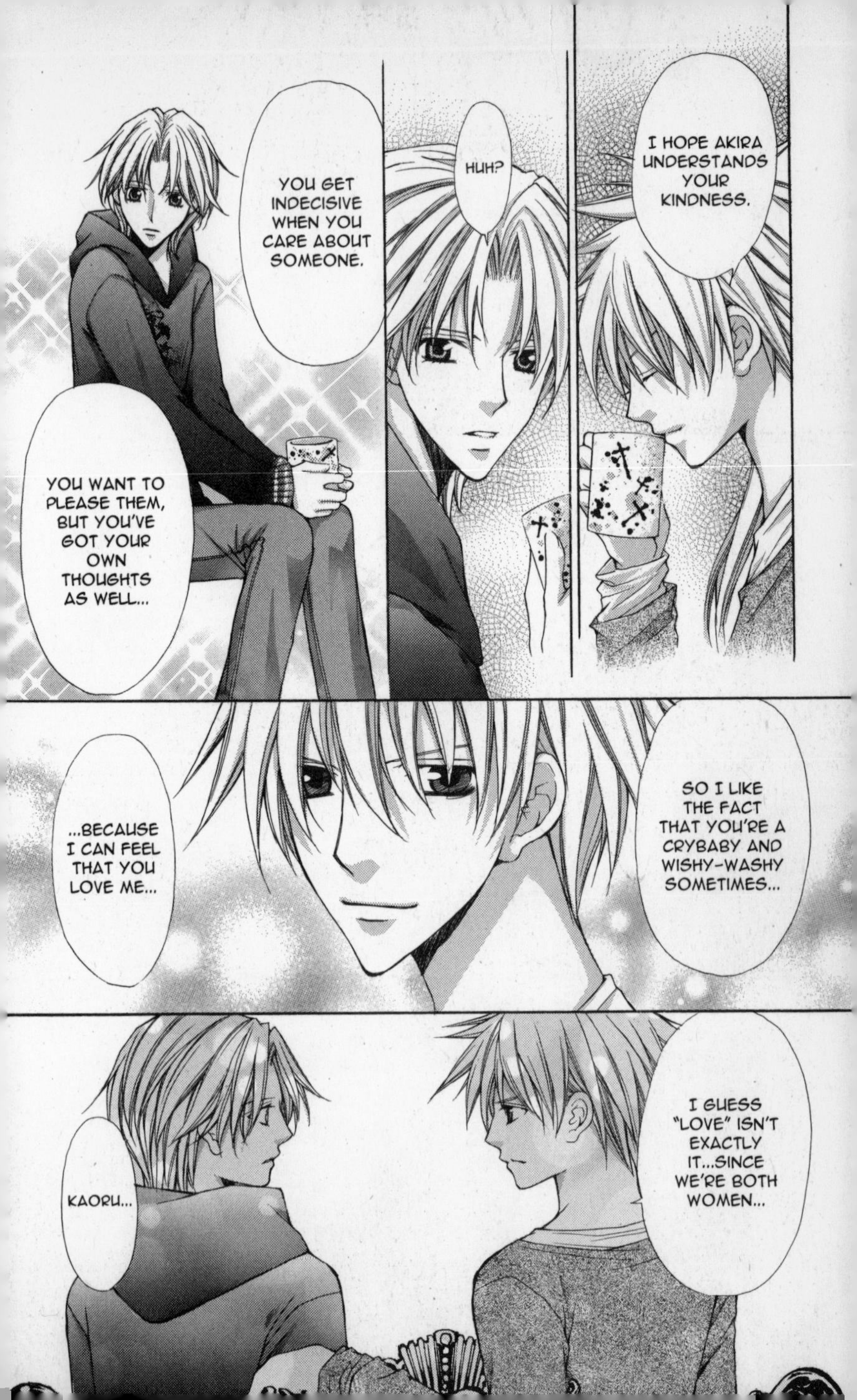
I HOPE AKIRA UNDERSTANDS YOUR KINDNESS.
HUH?
YOU GET INDECISIVE WHEN YOU CARE ABOUT SOMEONE.
YOU WANT TO PLEASE THEM, BUT YOU'VE GOT YOUR OWN THOUGHTS AS WELL...
SO I LIKE THE FACT THAT YOU'RE A CRYBABY AND WISHY-WASHY SOMETIMES...
...BECAUSE I CAN FEEL THAT YOU LOVE ME...
I GUESS "LOVE" ISN'T EXACTLY IT...SINCE WE'RE BOTH WOMEN...
KAORU...

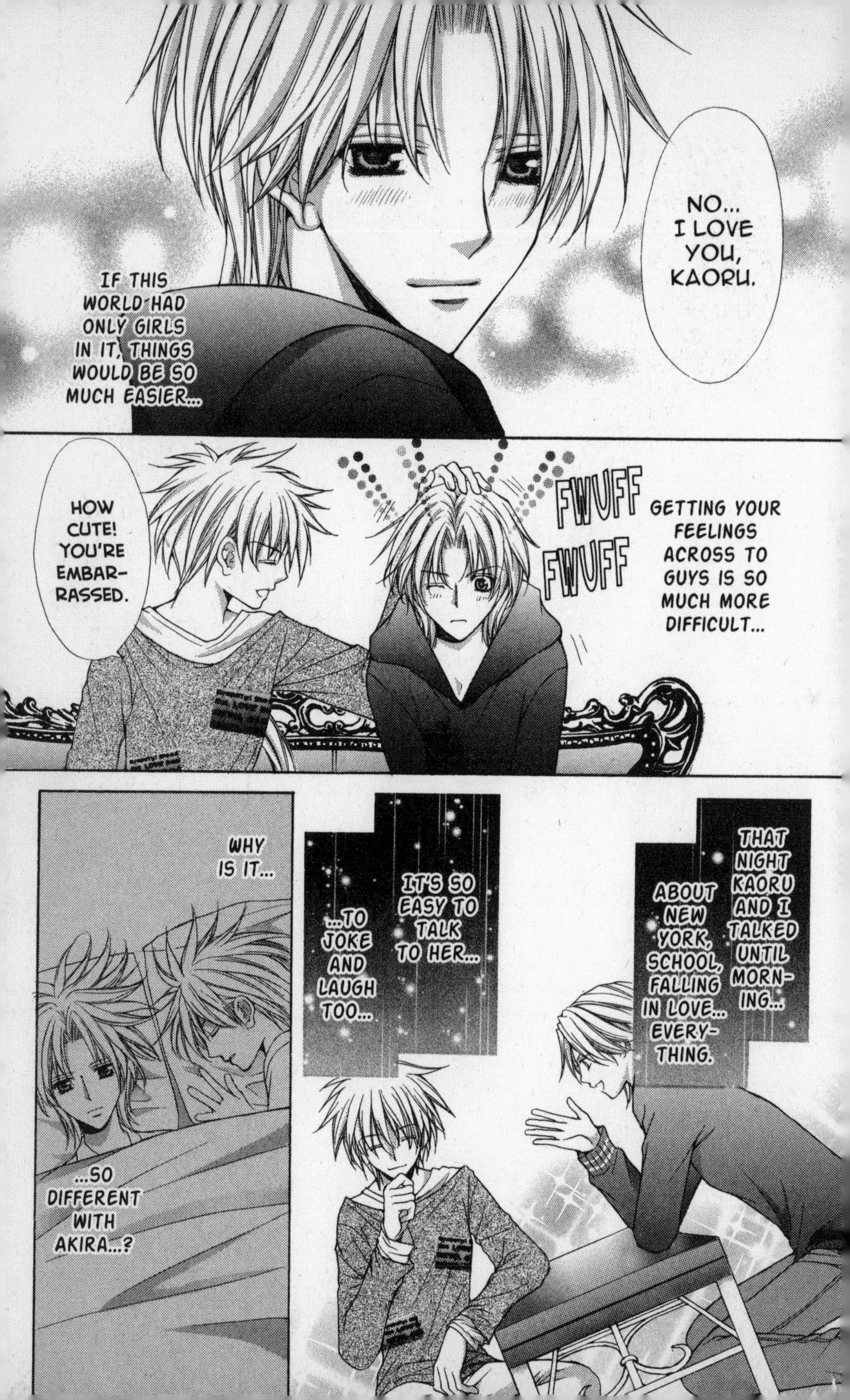
NO... I LOVE YOU, KAORU.
IF THIS WORLD HAD ONLY GIRLS IN IT, THINGS WOULD BE SO MUCH EASIER...
GETTING YOUR FEELINGS ACROSS TO GUYS IS SO MUCH MORE DIFFICULT...
FWUFF FWUFF
HOW CUTE! YOU'RE EMBAR-RASSED.
THAT NIGHT KAORU AND I TALKED UNTIL MORN-ING...
ABOUT NEW YORK, SCHOOL, FALLING IN LOVE... EVERY-THING.
IT'S SO EASY TO TALK TO HER...
...TO JOKE AND LAUGH TOO...
WHY IS IT...
...SO DIFFERENT WITH AKIRA...?

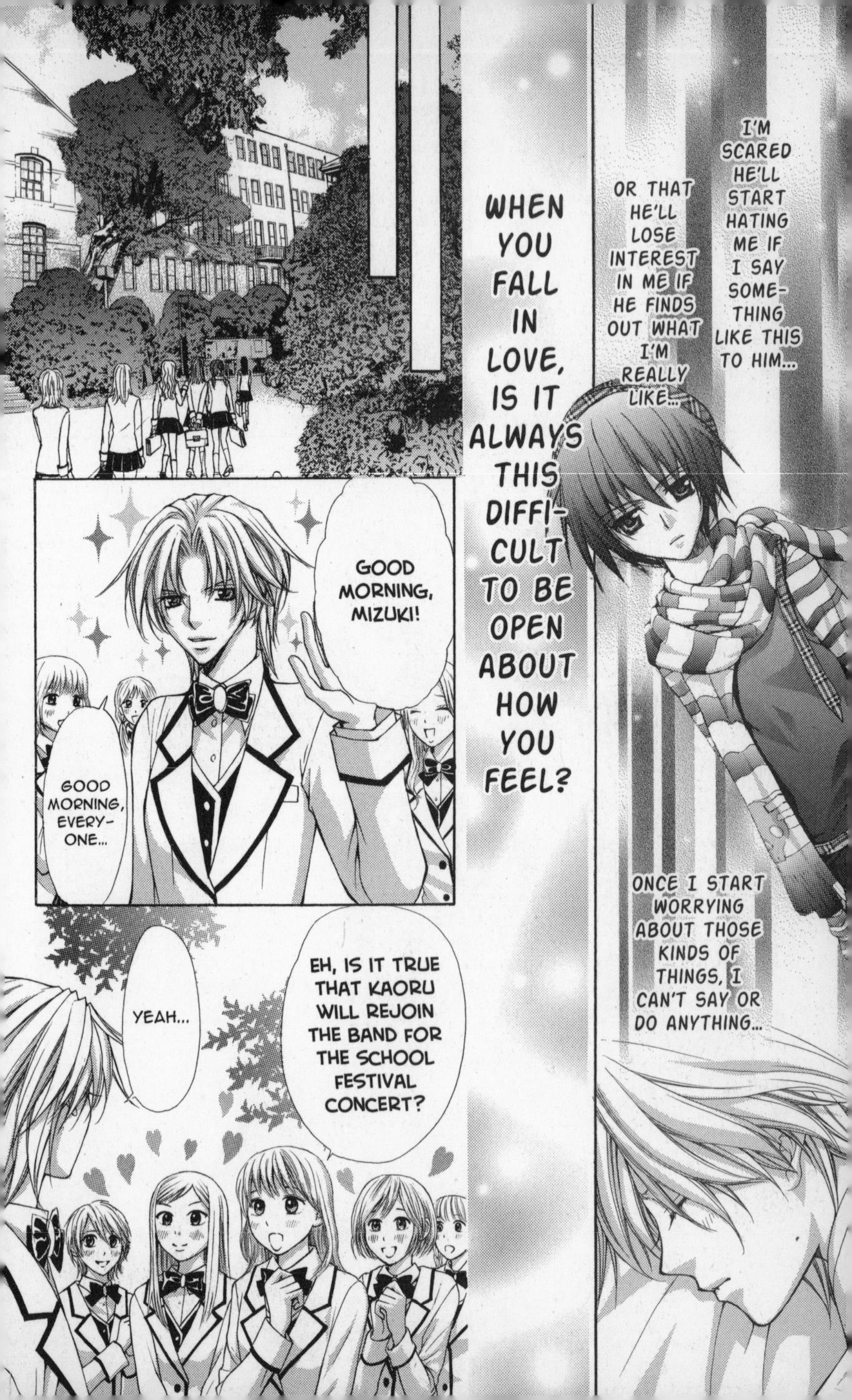
I'M SCARED HE'LL START HATING ME IF I SAY SOME-THING LIKE THIS TO HIM...
OR THAT HE'LL LOSE INTEREST IN ME IF HE FINDS OUT WHAT I'M REALLY LIKE...
ONCE I START WORRYING ABOUT THOSE KINDS OF THINGS, I CAN'T SAY OR DO ANYTHING...
WHEN YOU FALL IN LOVE, IS IT ALWAYS THIS DIFFI-CULT TO BE OPEN ABOUT HOW YOU FEEL?
GOOD MORNING, MIZUKI!
GOOD MORNING, EVERY-ONE...
EH, IS IT TRUE THAT KAORU WILL REJOIN THE BAND FOR THE SCHOOL FESTIVAL CONCERT?
YEAH...

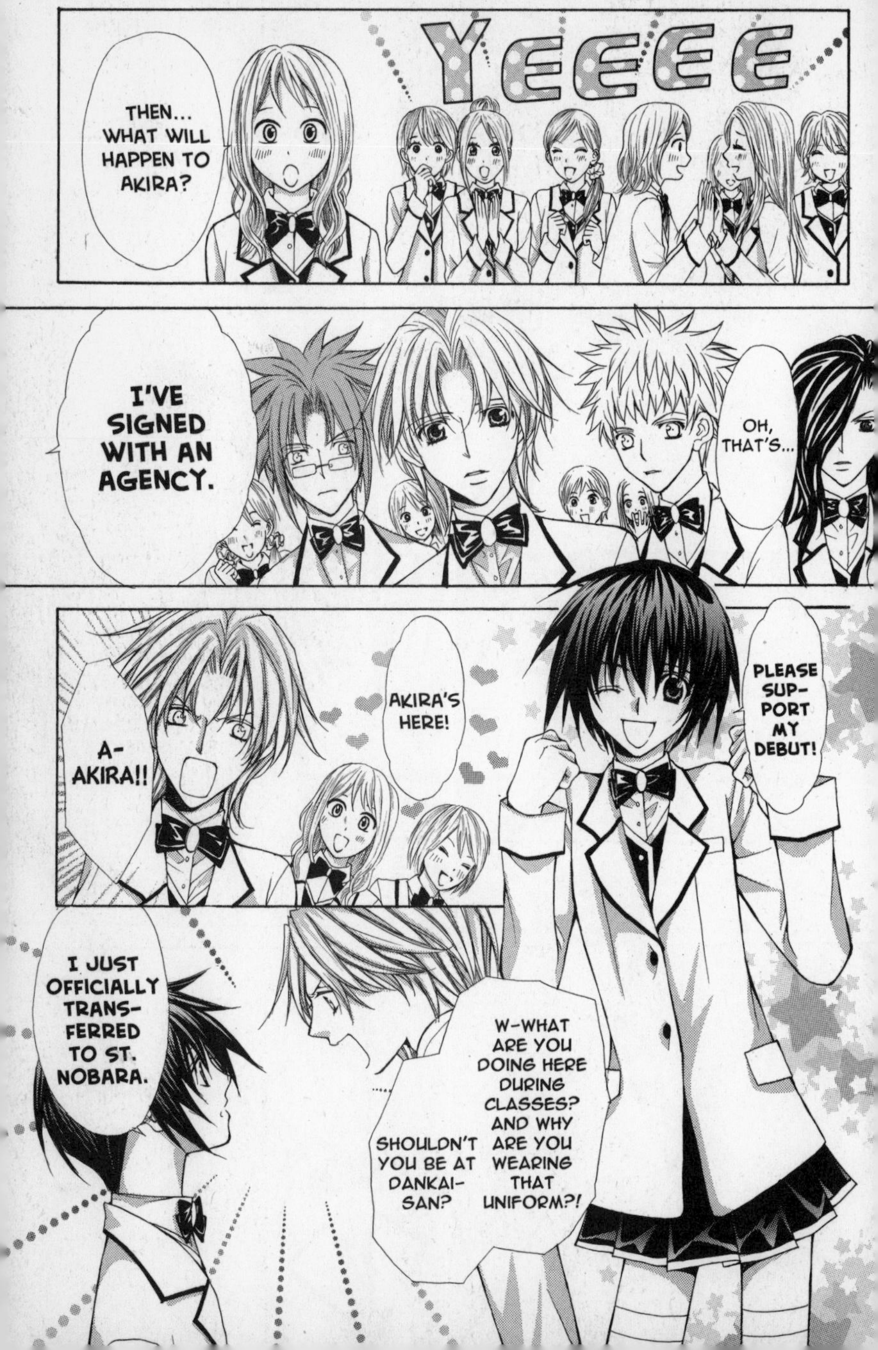
YEEEE
THEN... WHAT WILL HAPPEN TO AKIRA?
OH, THAT'S...
I'VE SIGNED WITH AN AGENCY.
PLEASE SUP-PORT MY DEBUT!
AKIRA'S HERE!
A-AKIRA!!
W-WHAT ARE YOU DOING HERE DURING CLASSES? AND WHY ARE YOU WEARING THAT UNIFORM?!
SHOULDN'T YOU BE AT DANKAI-SAN?
I JUST OFFICIALLY TRANS-FERRED TO ST. NOBARA.

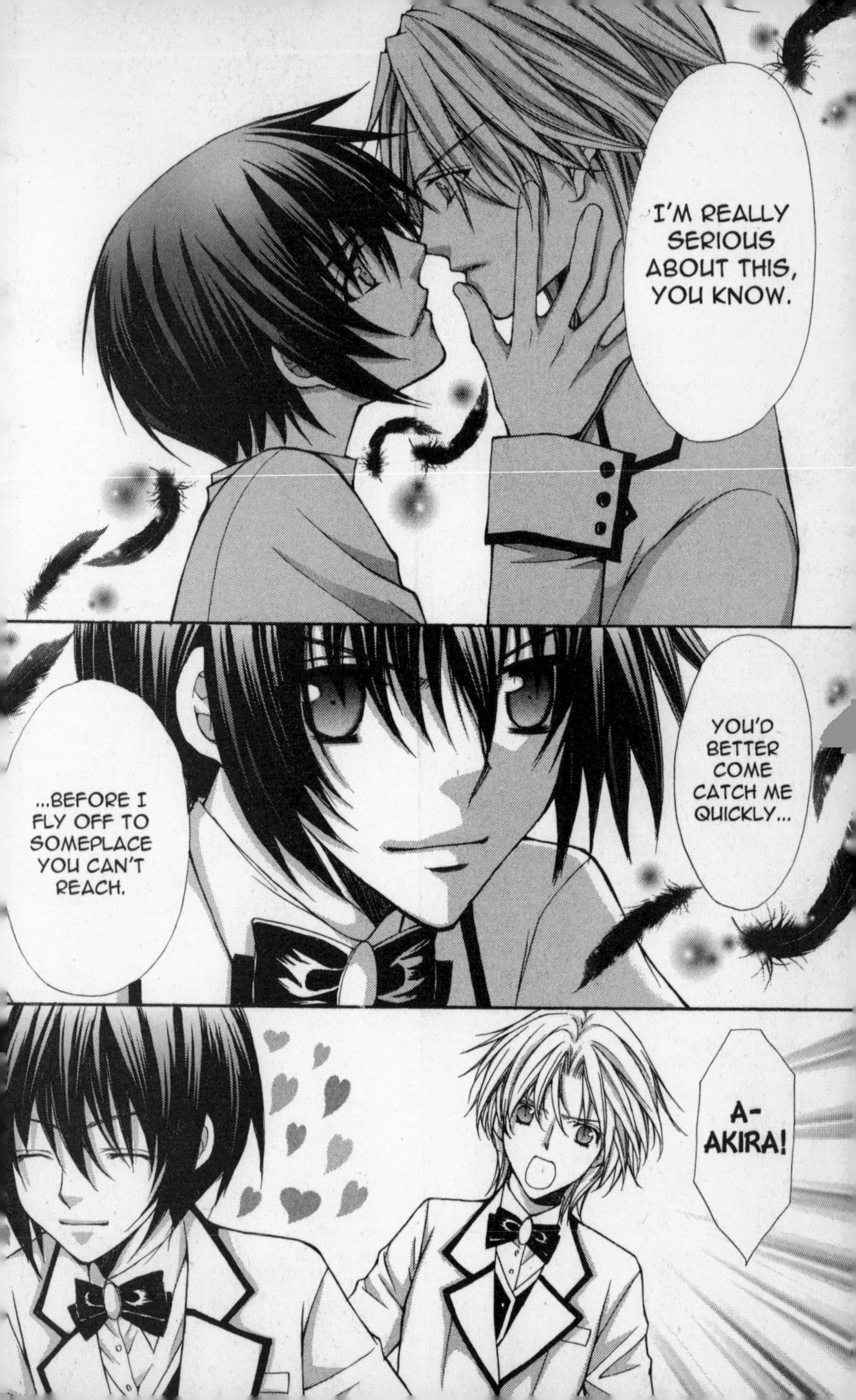
I'M REALLY SERIOUS ABOUT THIS, YOU KNOW.
YOU'D BETTER COME CATCH ME QUICKLY...
...BEFORE I FLY OFF TO SOMEPLACE YOU CAN'T REACH.
A-AKIRA!

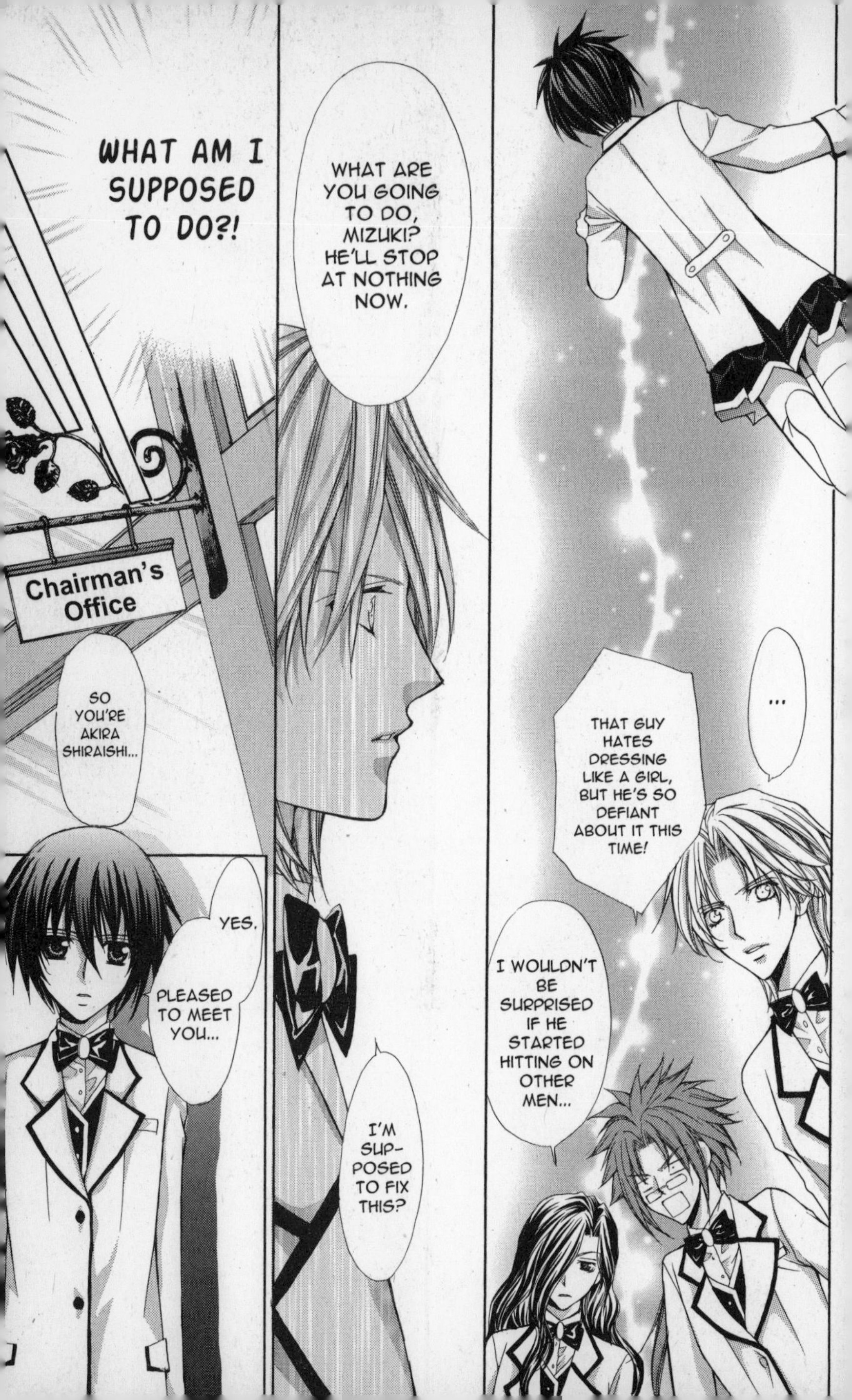
...
THAT GUY HATES DRESSING LIKE A GIRL, BUT HE'S SO DEFIANT ABOUT IT THIS TIME!
I WOULDN'T BE SURPRISED IF HE STARTED HITTING ON OTHER MEN...
WHAT ARE YOU GOING TO DO, MIZUKI? HE'LL STOP AT NOTHING NOW.
I'M SUP-POSED TO FIX THIS?
WHAT AM I SUPPOSED TO DO?!
Chairman's Office
SO YOU'RE AKIRA SHIRAISHI...
YES.
PLEASED TO MEET YOU...

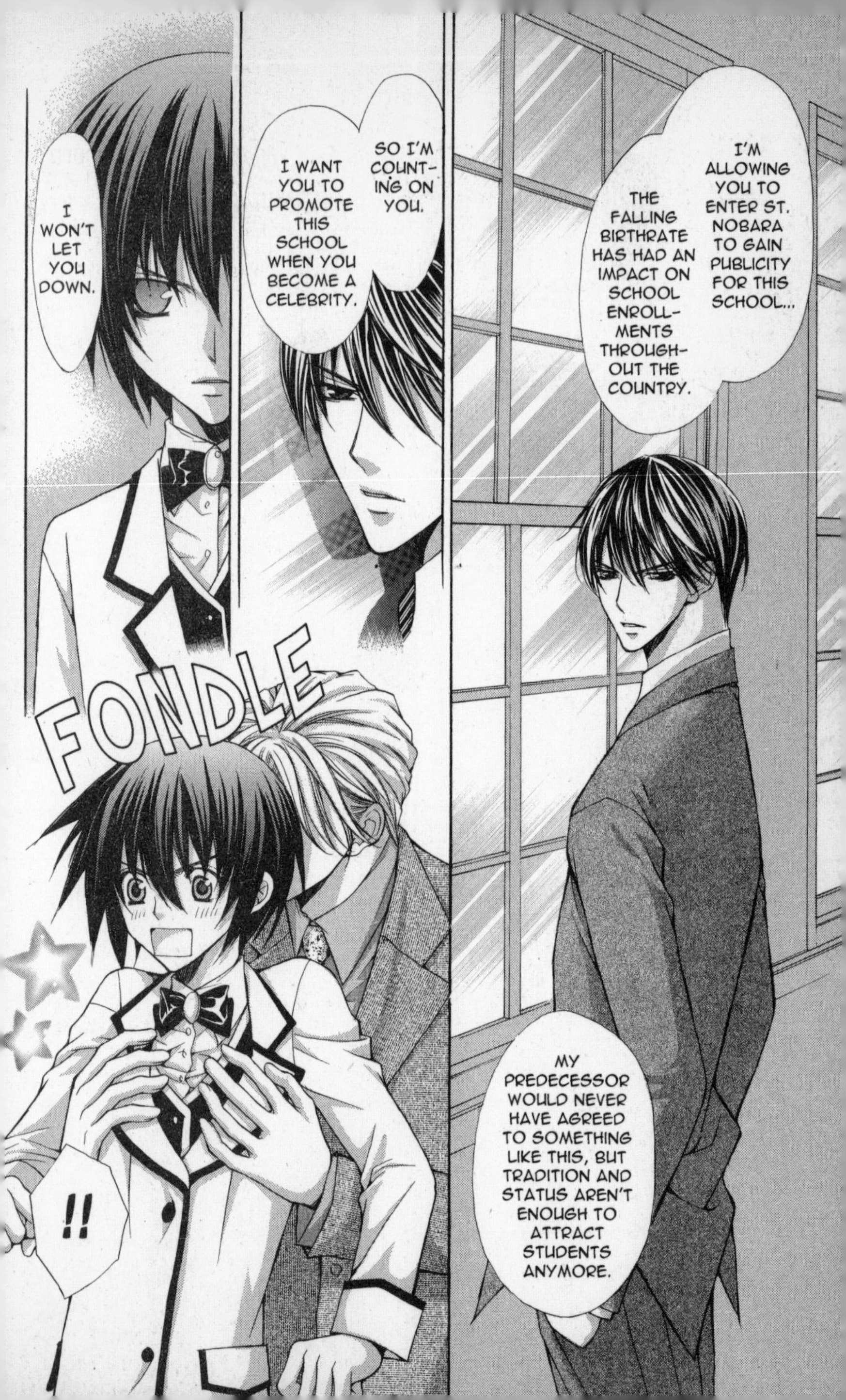
I'M ALLOWING YOU TO ENTER ST. NOBARA TO GAIN PUBLICITY FOR THIS SCHOOL...
THE FALLING BIRTHRATE HAS HAD AN IMPACT ON SCHOOL ENROLL-MENTS THROUGH-OUT THE COUNTRY.
MY PREDECESSOR WOULD NEVER HAVE AGREED TO SOMETHING LIKE THIS, BUT TRADITION AND STATUS AREN'T ENOUGH TO ATTRACT STUDENTS ANYMORE.
I WANT YOU TO PROMOTE THIS SCHOOL WHEN YOU BECOME A CELEBRITY.
SO I'M COUNT-ING ON YOU.
I WON'T LET YOU DOWN.
FONDLE
!!

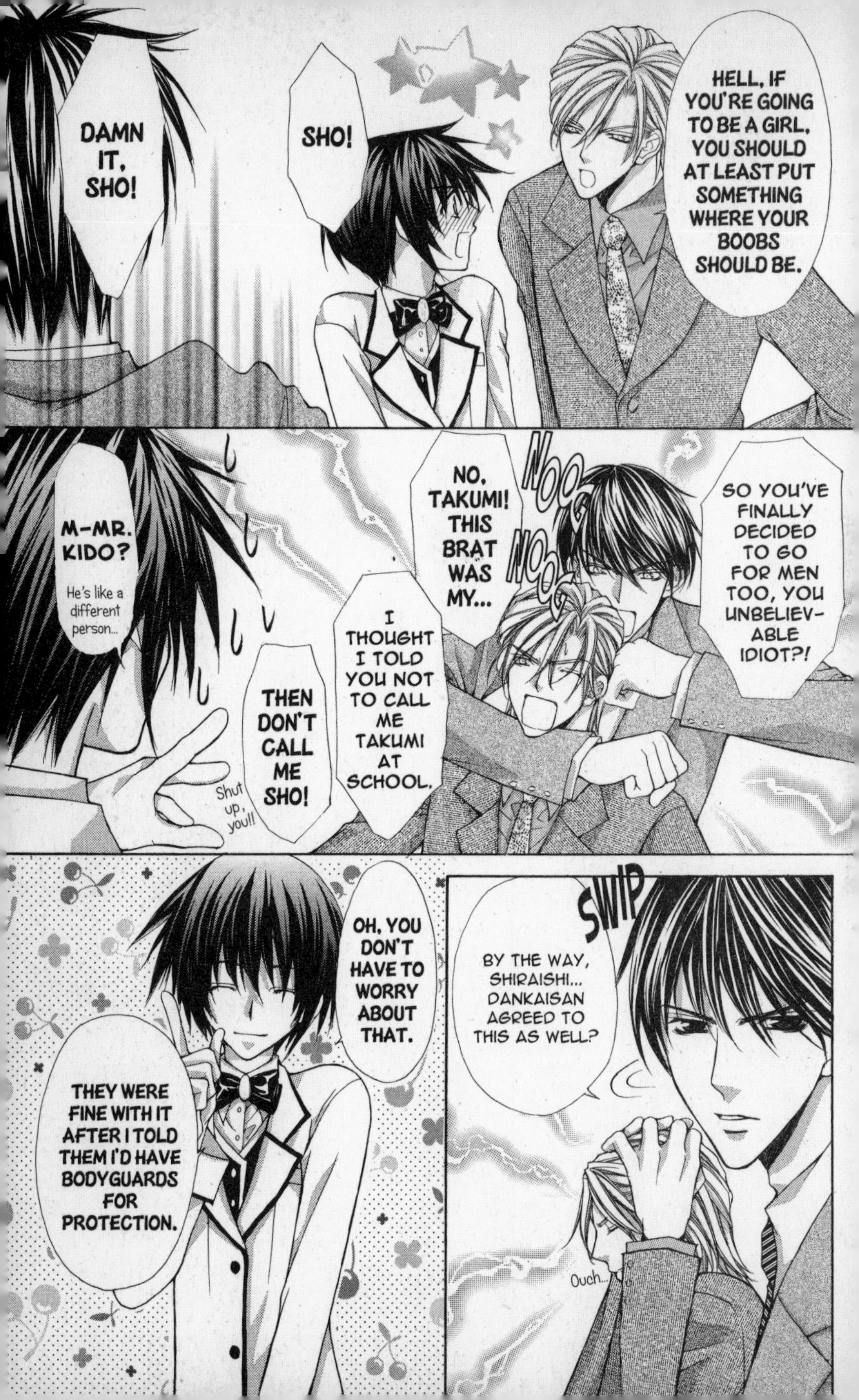
HELL, IF YOU'RE GOING TO BE A GIRL, YOU SHOULD AT LEAST PUT SOMETHING WHERE YOUR BOOBS SHOULD BE.
SHO!
DAMN IT, SHO!
SO YOU'VE FINALLY DECIDED TO GO FOR MEN TOO, YOU UNBELIEVABLE IDIOT?!
NOOG
NOOG
NO, TAKUMI! THIS BRAT WAS MY...
I THOUGHT I TOLD YOU NOT TO CALL ME TAKUMI AT SCHOOL.
THEN DON'T CALL ME SHO!
Shut up, you!!
M-MR. KIDO?
He's like a different person...
SWIP
BY THE WAY, SHIRAISHI... DANKAISAN AGREED TO THIS AS WELL?
Ouch...
OH, YOU DON'T HAVE TO WORRY ABOUT THAT.
THEY WERE FINE WITH IT AFTER I TOLD THEM I'D HAVE BODYGUARDS FOR PROTECTION.

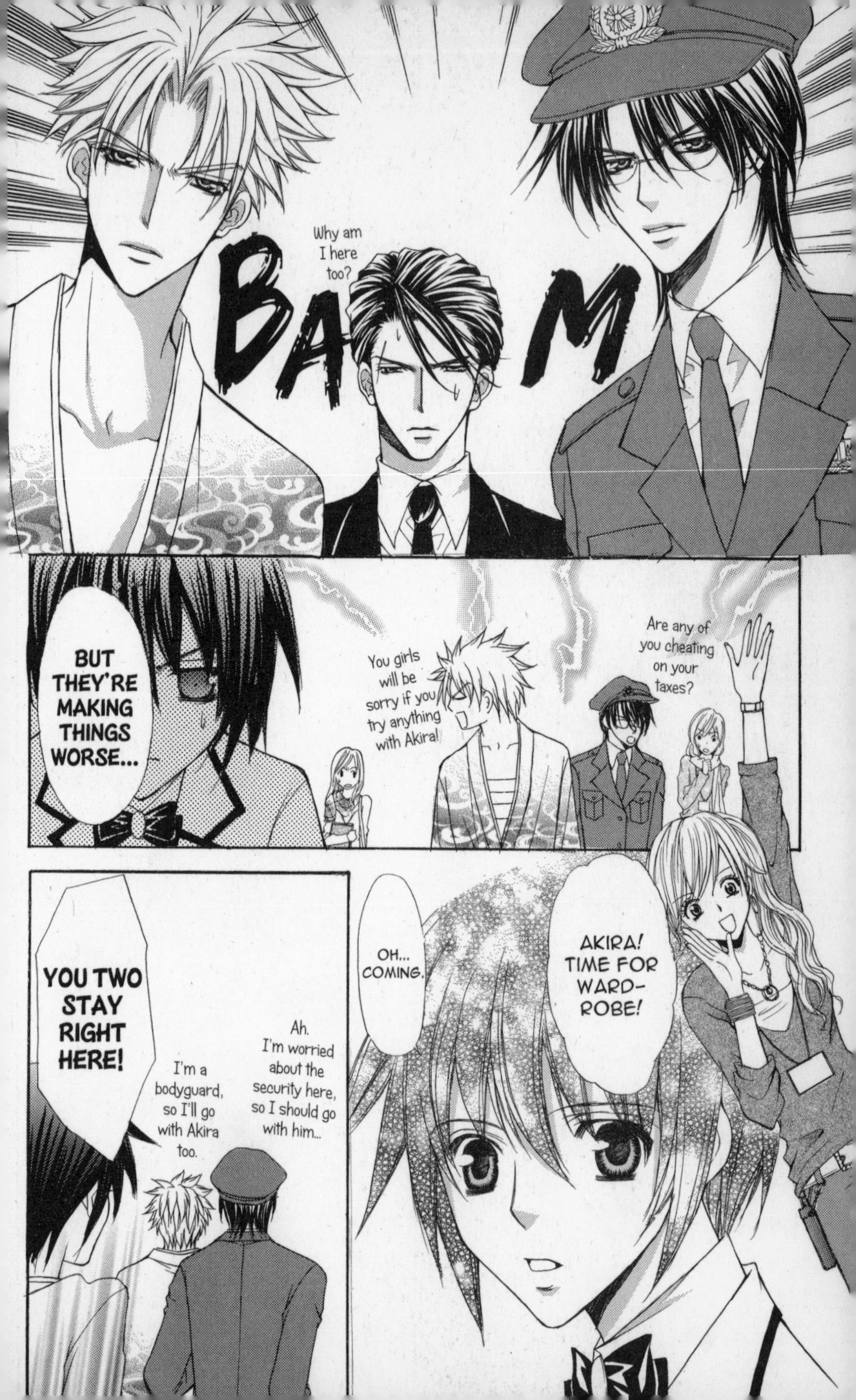
BAM
Why am I here too?
Are any of you cheating on your taxes?
You girls will be sorry if you try anything with Akira!
BUT THEY'RE MAKING THINGS WORSE...
AKIRA! TIME FOR WARD-ROBE!
OH... COMING.
Ah. I'm worried about the security here, so I should go with him...
I'm a bodyguard, so I'll go with Akira too.
YOU TWO STAY RIGHT HERE!

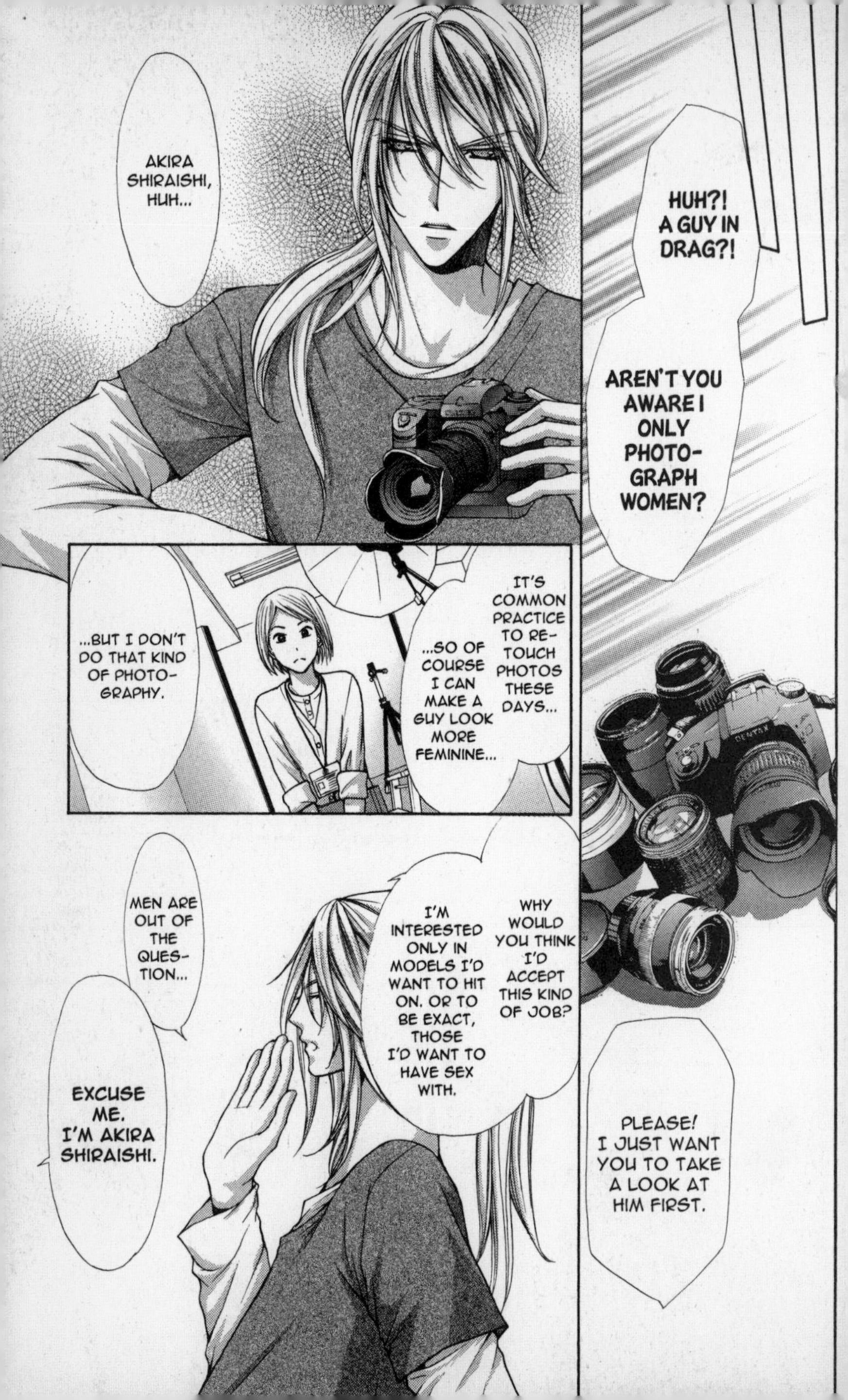
HUH?! A GUY IN DRAG?!
AREN'T YOU AWARE I ONLY PHOTO-GRAPH WOMEN?
PLEASE! I JUST WANT YOU TO TAKE A LOOK AT HIM FIRST.
AKIRA SHIRAISHI, HUH...
IT'S COMMON PRACTICE TO RE-TOUCH PHOTOS THESE DAYS...
...SO OF COURSE I CAN MAKE A GUY LOOK MORE FEMININE...
...BUT I DON'T DO THAT KIND OF PHOTO-GRAPHY.
WHY WOULD YOU THINK I'D ACCEPT THIS KIND OF JOB?
I'M INTERESTED ONLY IN MODELS I'D WANT TO HIT ON. OR TO BE EXACT, THOSE I'D WANT TO HAVE SEX WITH.
MEN ARE OUT OF THE QUES-TION...
EXCUSE ME. I'M AKIRA SHIRAISHI.

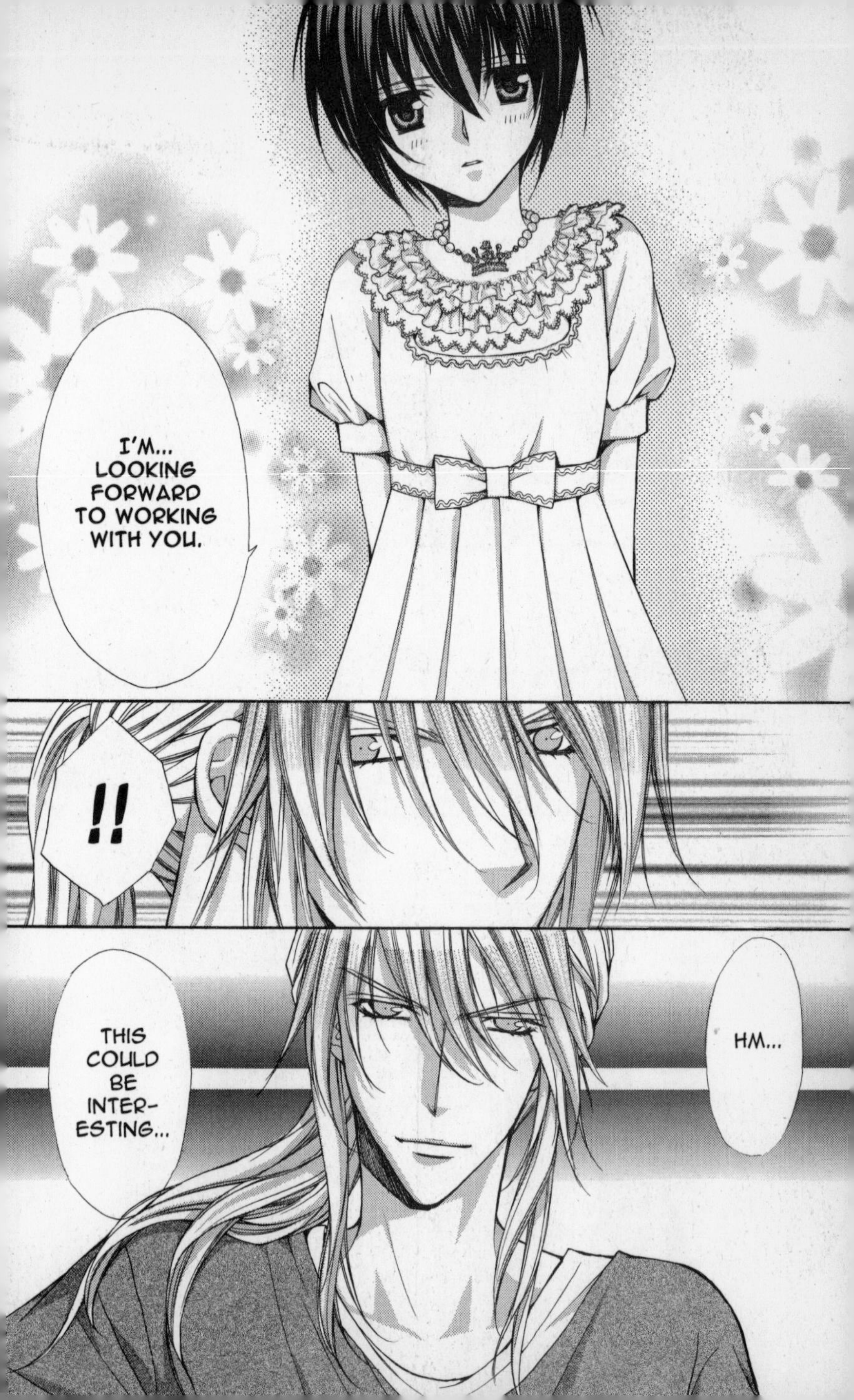
I'M... LOOKING FORWARD TO WORKING WITH YOU.
!!
HM...
THIS COULD BE INTER-ESTING...

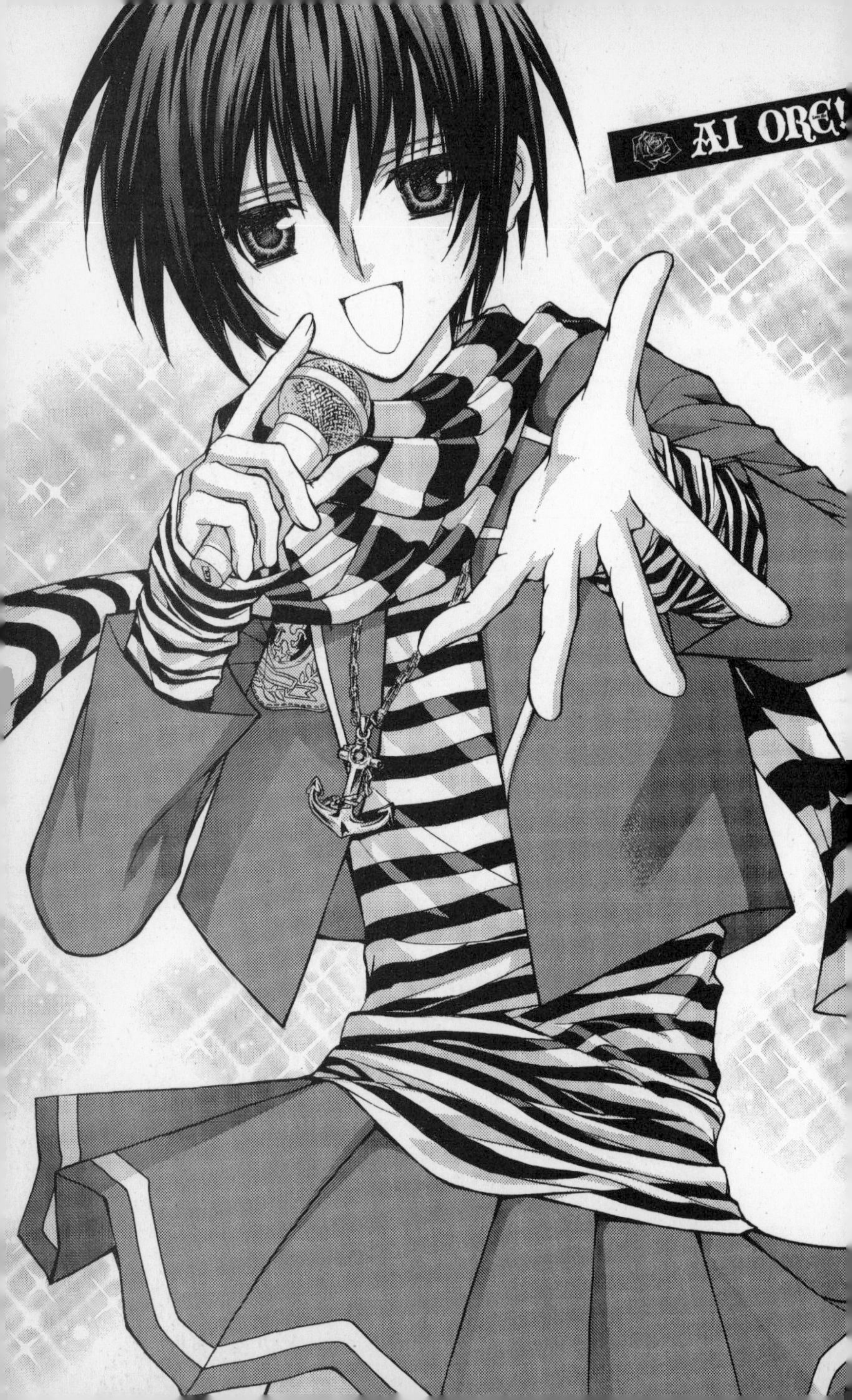
AI ORE!

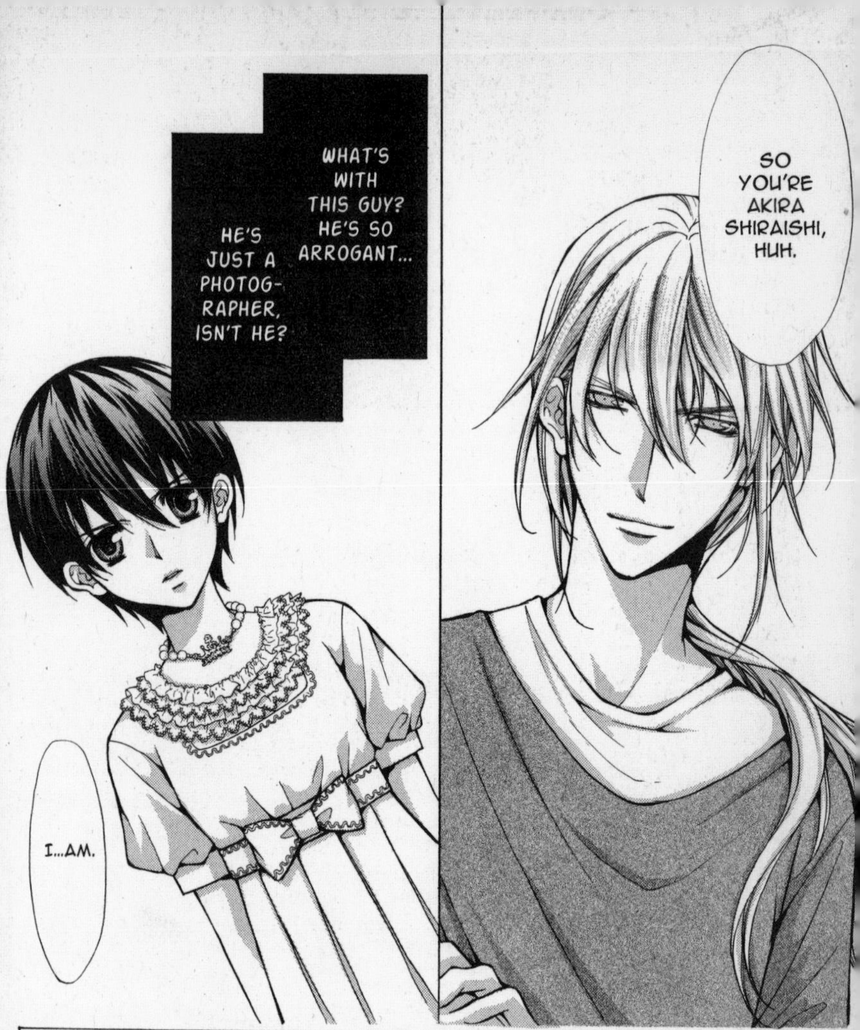
SO YOU'RE AKIRA SHIRAISHI, HUH.
WHAT'S WITH THIS GUY? HE'S SO ARROGANT...
HE'S JUST A PHOTOG-RAPHER, ISN'T HE?
I...AM.

Recent Events

Writing this section has been a pain... All I've been doing lately is working, so I haven't had anything to talk about here. But! There has been a change in my life!! You may think I'm late to the party, but for some reason I am now hooked on EXILE! For all those readers who know me well, I'm sure you've noticed I often listen to music by rock bands, but now I'm into dance music! Well, to be honest, it's because the vocalist of the group, Takahiro, is my type. He's over 5'9", has a baby face, and he's good looking: He's perfect. It all started when I saw the music video for a song called "Futatsu no Kuchibiru." Takahiro was wearing a coat in that music video, and he looked so cool! It may not seem so (?), but I think men in heavy layers of clothing are sexy! Coats, gloves, scarves... I adore it!

(Continues)

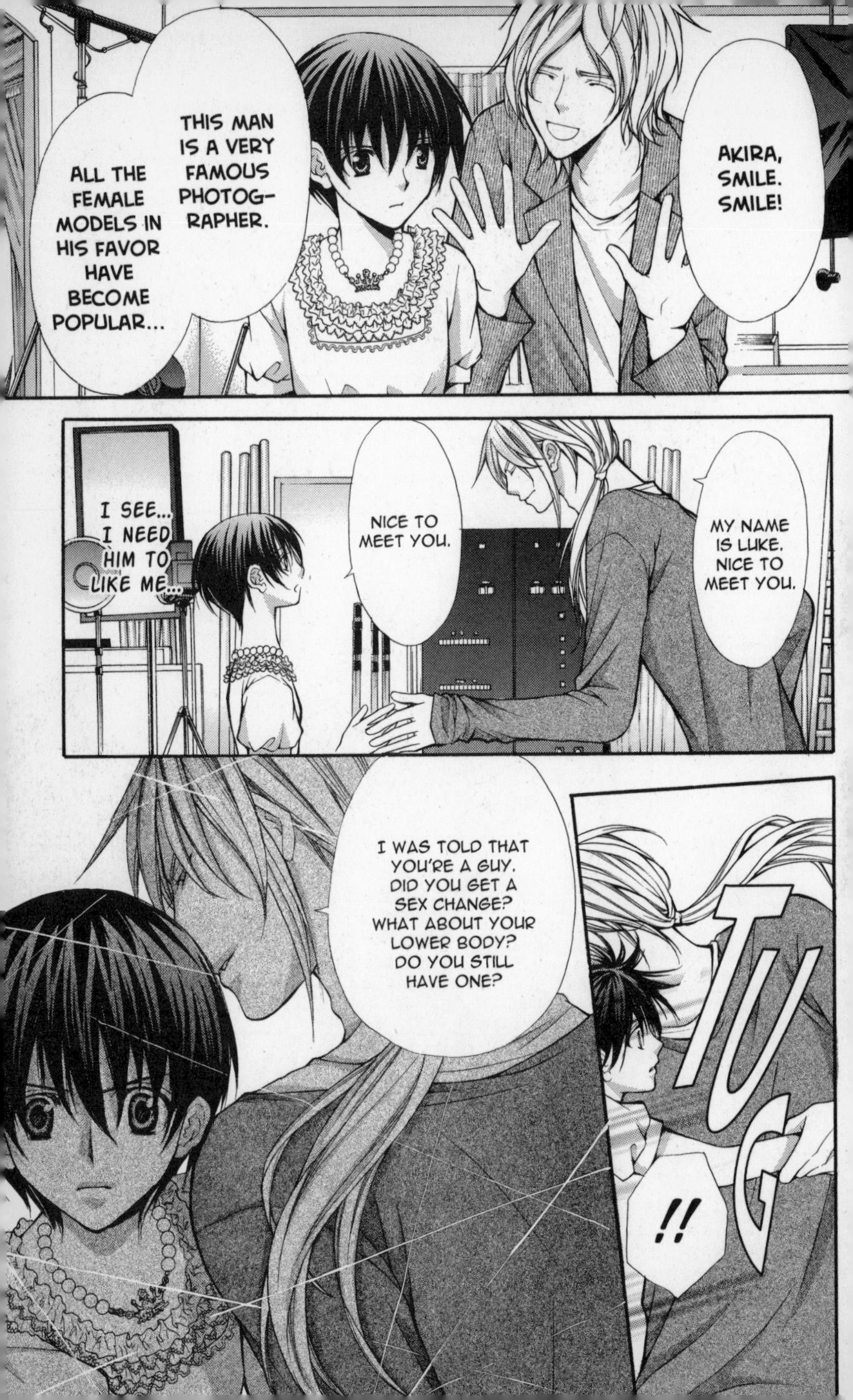
AKIRA, SMILE. SMILE!
THIS MAN IS A VERY FAMOUS PHOTOG-RAPHER.
ALL THE FEMALE MODELS IN HIS FAVOR HAVE BECOME POPULAR...
MY NAME IS LUKE. NICE TO MEET YOU.
NICE TO MEET YOU.
I SEE... I NEED HIM TO LIKE ME...
I WAS TOLD THAT YOU'RE A GUY. DID YOU GET A SEX CHANGE? WHAT ABOUT YOUR LOWER BODY? DO YOU STILL HAVE ONE?
TUG
!!

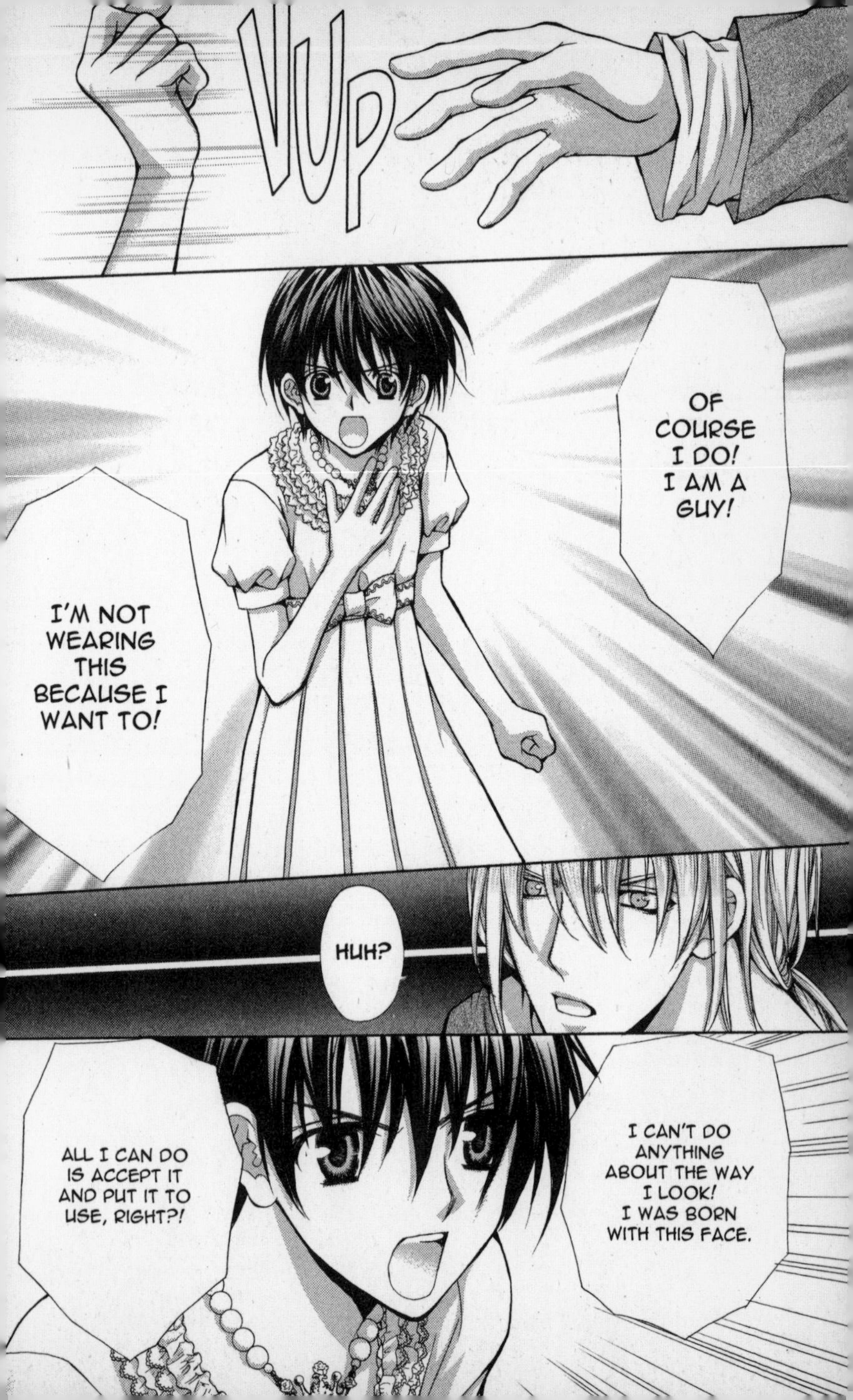
VUP
OF COURSE I DO! I AM A GUY!
I'M NOT WEARING THIS BECAUSE I WANT TO!
HUH?
I CAN'T DO ANYTHING ABOUT THE WAY I LOOK! I WAS BORN WITH THIS FACE.
ALL I CAN DO IS ACCEPT IT AND PUT IT TO USE, RIGHT?!

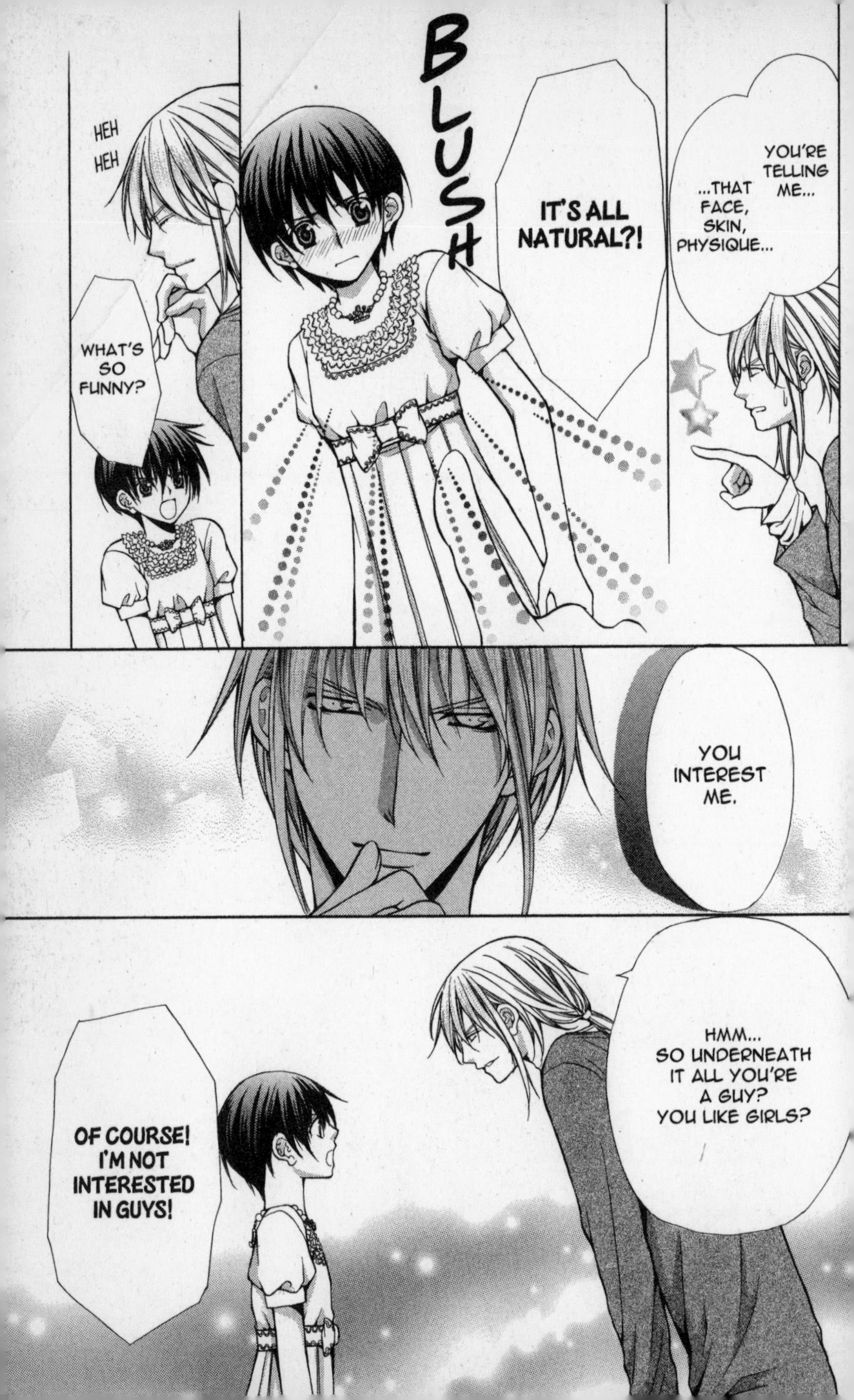
YOU'RE TELLING ME...
...THAT FACE, SKIN, PHYSIQUE...
IT'S ALL NATURAL?!
BLUSH
HEH HEH
WHAT'S SO FUNNY?
YOU INTEREST ME.
HMM... SO UNDERNEATH IT ALL YOU'RE A GUY? YOU LIKE GIRLS?
OF COURSE! I'M NOT INTERESTED IN GUYS!

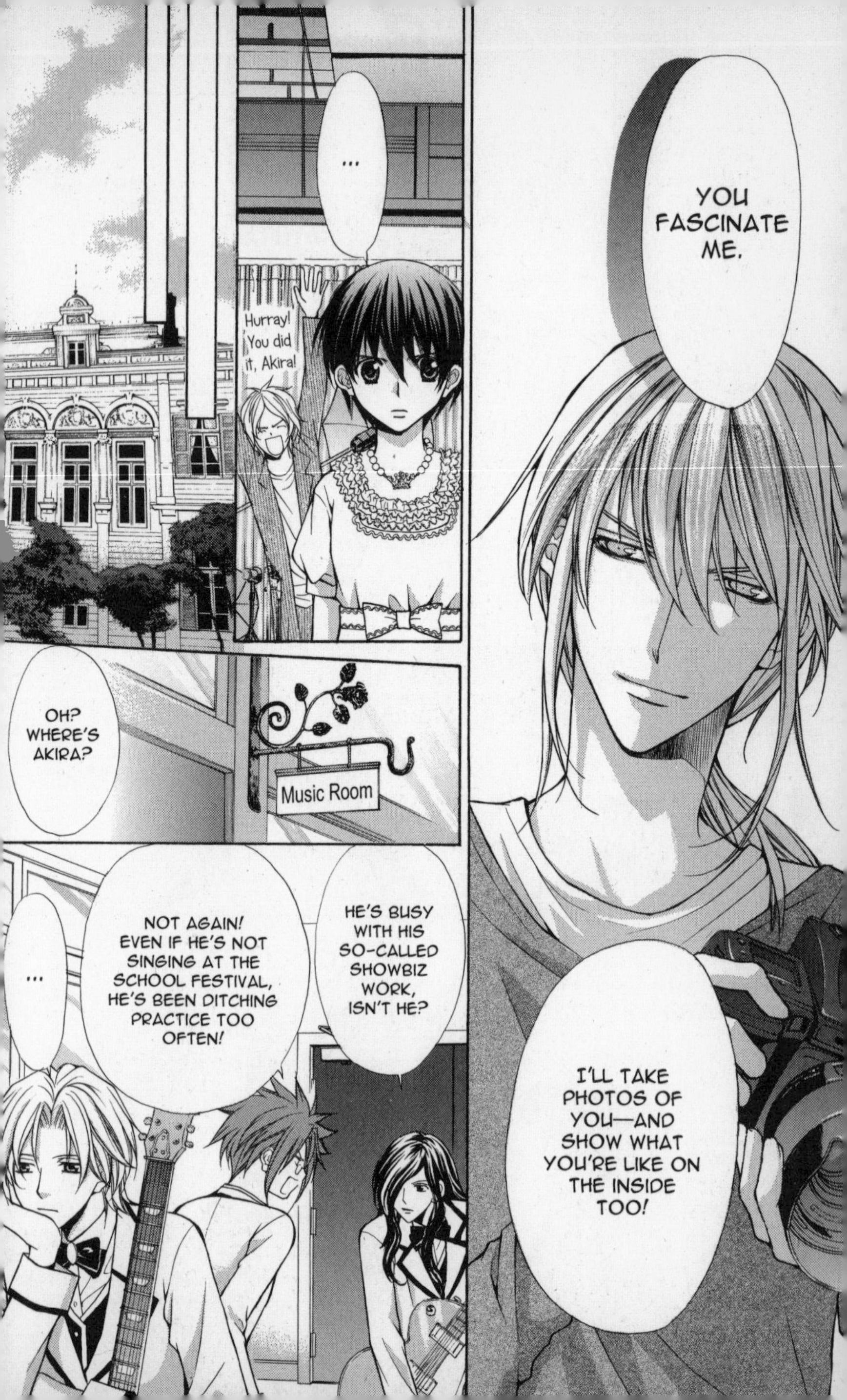
YOU FASCINATE ME.
I'LL TAKE PHOTOS OF YOU—AND SHOW WHAT YOU'RE LIKE ON THE INSIDE TOO!
...
Hurray! You did it, Akira!
OH? WHERE'S AKIRA?
Music Room
HE'S BUSY WITH HIS SO-CALLED SHOWBIZ WORK, ISN'T HE?
NOT AGAIN! EVEN IF HE'S NOT SINGING AT THE SCHOOL FESTIVAL, HE'S BEEN DITCHING PRACTICE TOO OFTEN!
...

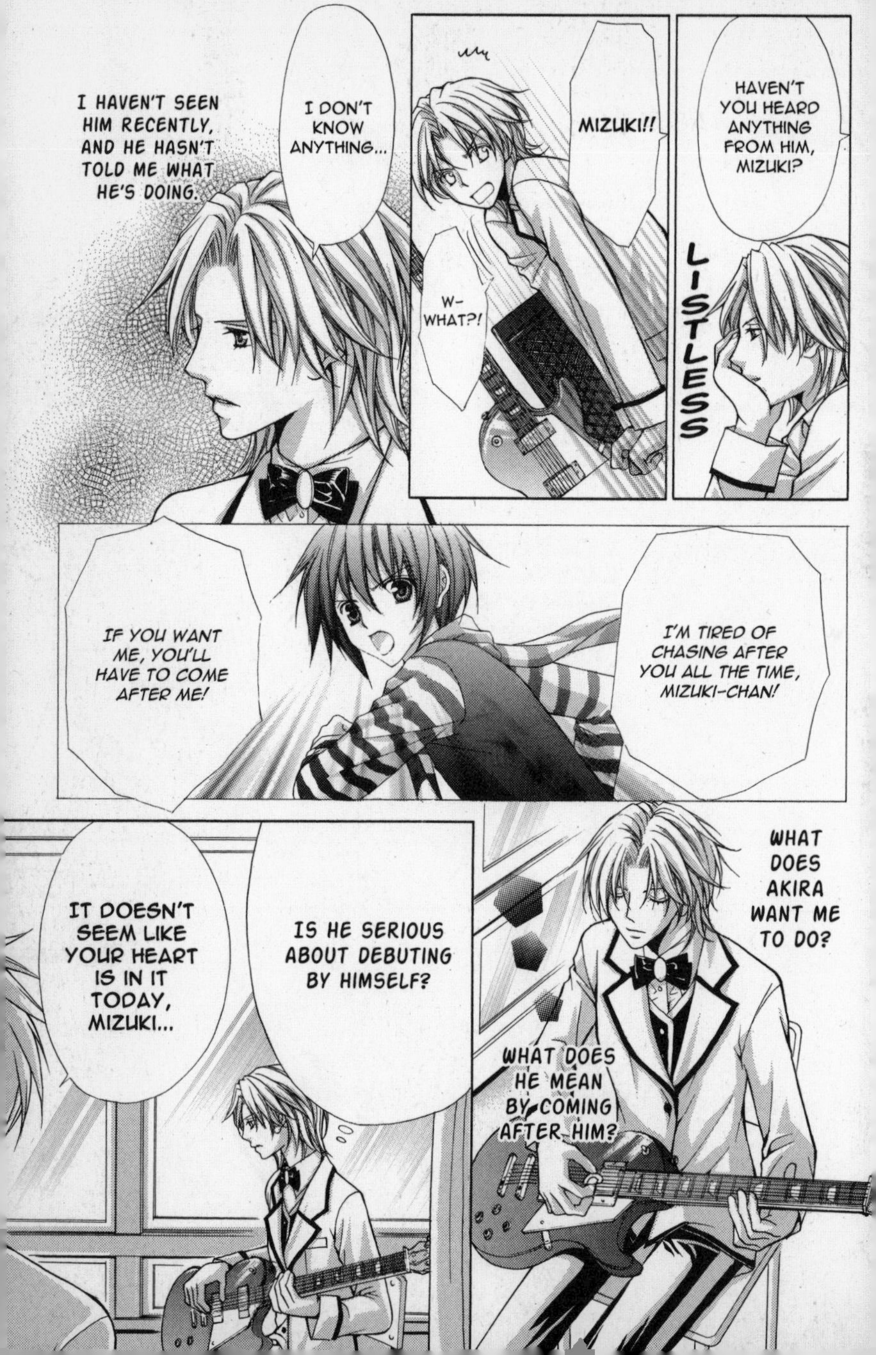
HAVEN'T YOU HEARD ANYTHING FROM HIM, MIZUKI?
LISTLESS
MIZUKI!!
W-WHAT?!
I DON'T KNOW ANYTHING...
I HAVEN'T SEEN HIM RECENTLY, AND HE HASN'T TOLD ME WHAT HE'S DOING.
I'M TIRED OF CHASING AFTER YOU ALL THE TIME, MIZUKI-CHAN!
IF YOU WANT ME, YOU'LL HAVE TO COME AFTER ME!
WHAT DOES AKIRA WANT ME TO DO?
WHAT DOES HE MEAN BY COMING AFTER HIM?
IS HE SERIOUS ABOUT DEBUTING BY HIMSELF?
IT DOESN'T SEEM LIKE YOUR HEART IS IN IT TODAY, MIZUKI...

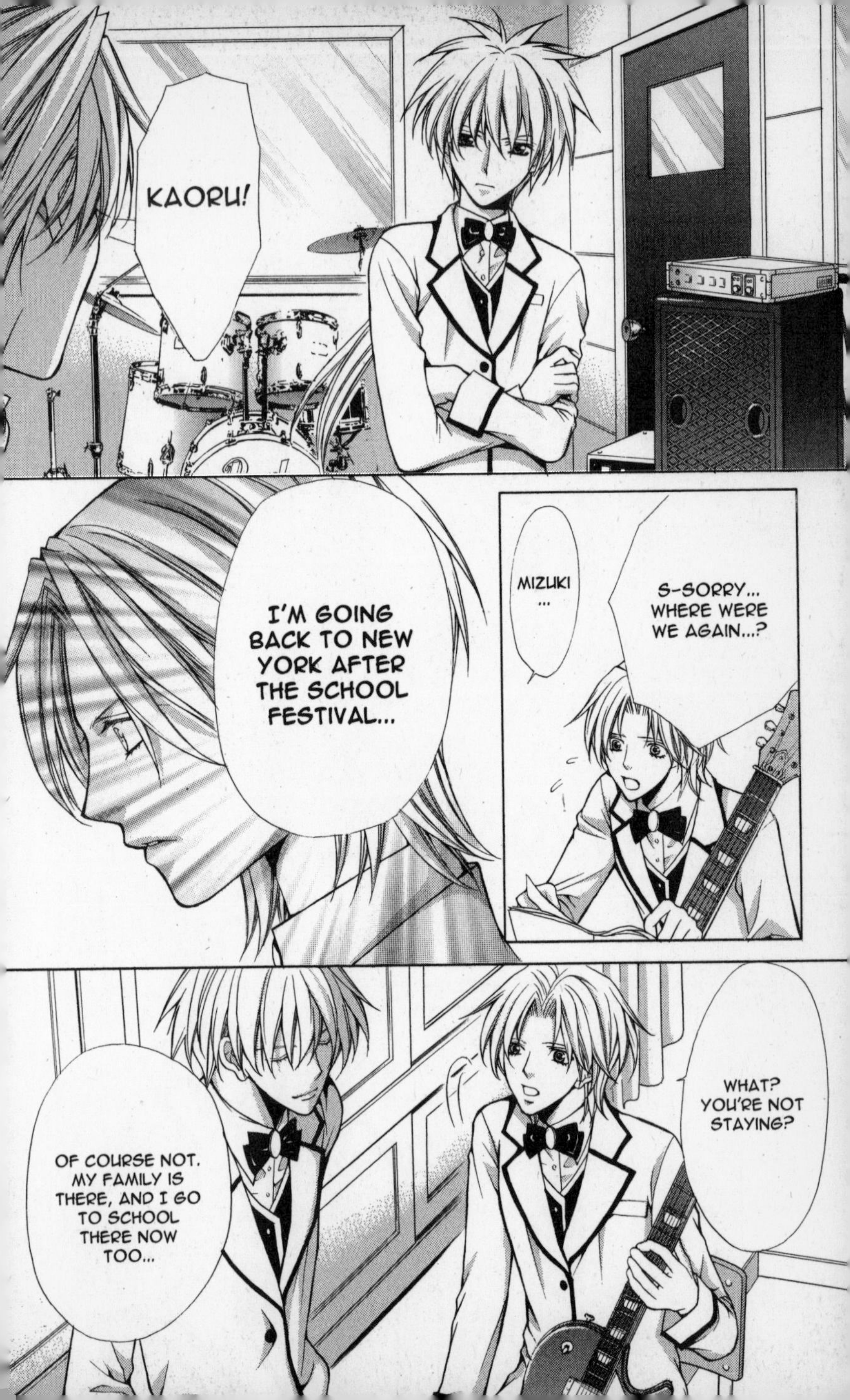
KAORU!
S-SORRY... WHERE WERE WE AGAIN...?
MIZUKI...
I'M GOING BACK TO NEW YORK AFTER THE SCHOOL FESTIVAL...
WHAT? YOU'RE NOT STAYING?
OF COURSE NOT. MY FAMILY IS THERE, AND I GO TO SCHOOL THERE NOW TOO...

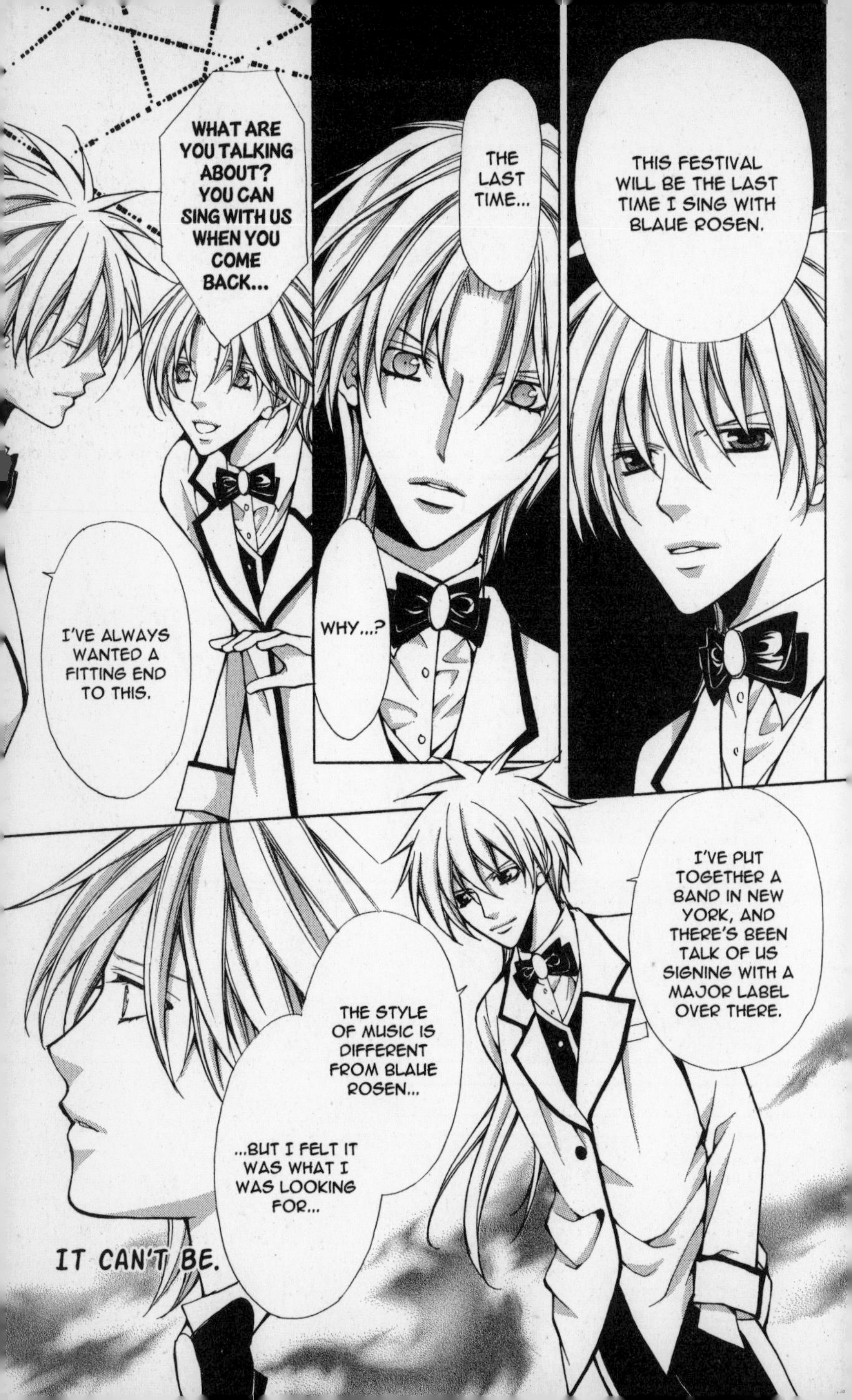
THIS FESTIVAL WILL BE THE LAST TIME I SING WITH BLAUE ROSEN.
THE LAST TIME...
WHY...?
WHAT ARE YOU TALKING ABOUT? YOU CAN SING WITH US WHEN YOU COME BACK...
I'VE ALWAYS WANTED A FITTING END TO THIS.
I'VE PUT TOGETHER A BAND IN NEW YORK, AND THERE'S BEEN TALK OF US SIGNING WITH A MAJOR LABEL OVER THERE.
THE STYLE OF MUSIC IS DIFFERENT FROM BLAUE ROSEN...
...BUT I FELT IT WAS WHAT I WAS LOOKING FOR...
IT CAN'T BE.

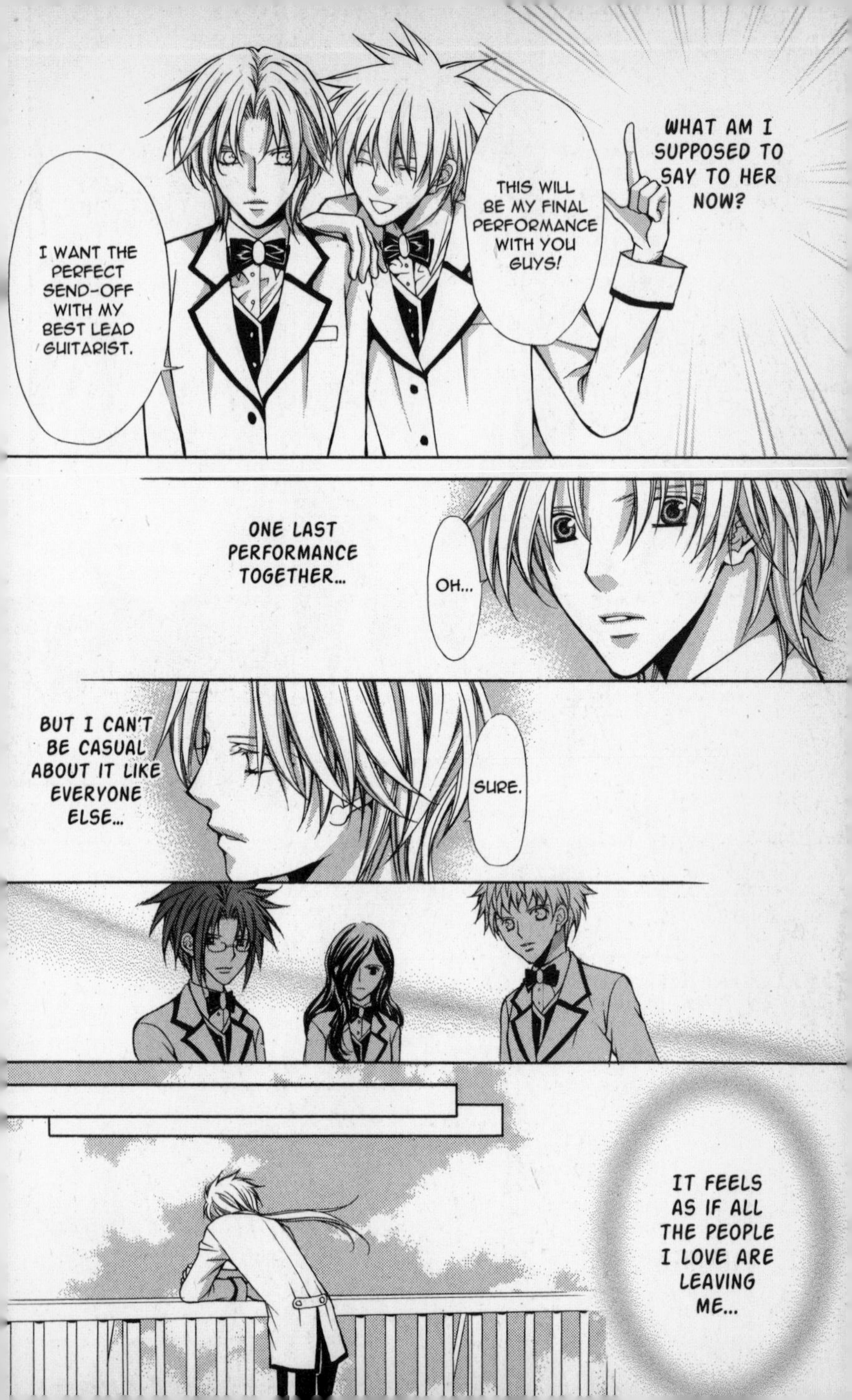
WHAT AM I SUPPOSED TO SAY TO HER NOW?
THIS WILL BE MY FINAL PERFORMANCE WITH YOU GUYS!
I WANT THE PERFECT SEND-OFF WITH MY BEST LEAD GUITARIST.
OH...
ONE LAST PERFORMANCE TOGETHER...
SURE.
BUT I CAN'T BE CASUAL ABOUT IT LIKE EVERYONE ELSE...
IT FEELS AS IF ALL THE PEOPLE I LOVE ARE LEAVING ME...

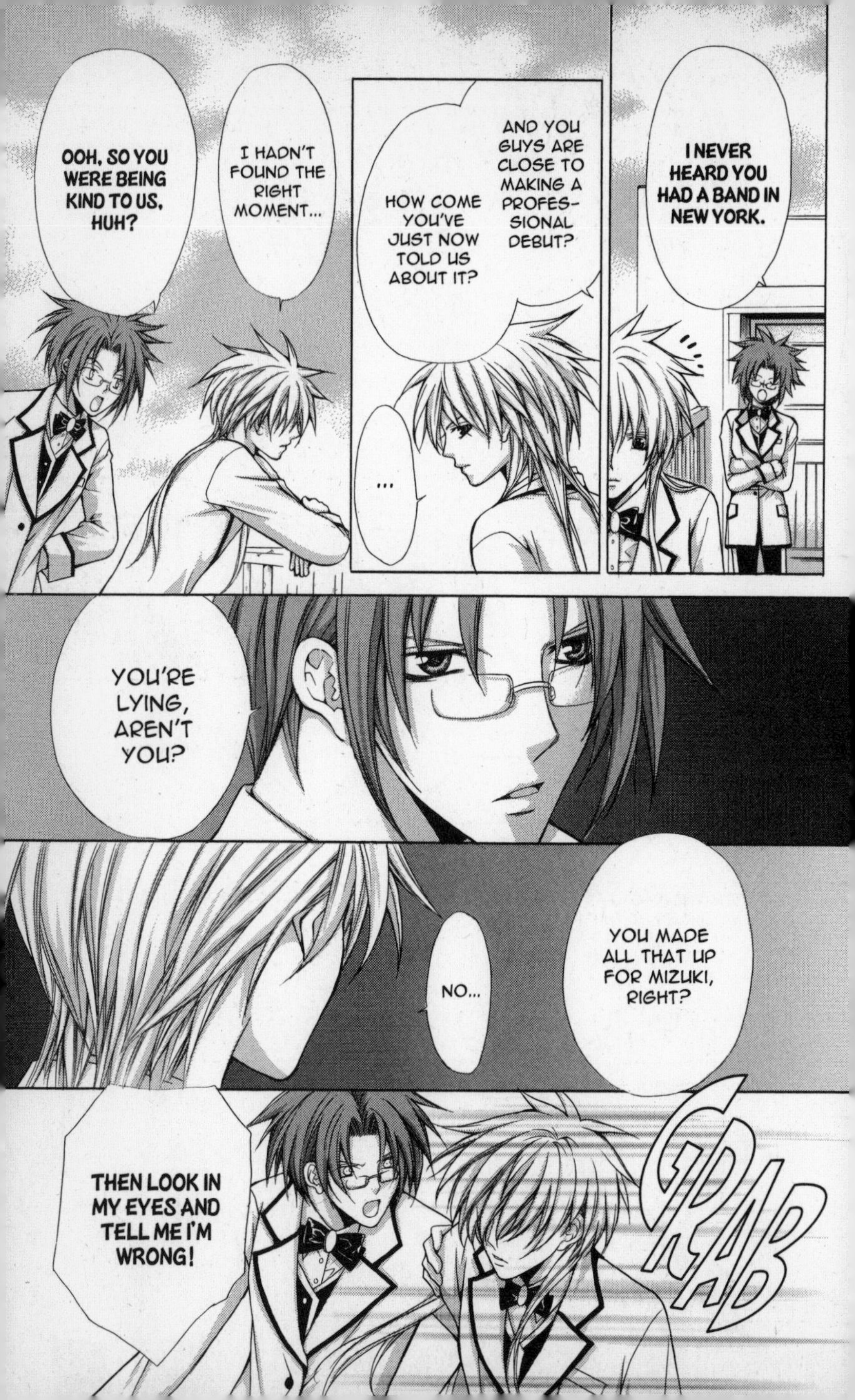
I NEVER HEARD YOU HAD A BAND IN NEW YORK.
AND YOU GUYS ARE CLOSE TO MAKING A PROFESSIONAL DEBUT?
HOW COME YOU'VE JUST NOW TOLD US ABOUT IT?
...
I HADN'T FOUND THE RIGHT MOMENT...
OOH, SO YOU WERE BEING KIND TO US, HUH?
YOU'RE LYING, AREN'T YOU?
YOU MADE ALL THAT UP FOR MIZUKI, RIGHT?
NO...
GRAB
THEN LOOK IN MY EYES AND TELL ME I'M WRONG!

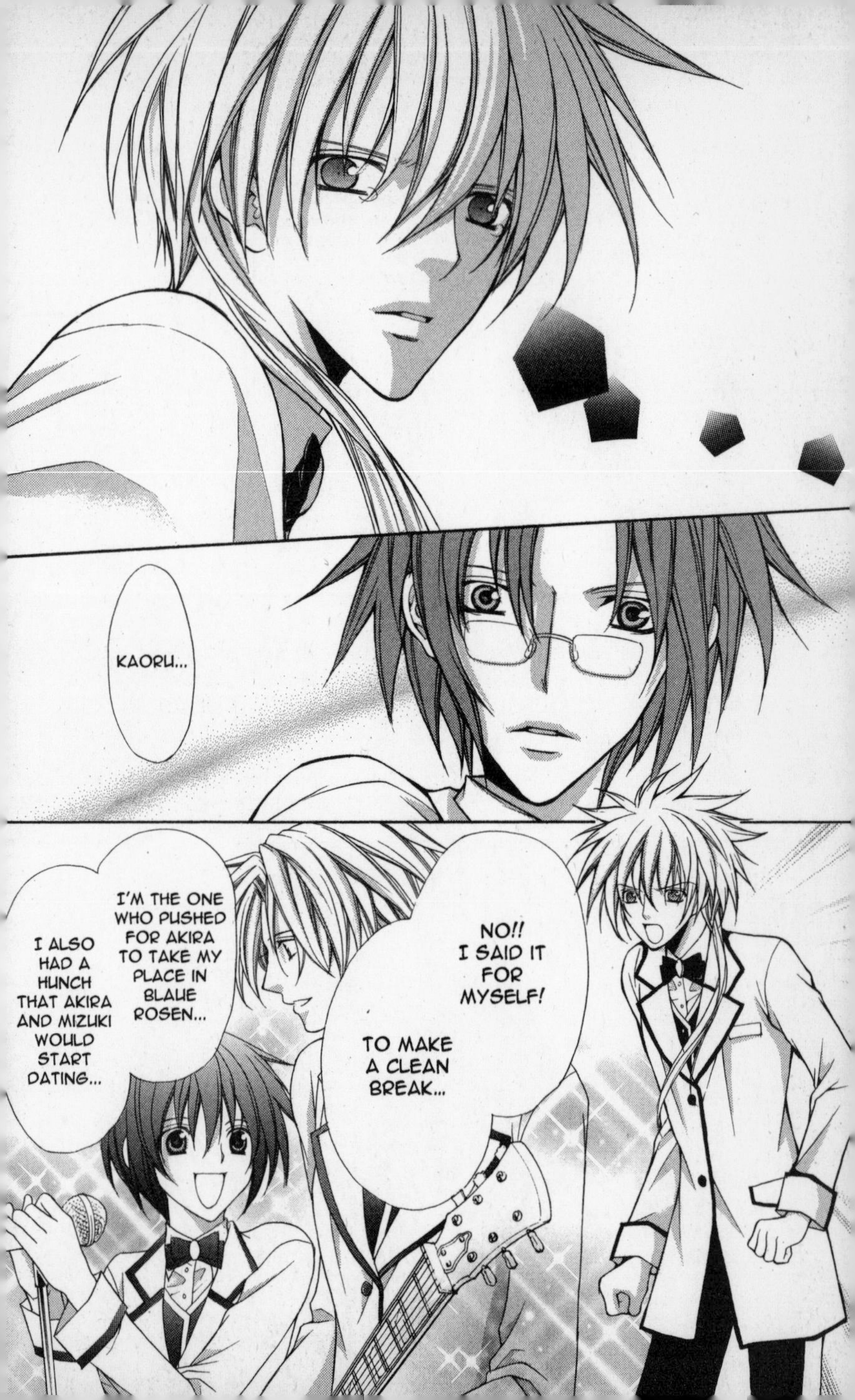
KAORU...
NO!! I SAID IT FOR MYSELF!
TO MAKE A CLEAN BREAK...
I'M THE ONE WHO PUSHED FOR AKIRA TO TAKE MY PLACE IN BLAUE ROSEN...
I ALSO HAD A HUNCH THAT AKIRA AND MIZUKI WOULD START DATING...

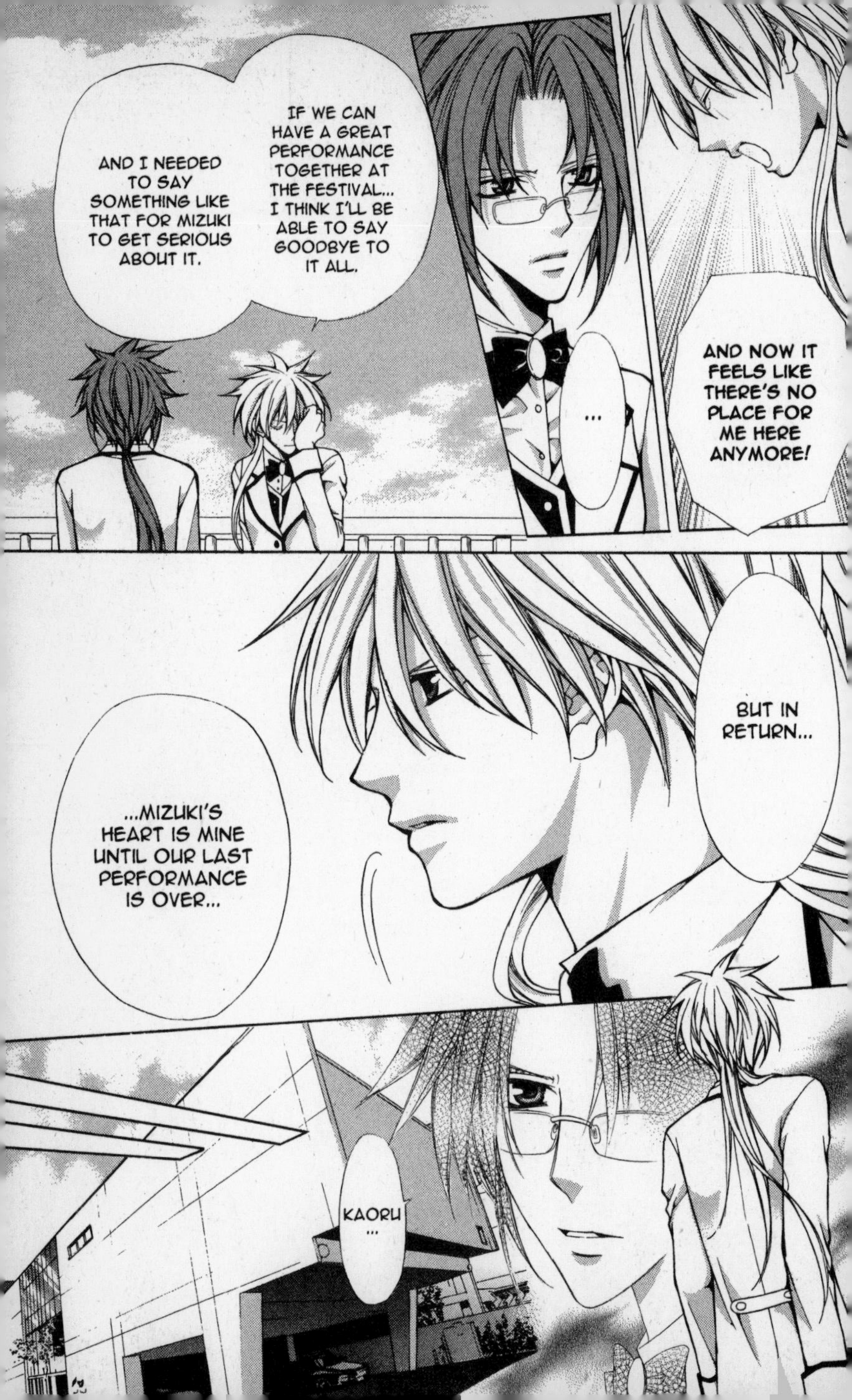
AND NOW IT FEELS LIKE THERE'S NO PLACE FOR ME HERE ANYMORE!
...
IF WE CAN HAVE A GREAT PERFORMANCE TOGETHER AT THE FESTIVAL... I THINK I'LL BE ABLE TO SAY GOODBYE TO IT ALL.
AND I NEEDED TO SAY SOMETHING LIKE THAT FOR MIZUKI TO GET SERIOUS ABOUT IT.
BUT IN RETURN...
...MIZUKI'S HEART IS MINE UNTIL OUR LAST PERFORMANCE IS OVER...
KAORU ...

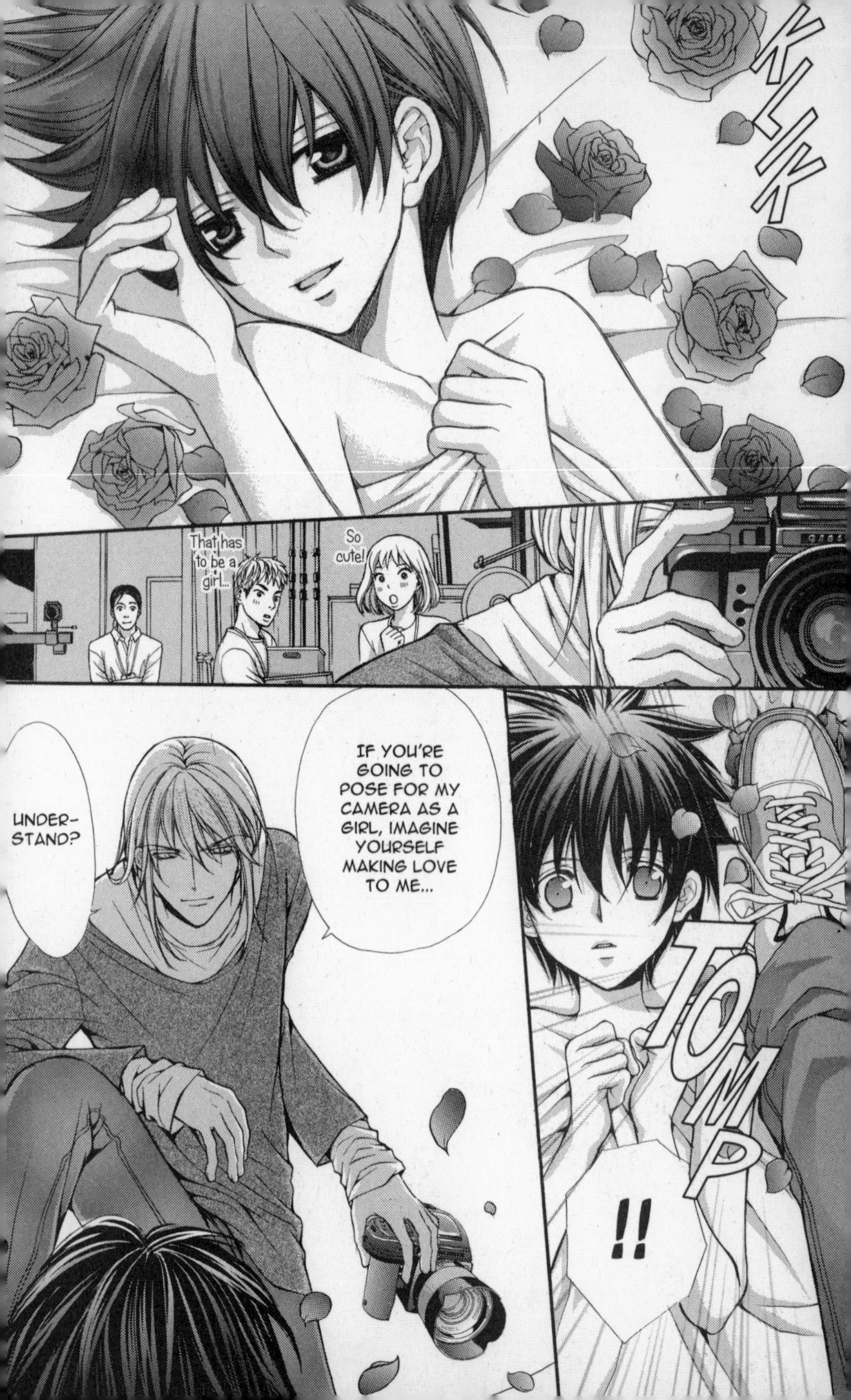
KLIK
So cute!
That has to be a girl...
TOMP
!!
IF YOU'RE GOING TO POSE FOR MY CAMERA AS A GIRL, IMAGINE YOURSELF MAKING LOVE TO ME...
UNDER-STAND?

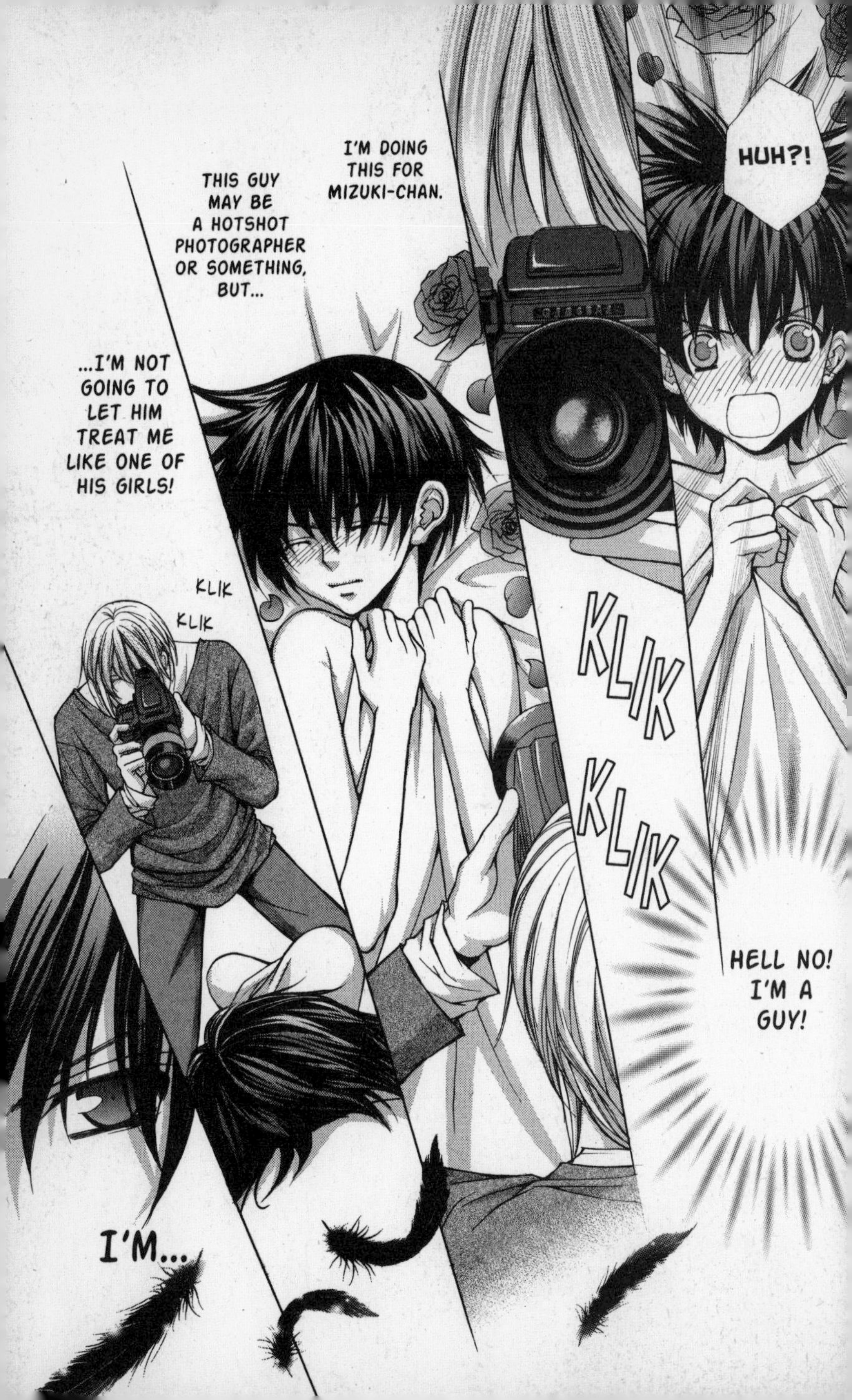
HUH?!
HELL NO! I'M A GUY!
KLIK
KLIK
I'M DOING THIS FOR MIZUKI-CHAN.
THIS GUY MAY BE A HOTSHOT PHOTOGRAPHER OR SOMETHING, BUT...
...I'M NOT GOING TO LET HIM TREAT ME LIKE ONE OF HIS GIRLS!
KLIK
KLIK
I'M...

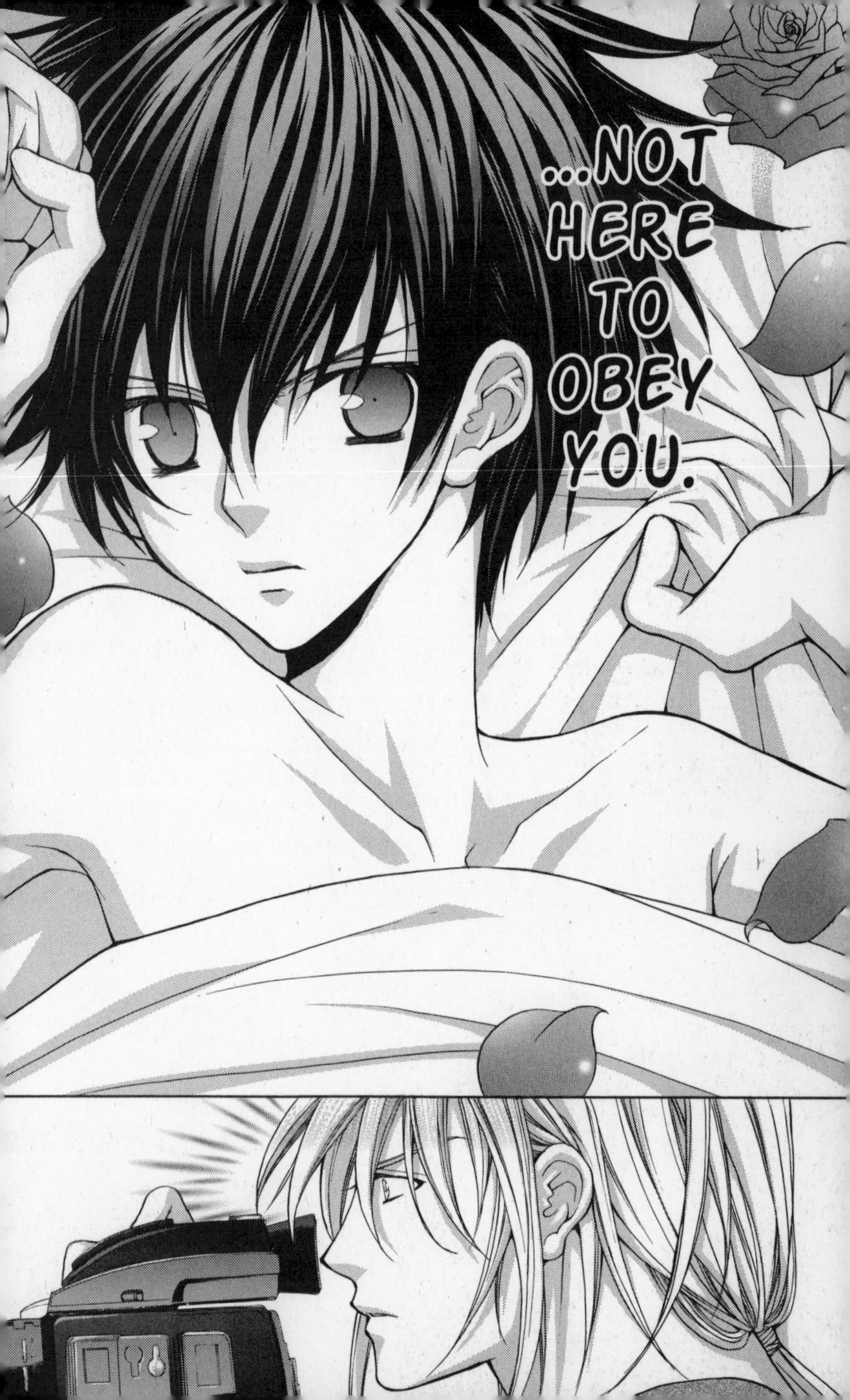
...NOT HERE TO OBEY YOU.

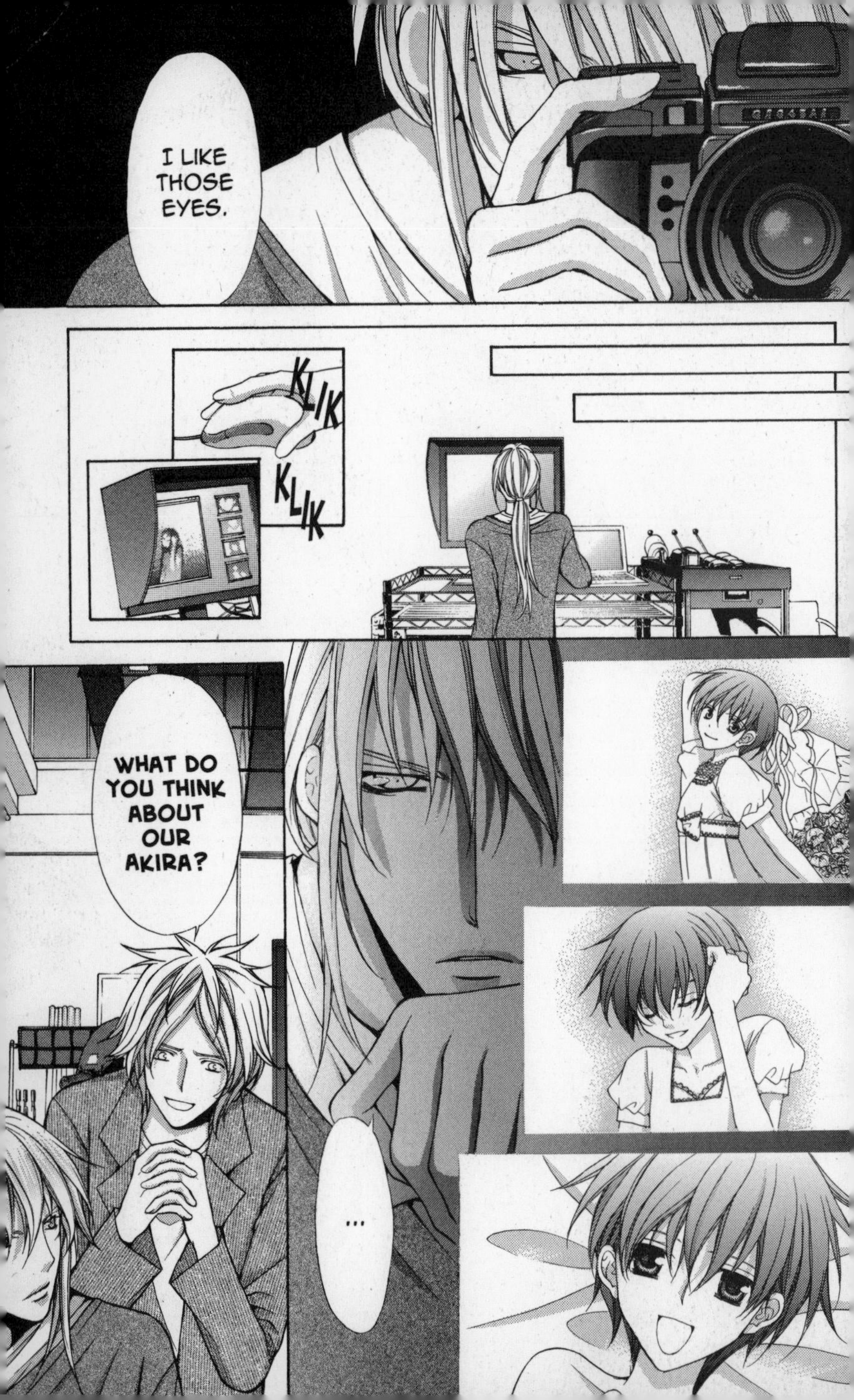
I LIKE THOSE EYES.
KLIK
KLIK
WHAT DO YOU THINK ABOUT OUR AKIRA?
...

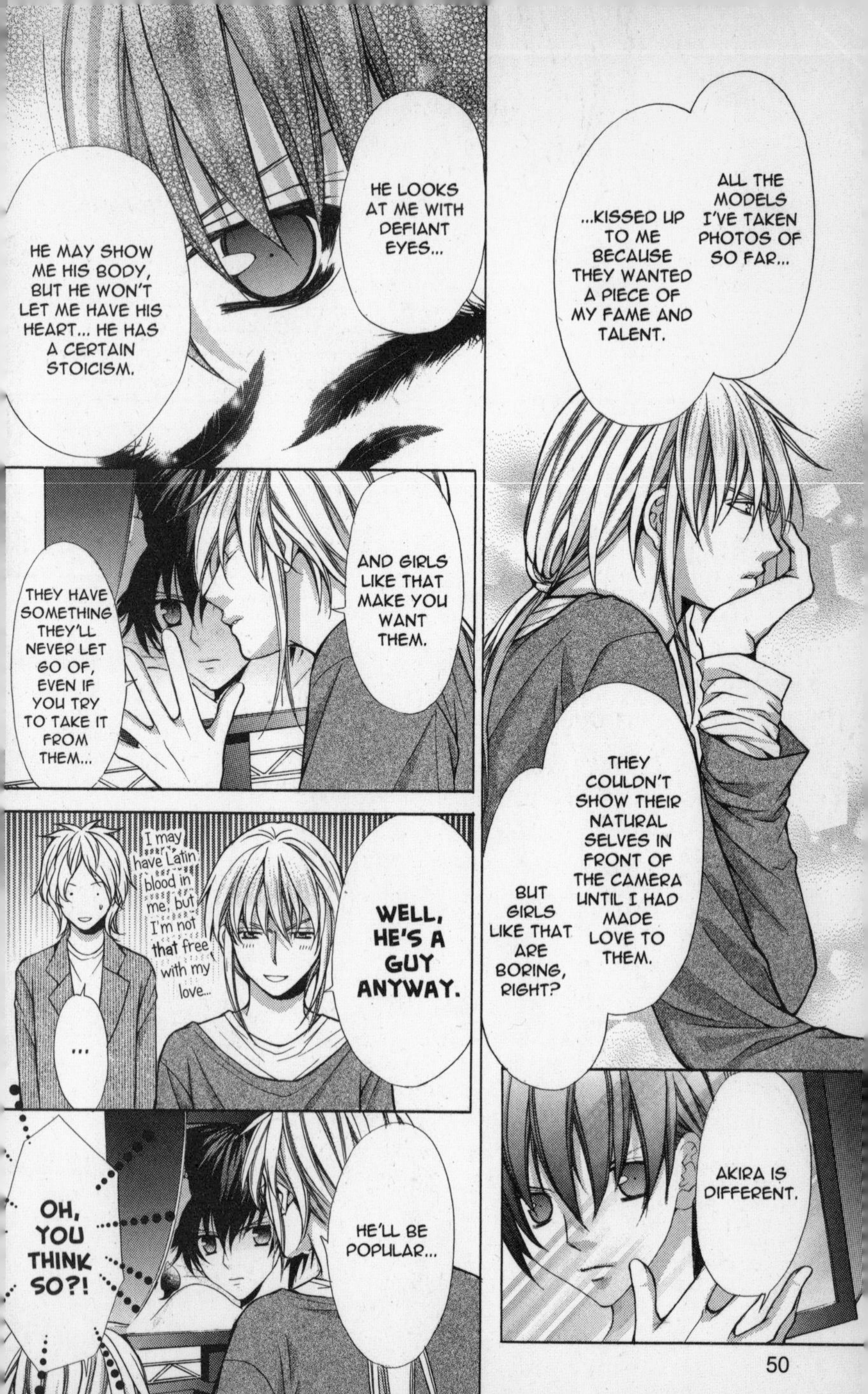
ALL THE MODELS I'VE TAKEN PHOTOS OF SO FAR...
...KISSED UP TO ME BECAUSE THEY WANTED A PIECE OF MY FAME AND TALENT.
THEY COULDN'T SHOW THEIR NATURAL SELVES IN FRONT OF THE CAMERA UNTIL I HAD MADE LOVE TO THEM.
BUT GIRLS LIKE THAT ARE BORING, RIGHT?
AKIRA IS DIFFERENT.
HE LOOKS AT ME WITH DEFIANT EYES...
HE MAY SHOW ME HIS BODY, BUT HE WON'T LET ME HAVE HIS HEART... HE HAS A CERTAIN STOICISM.
AND GIRLS LIKE THAT MAKE YOU WANT THEM.
THEY HAVE SOMETHING THEY'LL NEVER LET GO OF, EVEN IF YOU TRY TO TAKE IT FROM THEM...
WELL, HE'S A GUY ANYWAY.
I may have Latin blood in me, but I'm not that free with my love...
...
HE'LL BE POPULAR...
OH, YOU THINK SO?!

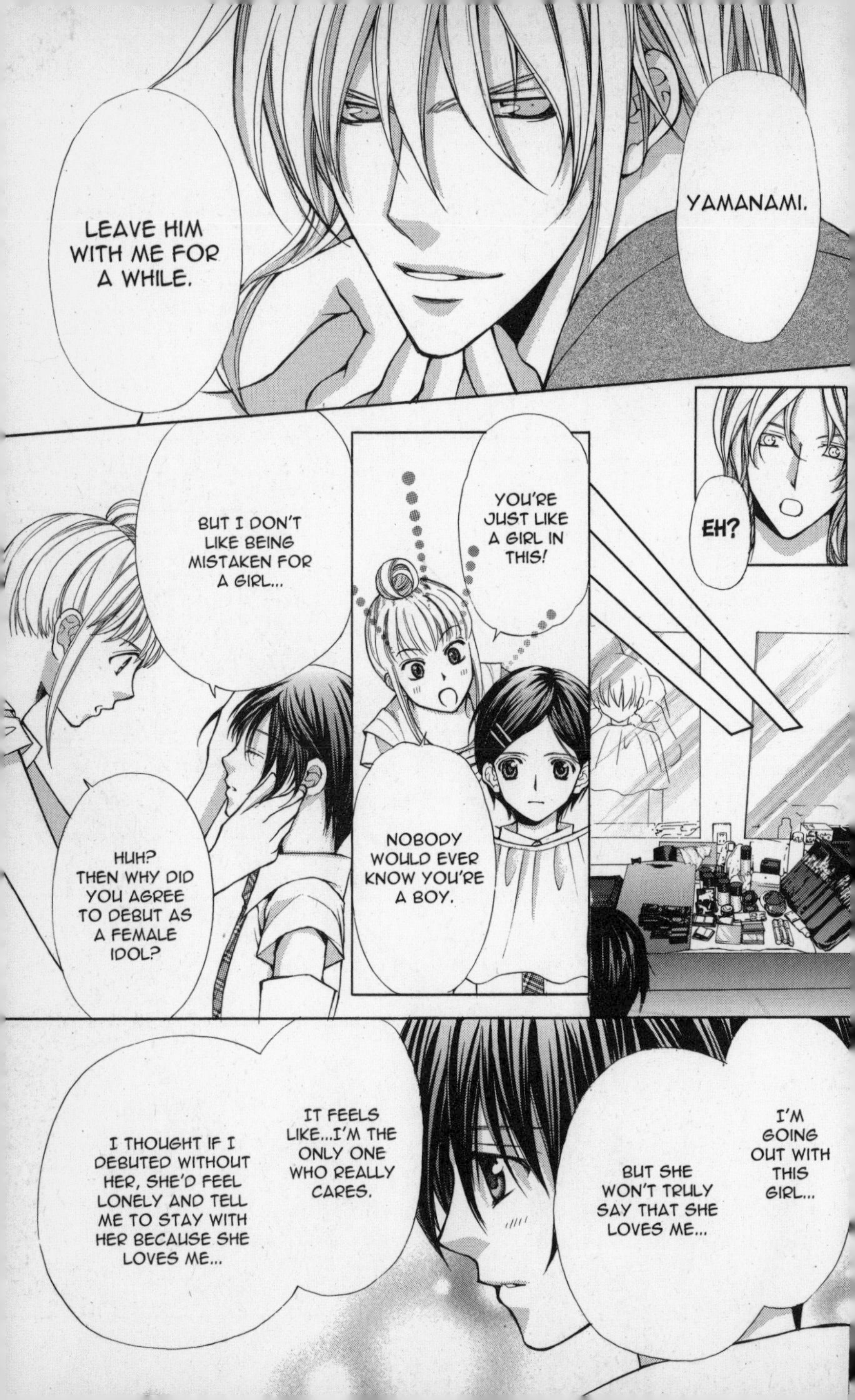
YAMANAMI.
LEAVE HIM WITH ME FOR A WHILE.
EH?
YOU'RE JUST LIKE A GIRL IN THIS!
NOBODY WOULD EVER KNOW YOU'RE A BOY.
BUT I DON'T LIKE BEING MISTAKEN FOR A GIRL...
HUH? THEN WHY DID YOU AGREE TO DEBUT AS A FEMALE IDOL?
I'M GOING OUT WITH THIS GIRL...
BUT SHE WON'T TRULY SAY THAT SHE LOVES ME...
IT FEELS LIKE...I'M THE ONLY ONE WHO REALLY CARES.
I THOUGHT IF I DEBUTED WITHOUT HER, SHE'D FEEL LONELY AND TELL ME TO STAY WITH HER BECAUSE SHE LOVES ME...

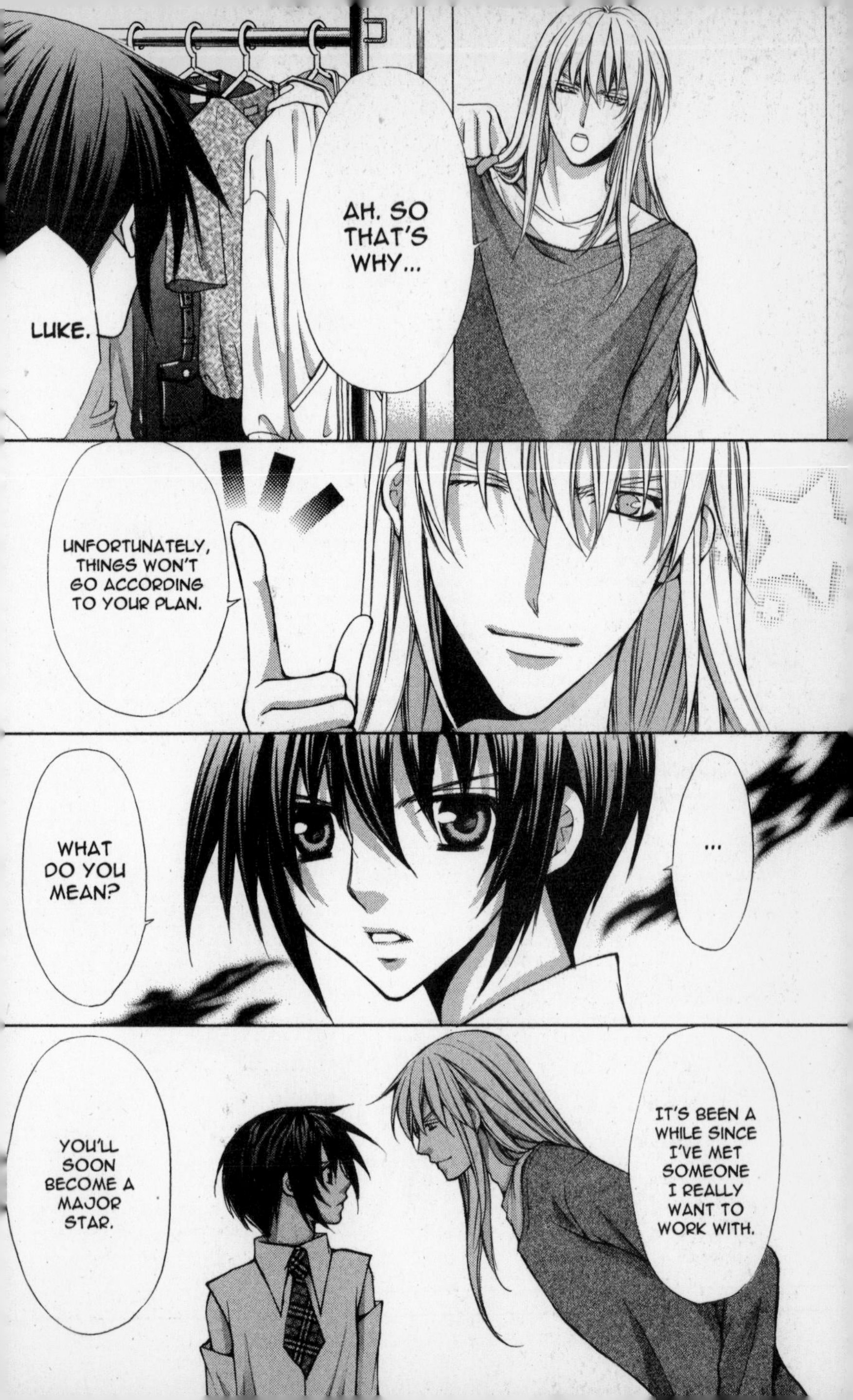
AH. SO THAT'S WHY...
LUKE.
UNFORTUNATELY, THINGS WON'T GO ACCORDING TO YOUR PLAN.
...
WHAT DO YOU MEAN?
IT'S BEEN A WHILE SINCE I'VE MET SOMEONE I REALLY WANT TO WORK WITH.
YOU'LL SOON BECOME A MAJOR STAR.

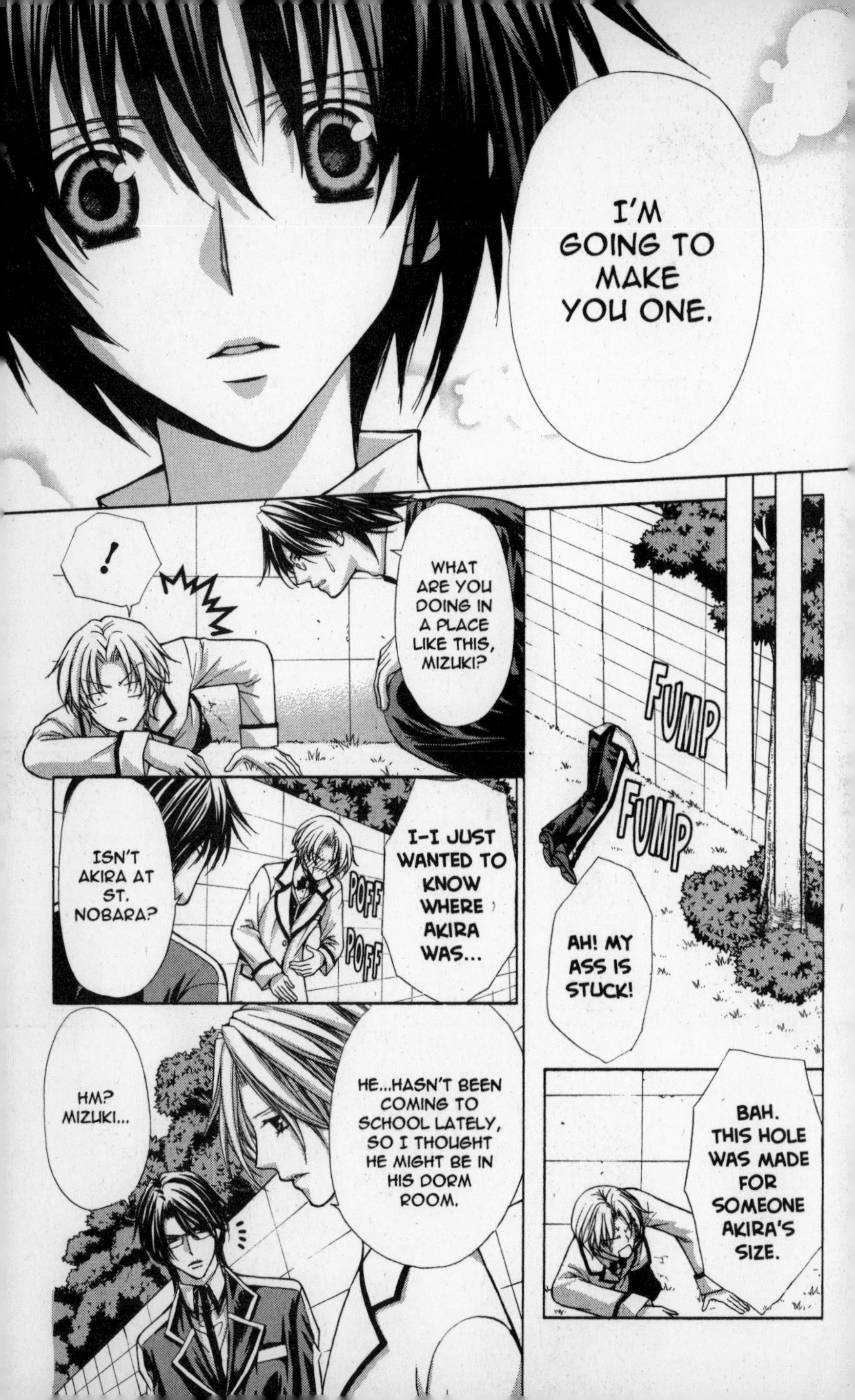

I'M GOING TO MAKE YOU ONE.
FUMP
FUMP
AH! MY ASS IS STUCK!
BAH. THIS HOLE WAS MADE FOR SOMEONE AKIRA'S SIZE.
WHAT ARE YOU DOING IN A PLACE LIKE THIS, MIZUKI?
!
I-I JUST WANTED TO KNOW WHERE AKIRA WAS...
POFF
POFF
ISN'T AKIRA AT ST. NOBARA?
HE...HASN'T BEEN COMING TO SCHOOL LATELY, SO I THOUGHT HE MIGHT BE IN HIS DORM ROOM.
HM? MIZUKI...

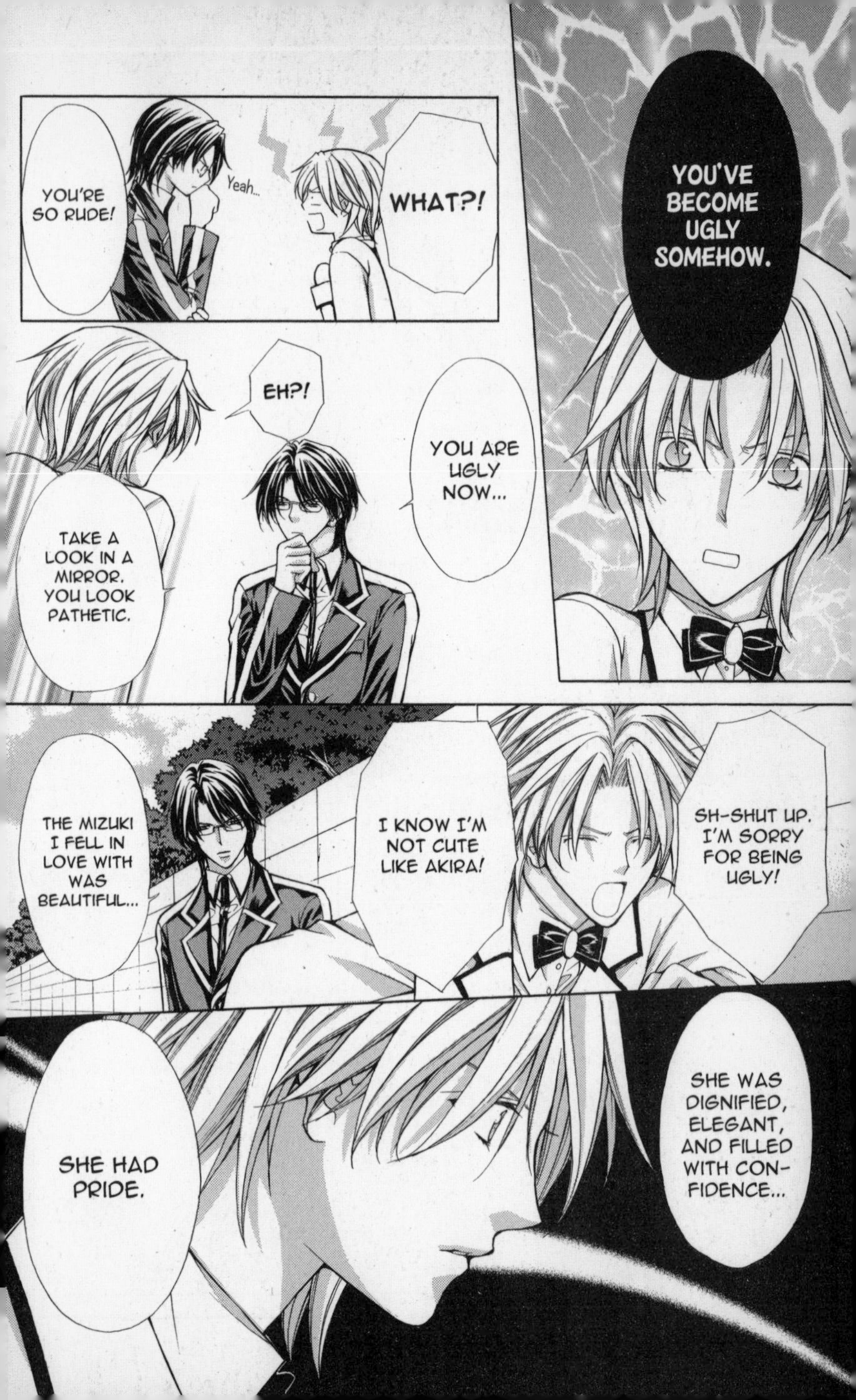

YOU'VE BECOME UGLY SOMEHOW.
WHAT?!
Yeah...
YOU'RE SO RUDE!
YOU ARE UGLY NOW...
EH?!
TAKE A LOOK IN A MIRROR. YOU LOOK PATHETIC.
SH-SHUT UP. I'M SORRY FOR BEING UGLY!
I KNOW I'M NOT CUTE LIKE AKIRA!
THE MIZUKI I FELL IN LOVE WITH WAS BEAUTIFUL...
SHE WAS DIGNIFIED, ELEGANT, AND FILLED WITH CON-FIDENCE...
SHE HAD PRIDE.

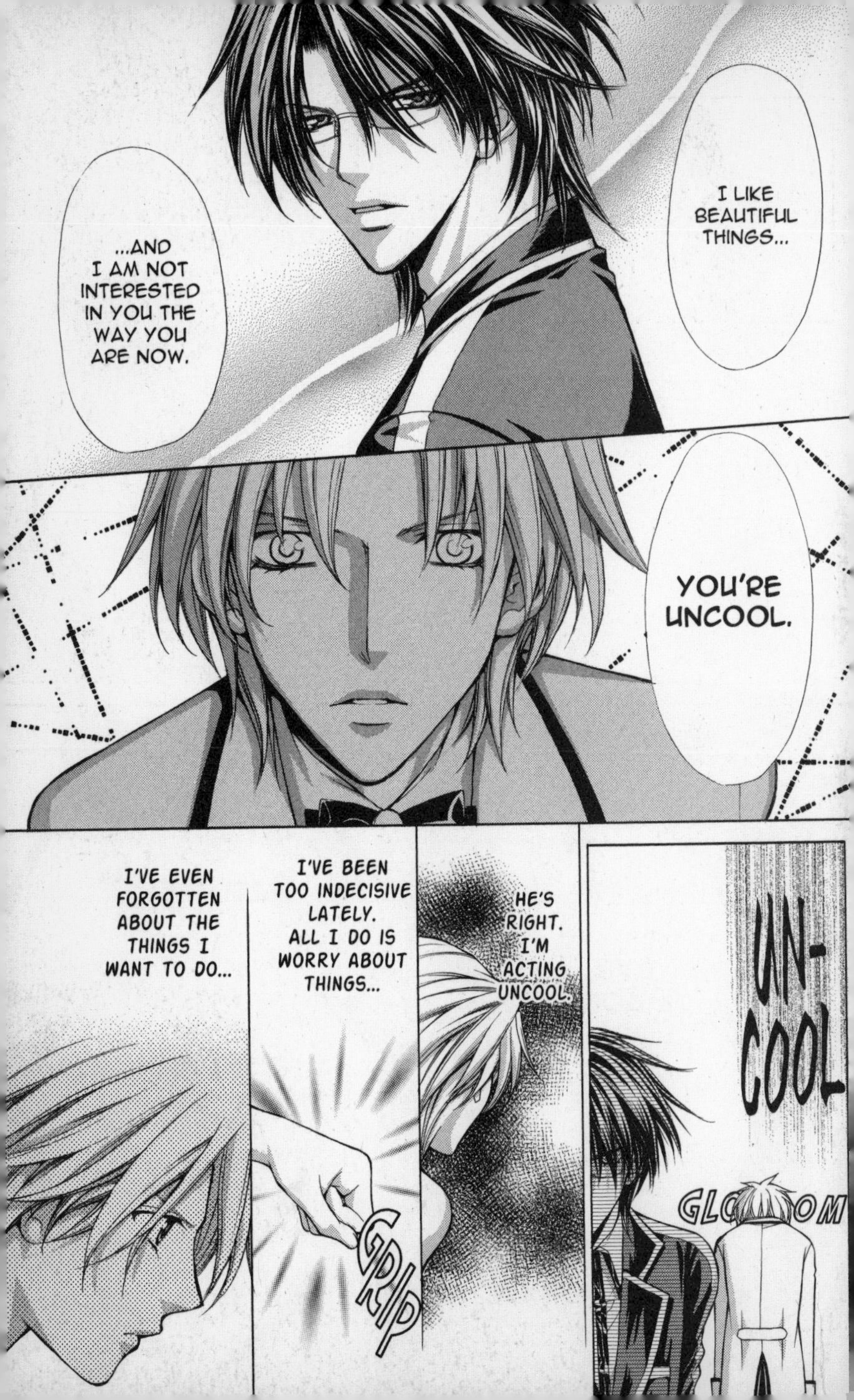
I LIKE BEAUTIFUL THINGS...
...AND I AM NOT INTERESTED IN YOU THE WAY YOU ARE NOW.
YOU'RE UNCOOL.
UN-COOL
GLO OM
HE'S RIGHT. I'M ACTING UNCOOL.
I'VE BEEN TOO INDECISIVE LATELY. ALL I DO IS WORRY ABOUT THINGS...
GRIP
I'VE EVEN FORGOTTEN ABOUT THE THINGS I WANT TO DO...

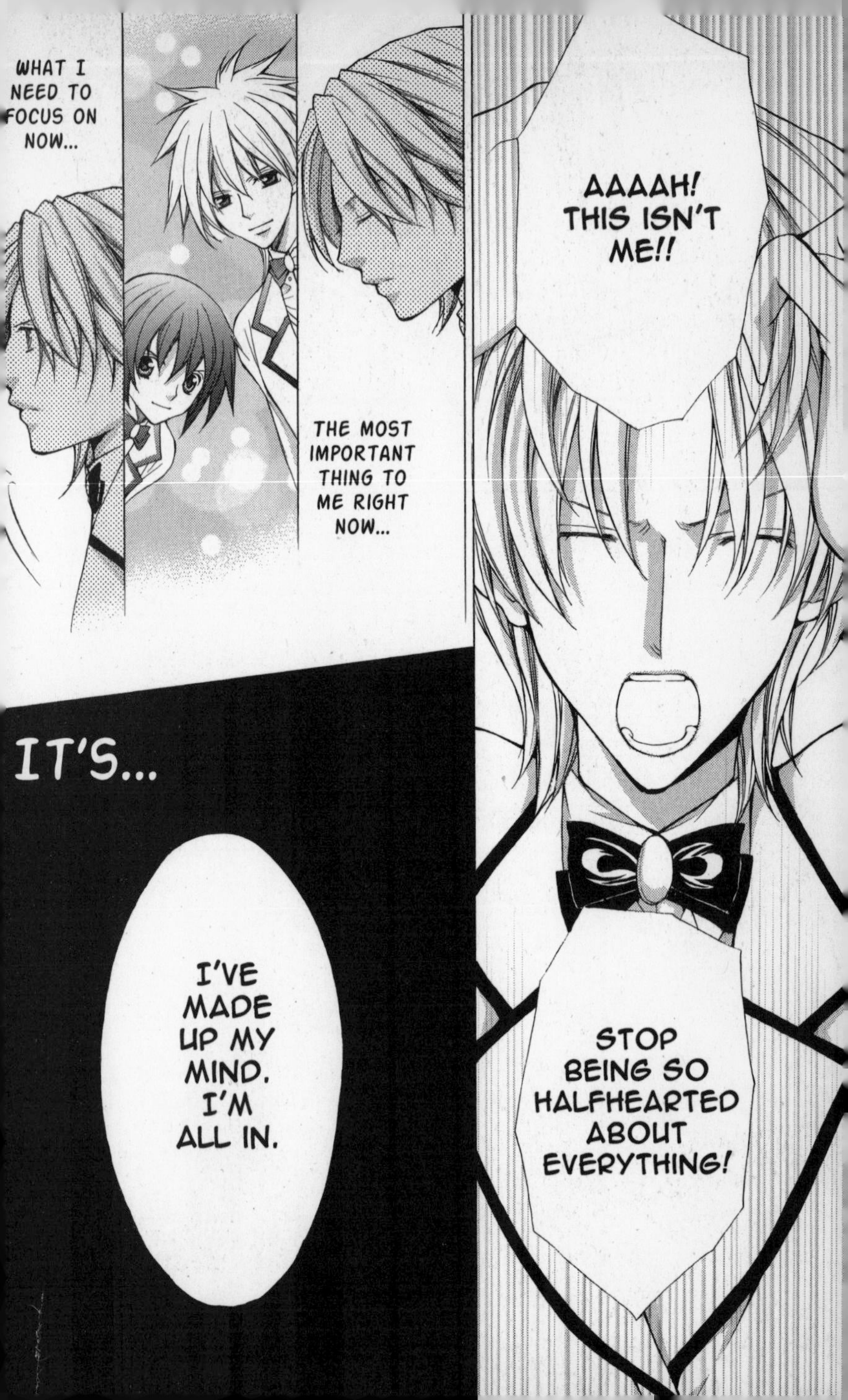
AAAAH! THIS ISN'T ME!!
STOP BEING SO HALFHEARTED ABOUT EVERYTHING!
THE MOST IMPORTANT THING TO ME RIGHT NOW...
WHAT I NEED TO FOCUS ON NOW...
IT'S...
I'VE MADE UP MY MIND. I'M ALL IN.

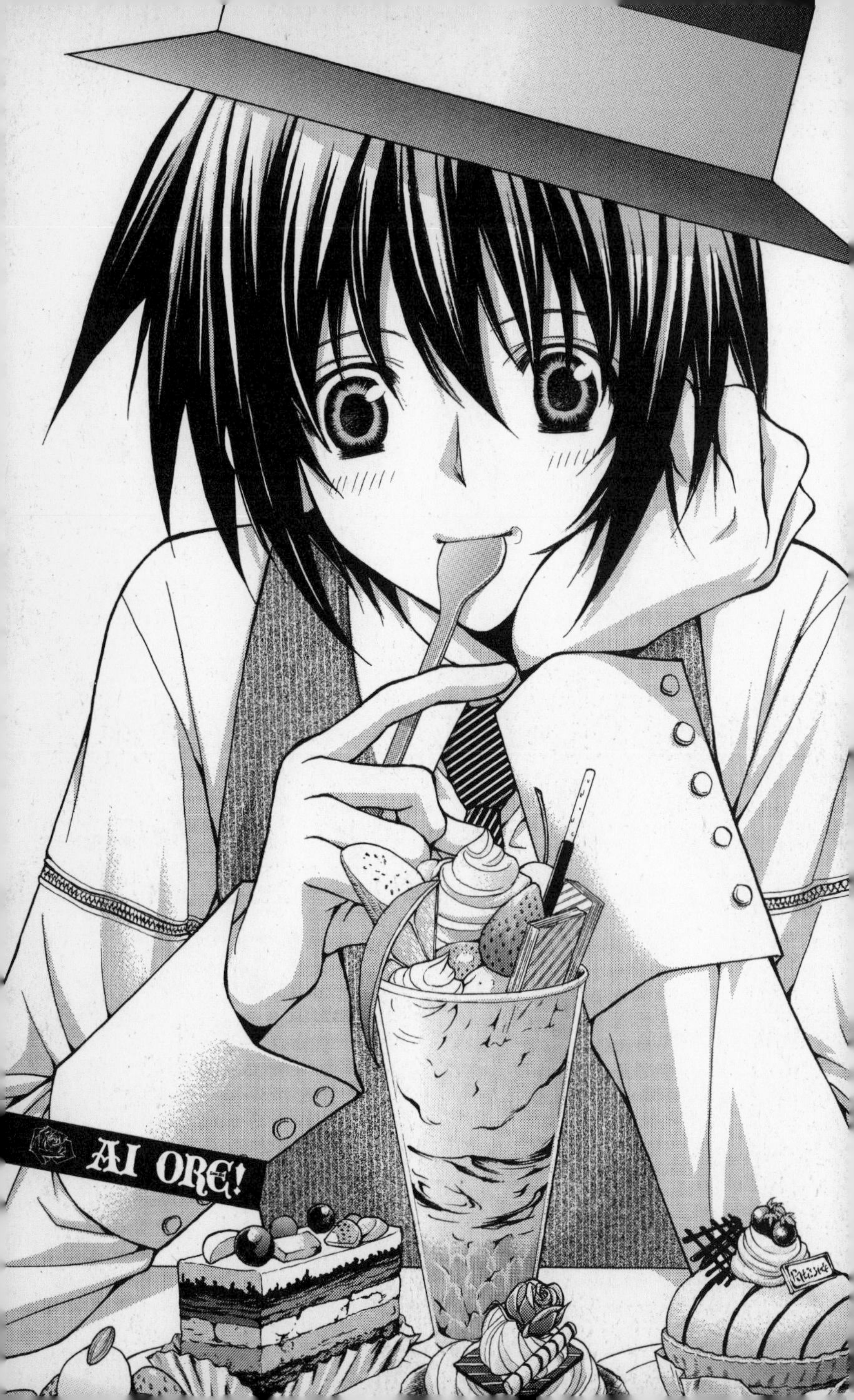
AI ORE!

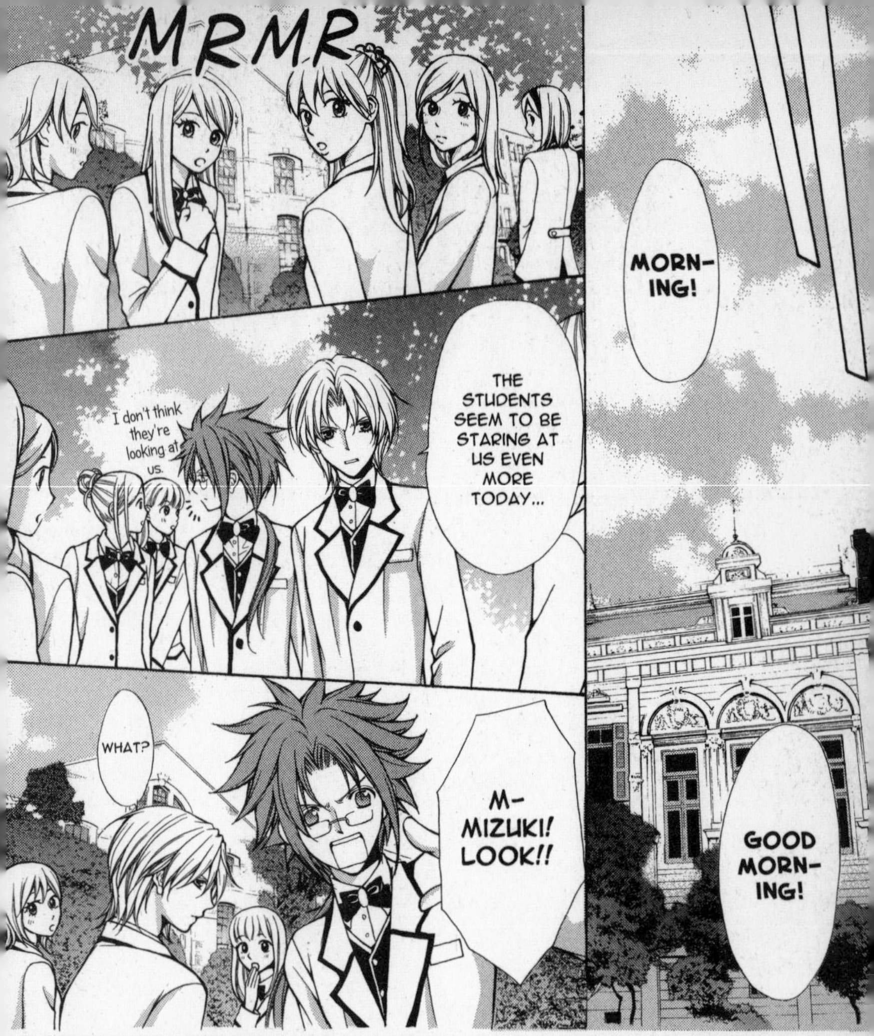
MORN-ING!
GOOD MORN-ING!
MRMR
THE STUDENTS SEEM TO BE STARING AT US EVEN MORE TODAY...
I don't think they're looking at us.
M-MIZUKI! LOOK!!
WHAT?

Recent Events

Hurray for heavy clothing! Men are at their best when they're wearing layers! Winter is my favorite season because the cold wind forces men to wear more layers! (Said in Sgt. Frog-style) Oh... What was I talking about again? Ah, yes, EXILE's Takahiro. If you ever get the chance to see the music video for "Futatsu no Kuchibiru," please pay attention to Takahiro and his coat. By the way, Takahiro is from Sasebo, Nagasaki, just like me. He's exactly my type of guy, but my mother said, "He looks like a host from a host club, so I don't like him!!" (cries) D-Does he...? I'll try to show her the music video for "Super Shine" next time. I love how sadistic he looks in those boots. It's pretty amazing that he looks so good in them. I'm listening to EXILE every day nowadays!!

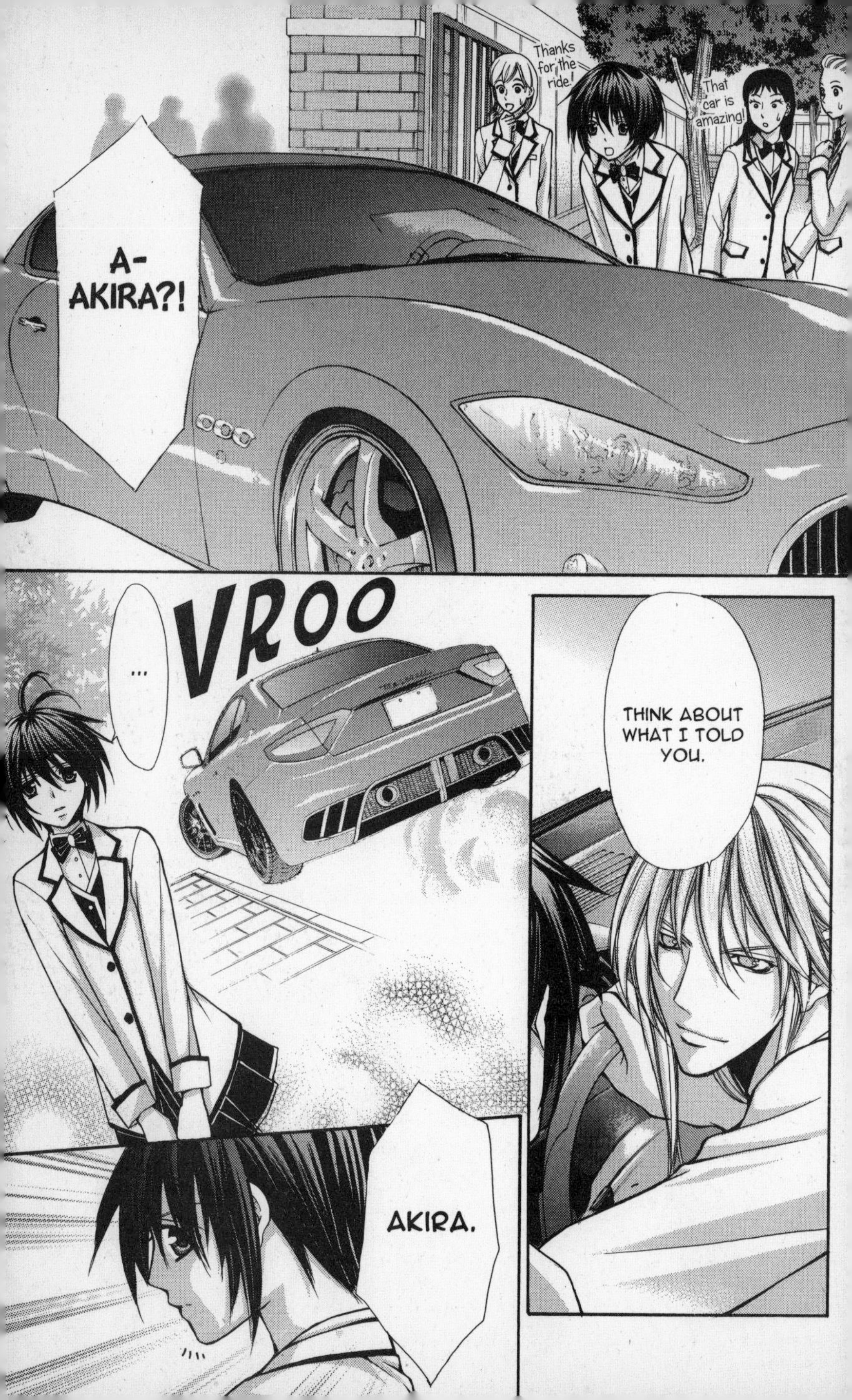
That car is amazing!
Thanks for the ride!
A-AKIRA?!
THINK ABOUT WHAT I TOLD YOU.
VROO
...
AKIRA.

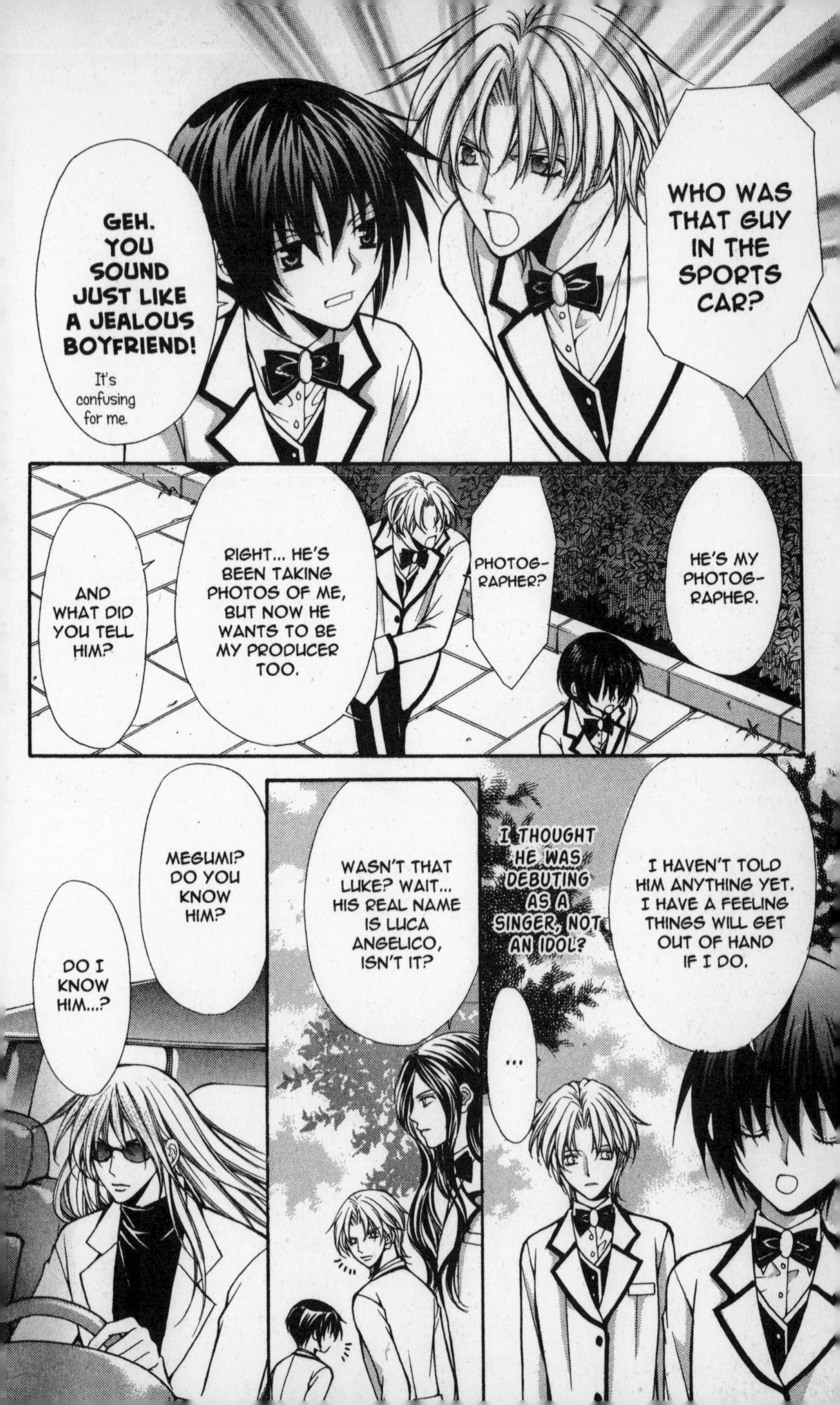
WHO WAS THAT GUY IN THE SPORTS CAR?
GEH. YOU SOUND JUST LIKE A JEALOUS BOYFRIEND!
It's confusing for me.
HE'S MY PHOTOG-RAPHER.
PHOTOG-RAPHER?
RIGHT... HE'S BEEN TAKING PHOTOS OF ME, BUT NOW HE WANTS TO BE MY PRODUCER TOO.
AND WHAT DID YOU TELL HIM?
I HAVEN'T TOLD HIM ANYTHING YET. I HAVE A FEELING THINGS WILL GET OUT OF HAND IF I DO.
I THOUGHT HE WAS DEBUTING AS A SINGER, NOT AN IDOL?
...
WASN'T THAT LUKE? WAIT... HIS REAL NAME IS LUCA ANGELICO, ISN'T IT?
MEGUMI? DO YOU KNOW HIM?
DO I KNOW HIM...?

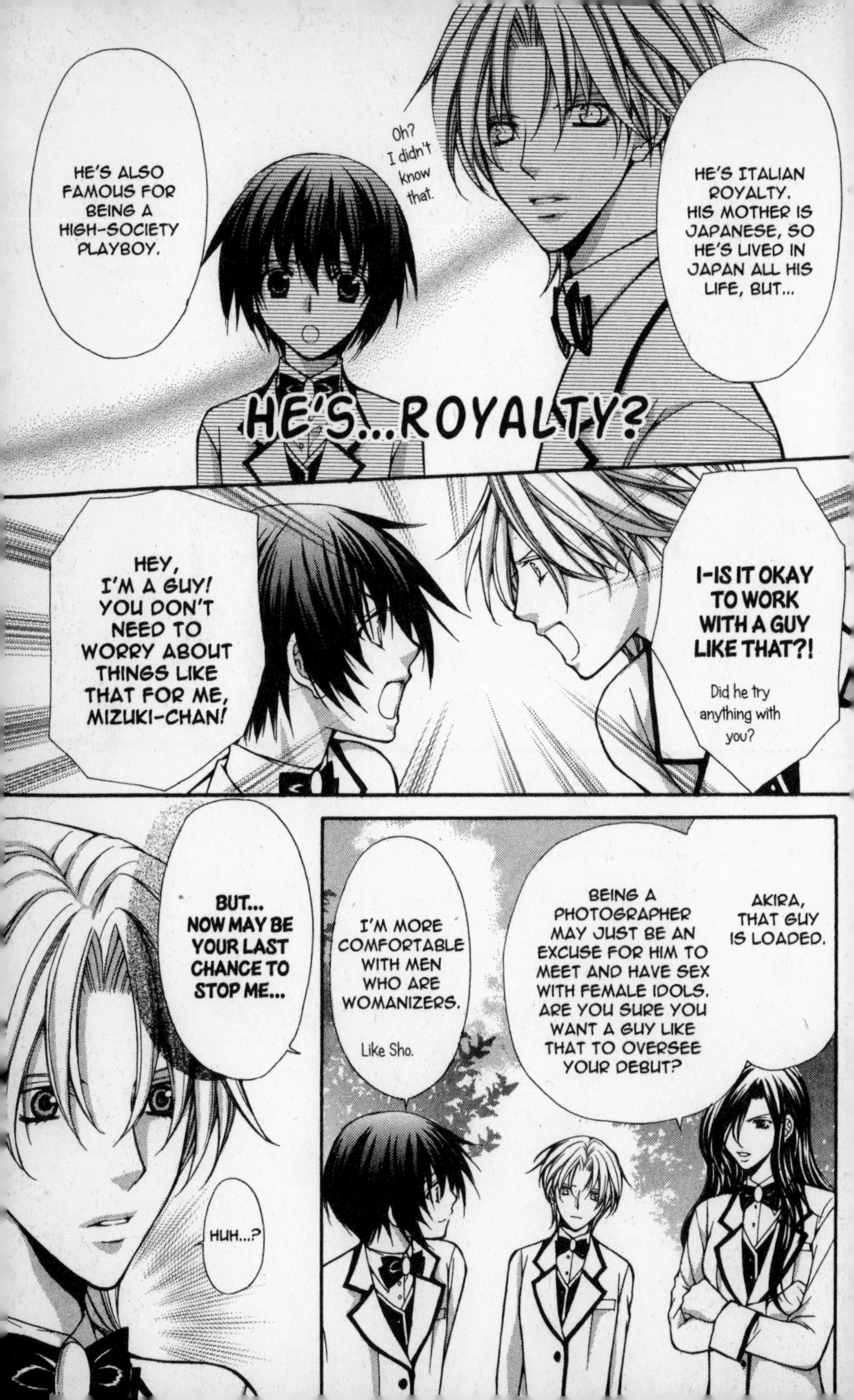
HE'S ITALIAN ROYALTY. HIS MOTHER IS JAPANESE, SO HE'S LIVED IN JAPAN ALL HIS LIFE, BUT...
Oh? I didn't know that.
HE'S ALSO FAMOUS FOR BEING A HIGH-SOCIETY PLAYBOY.
HE'S...ROYALTY?
I-IS IT OKAY TO WORK WITH A GUY LIKE THAT?!
Did he try anything with you?
HEY, I'M A GUY! YOU DON'T NEED TO WORRY ABOUT THINGS LIKE THAT FOR ME, MIZUKI-CHAN!
AKIRA, THAT GUY IS LOADED.
BEING A PHOTOGRAPHER MAY JUST BE AN EXCUSE FOR HIM TO MEET AND HAVE SEX WITH FEMALE IDOLS. ARE YOU SURE YOU WANT A GUY LIKE THAT TO OVERSEE YOUR DEBUT?
I'M MORE COMFORTABLE WITH MEN WHO ARE WOMANIZERS.
Like Sho.
BUT... NOW MAY BE YOUR LAST CHANCE TO STOP ME...
HUH...?

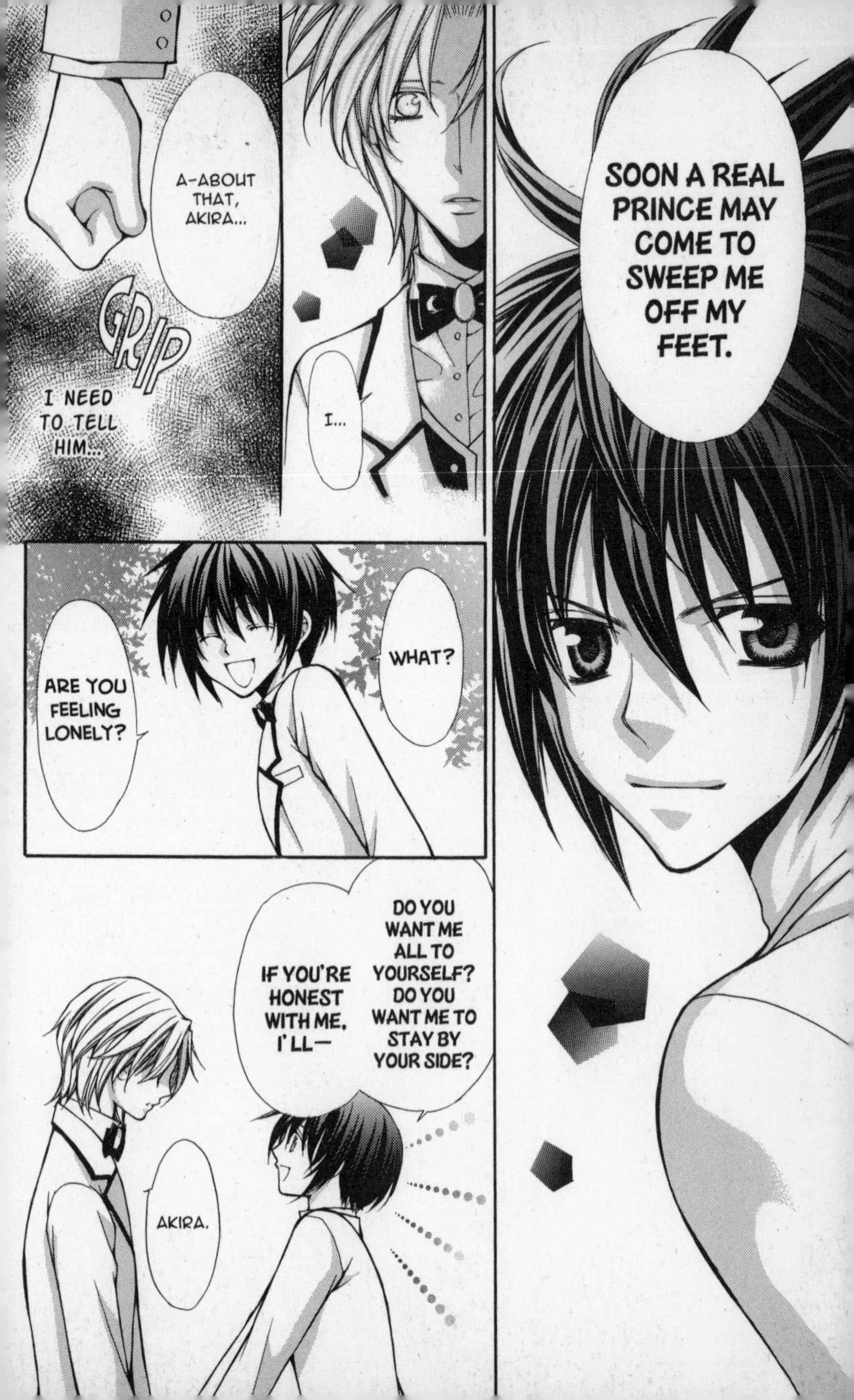
SOON A REAL PRINCE MAY COME TO SWEEP ME OFF MY FEET.
I...
A-ABOUT THAT, AKIRA...
GRIP
I NEED TO TELL HIM...
WHAT?
ARE YOU FEELING LONELY?
DO YOU WANT ME ALL TO YOURSELF? DO YOU WANT ME TO STAY BY YOUR SIDE?
IF YOU'RE HONEST WITH ME, I'LL—
AKIRA.

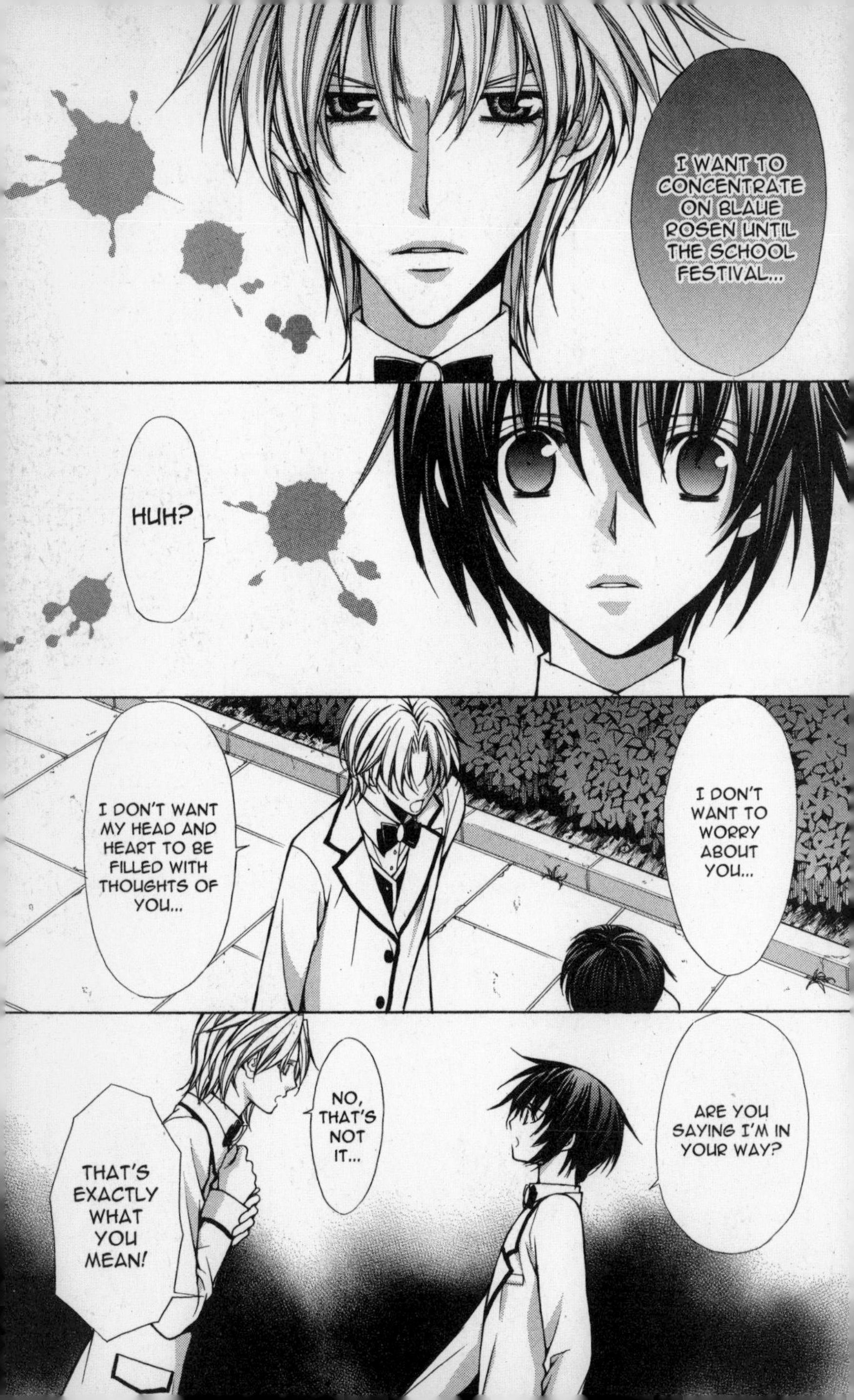
I WANT TO CONCENTRATE ON BLAUE ROSEN UNTIL THE SCHOOL FESTIVAL...
HUH?
I DON'T WANT TO WORRY ABOUT YOU...
I DON'T WANT MY HEAD AND HEART TO BE FILLED WITH THOUGHTS OF YOU...
ARE YOU SAYING I'M IN YOUR WAY?
NO, THAT'S NOT IT...
THAT'S EXACTLY WHAT YOU MEAN!

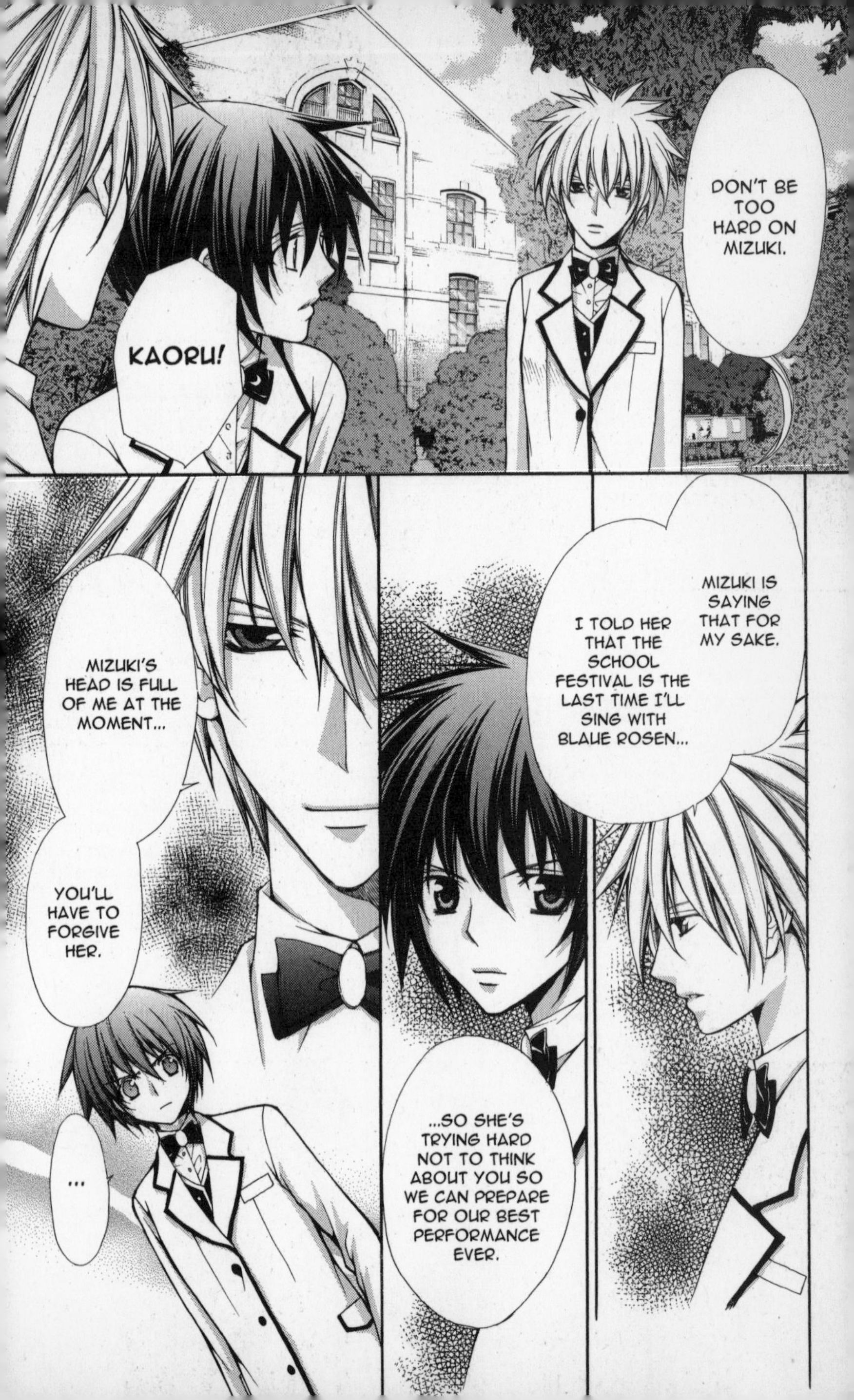
DON'T BE TOO HARD ON MIZUKI.
KAORU!
MIZUKI IS SAYING THAT FOR MY SAKE.
I TOLD HER THAT THE SCHOOL FESTIVAL IS THE LAST TIME I'LL SING WITH BLAUE ROSEN...
...SO SHE'S TRYING HARD NOT TO THINK ABOUT YOU SO WE CAN PREPARE FOR OUR BEST PERFORMANCE EVER.
MIZUKI'S HEAD IS FULL OF ME AT THE MOMENT...
YOU'LL HAVE TO FORGIVE HER.
...

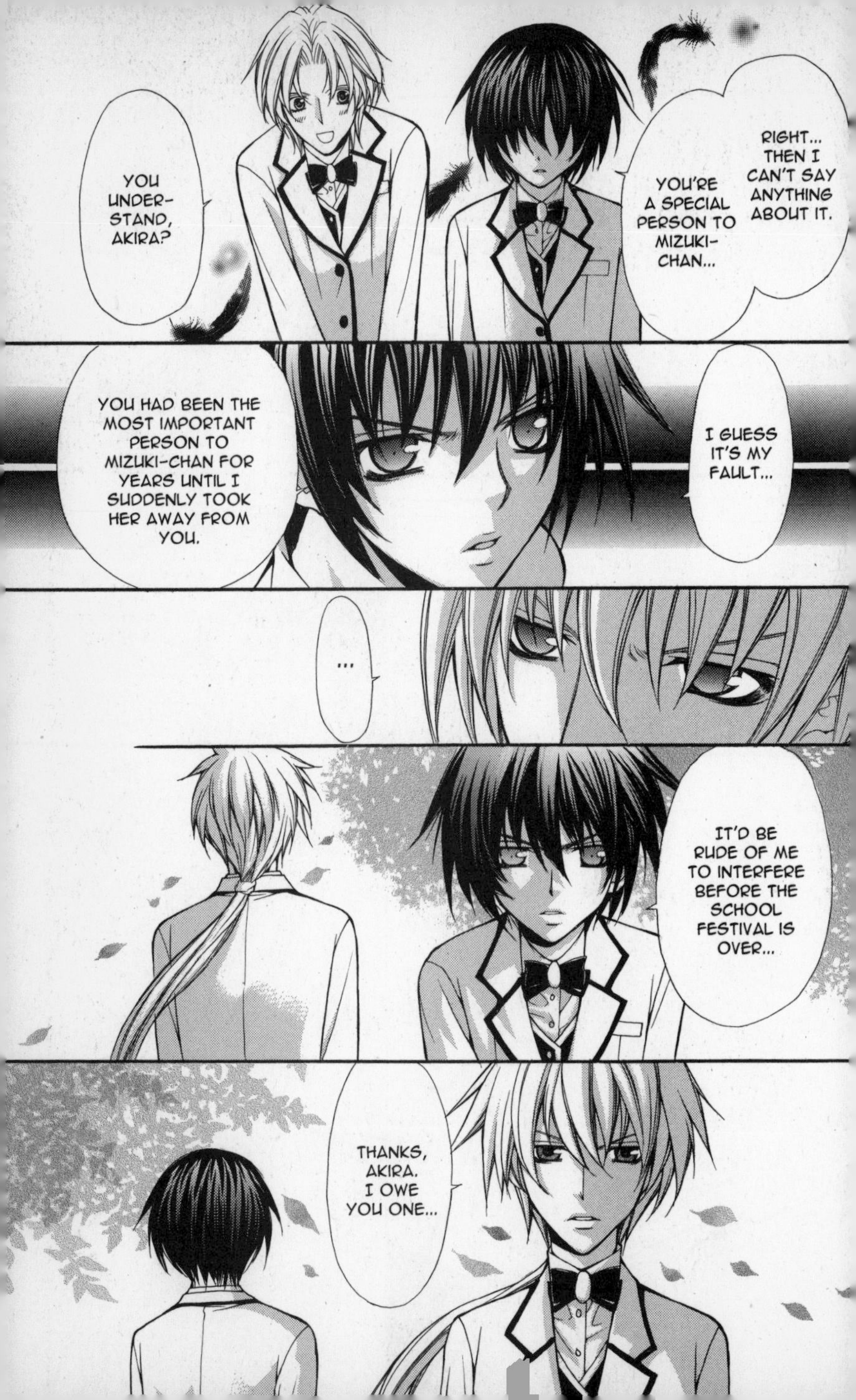
RIGHT... THEN I CAN'T SAY ANYTHING ABOUT IT.
YOU'RE A SPECIAL PERSON TO MIZUKI-CHAN...
YOU UNDER-STAND, AKIRA?
I GUESS IT'S MY FAULT...
YOU HAD BEEN THE MOST IMPORTANT PERSON TO MIZUKI-CHAN FOR YEARS UNTIL I SUDDENLY TOOK HER AWAY FROM YOU.
...
IT'D BE RUDE OF ME TO INTERFERE BEFORE THE SCHOOL FESTIVAL IS OVER...
THANKS, AKIRA. I OWE YOU ONE...

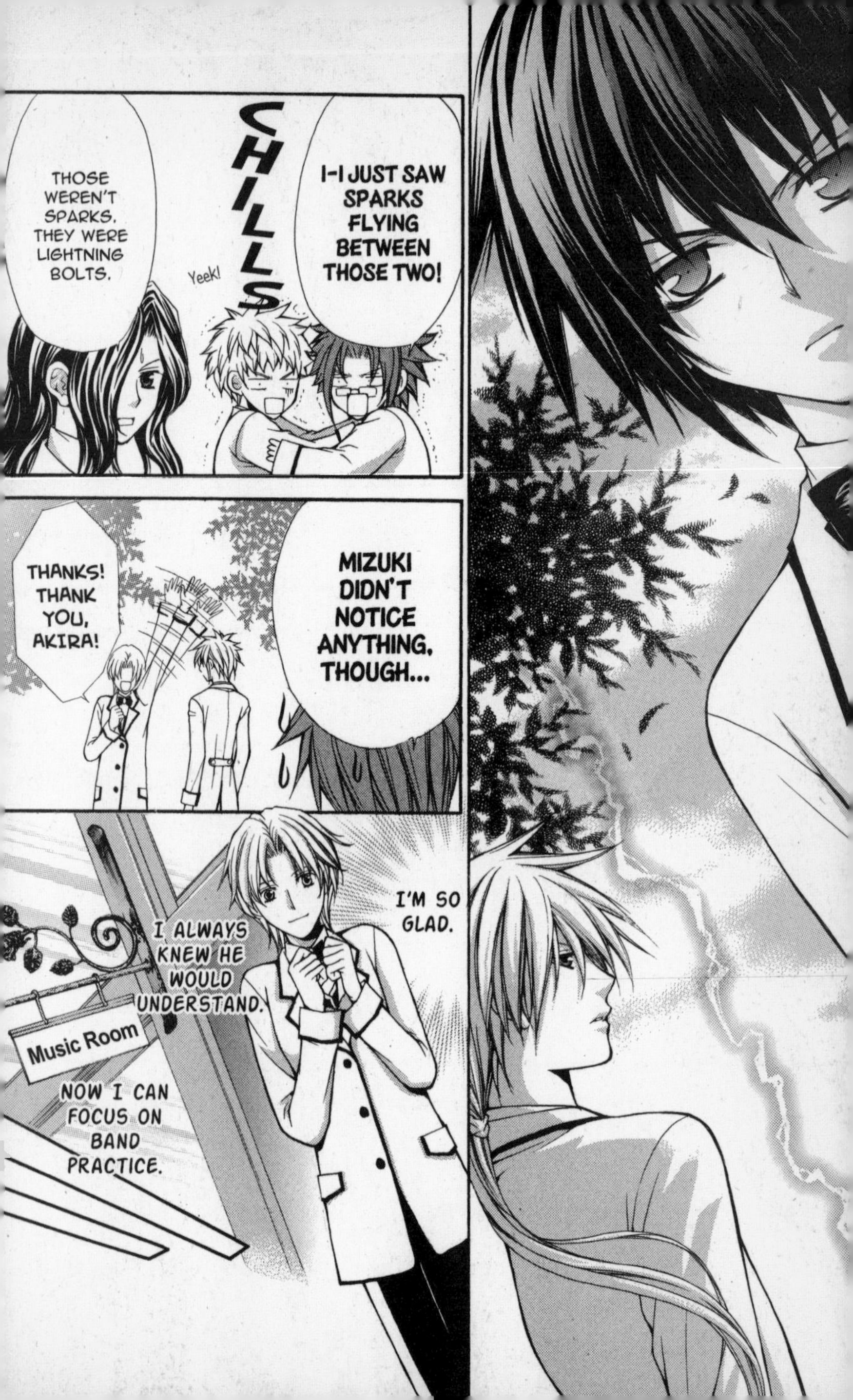
I-I JUST SAW SPARKS FLYING BETWEEN THOSE TWO!
CHILLS
Yeek!
THOSE WEREN'T SPARKS. THEY WERE LIGHTNING BOLTS.
MIZUKI DIDN'T NOTICE ANYTHING, THOUGH...
THANKS! THANK YOU, AKIRA!
I'M SO GLAD.
I ALWAYS KNEW HE WOULD UNDERSTAND.
Music Room
NOW I CAN FOCUS ON BAND PRACTICE.

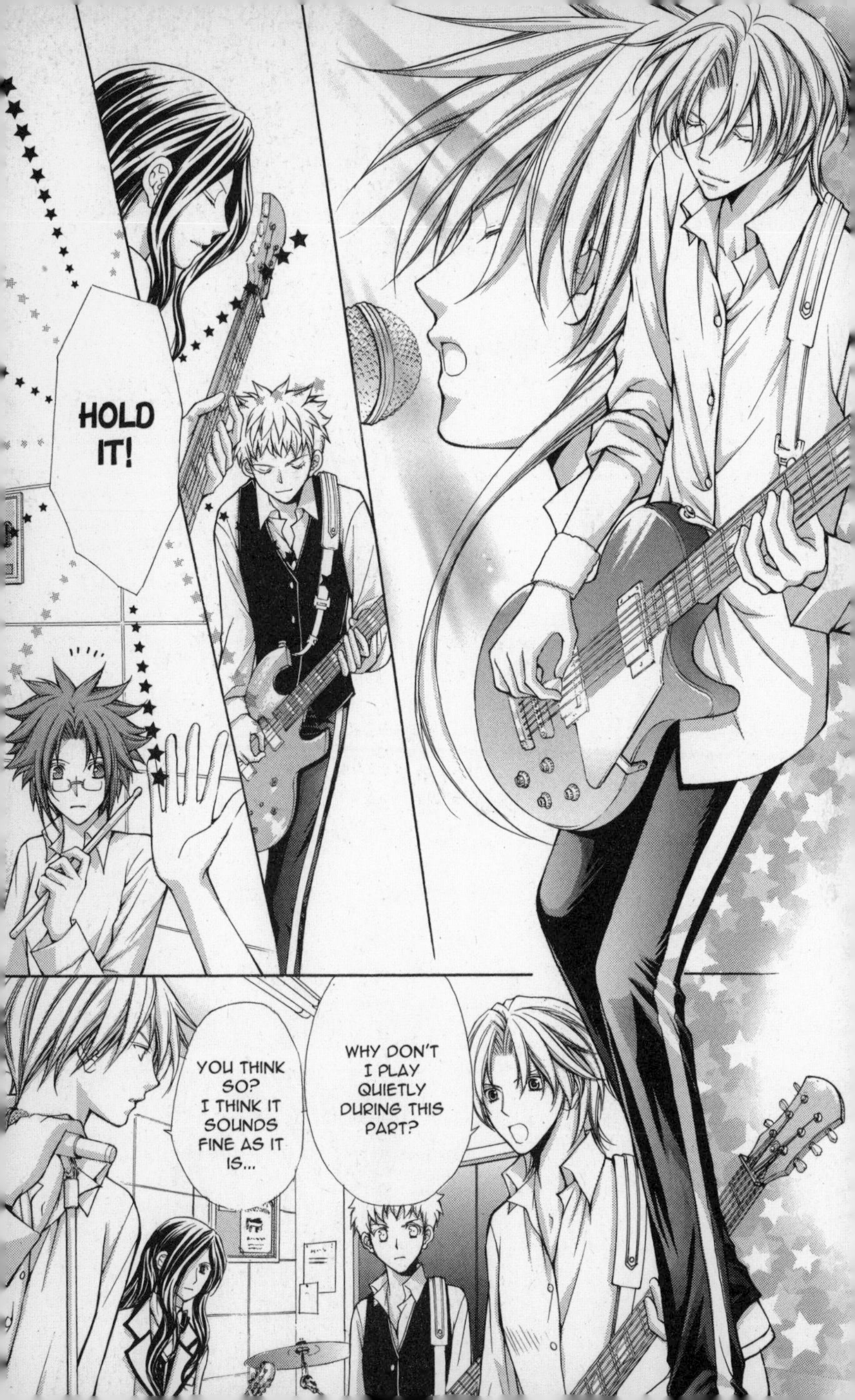
HOLD IT!
WHY DON'T I PLAY QUIETLY DURING THIS PART?
YOU THINK SO? I THINK IT SOUNDS FINE AS IT IS...

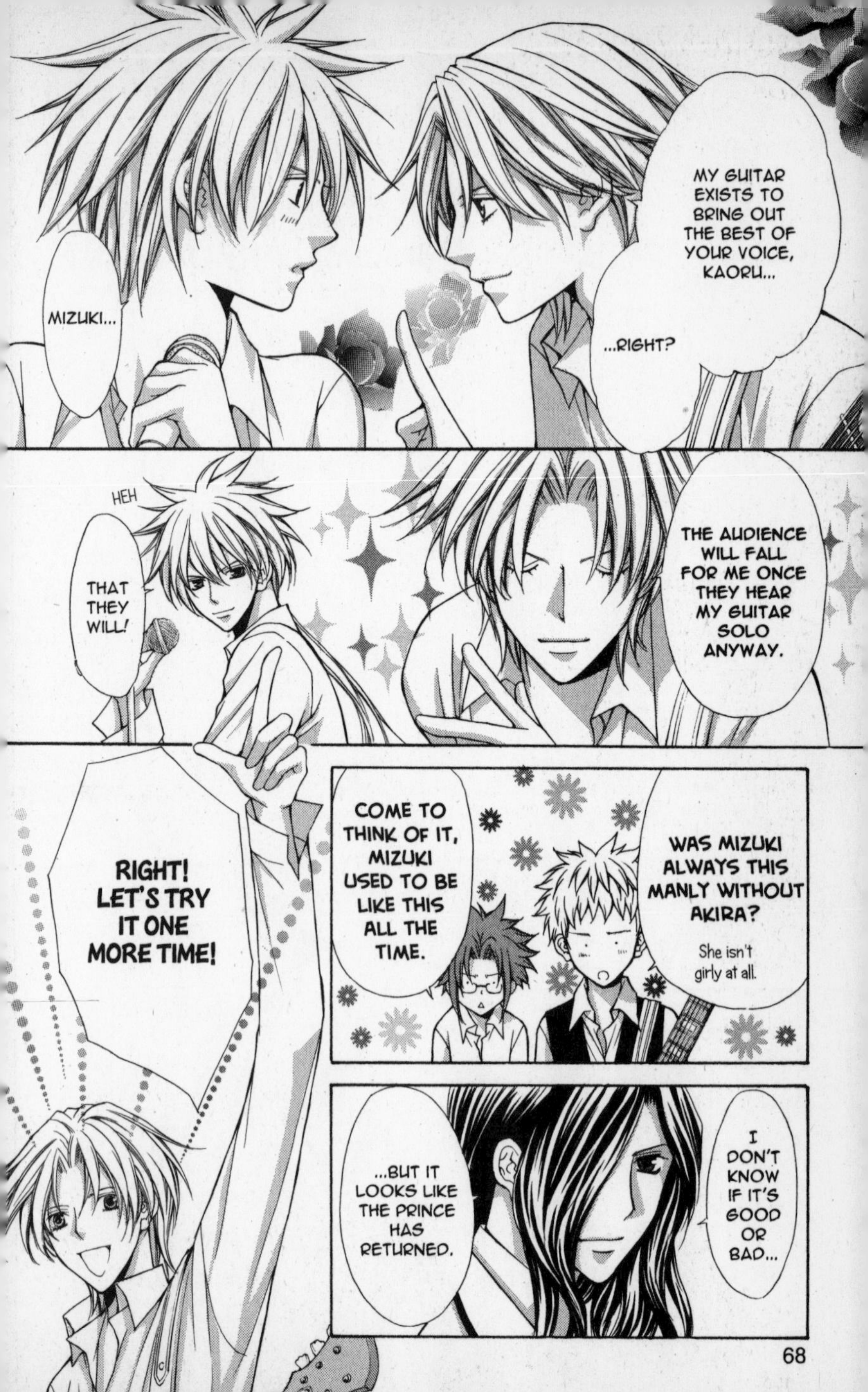
MY GUITAR EXISTS TO BRING OUT THE BEST OF YOUR VOICE, KAORU...
...RIGHT?
MIZUKI...
THE AUDIENCE WILL FALL FOR ME ONCE THEY HEAR MY GUITAR SOLO ANYWAY.
HEH
THAT THEY WILL!
WAS MIZUKI ALWAYS THIS MANLY WITHOUT AKIRA?
She isn't girly at all.
COME TO THINK OF IT, MIZUKI USED TO BE LIKE THIS ALL THE TIME.
I DON'T KNOW IF IT'S GOOD OR BAD...
...BUT IT LOOKS LIKE THE PRINCE HAS RETURNED.
RIGHT! LET'S TRY IT ONE MORE TIME!

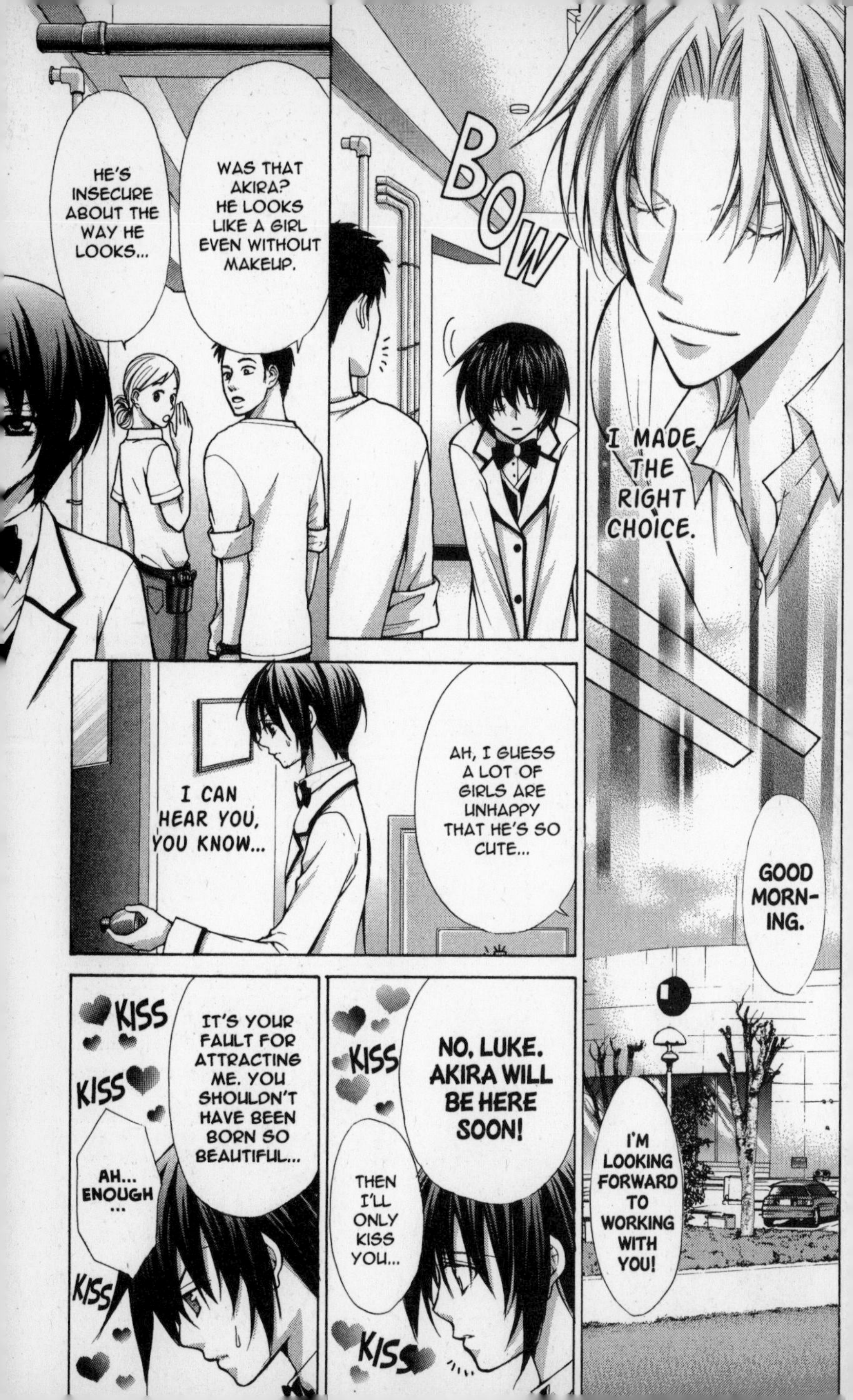
I MADE THE RIGHT CHOICE.
GOOD MORN-ING.
I'M LOOKING FORWARD TO WORKING WITH YOU!
BOW
WAS THAT AKIRA? HE LOOKS LIKE A GIRL EVEN WITHOUT MAKEUP.
HE'S INSECURE ABOUT THE WAY HE LOOKS...
AH, I GUESS A LOT OF GIRLS ARE UNHAPPY THAT HE'S SO CUTE...
I CAN HEAR YOU, YOU KNOW...
NO, LUKE. AKIRA WILL BE HERE SOON!
KISS
THEN I'LL ONLY KISS YOU...
KISS
KISS
IT'S YOUR FAULT FOR ATTRACTING ME. YOU SHOULDN'T HAVE BEEN BORN SO BEAUTIFUL...
KISS
AH... ENOUGH ...
KISS

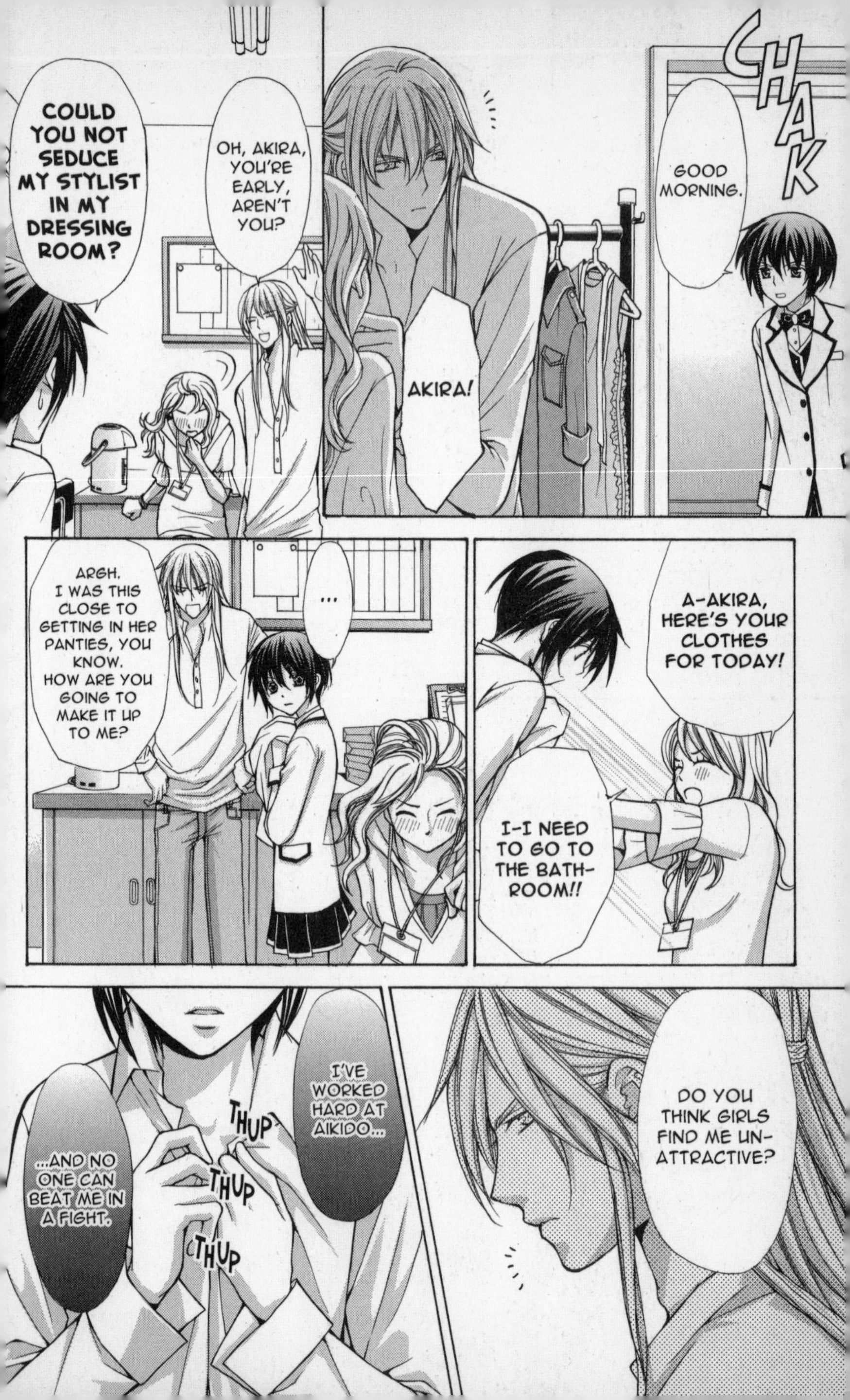
CHAK
GOOD MORNING.
AKIRA!
OH, AKIRA, YOU'RE EARLY, AREN'T YOU?
COULD YOU NOT SEDUCE MY STYLIST IN MY DRESSING ROOM?
A-AKIRA, HERE'S YOUR CLOTHES FOR TODAY!
I-I NEED TO GO TO THE BATHROOM!!
...
ARGH. I WAS THIS CLOSE TO GETTING IN HER PANTIES, YOU KNOW. HOW ARE YOU GOING TO MAKE IT UP TO ME?
DO YOU THINK GIRLS FIND ME UN-ATTRACTIVE?
I'VE WORKED HARD AT AIKIDO...
THUP
THUP
THUP
...AND NO ONE CAN BEAT ME IN A FIGHT.

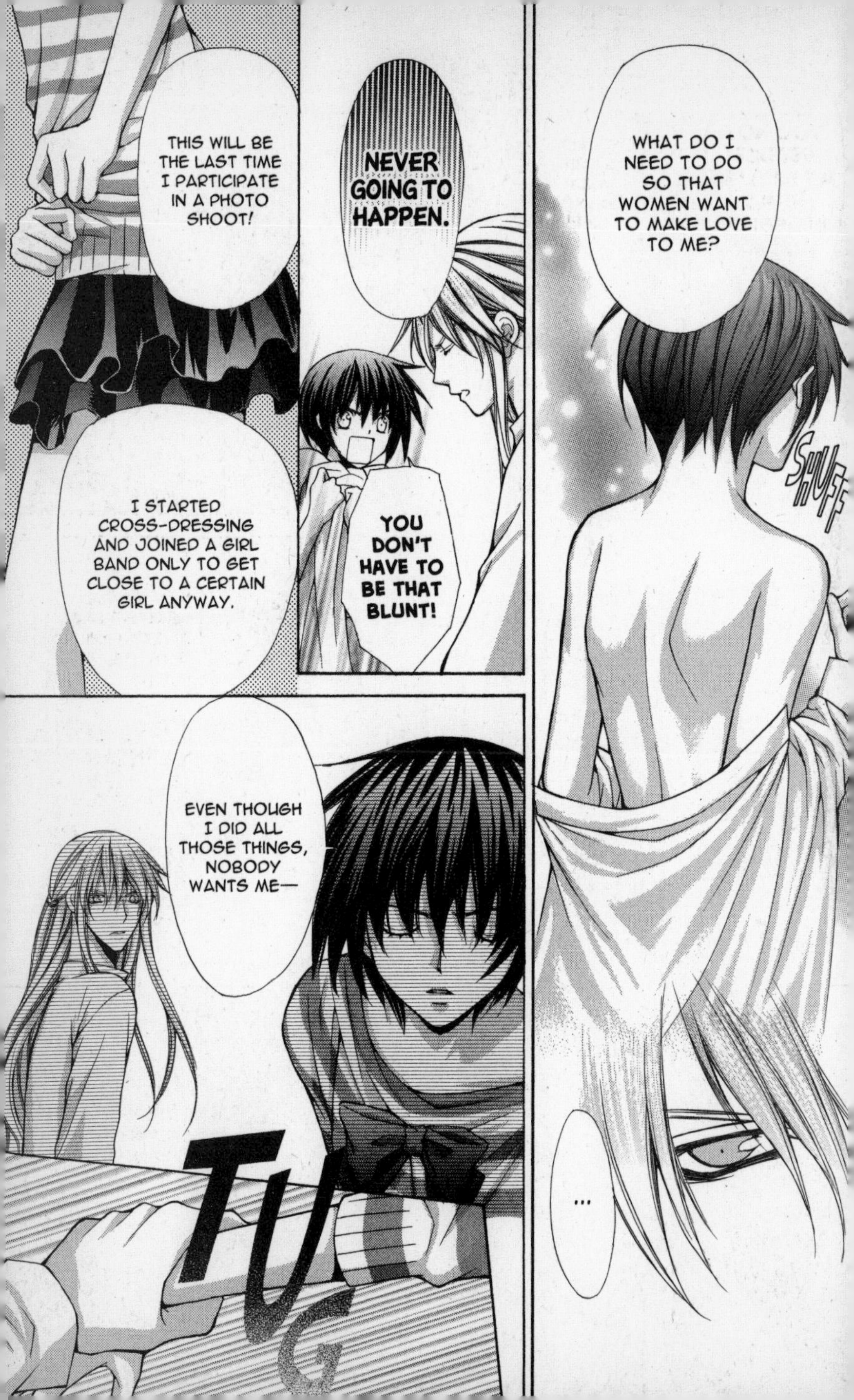
THIS WILL BE THE LAST TIME I PARTICIPATE IN A PHOTO SHOOT!
I STARTED CROSS-DRESSING AND JOINED A GIRL BAND ONLY TO GET CLOSE TO A CERTAIN GIRL ANYWAY.
NEVER GOING TO HAPPEN.
YOU DON'T HAVE TO BE THAT BLUNT!
EVEN THOUGH I DID ALL THOSE THINGS, NOBODY WANTS ME—
TUG
WHAT DO I NEED TO DO SO THAT WOMEN WANT TO MAKE LOVE TO ME?
SHUFF
...

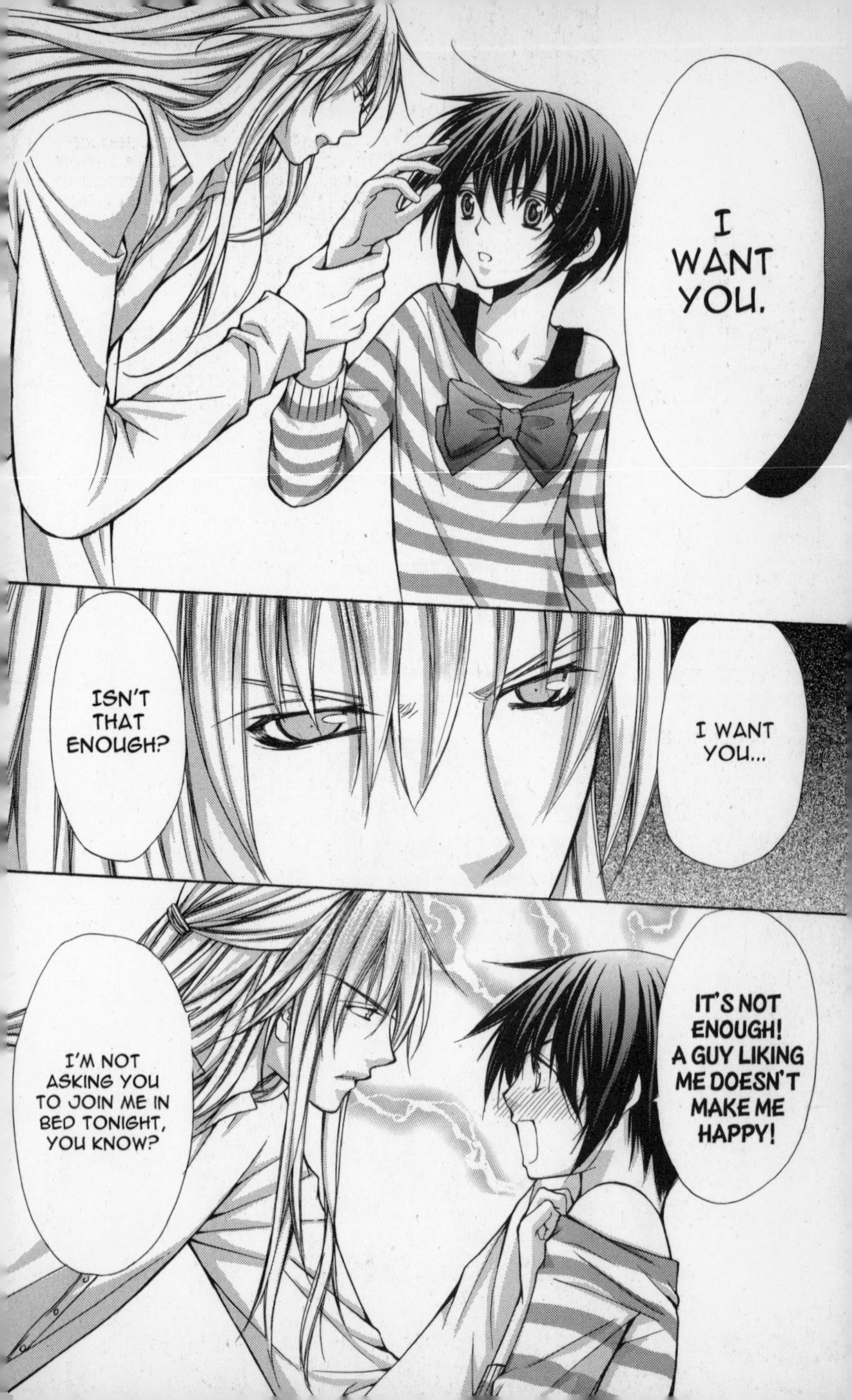
I WANT YOU.
I WANT YOU...
ISN'T THAT ENOUGH?
IT'S NOT ENOUGH! A GUY LIKING ME DOESN'T MAKE ME HAPPY!
I'M NOT ASKING YOU TO JOIN ME IN BED TONIGHT, YOU KNOW?

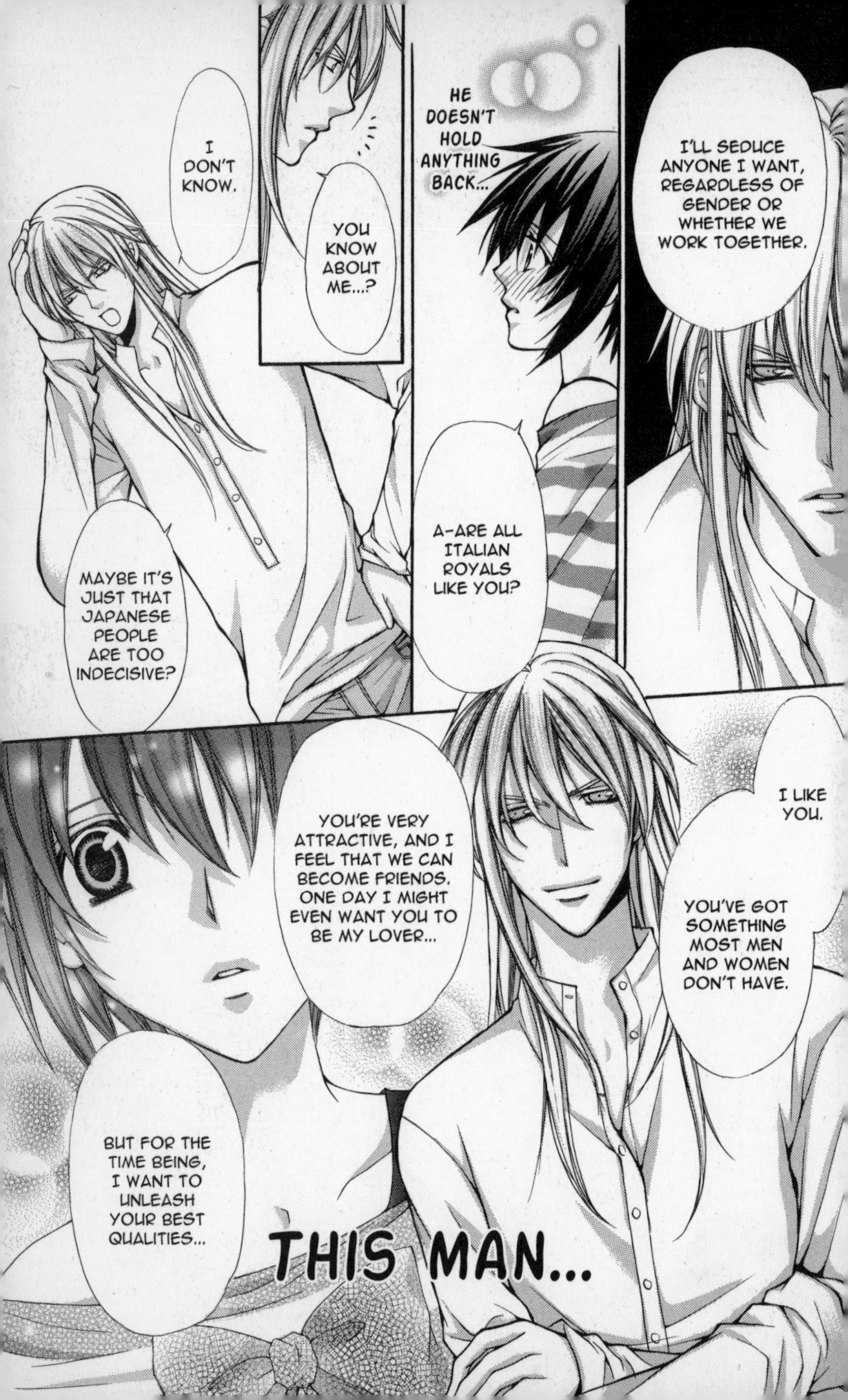
I'LL SEDUCE ANYONE I WANT, REGARDLESS OF GENDER OR WHETHER WE WORK TOGETHER.
HE DOESN'T HOLD ANYTHING BACK...
A-ARE ALL ITALIAN ROYALS LIKE YOU?
YOU KNOW ABOUT ME...?
I DON'T KNOW.
MAYBE IT'S JUST THAT JAPANESE PEOPLE ARE TOO INDECISIVE?
I LIKE YOU.
YOU'VE GOT SOMETHING MOST MEN AND WOMEN DON'T HAVE.
YOU'RE VERY ATTRACTIVE, AND I FEEL THAT WE CAN BECOME FRIENDS. ONE DAY I MIGHT EVEN WANT YOU TO BE MY LOVER...
BUT FOR THE TIME BEING, I WANT TO UNLEASH YOUR BEST QUALITIES...
THIS MAN...

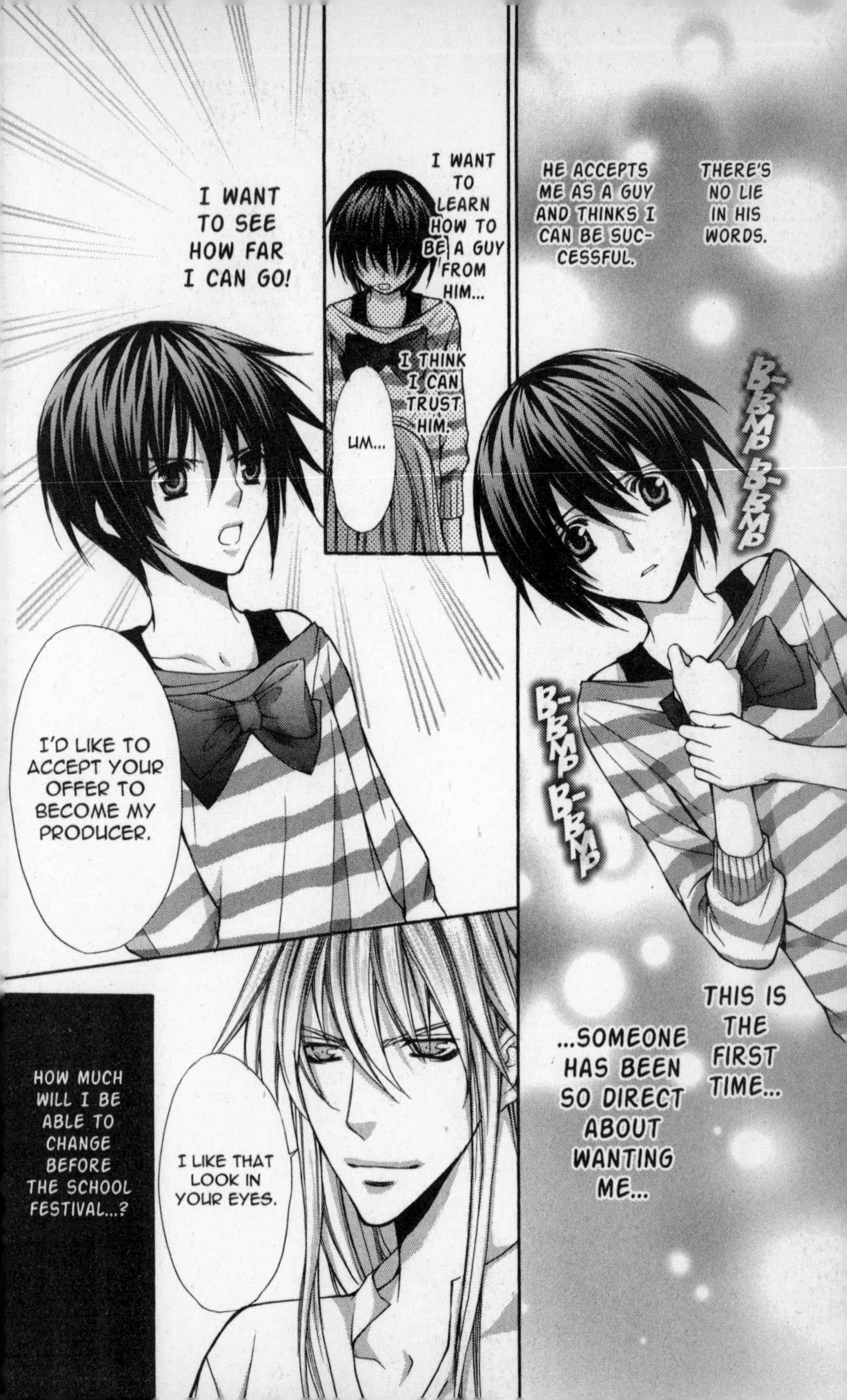
THERE'S NO LIE IN HIS WORDS.
HE ACCEPTS ME AS A GUY AND THINKS I CAN BE SUC-CESSFUL.
B-BMP B-BMP
B-BMP B-BMP
THIS IS THE FIRST TIME...
...SOMEONE HAS BEEN SO DIRECT ABOUT WANTING ME...
I WANT TO LEARN HOW TO BE A GUY FROM HIM...
I THINK I CAN TRUST HIM.
UM...
I WANT TO SEE HOW FAR I CAN GO!
I'D LIKE TO ACCEPT YOUR OFFER TO BECOME MY PRODUCER.
I LIKE THAT LOOK IN YOUR EYES.
HOW MUCH WILL I BE ABLE TO CHANGE BEFORE THE SCHOOL FESTIVAL...?

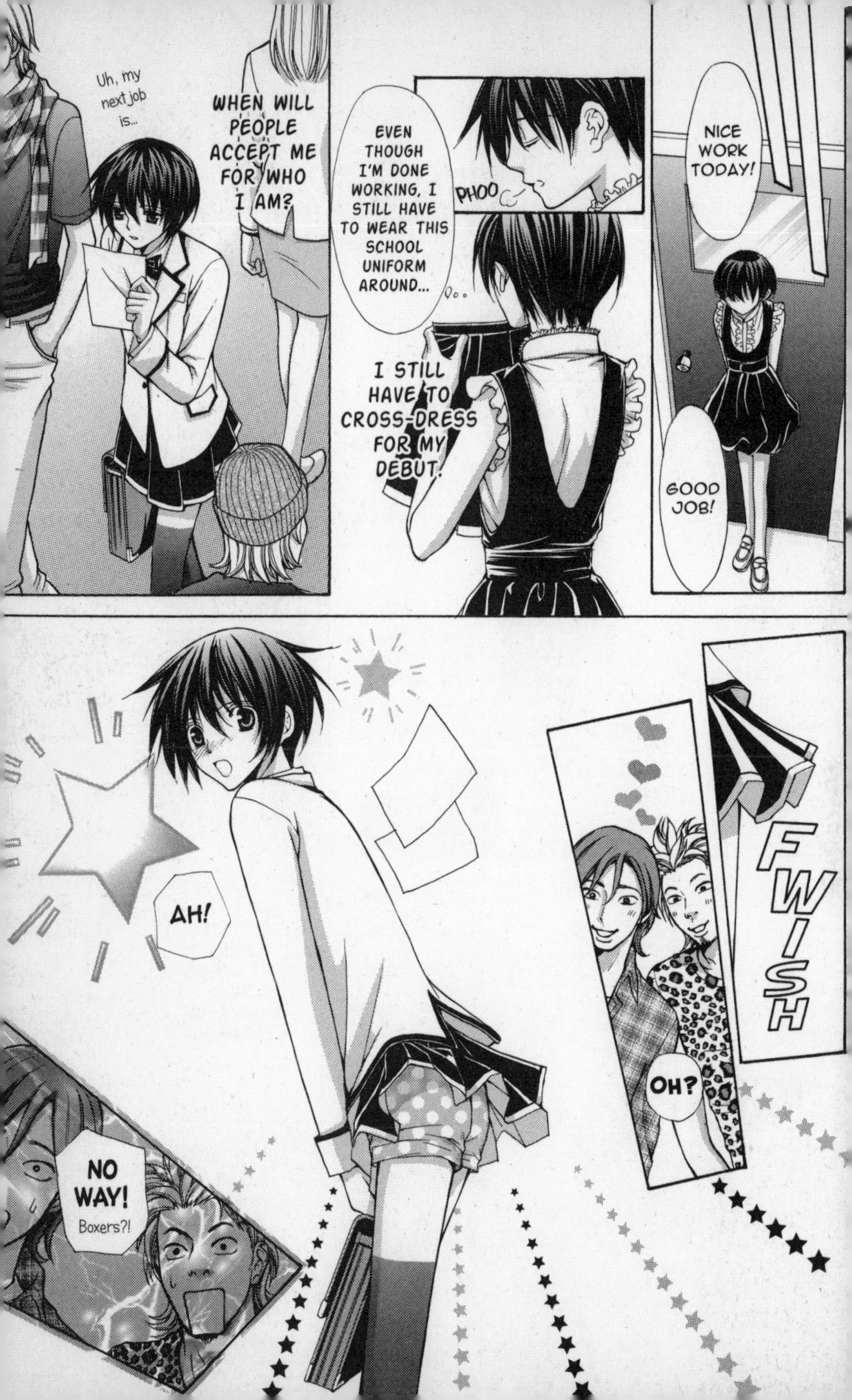
NICE WORK TODAY!
GOOD JOB!
PHOO
EVEN THOUGH I'M DONE WORKING, I STILL HAVE TO WEAR THIS SCHOOL UNIFORM AROUND...
I STILL HAVE TO CROSS-DRESS FOR MY DEBUT.
WHEN WILL PEOPLE ACCEPT ME FOR WHO I AM?
Uh, my next job is...
FWISH
OH?
AH!
NO WAY!
Boxers?!

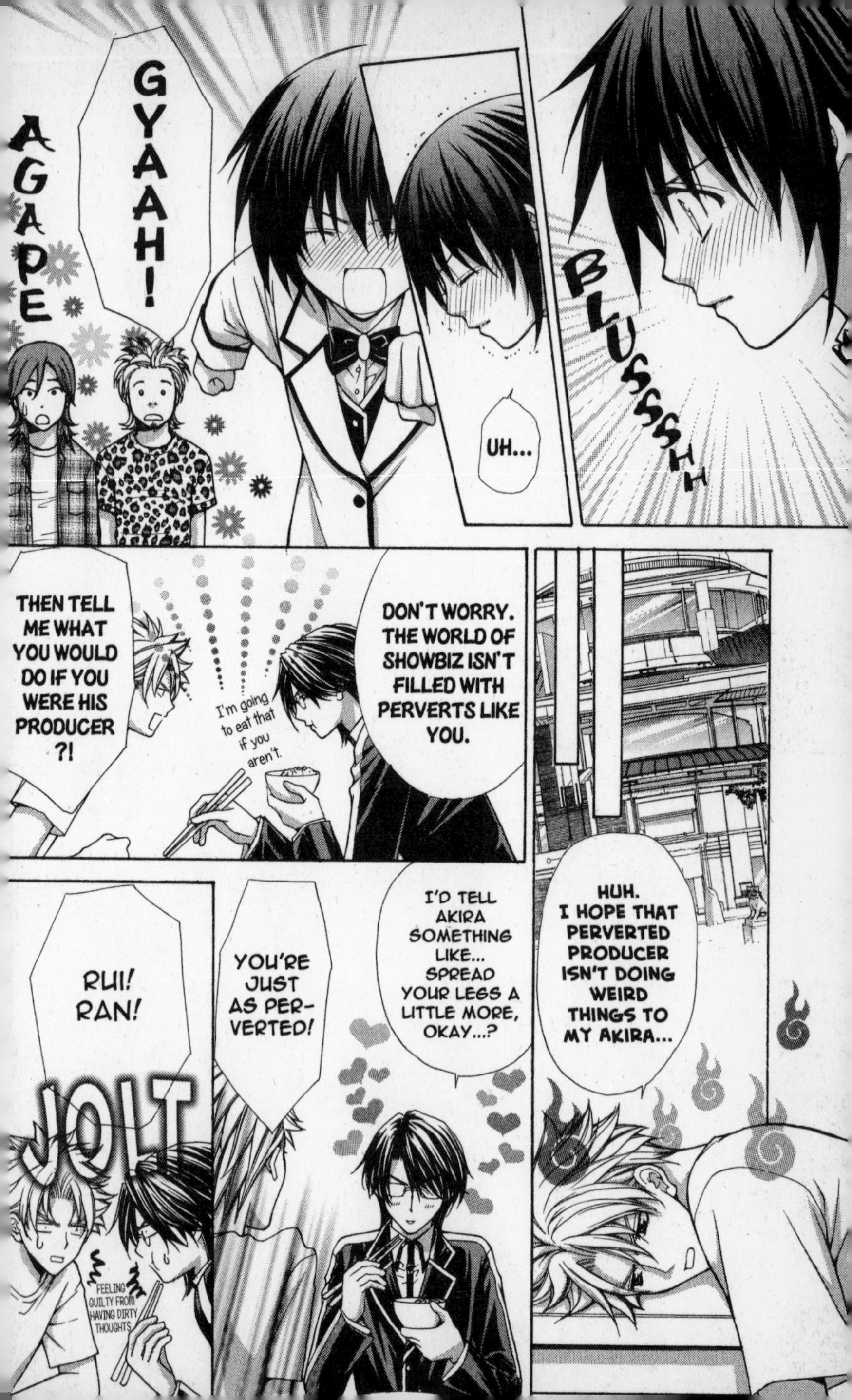
BLUSSSHH
UH...
GYAAH!
AGAPE
HUH. I HOPE THAT PERVERTED PRODUCER ISN'T DOING WEIRD THINGS TO MY AKIRA...
DON'T WORRY. THE WORLD OF SHOWBIZ ISN'T FILLED WITH PERVERTS LIKE YOU.
I'm going to eat that if you aren't.
THEN TELL ME WHAT YOU WOULD DO IF YOU WERE HIS PRODUCER ?!
I'D TELL AKIRA SOMETHING LIKE... SPREAD YOUR LEGS A LITTLE MORE, OKAY...?
YOU'RE JUST AS PER-VERTED!
RUI! RAN!
JOLT
FEELING GUILTY FROM HAVING DIRTY THOUGHTS

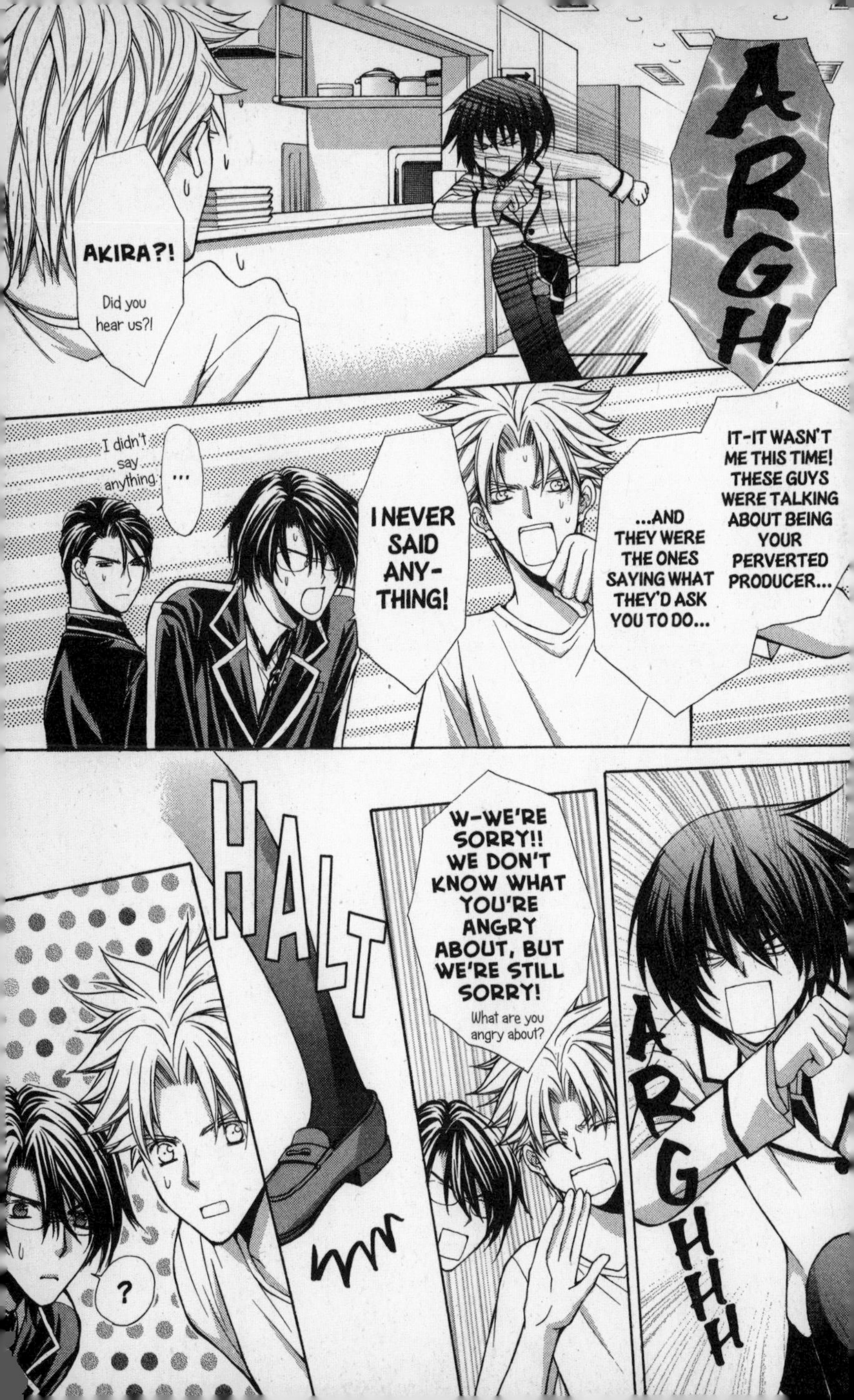
ARGH
AKIRA?!
Did you hear us?!
IT-IT WASN'T ME THIS TIME! THESE GUYS WERE TALKING ABOUT BEING YOUR PERVERTED PRODUCER...
...AND THEY WERE THE ONES SAYING WHAT THEY'D ASK YOU TO DO...
I NEVER SAID ANY-THING!
...
I didn't say anything.
ARGHHH
W-WE'RE SORRY!! WE DON'T KNOW WHAT YOU'RE ANGRY ABOUT, BUT WE'RE STILL SORRY!
What are you angry about?
HALT
?

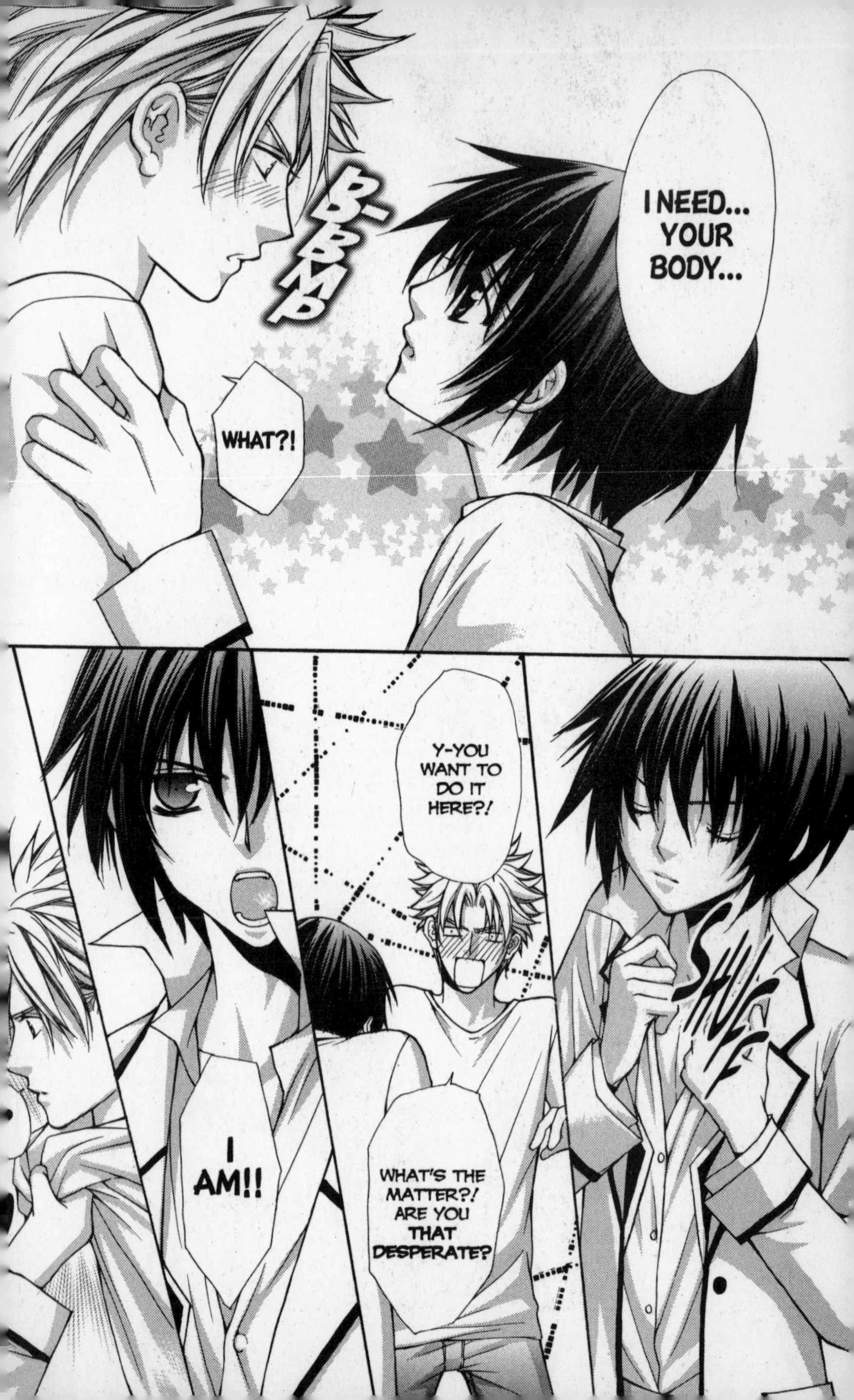
I NEED... YOUR BODY...
B-BMP
WHAT?!
SHUF
Y-YOU WANT TO DO IT HERE?!
WHAT'S THE MATTER?! ARE YOU THAT DESPERATE?
I AM!!

HI-YAH!
SHWUNK
I'M A BOY!
THUD
EVERYONE TREATS ME LIKE A GIRL, DAMN IT!!
FWAK
AKIRA?
BAM
KRAK
DON'T LOOK AT ME LIKE I'M A GIRL. STOP SAYING I'M CUTE!

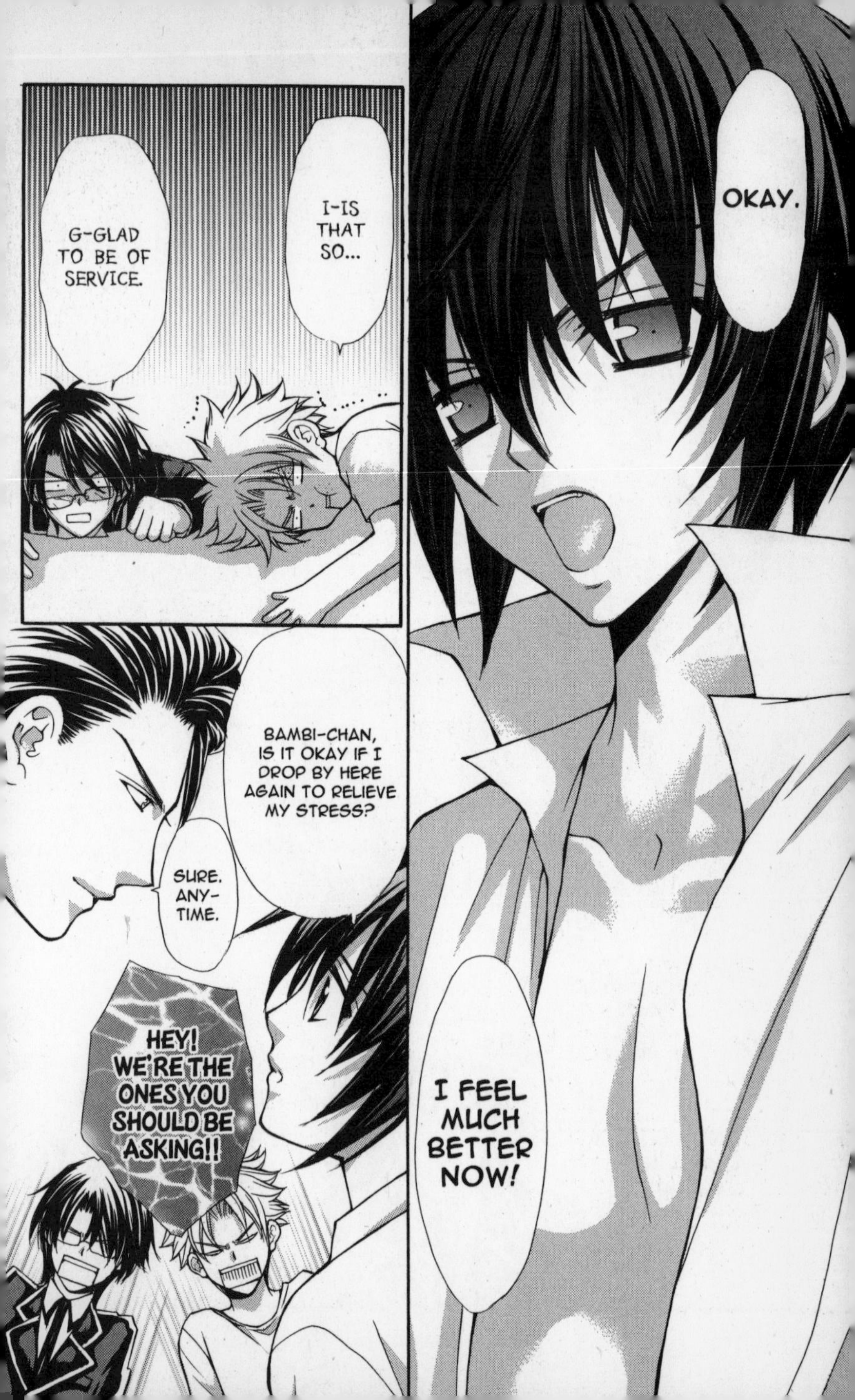
OKAY.
I FEEL MUCH BETTER NOW!
I-IS THAT SO...
G-GLAD TO BE OF SERVICE.
BAMBI-CHAN, IS IT OKAY IF I DROP BY HERE AGAIN TO RELIEVE MY STRESS?
SURE. ANY-TIME.
HEY! WE'RE THE ONES YOU SHOULD BE ASKING!!

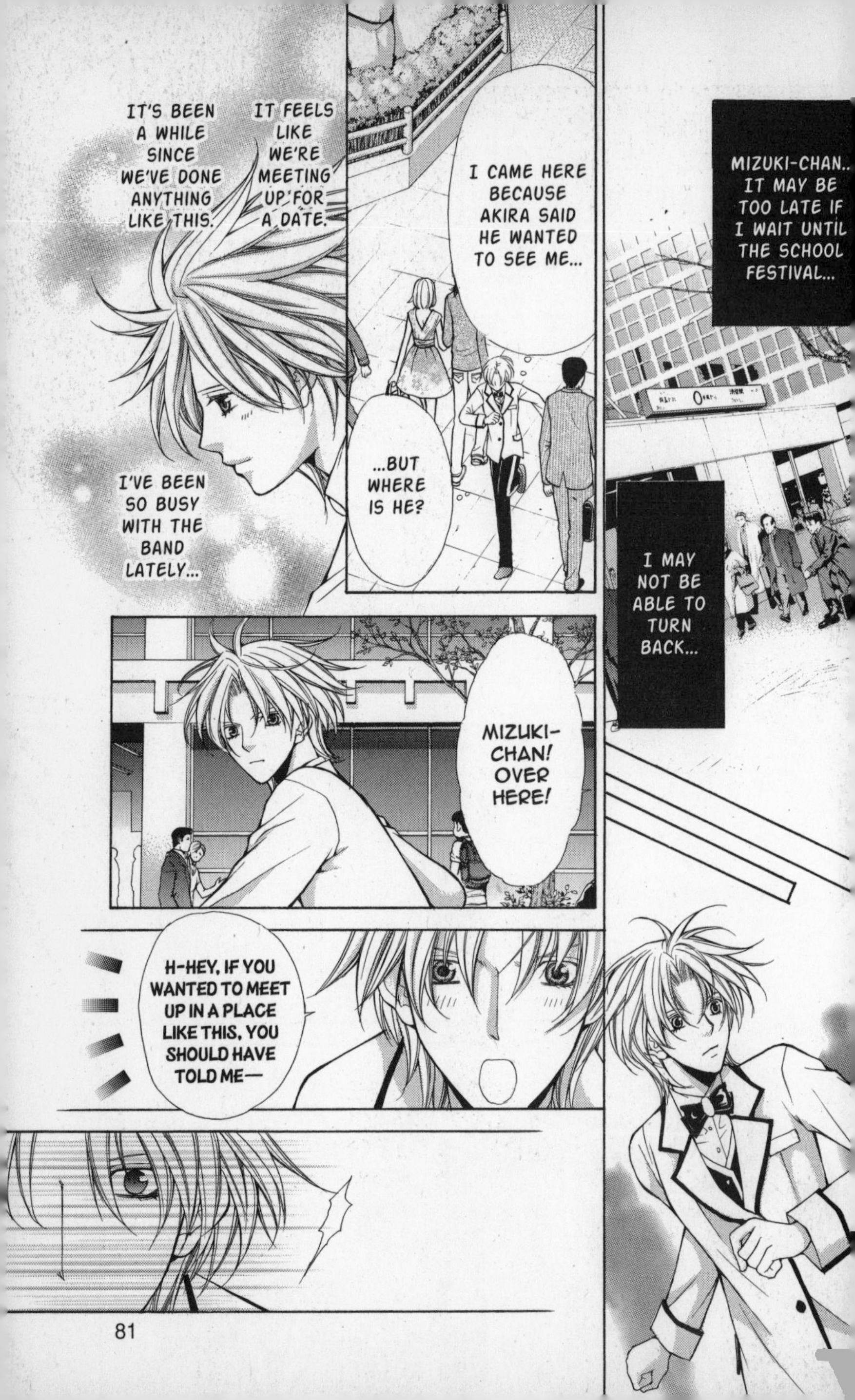
MIZUKI-CHAN... IT MAY BE TOO LATE IF I WAIT UNTIL THE SCHOOL FESTIVAL...
I MAY NOT BE ABLE TO TURN BACK...
I CAME HERE BECAUSE AKIRA SAID HE WANTED TO SEE ME...
...BUT WHERE IS HE?
IT FEELS LIKE WE'RE MEETING UP FOR A DATE.
IT'S BEEN A WHILE SINCE WE'VE DONE ANYTHING LIKE THIS.
I'VE BEEN SO BUSY WITH THE BAND LATELY...
MIZUKI-CHAN! OVER HERE!
H-HEY, IF YOU WANTED TO MEET UP IN A PLACE LIKE THIS, YOU SHOULD HAVE TOLD ME—

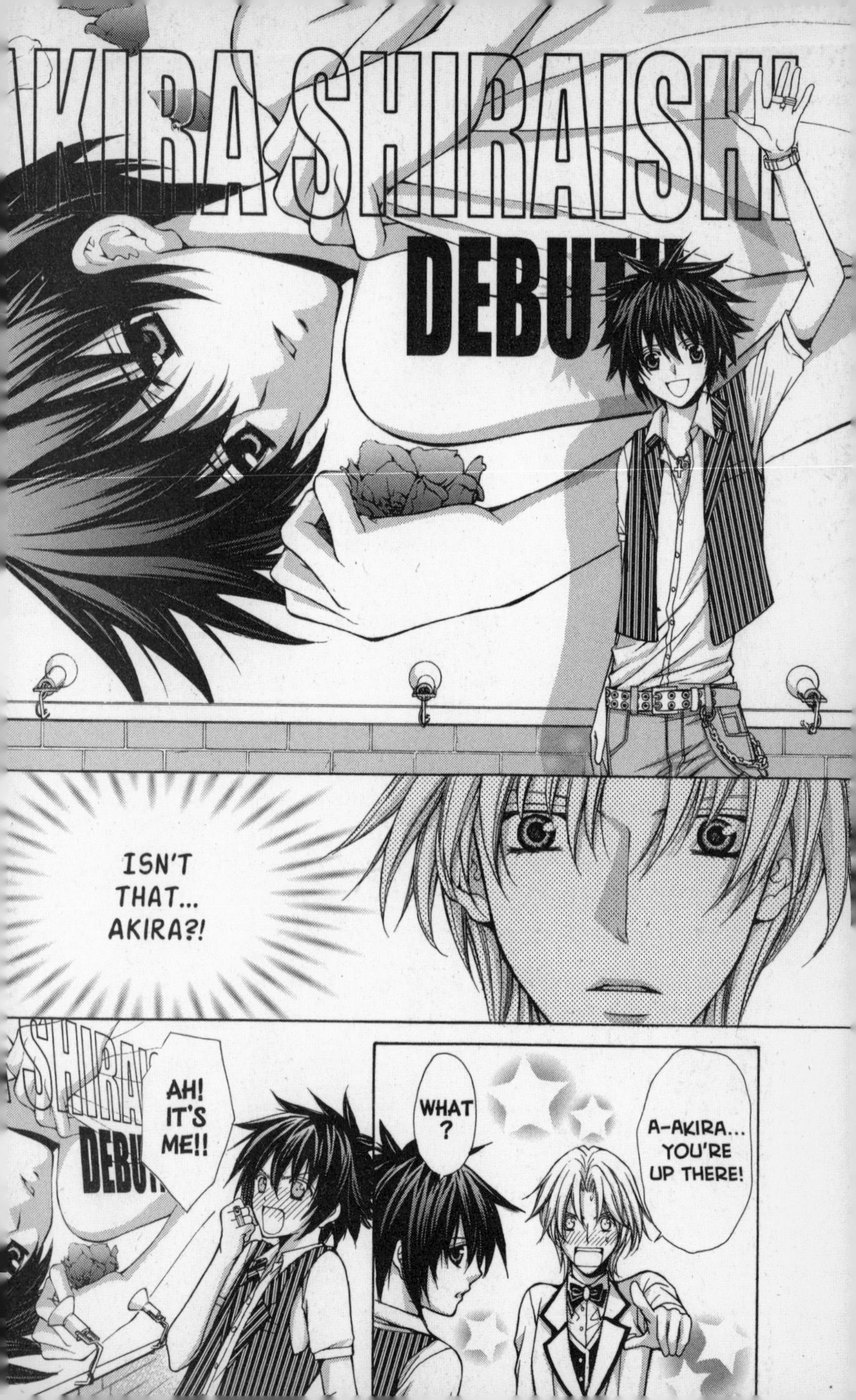
KIRA SHIRAISHI
DEBUT
ISN'T THAT... AKIRA?!
A-AKIRA... YOU'RE UP THERE!
WHAT?
AH! IT'S ME!!

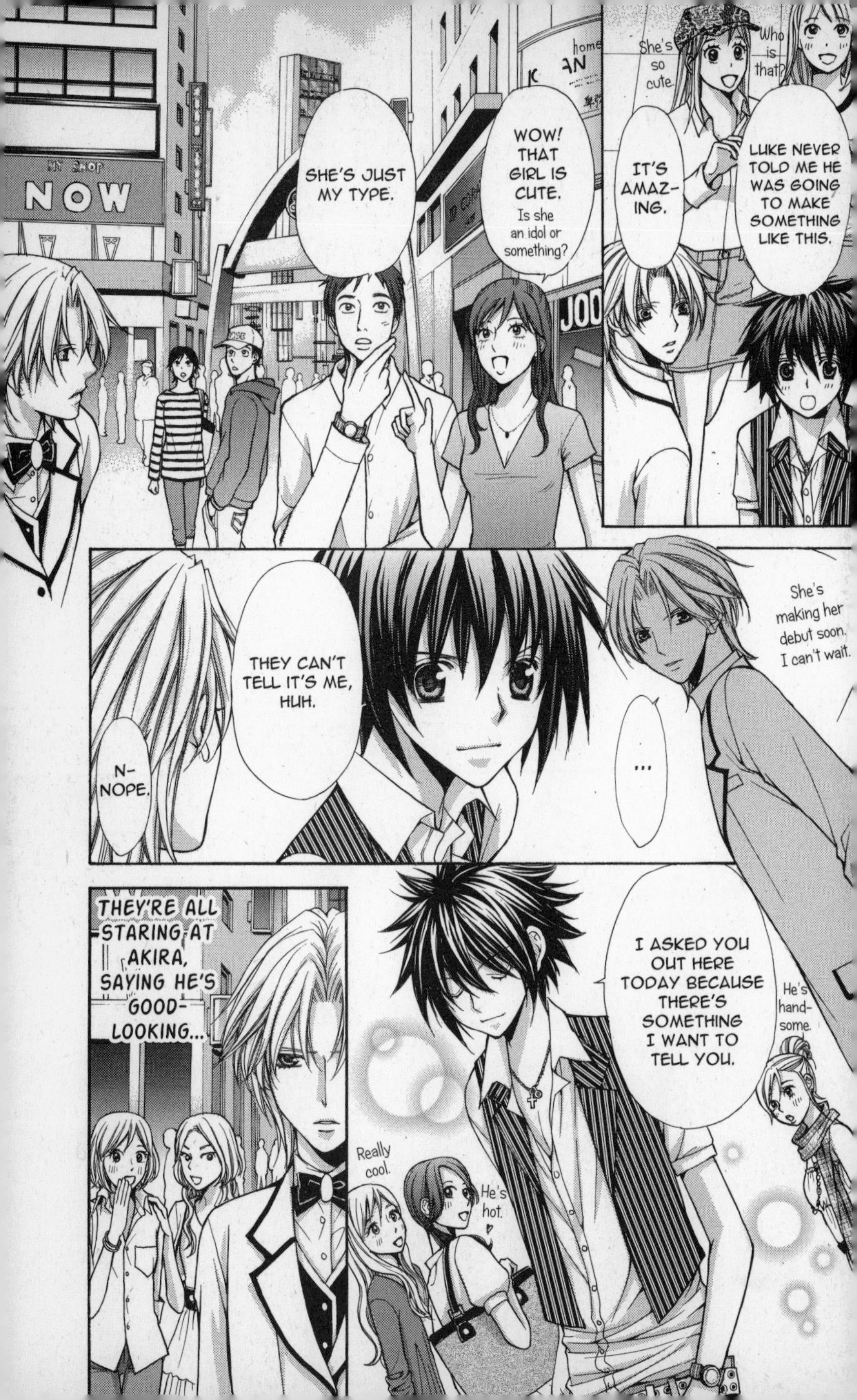
Who is that?
She's so cute.
LUKE NEVER TOLD ME HE WAS GOING TO MAKE SOMETHING LIKE THIS.
IT'S AMAZ-ING.
WOW! THAT GIRL IS CUTE. Is she an idol or something?
SHE'S JUST MY TYPE.
MY SHOP NOW
She's making her debut soon. I can't wait.
...
THEY CAN'T TELL IT'S ME, HUH.
N-NOPE.
He's hand-some.
I ASKED YOU OUT HERE TODAY BECAUSE THERE'S SOMETHING I WANT TO TELL YOU.
He's hot.
Really cool.
THEY'RE ALL STARING AT AKIRA, SAYING HE'S GOOD-LOOKING...

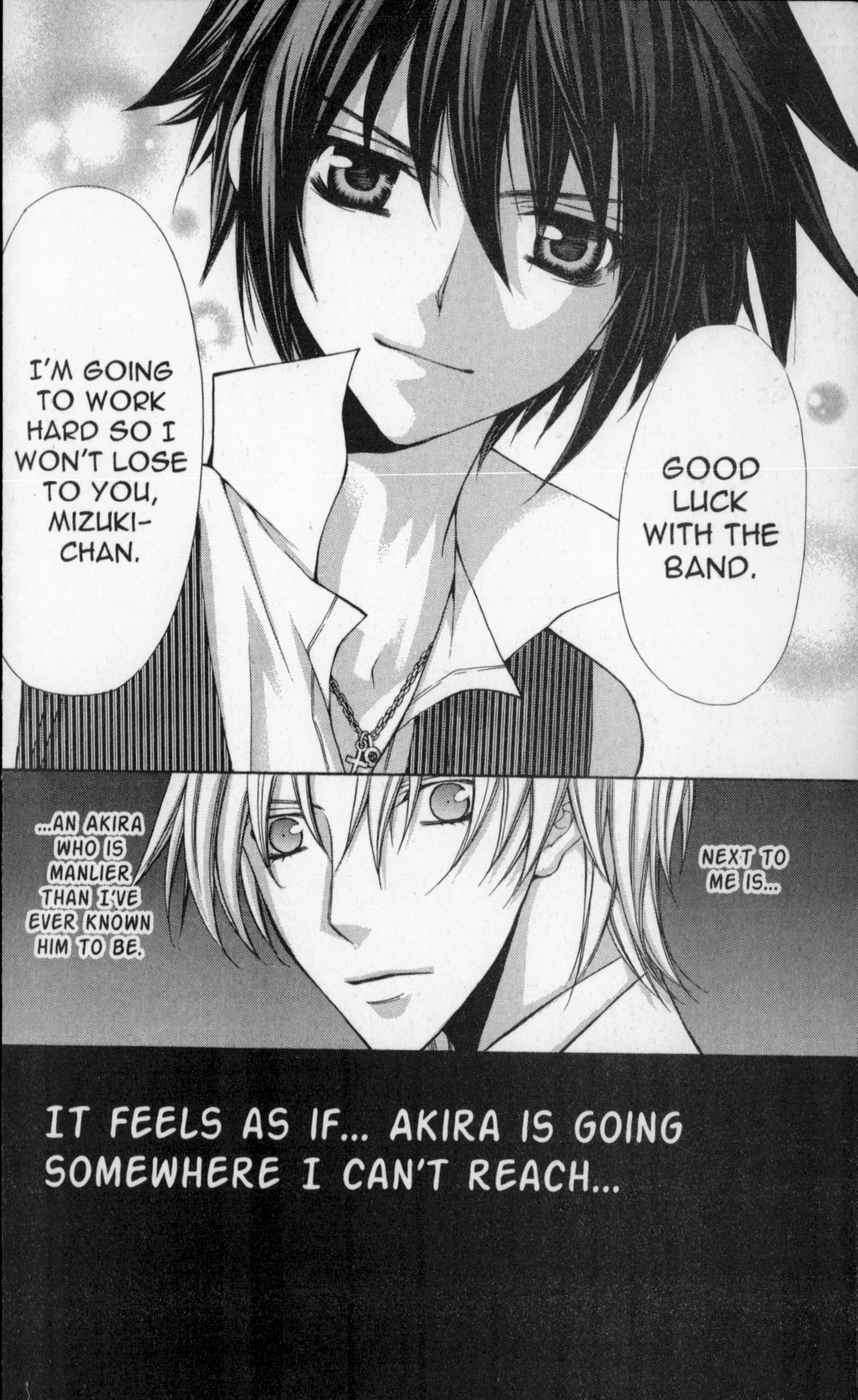
GOOD LUCK WITH THE BAND.
I'M GOING TO WORK HARD SO I WON'T LOSE TO YOU, MIZUKI-CHAN.
NEXT TO ME IS...
...AN AKIRA WHO IS MANLIER THAN I'VE EVER KNOWN HIM TO BE.
IT FEELS AS IF... AKIRA IS GOING SOMEWHERE I CAN'T REACH...

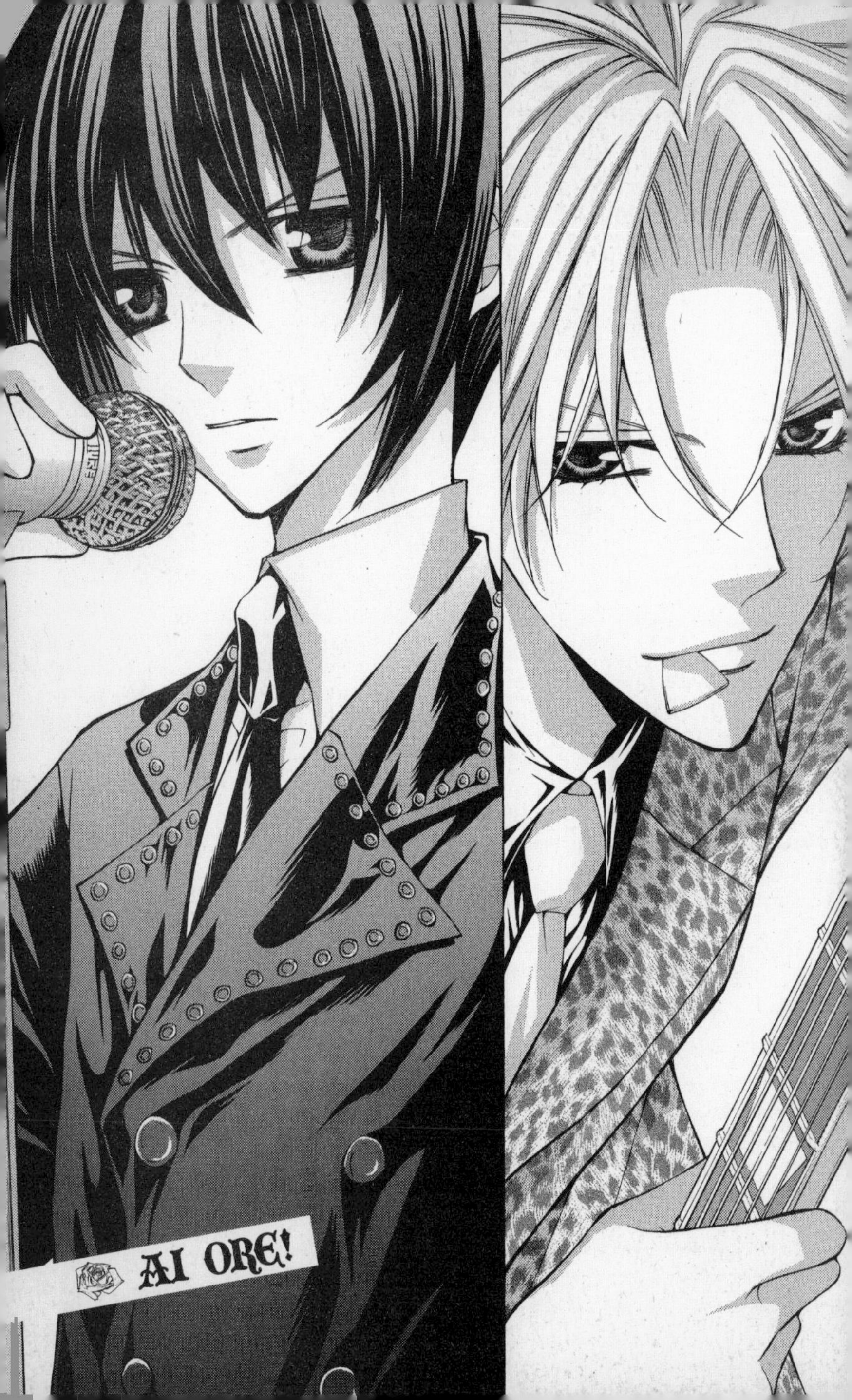
AI ORE!

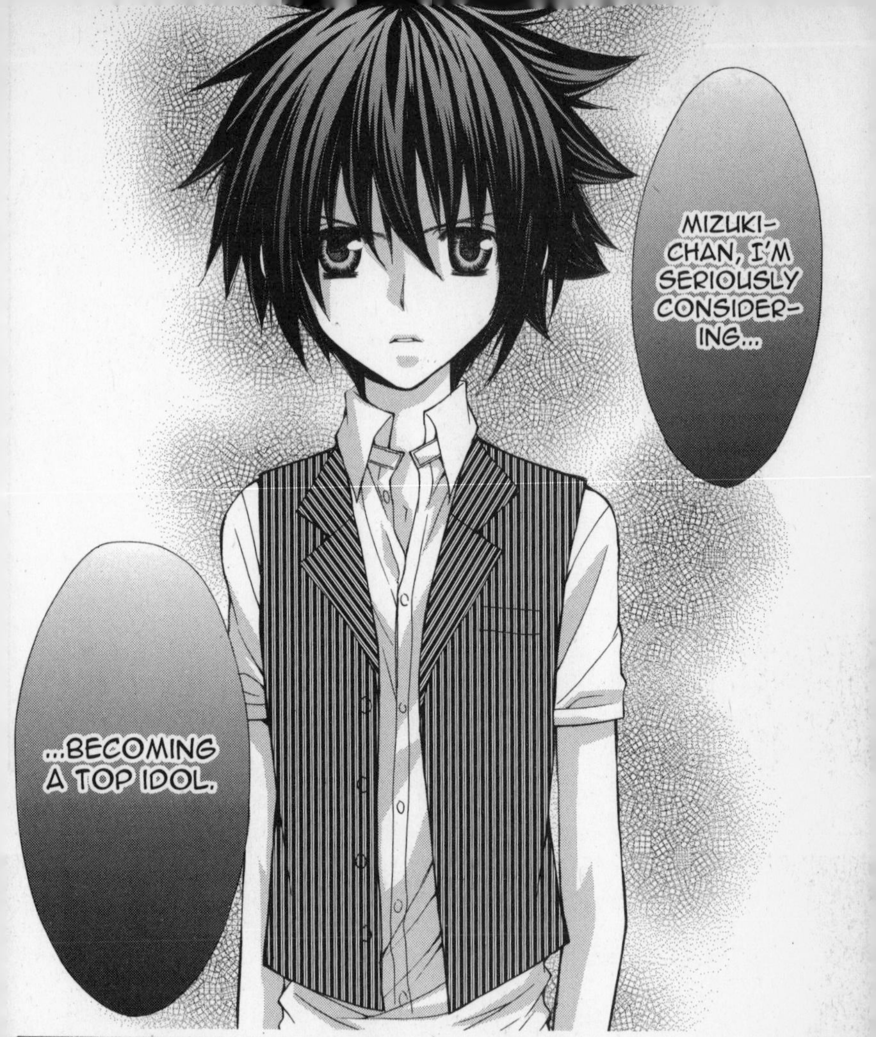
MIZUKI-CHAN, I'M SERIOUSLY CONSIDERING...
...BECOMING A TOP IDOL.

About *Ai Ore!*

Ai Ore! is now bimonthly in *Asuka*, and because of my work schedule it took me a while to notice that cross-dressing seems to have gathered some popularity among the public. Visual Kei girl bands are popular nowadays too. When I hear about things like that, I feel glad to have continued creating a manga like this. But then again, Akira doesn't enjoy dressing like a girl—he'll only do it when Mizuki is involved. But in this chapter Akira chooses to dress this way for himself. I think that's important. He must have thought about the possibilities open to him for the first time and realized that having a girlish face is not something to be embarrassed about... Right! He should have figured out that ages ago. Being cute is good!

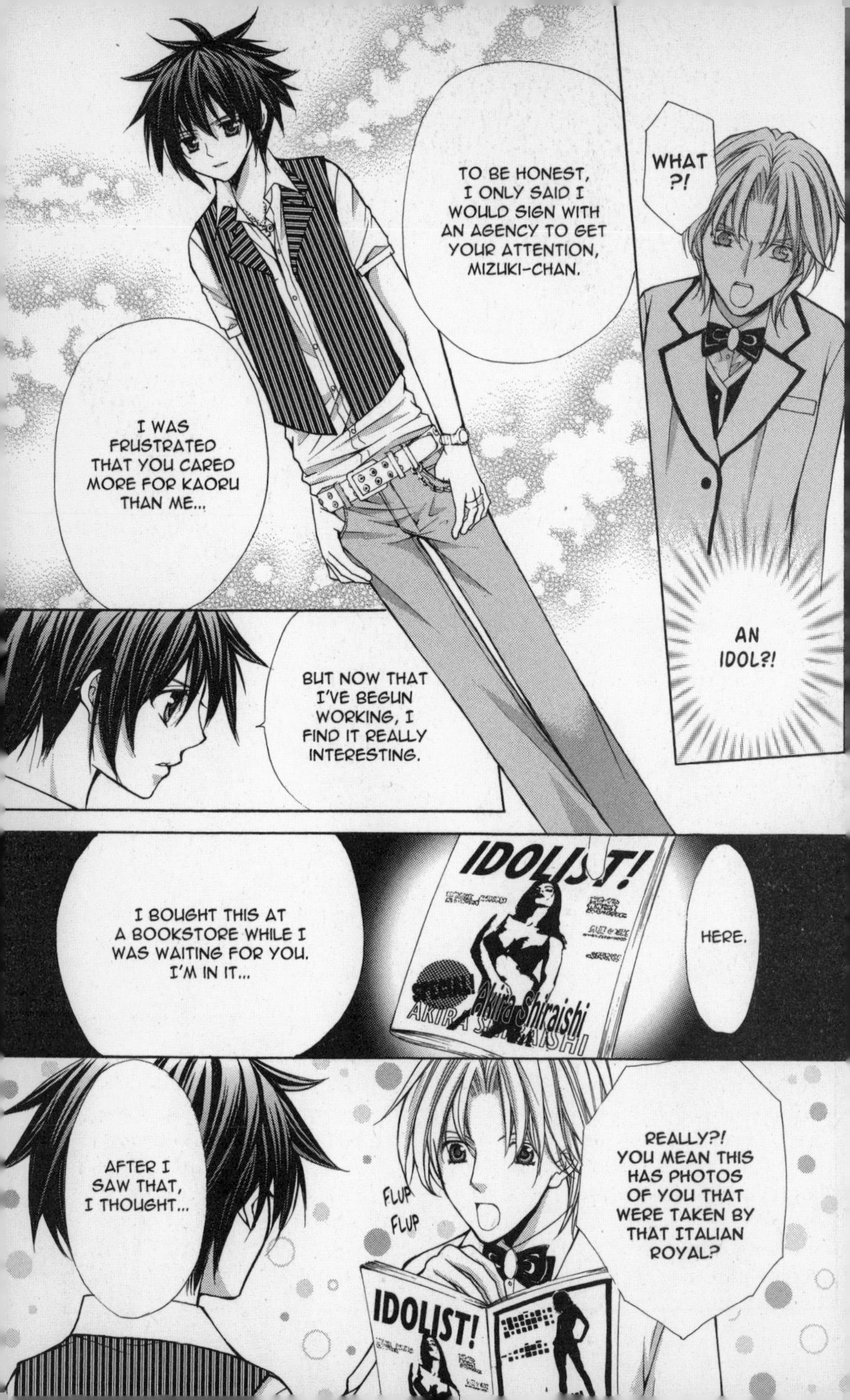
WHAT ?!
AN IDOL?!
TO BE HONEST, I ONLY SAID I WOULD SIGN WITH AN AGENCY TO GET YOUR ATTENTION, MIZUKI-CHAN.
I WAS FRUSTRATED THAT YOU CARED MORE FOR KAORU THAN ME...
BUT NOW THAT I'VE BEGUN WORKING, I FIND IT REALLY INTERESTING.
HERE.
IDOLIST!
Akira Shiraishi
I BOUGHT THIS AT A BOOKSTORE WHILE I WAS WAITING FOR YOU. I'M IN IT...
REALLY?! YOU MEAN THIS HAS PHOTOS OF YOU THAT WERE TAKEN BY THAT ITALIAN ROYAL?
FLUP FLUP
IDOLIST!
AFTER I SAW THAT, I THOUGHT...

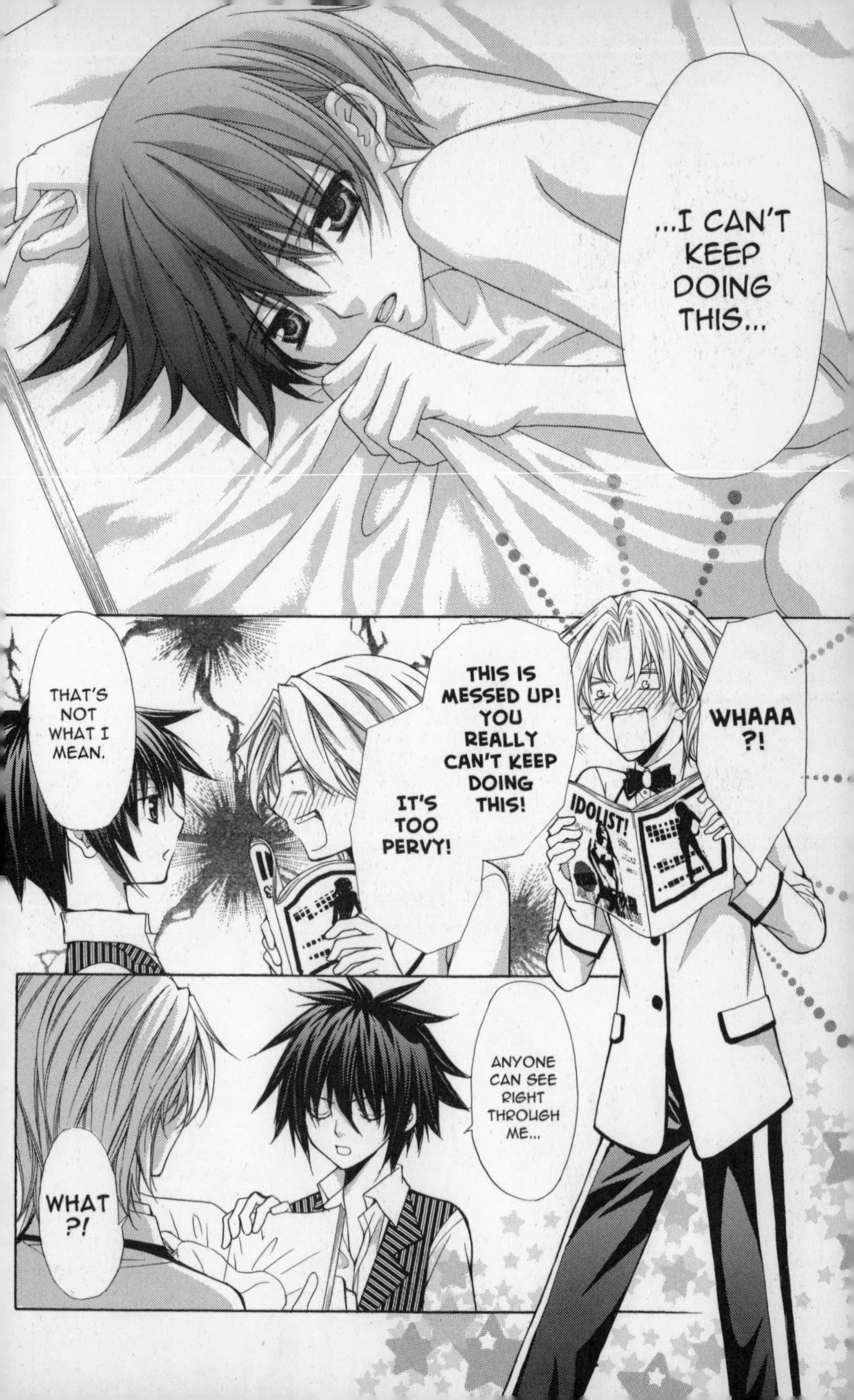
...I CAN'T KEEP DOING THIS...
WHAAA ?!
THIS IS MESSED UP! YOU REALLY CAN'T KEEP DOING THIS!
IT'S TOO PERVY!
THAT'S NOT WHAT I MEAN.
ANYONE CAN SEE RIGHT THROUGH ME...
WHAT ?!
IDOLIST!

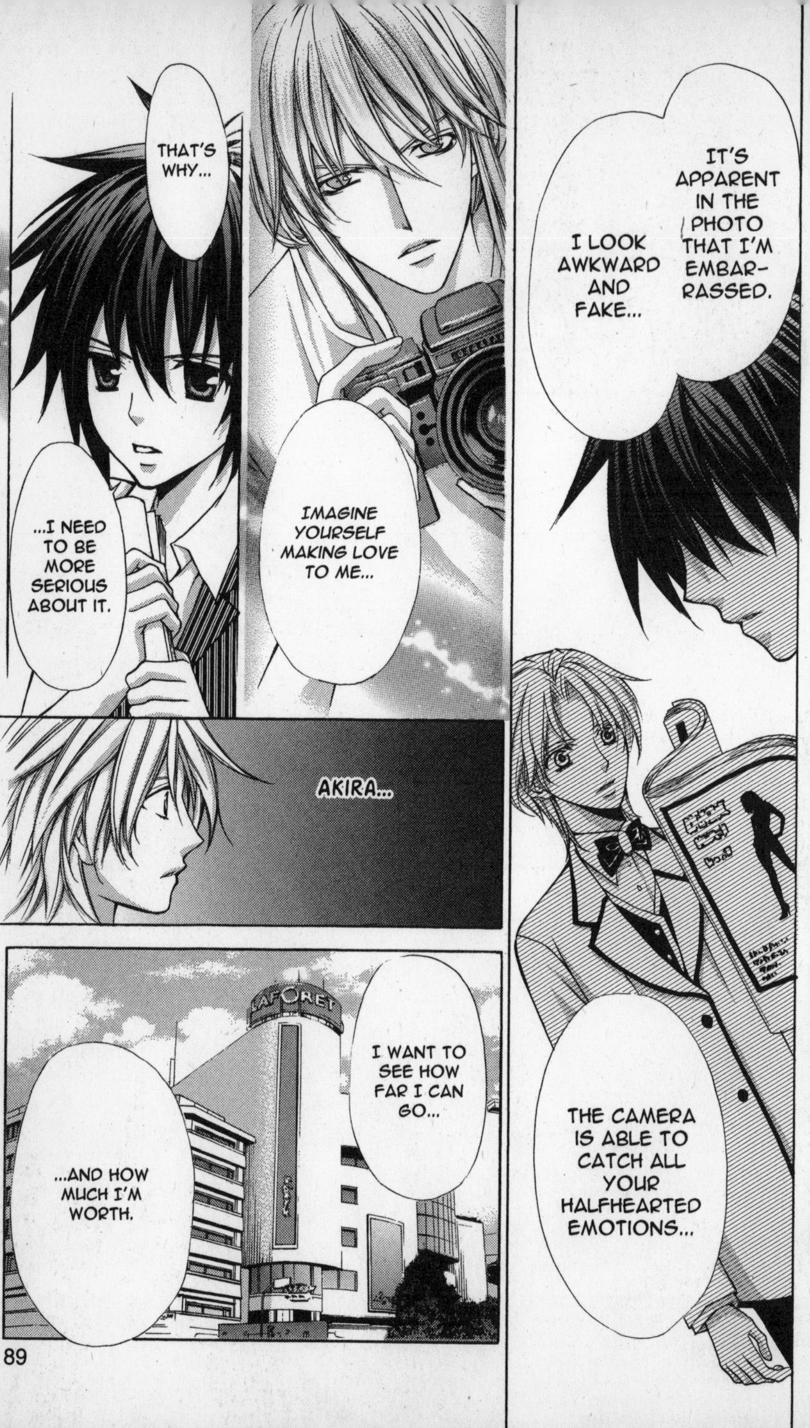
IT'S APPARENT IN THE PHOTO THAT I'M EMBAR-RASSED.
I LOOK AWKWARD AND FAKE...
THE CAMERA IS ABLE TO CATCH ALL YOUR HALFHEARTED EMOTIONS...
IMAGINE YOURSELF MAKING LOVE TO ME...
THAT'S WHY...
...I NEED TO BE MORE SERIOUS ABOUT IT.
AKIRA...
I WANT TO SEE HOW FAR I CAN GO...
...AND HOW MUCH I'M WORTH.

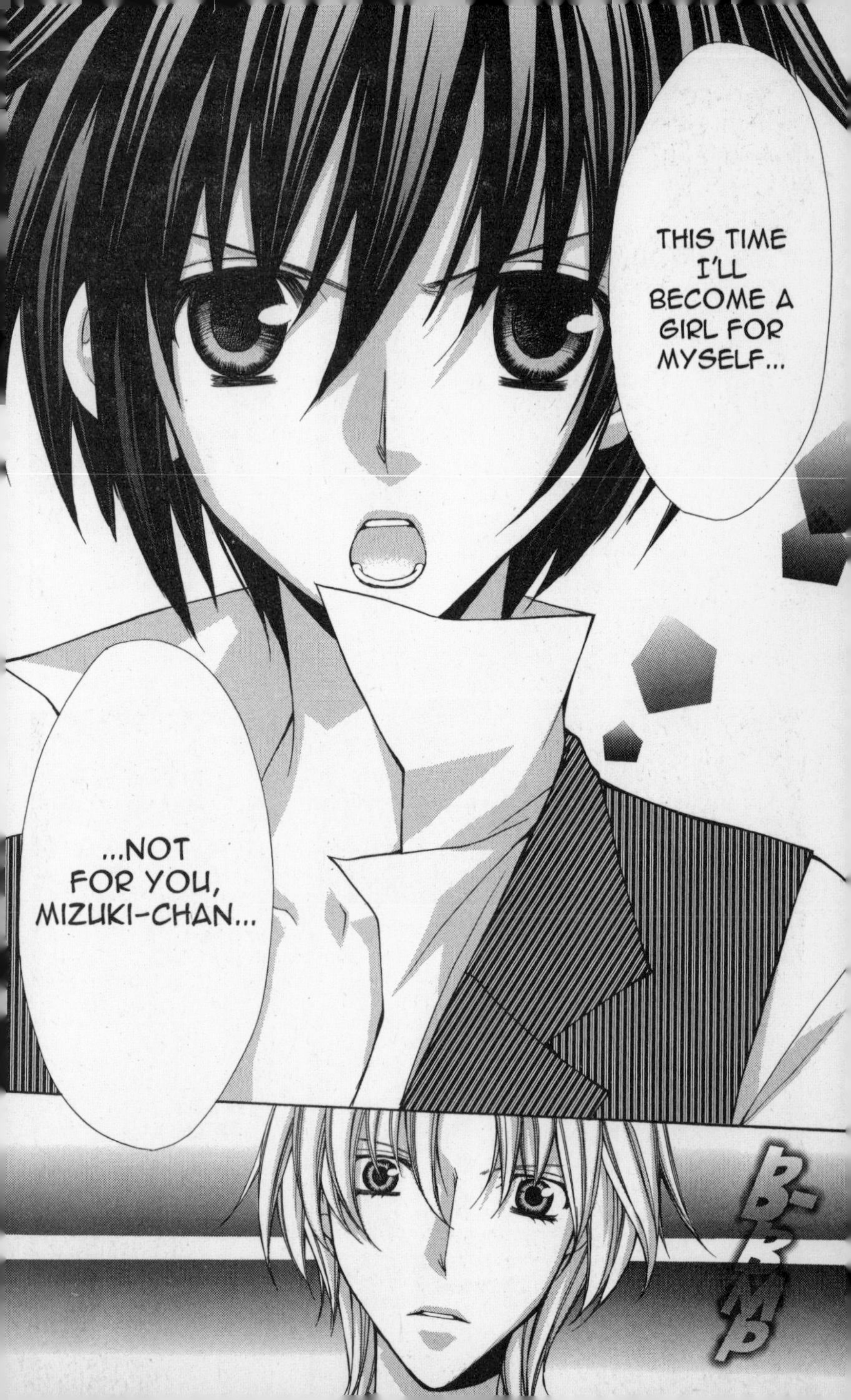
THIS TIME I'LL BECOME A GIRL FOR MYSELF...
...NOT FOR YOU, MIZUKI-CHAN...
B-BMP

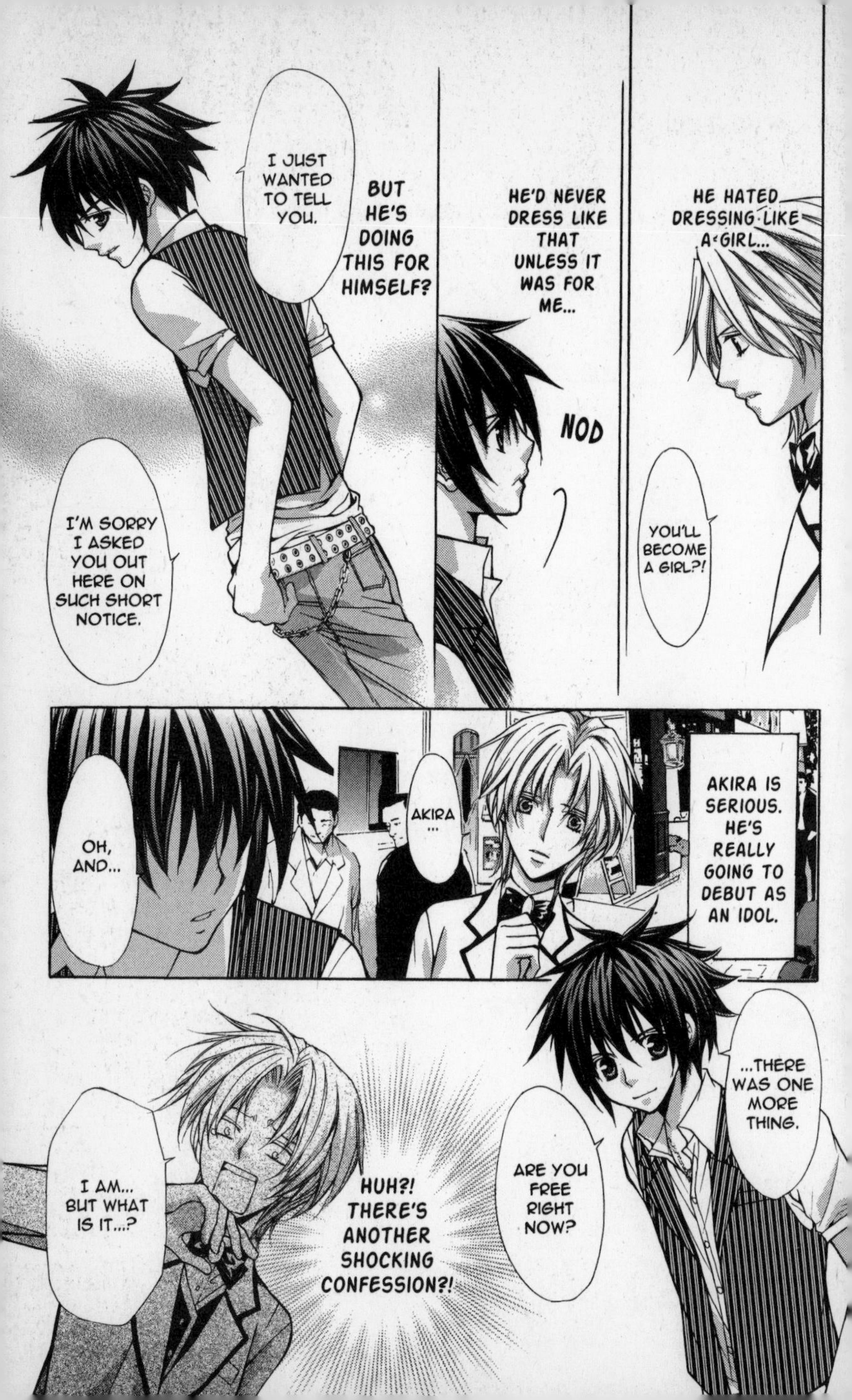
HE HATED DRESSING LIKE A GIRL...
YOU'LL BECOME A GIRL?!
HE'D NEVER DRESS LIKE THAT UNLESS IT WAS FOR ME...
NOD
I JUST WANTED TO TELL YOU.
BUT HE'S DOING THIS FOR HIMSELF?
I'M SORRY I ASKED YOU OUT HERE ON SUCH SHORT NOTICE.
AKIRA IS SERIOUS. HE'S REALLY GOING TO DEBUT AS AN IDOL.
AKIRA...
OH, AND...
...THERE WAS ONE MORE THING.
ARE YOU FREE RIGHT NOW?
HUH?! THERE'S ANOTHER SHOCKING CONFESSION?!
I AM... BUT WHAT IS IT...?

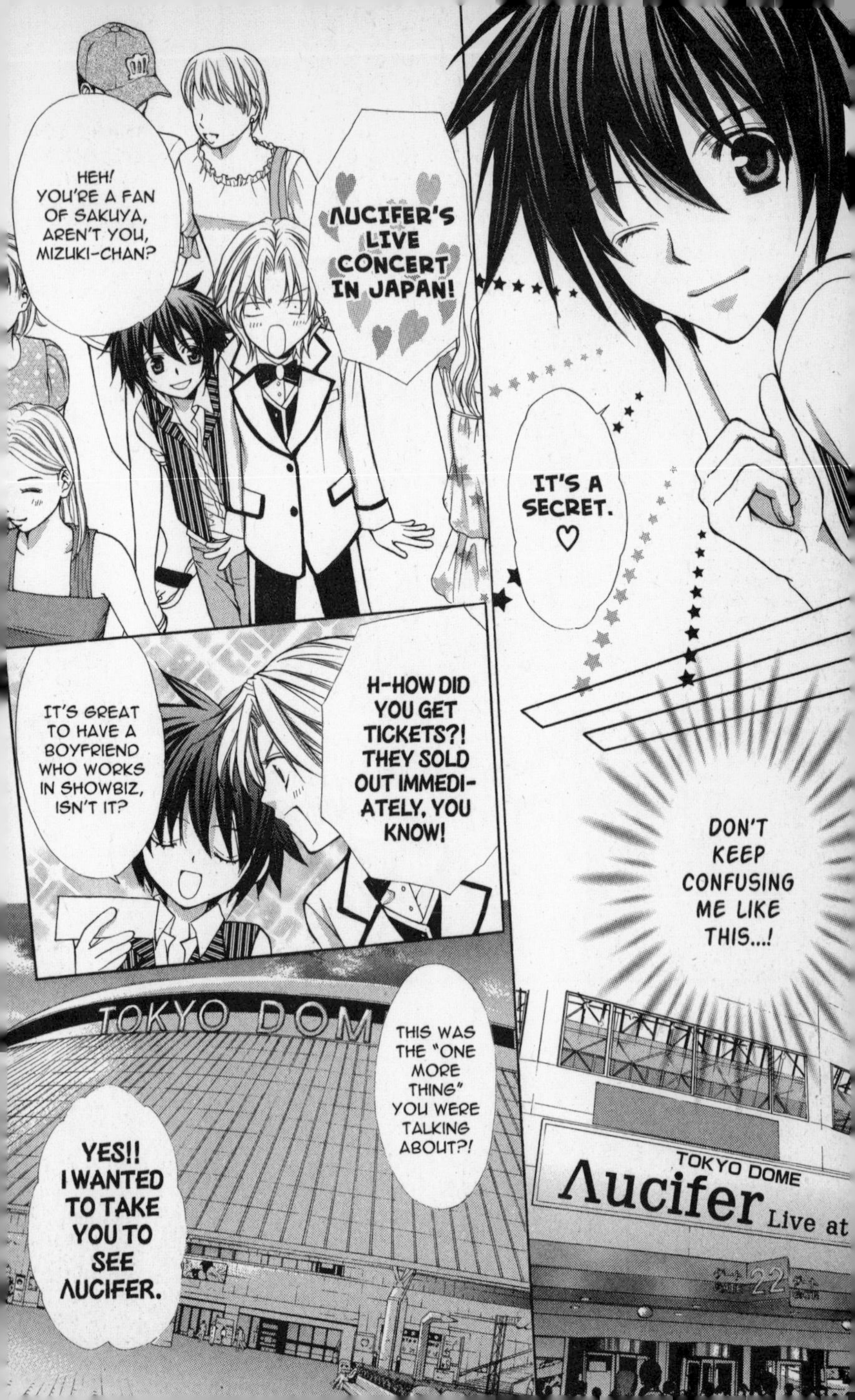
IT'S A SECRET. ♡
DON'T KEEP CONFUSING ME LIKE THIS...!
TOKYO DOME Λucifer Live at
ΛUCIFER'S LIVE CONCERT IN JAPAN!
HEH! YOU'RE A FAN OF SAKUYA, AREN'T YOU, MIZUKI-CHAN?
H-HOW DID YOU GET TICKETS?! THEY SOLD OUT IMMEDI-ATELY, YOU KNOW!
IT'S GREAT TO HAVE A BOYFRIEND WHO WORKS IN SHOWBIZ, ISN'T IT?
TOKYO DOM
THIS WAS THE "ONE MORE THING" YOU WERE TALKING ABOUT?!
YES!! I WANTED TO TAKE YOU TO SEE ΛUCIFER.

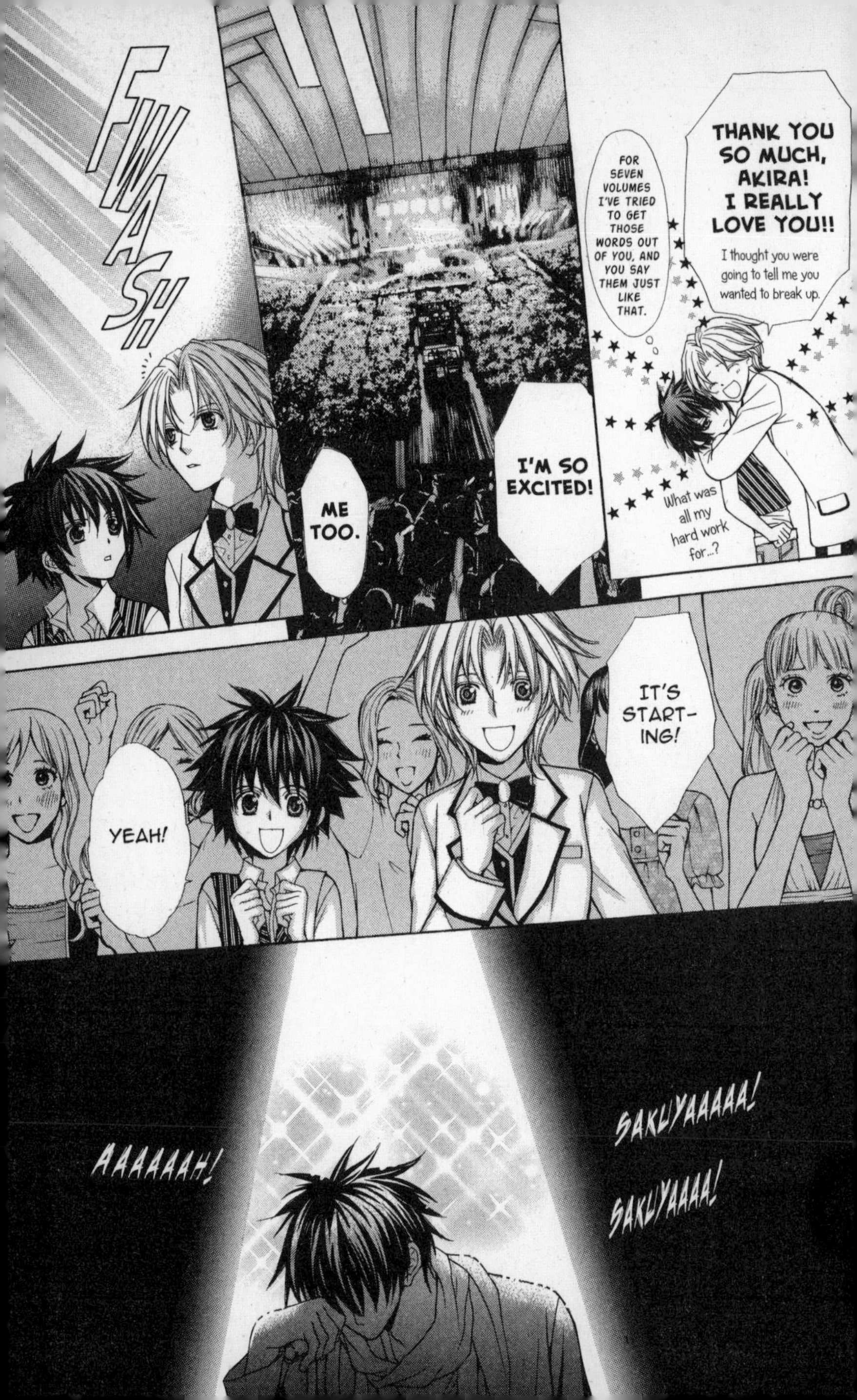
THANK YOU SO MUCH, AKIRA! I REALLY LOVE YOU!!
I thought you were going to tell me you wanted to break up.
FOR SEVEN VOLUMES I'VE TRIED TO GET THOSE WORDS OUT OF YOU, AND YOU SAY THEM JUST LIKE THAT.
What was all my hard work for...?
I'M SO EXCITED!
ME TOO.
FWASH
IT'S START-ING!
YEAH!
SAKUYAAAAA!
SAKUYAAAA!
AAAAAAH!

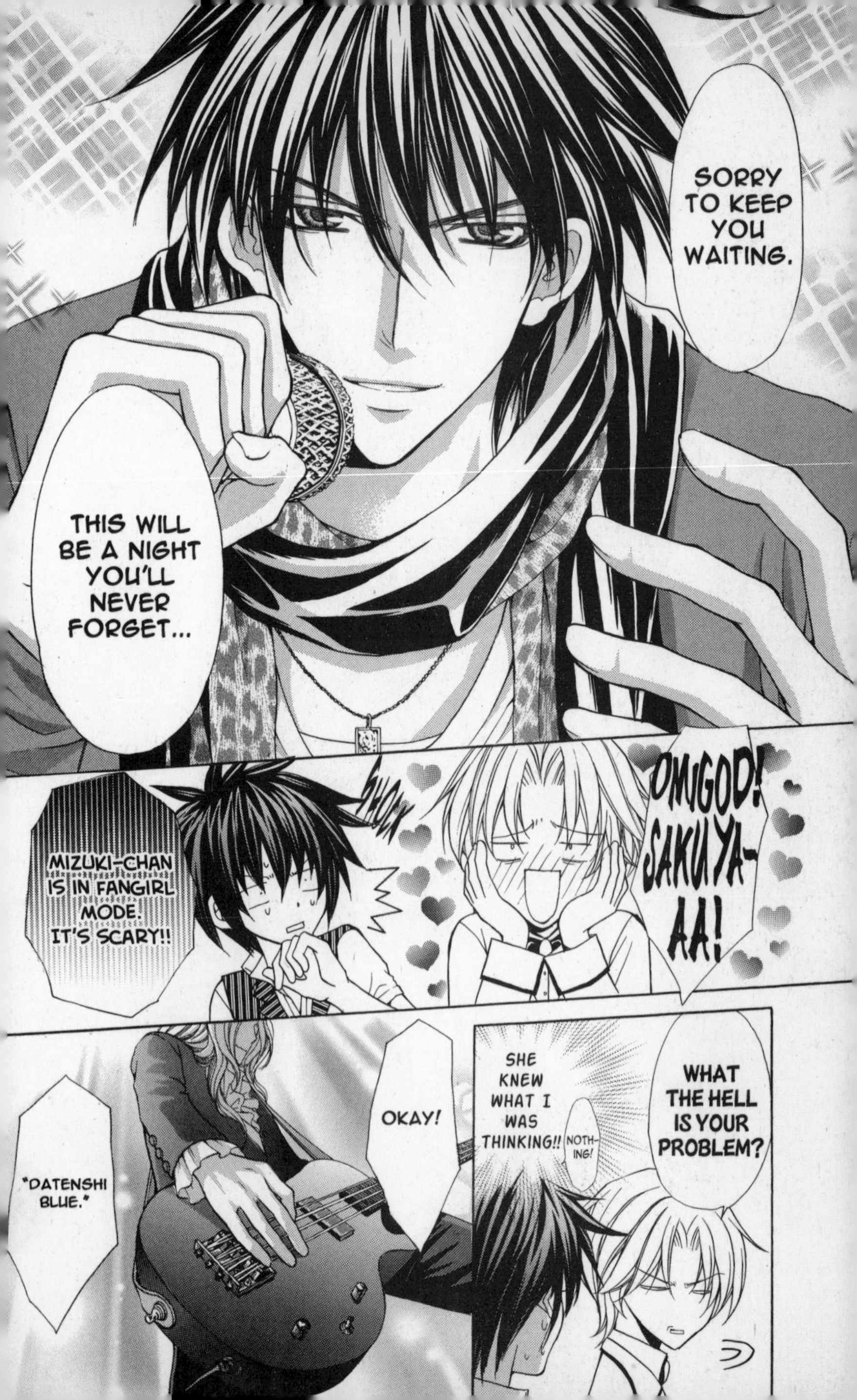
SORRY TO KEEP YOU WAITING.
THIS WILL BE A NIGHT YOU'LL NEVER FORGET...
OMIGOD! SAKUYA-AA!
SHOCK
MIZUKI-CHAN IS IN FANGIRL MODE. IT'S SCARY!!
WHAT THE HELL IS YOUR PROBLEM?
NOTH-ING!
SHE KNEW WHAT I WAS THINKING!!
OKAY!
"DATENSHI BLUE."

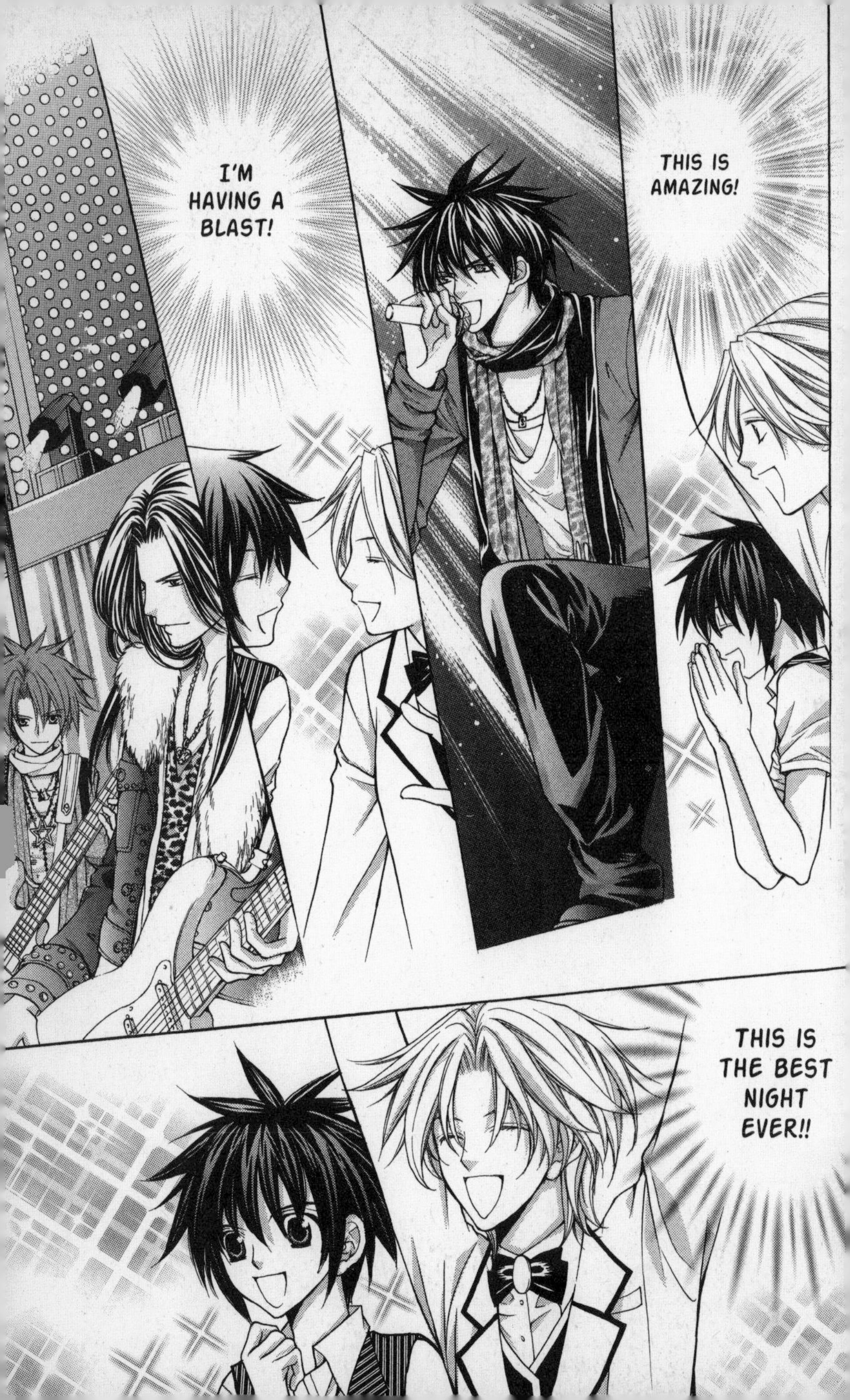
THIS IS AMAZING!
I'M HAVING A BLAST!
THIS IS THE BEST NIGHT EVER!!

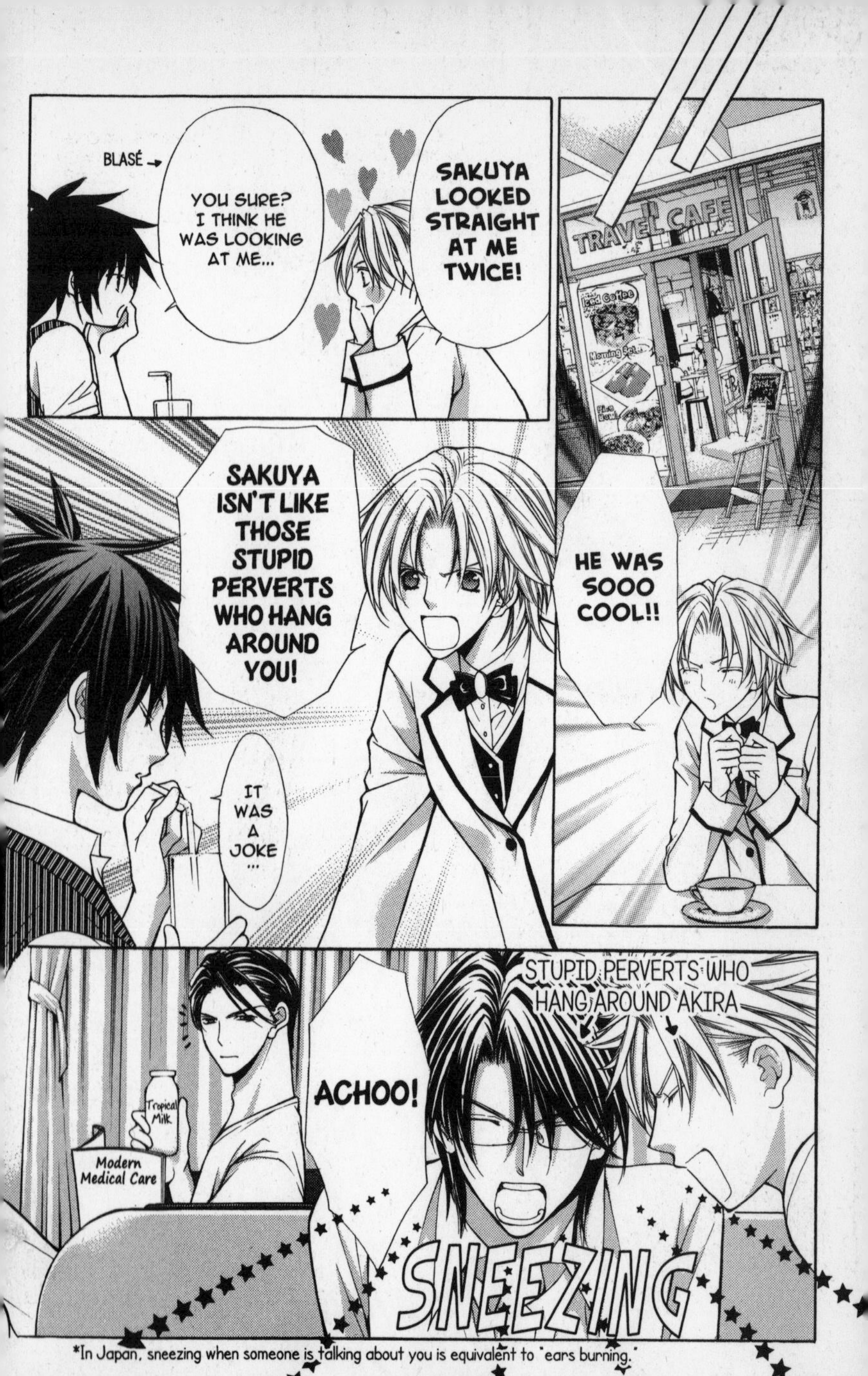
TRAVEL CAFE
Iced Coffee
Morning Set
HE WAS SOOO COOL!!
SAKUYA LOOKED STRAIGHT AT ME TWICE!
YOU SURE? I THINK HE WAS LOOKING AT ME...
BLASÉ →
SAKUYA ISN'T LIKE THOSE STUPID PERVERTS WHO HANG AROUND YOU!
IT WAS A JOKE ...
STUPID PERVERTS WHO HANG AROUND AKIRA
ACHOO!
SNEEZING
Tropical Milk
Modern Medical Care

*In Japan, sneezing when someone is talking about you is equivalent to "ears burning."

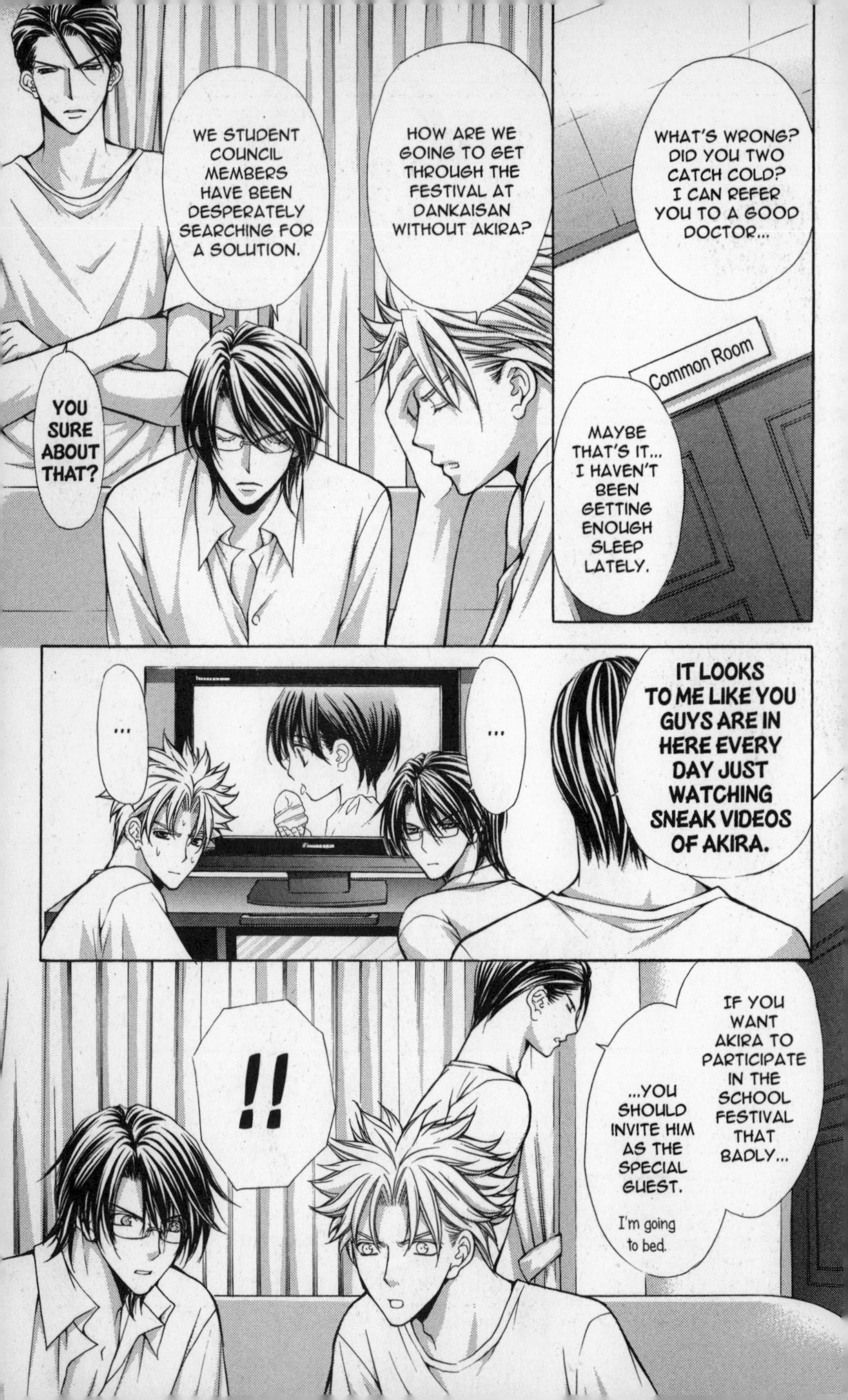
WHAT'S WRONG? DID YOU TWO CATCH COLD? I CAN REFER YOU TO A GOOD DOCTOR...
Common Room
MAYBE THAT'S IT... I HAVEN'T BEEN GETTING ENOUGH SLEEP LATELY.
HOW ARE WE GOING TO GET THROUGH THE FESTIVAL AT DANKAISAN WITHOUT AKIRA?
WE STUDENT COUNCIL MEMBERS HAVE BEEN DESPERATELY SEARCHING FOR A SOLUTION.
YOU SURE ABOUT THAT?
IT LOOKS TO ME LIKE YOU GUYS ARE IN HERE EVERY DAY JUST WATCHING SNEAK VIDEOS OF AKIRA.
...
...
IF YOU WANT AKIRA TO PARTICIPATE IN THE SCHOOL FESTIVAL THAT BADLY...
...YOU SHOULD INVITE HIM AS THE SPECIAL GUEST.
I'm going to bed.
!!

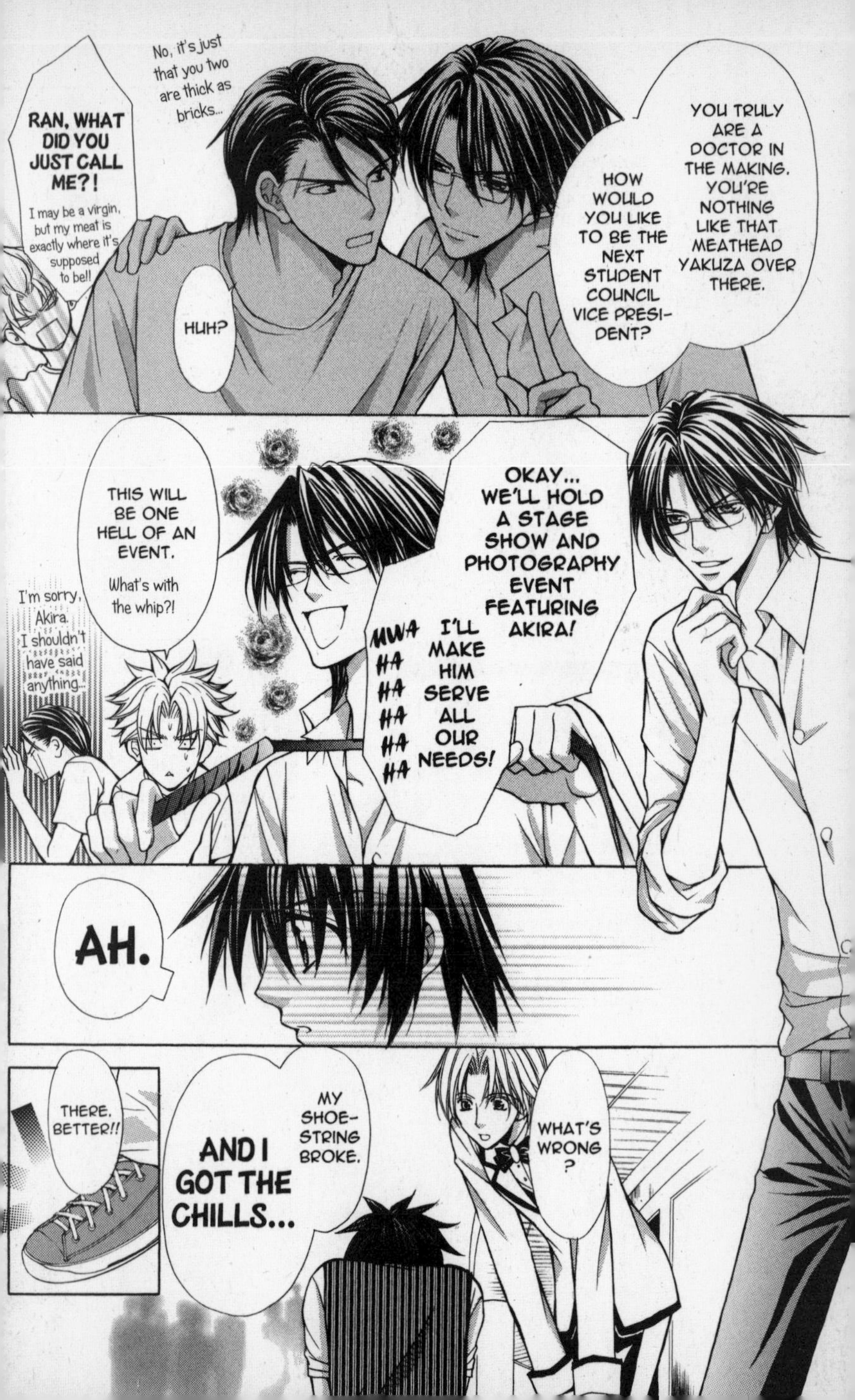
YOU TRULY ARE A DOCTOR IN THE MAKING. YOU'RE NOTHING LIKE THAT MEATHEAD YAKUZA OVER THERE.
HOW WOULD YOU LIKE TO BE THE NEXT STUDENT COUNCIL VICE PRESI-DENT?
HUH?
No, it's just that you two are thick as bricks...
RAN, WHAT DID YOU JUST CALL ME?!
I may be a virgin, but my meat is exactly where it's supposed to be!!
OKAY... WE'LL HOLD A STAGE SHOW AND PHOTOGRAPHY EVENT FEATURING AKIRA!
I'LL MAKE HIM SERVE ALL OUR NEEDS!
MWA HA HA HA HA HA
THIS WILL BE ONE HELL OF AN EVENT.
What's with the whip?!
I'm sorry, Akira. I shouldn't have said anything...
AH.
WHAT'S WRONG?
MY SHOE-STRING BROKE.
AND I GOT THE CHILLS...
THERE. BETTER!!

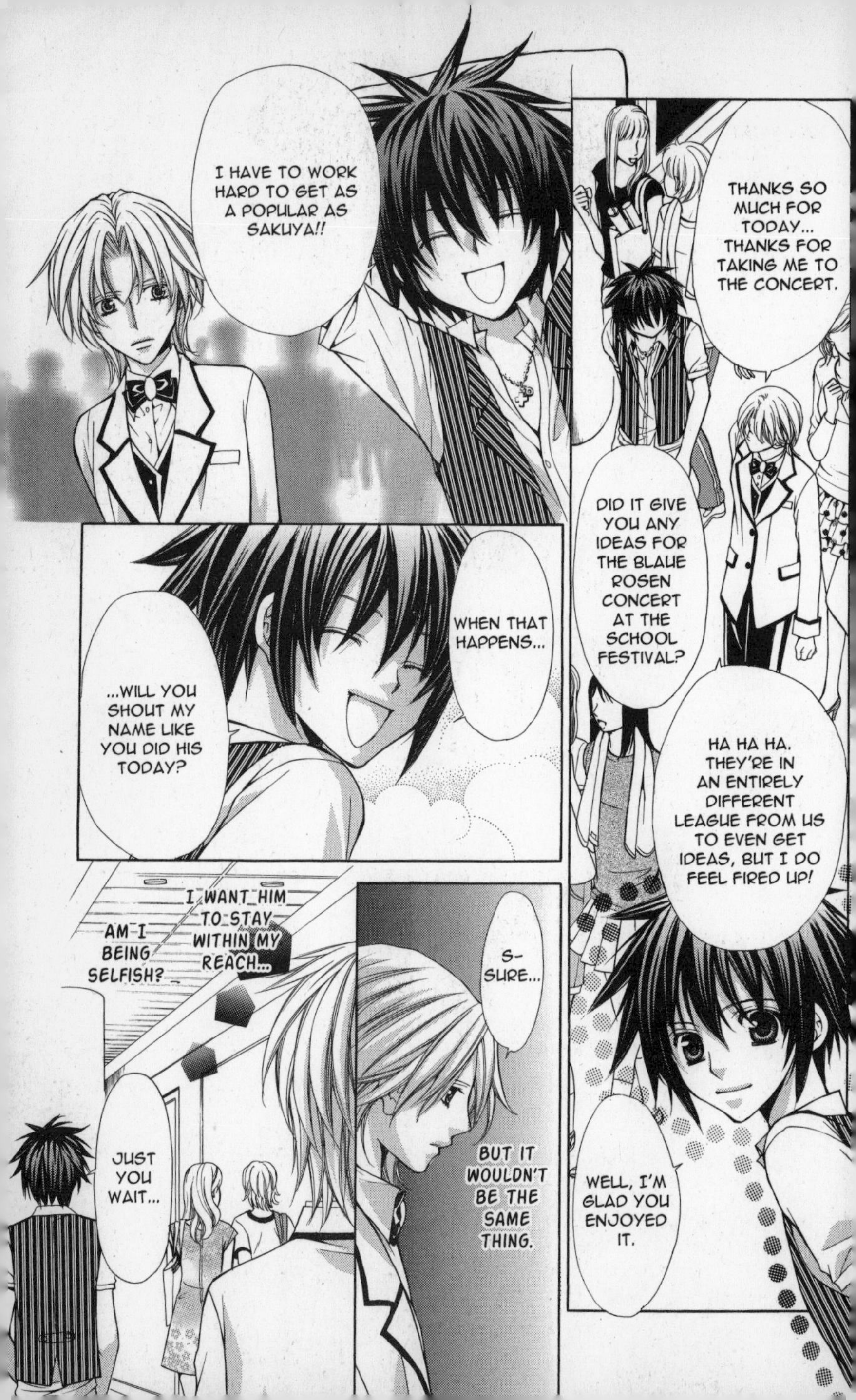
THANKS SO MUCH FOR TODAY... THANKS FOR TAKING ME TO THE CONCERT.
DID IT GIVE YOU ANY IDEAS FOR THE BLAUE ROSEN CONCERT AT THE SCHOOL FESTIVAL?
HA HA HA. THEY'RE IN AN ENTIRELY DIFFERENT LEAGUE FROM US TO EVEN GET IDEAS, BUT I DO FEEL FIRED UP!
WELL, I'M GLAD YOU ENJOYED IT.
I HAVE TO WORK HARD TO GET AS A POPULAR AS SAKUYA!!
WHEN THAT HAPPENS...
...WILL YOU SHOUT MY NAME LIKE YOU DID HIS TODAY?
S-SURE...
I WANT HIM TO STAY WITHIN MY REACH...
AM I BEING SELFISH?
BUT IT WOULDN'T BE THE SAME THING.
JUST YOU WAIT...

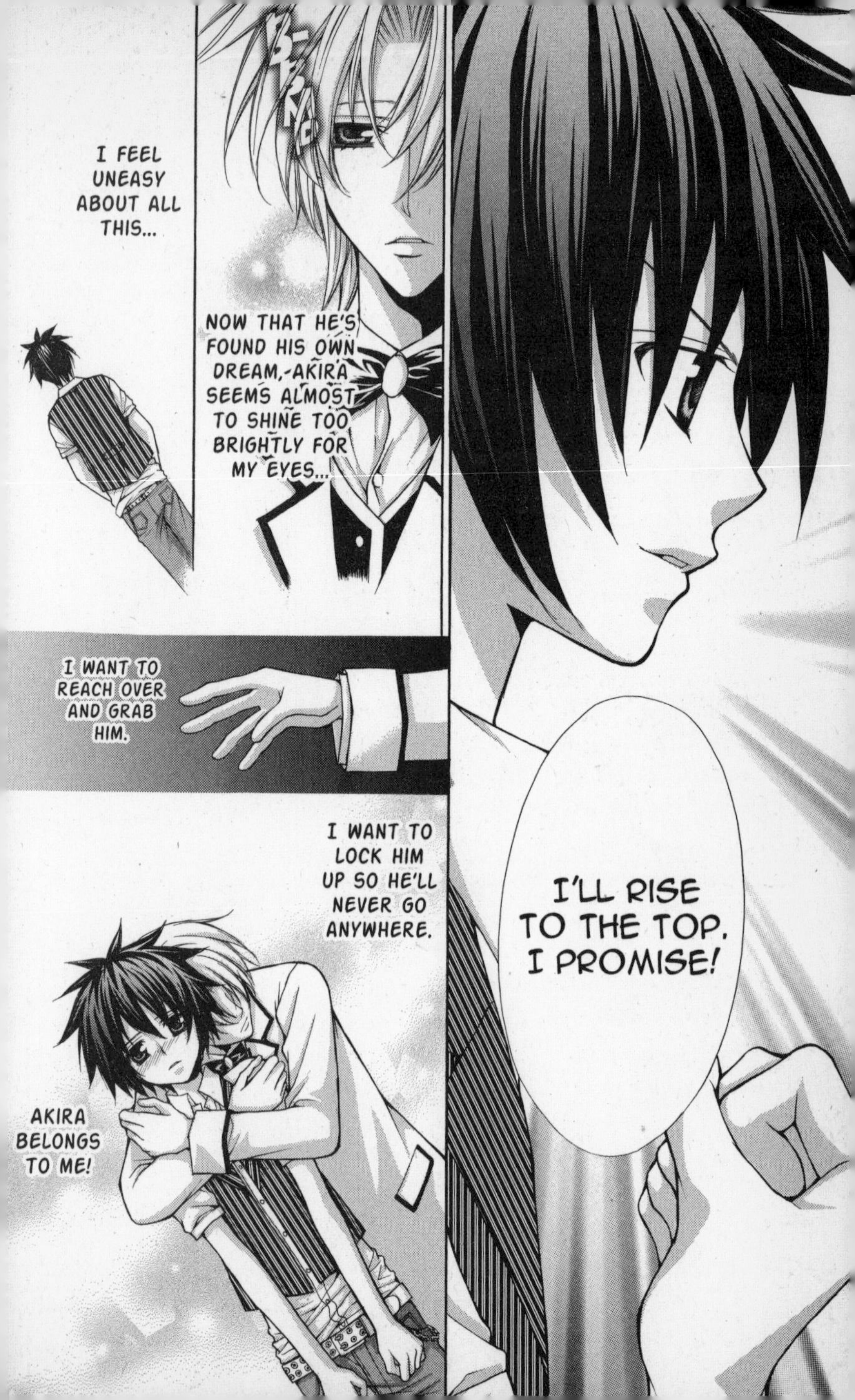
I'LL RISE TO THE TOP. I PROMISE!
B-RNG
NOW THAT HE'S FOUND HIS OWN DREAM, AKIRA SEEMS ALMOST TO SHINE TOO BRIGHTLY FOR MY EYES...
I FEEL UNEASY ABOUT ALL THIS...
I WANT TO REACH OVER AND GRAB HIM.
I WANT TO LOCK HIM UP SO HE'LL NEVER GO ANYWHERE.
AKIRA BELONGS TO ME!

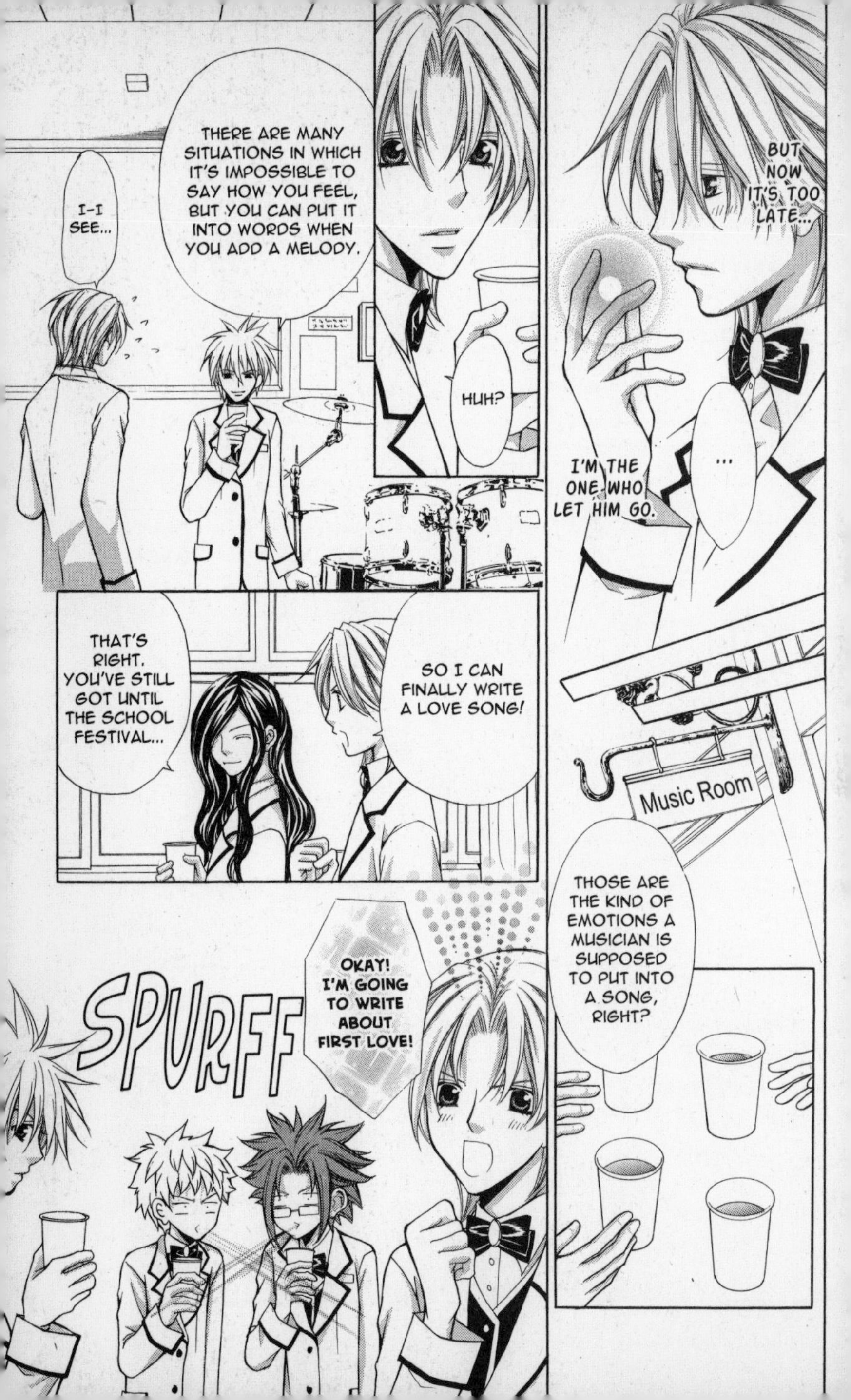
BUT NOW IT'S TOO LATE...
...
I'M THE ONE WHO LET HIM GO.
Music Room
THOSE ARE THE KIND OF EMOTIONS A MUSICIAN IS SUPPOSED TO PUT INTO A SONG, RIGHT?
HUH?
THERE ARE MANY SITUATIONS IN WHICH IT'S IMPOSSIBLE TO SAY HOW YOU FEEL, BUT YOU CAN PUT IT INTO WORDS WHEN YOU ADD A MELODY.
I-I SEE...
SO I CAN FINALLY WRITE A LOVE SONG!
THAT'S RIGHT. YOU'VE STILL GOT UNTIL THE SCHOOL FESTIVAL...
OKAY! I'M GOING TO WRITE ABOUT FIRST LOVE!
SPURFF

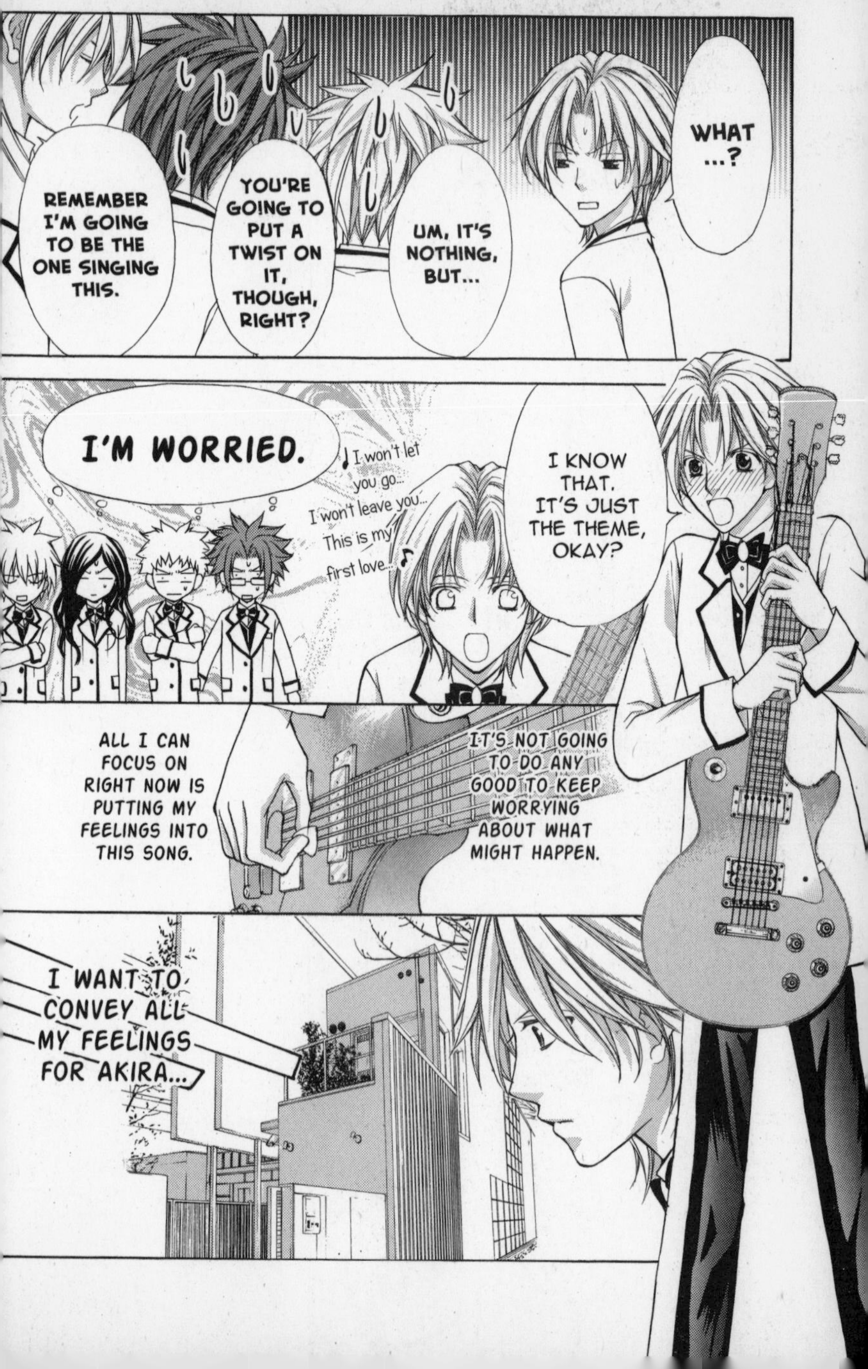
WHAT ...?
UM, IT'S NOTHING, BUT...
YOU'RE GOING TO PUT A TWIST ON IT, THOUGH, RIGHT?
REMEMBER I'M GOING TO BE THE ONE SINGING THIS.
I KNOW THAT. IT'S JUST THE THEME, OKAY?
I won't let you go... I won't leave you... This is my first love...
I'M WORRIED.
IT'S NOT GOING TO DO ANY GOOD TO KEEP WORRYING ABOUT WHAT MIGHT HAPPEN.
ALL I CAN FOCUS ON RIGHT NOW IS PUTTING MY FEELINGS INTO THIS SONG.
I WANT TO CONVEY ALL MY FEELINGS FOR AKIRA...

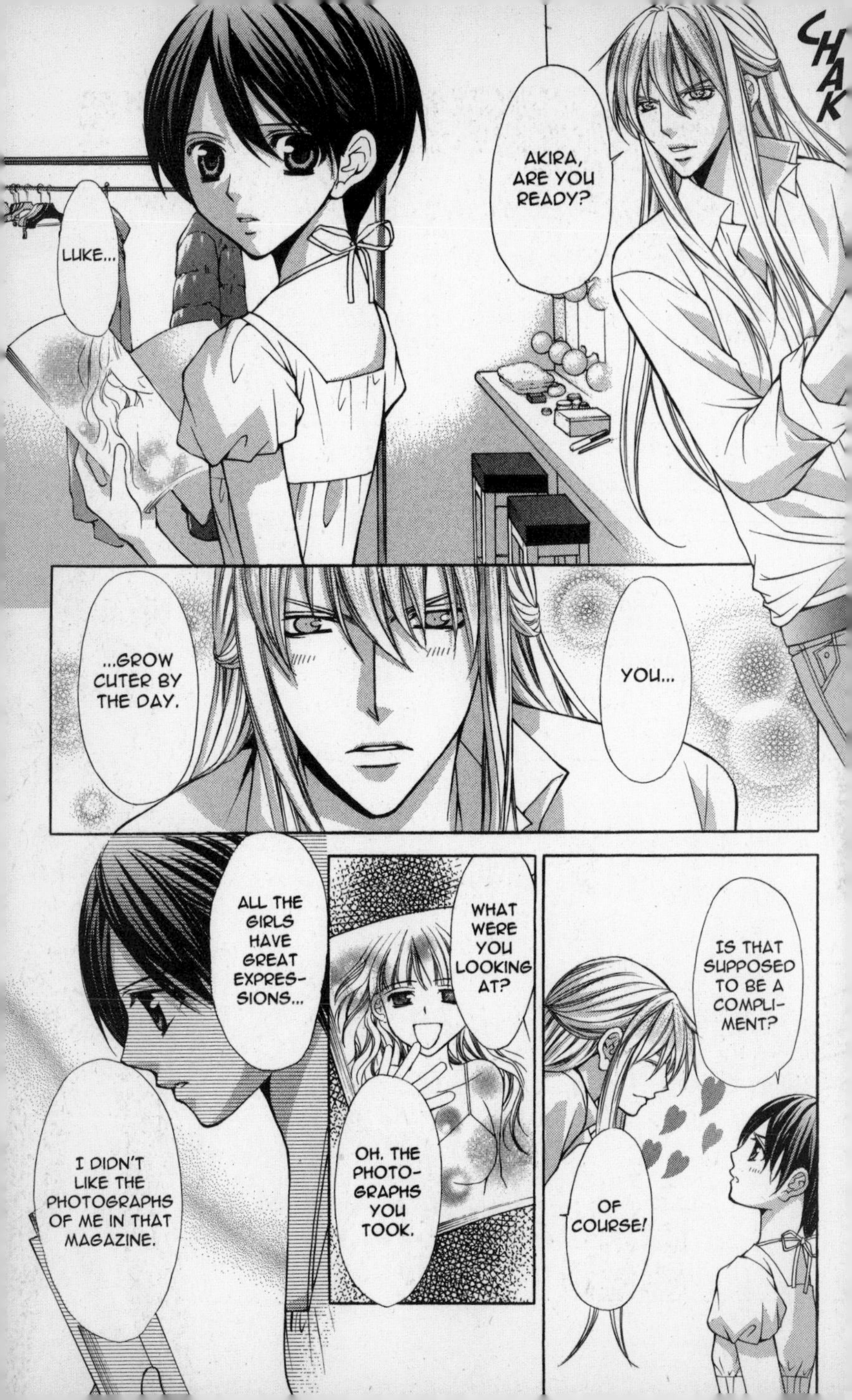
CHAK
AKIRA, ARE YOU READY?
LUKE...
YOU...
...GROW CUTER BY THE DAY.
IS THAT SUPPOSED TO BE A COMPLI-MENT?
OF COURSE!
WHAT WERE YOU LOOKING AT?
OH. THE PHOTO-GRAPHS YOU TOOK.
ALL THE GIRLS HAVE GREAT EXPRES-SIONS...
I DIDN'T LIKE THE PHOTOGRAPHS OF ME IN THAT MAGAZINE.

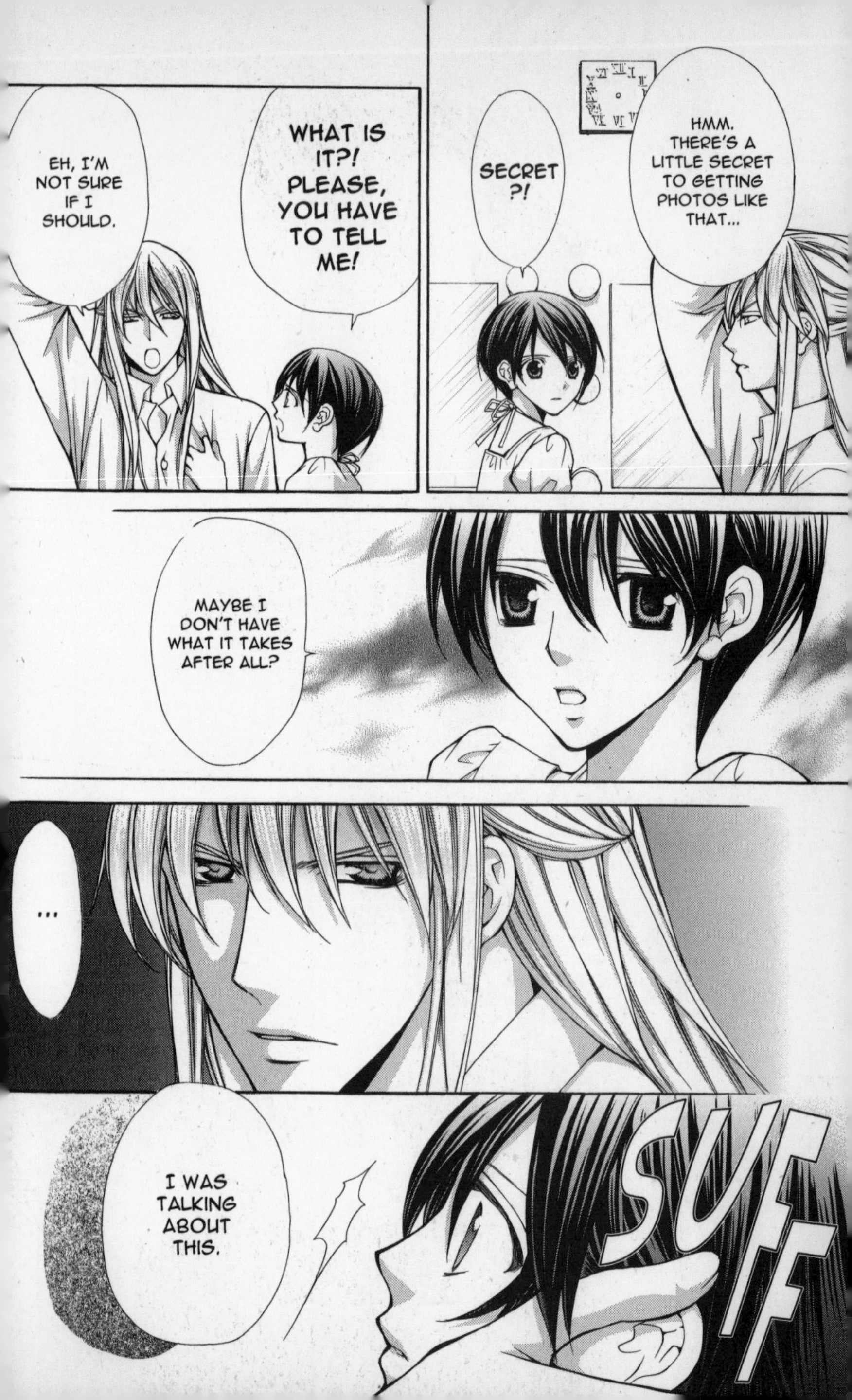
HMM. THERE'S A LITTLE SECRET TO GETTING PHOTOS LIKE THAT...
SECRET?!
WHAT IS IT?! PLEASE, YOU HAVE TO TELL ME!
EH, I'M NOT SURE IF I SHOULD.
MAYBE I DON'T HAVE WHAT IT TAKES AFTER ALL?
...
I WAS TALKING ABOUT THIS.
SUFF

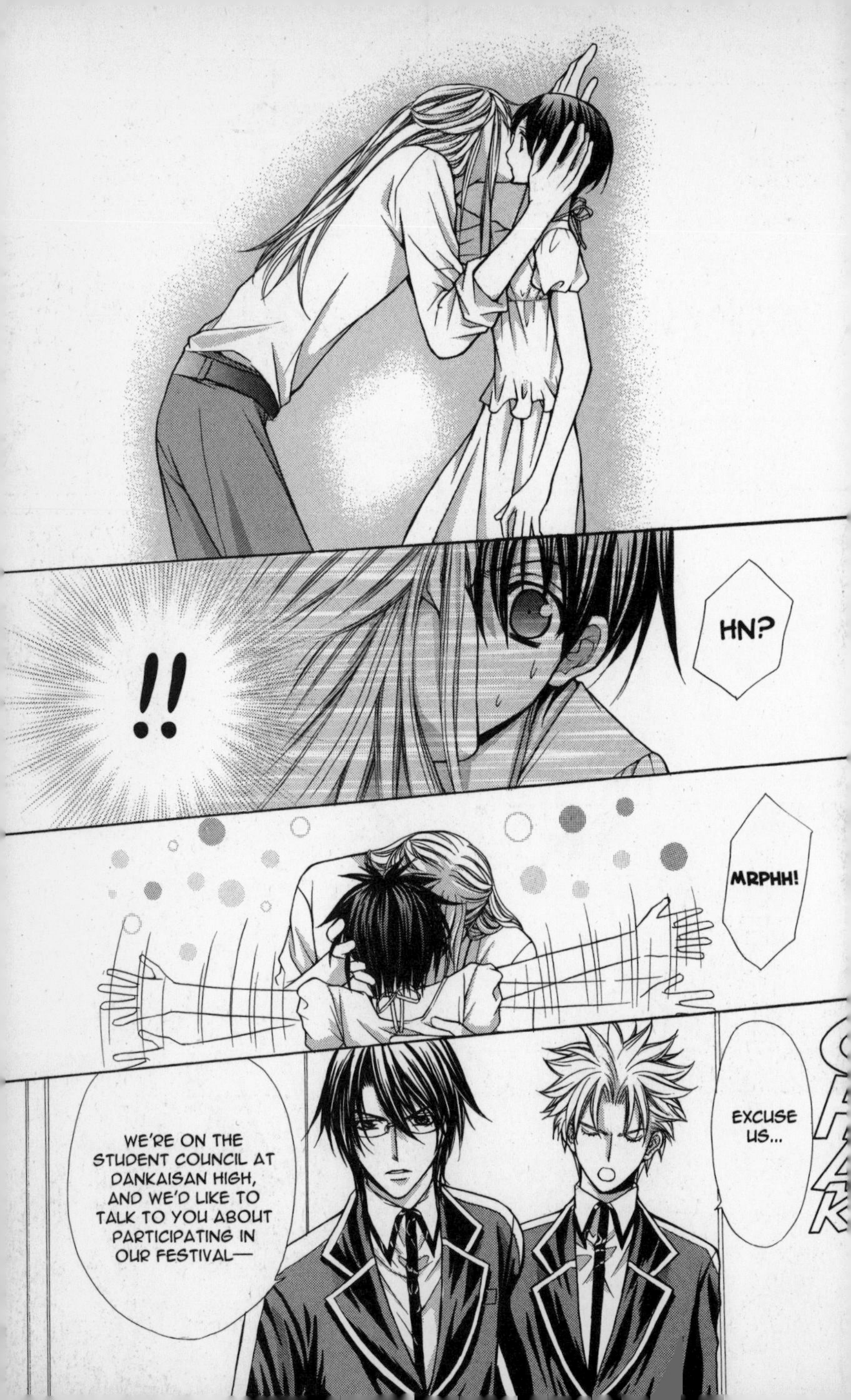
HN?
!!
MRPHH!
EXCUSE US...
WE'RE ON THE STUDENT COUNCIL AT DANKAISAN HIGH, AND WE'D LIKE TO TALK TO YOU ABOUT PARTICIPATING IN OUR FESTIVAL—

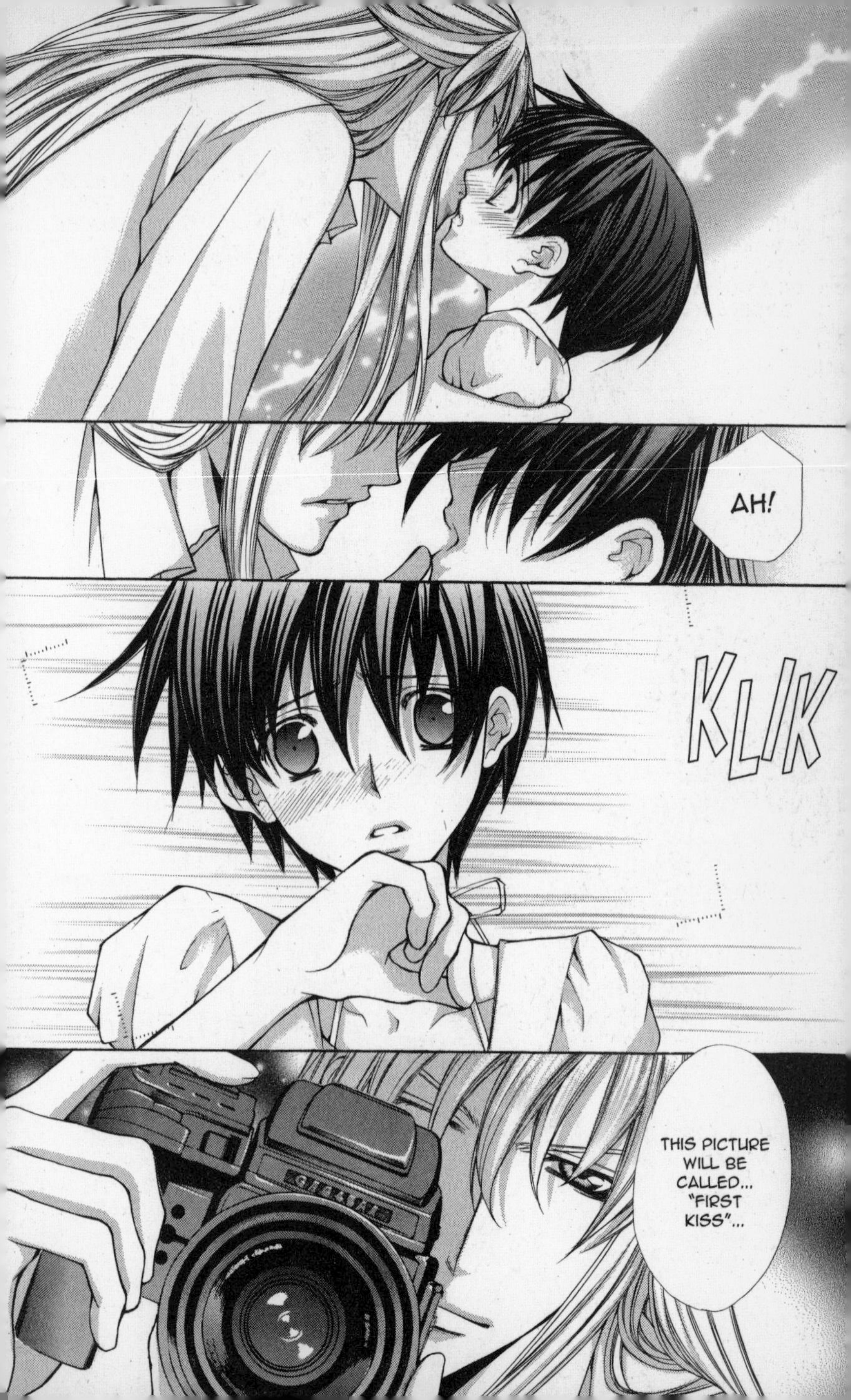
AH!
KLIK
THIS PICTURE WILL BE CALLED... "FIRST KISS"...

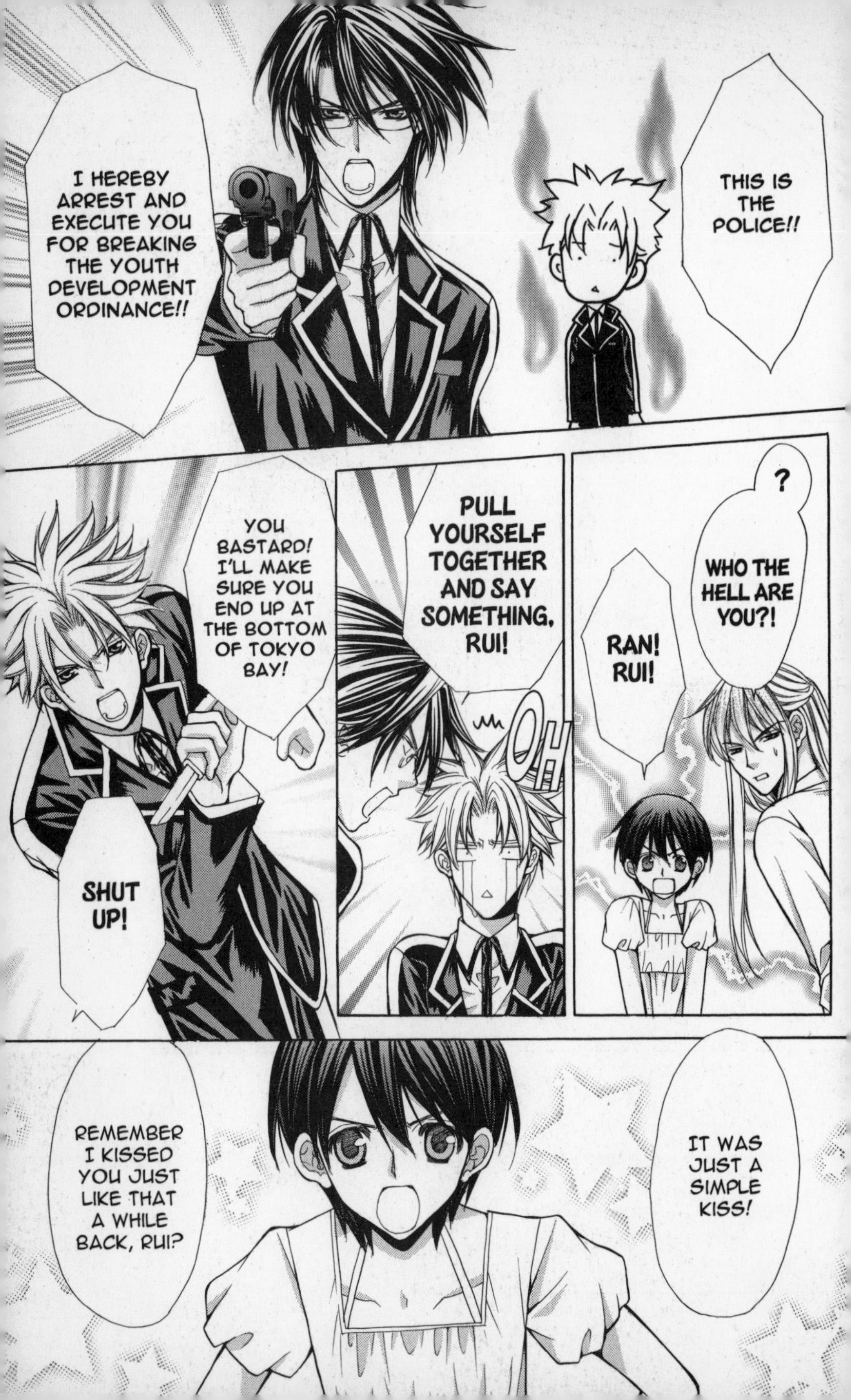
THIS IS THE POLICE!!
I HEREBY ARREST AND EXECUTE YOU FOR BREAKING THE YOUTH DEVELOPMENT ORDINANCE!!
?
WHO THE HELL ARE YOU?!
RAN! RUI!
PULL YOURSELF TOGETHER AND SAY SOMETHING, RUI!
OH
YOU BASTARD! I'LL MAKE SURE YOU END UP AT THE BOTTOM OF TOKYO BAY!
SHUT UP!
IT WAS JUST A SIMPLE KISS!
REMEMBER I KISSED YOU JUST LIKE THAT A WHILE BACK, RUI?

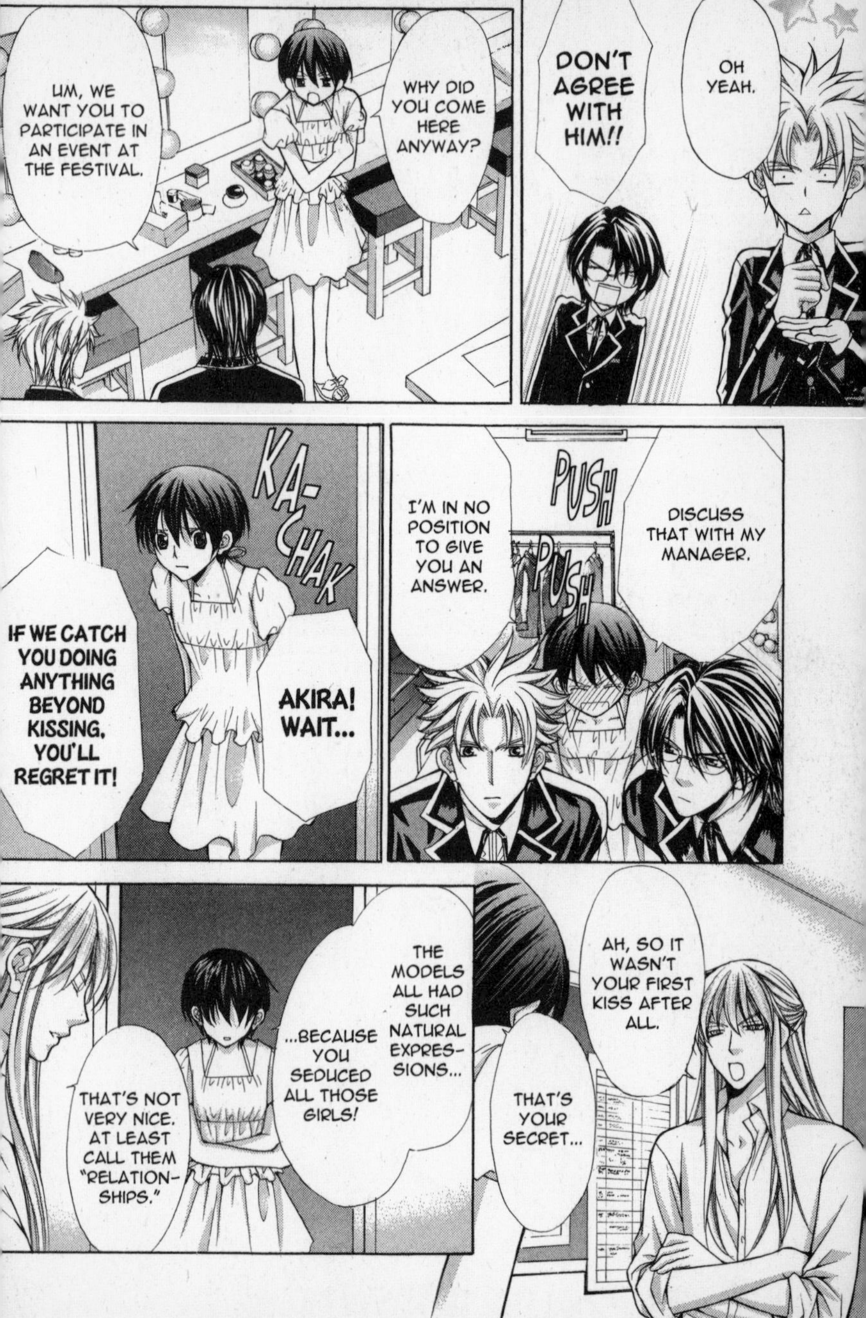
OH YEAH.
DON'T AGREE WITH HIM!!
WHY DID YOU COME HERE ANYWAY?
UM, WE WANT YOU TO PARTICIPATE IN AN EVENT AT THE FESTIVAL.
DISCUSS THAT WITH MY MANAGER.
PUSH
PUSH
I'M IN NO POSITION TO GIVE YOU AN ANSWER.
KA-CHAK
AKIRA! WAIT...
IF WE CATCH YOU DOING ANYTHING BEYOND KISSING, YOU'LL REGRET IT!
AH, SO IT WASN'T YOUR FIRST KISS AFTER ALL.
THAT'S YOUR SECRET...
THE MODELS ALL HAD SUCH NATURAL EXPRESSIONS...
...BECAUSE YOU SEDUCED ALL THOSE GIRLS!
THAT'S NOT VERY NICE. AT LEAST CALL THEM "RELATIONSHIPS."

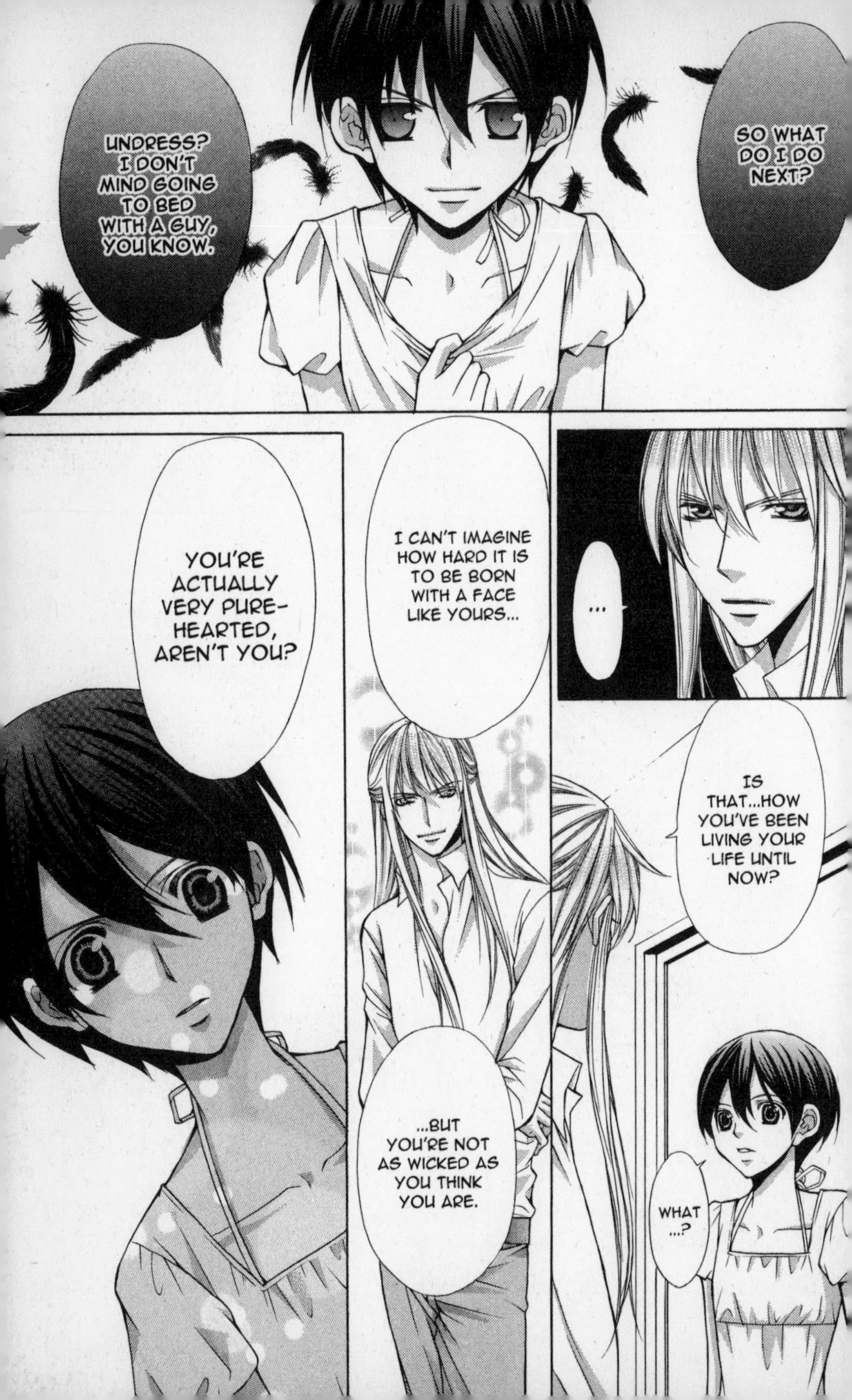
SO WHAT DO I DO NEXT?
UNDRESS? I DON'T MIND GOING TO BED WITH A GUY, YOU KNOW.
...
IS THAT...HOW YOU'VE BEEN LIVING YOUR LIFE UNTIL NOW?
WHAT ...?
I CAN'T IMAGINE HOW HARD IT IS TO BE BORN WITH A FACE LIKE YOURS...
...BUT YOU'RE NOT AS WICKED AS YOU THINK YOU ARE.
YOU'RE ACTUALLY VERY PURE-HEARTED, AREN'T YOU?

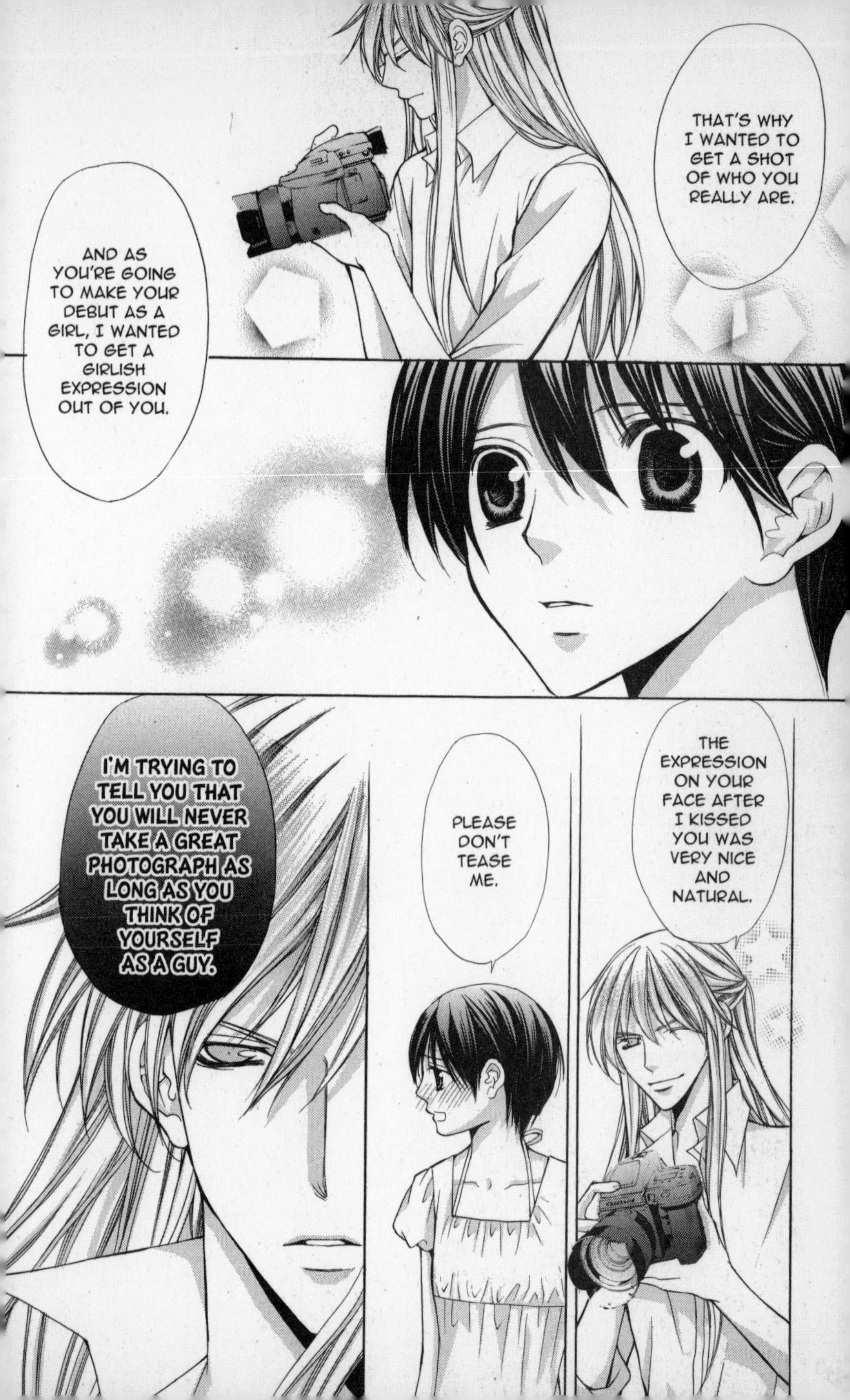
THAT'S WHY I WANTED TO GET A SHOT OF WHO YOU REALLY ARE.
AND AS YOU'RE GOING TO MAKE YOUR DEBUT AS A GIRL, I WANTED TO GET A GIRLISH EXPRESSION OUT OF YOU.
THE EXPRESSION ON YOUR FACE AFTER I KISSED YOU WAS VERY NICE AND NATURAL.
PLEASE DON'T TEASE ME.
I'M TRYING TO TELL YOU THAT YOU WILL NEVER TAKE A GREAT PHOTOGRAPH AS LONG AS YOU THINK OF YOURSELF AS A GUY.

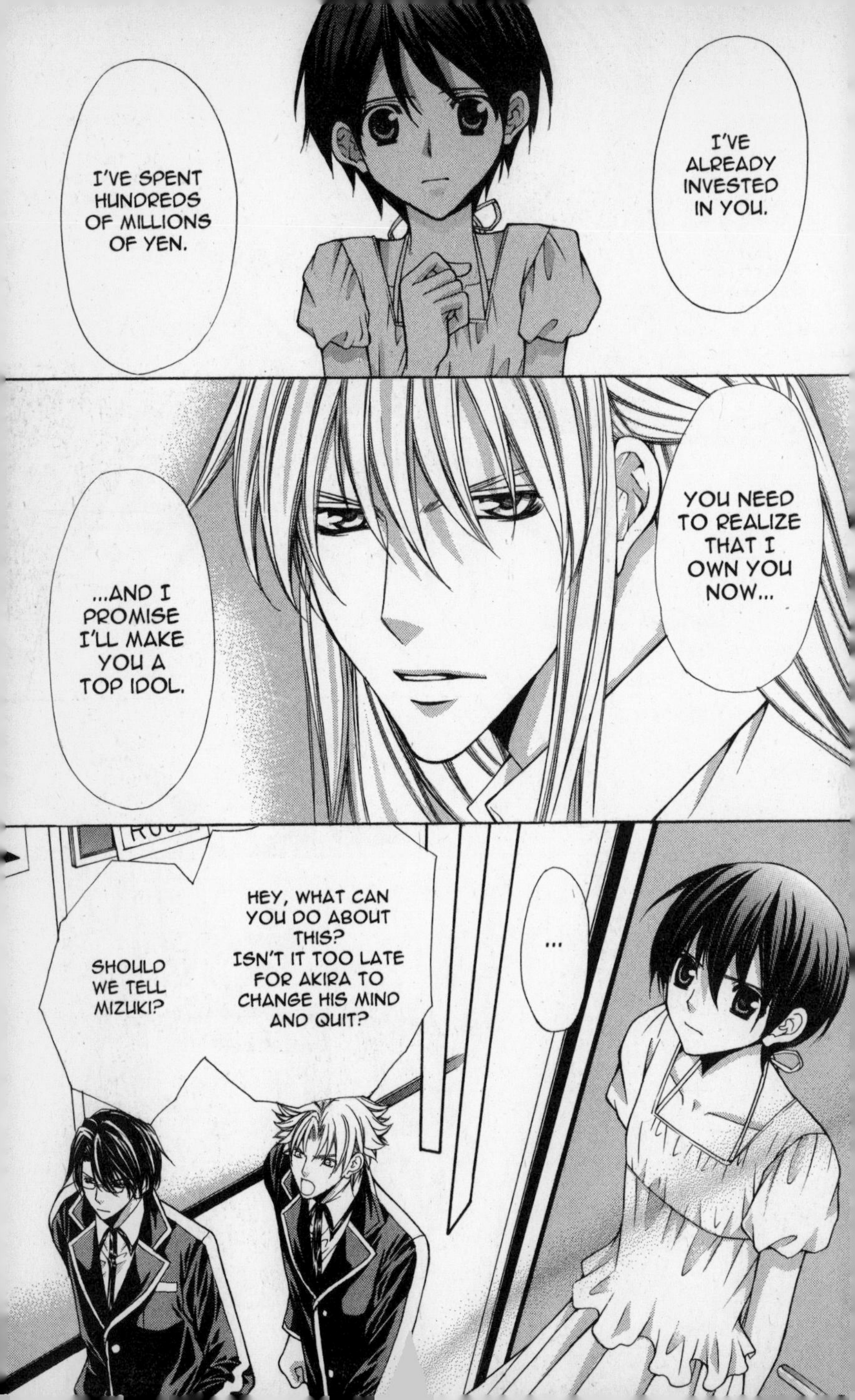
I'VE ALREADY INVESTED IN YOU.
I'VE SPENT HUNDREDS OF MILLIONS OF YEN.
YOU NEED TO REALIZE THAT I OWN YOU NOW...
...AND I PROMISE I'LL MAKE YOU A TOP IDOL.
...
HEY, WHAT CAN YOU DO ABOUT THIS? ISN'T IT TOO LATE FOR AKIRA TO CHANGE HIS MIND AND QUIT?
SHOULD WE TELL MIZUKI?

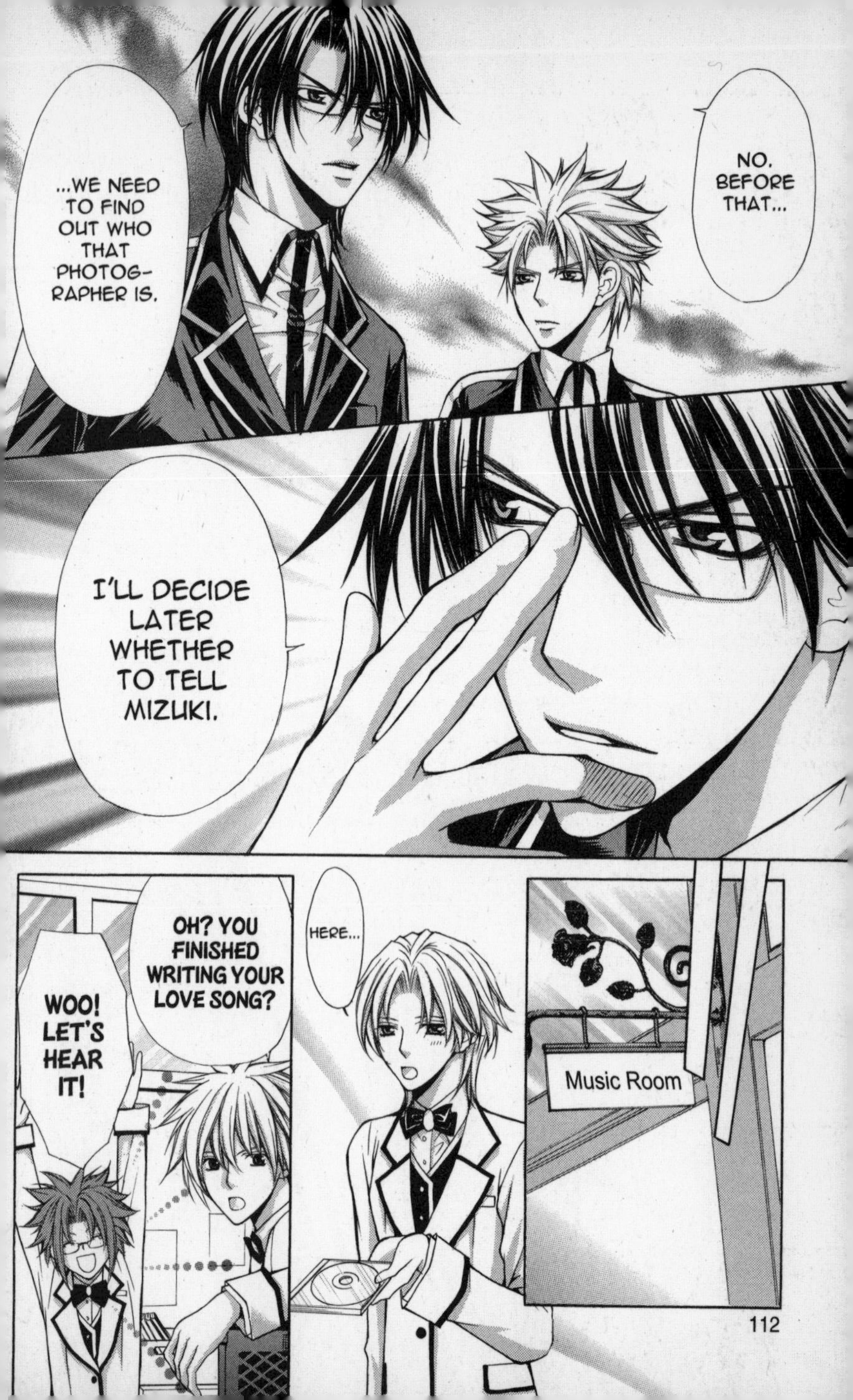
NO. BEFORE THAT...
...WE NEED TO FIND OUT WHO THAT PHOTOG-RAPHER IS.
I'LL DECIDE LATER WHETHER TO TELL MIZUKI.
Music Room
HERE...
OH? YOU FINISHED WRITING YOUR LOVE SONG?
WOO! LET'S HEAR IT!

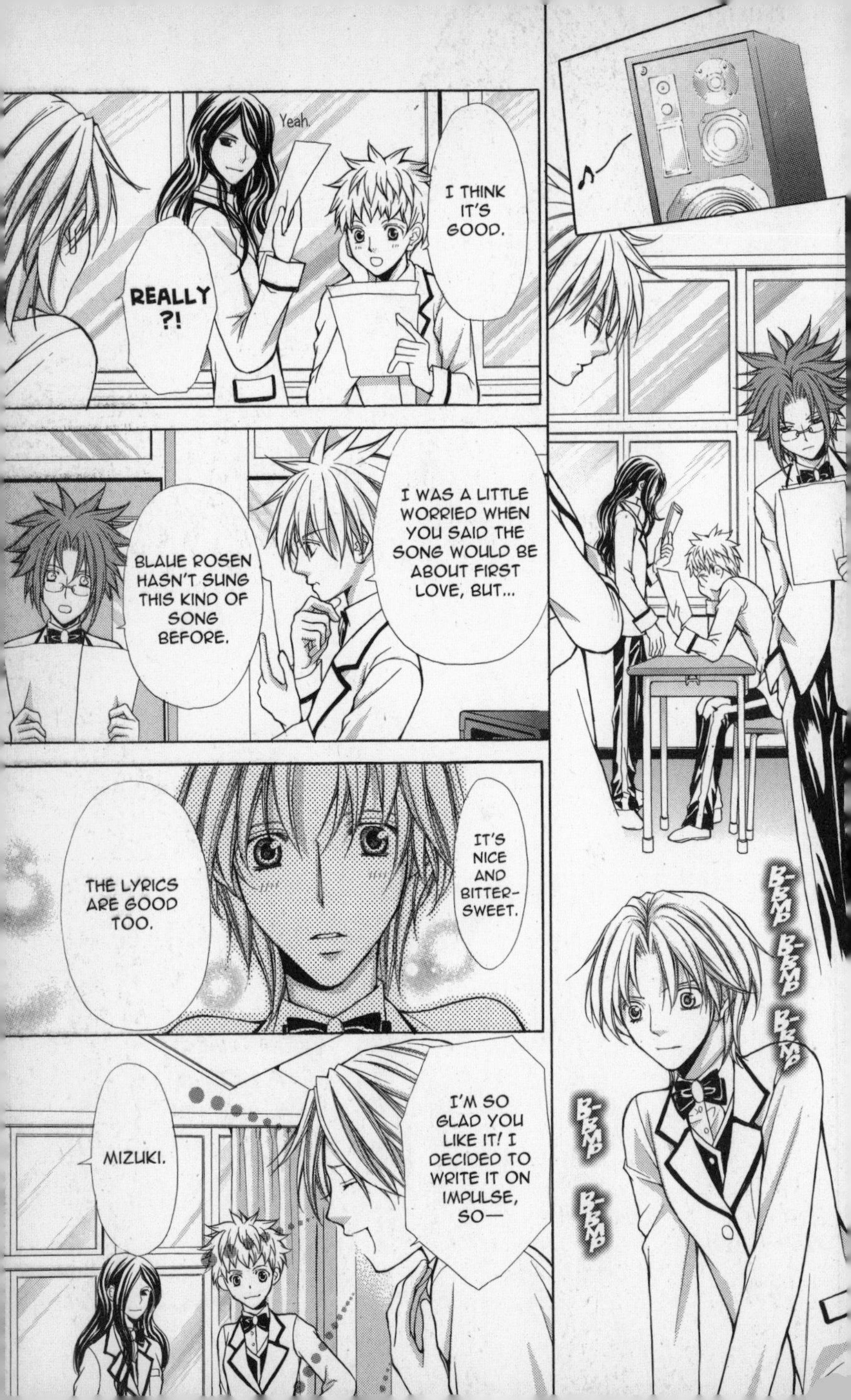
B-BMP B-BMP B-BMP
B-BMP B-BMP
I THINK IT'S GOOD.
Yeah.
REALLY ?!
I WAS A LITTLE WORRIED WHEN YOU SAID THE SONG WOULD BE ABOUT FIRST LOVE, BUT...
BLAUE ROSEN HASN'T SUNG THIS KIND OF SONG BEFORE.
IT'S NICE AND BITTER-SWEET.
THE LYRICS ARE GOOD TOO.
I'M SO GLAD YOU LIKE IT! I DECIDED TO WRITE IT ON IMPULSE, SO—
MIZUKI.

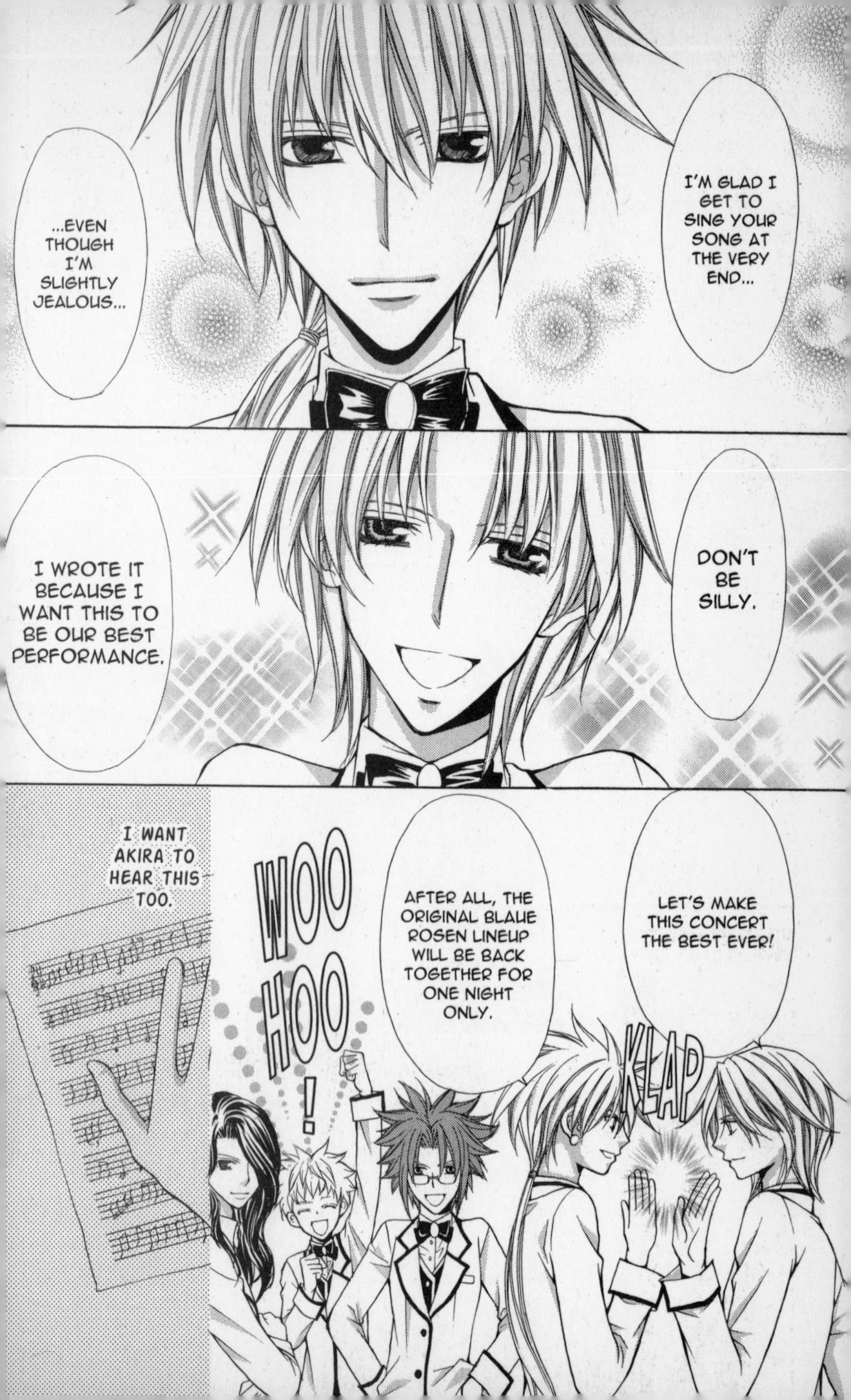
I'M GLAD I GET TO SING YOUR SONG AT THE VERY END...
...EVEN THOUGH I'M SLIGHTLY JEALOUS...
DON'T BE SILLY.
I WROTE IT BECAUSE I WANT THIS TO BE OUR BEST PERFORMANCE.
LET'S MAKE THIS CONCERT THE BEST EVER!
KLAP
AFTER ALL, THE ORIGINAL BLAUE ROSEN LINEUP WILL BE BACK TOGETHER FOR ONE NIGHT ONLY.
WOO HOO!
I WANT AKIRA TO HEAR THIS TOO.

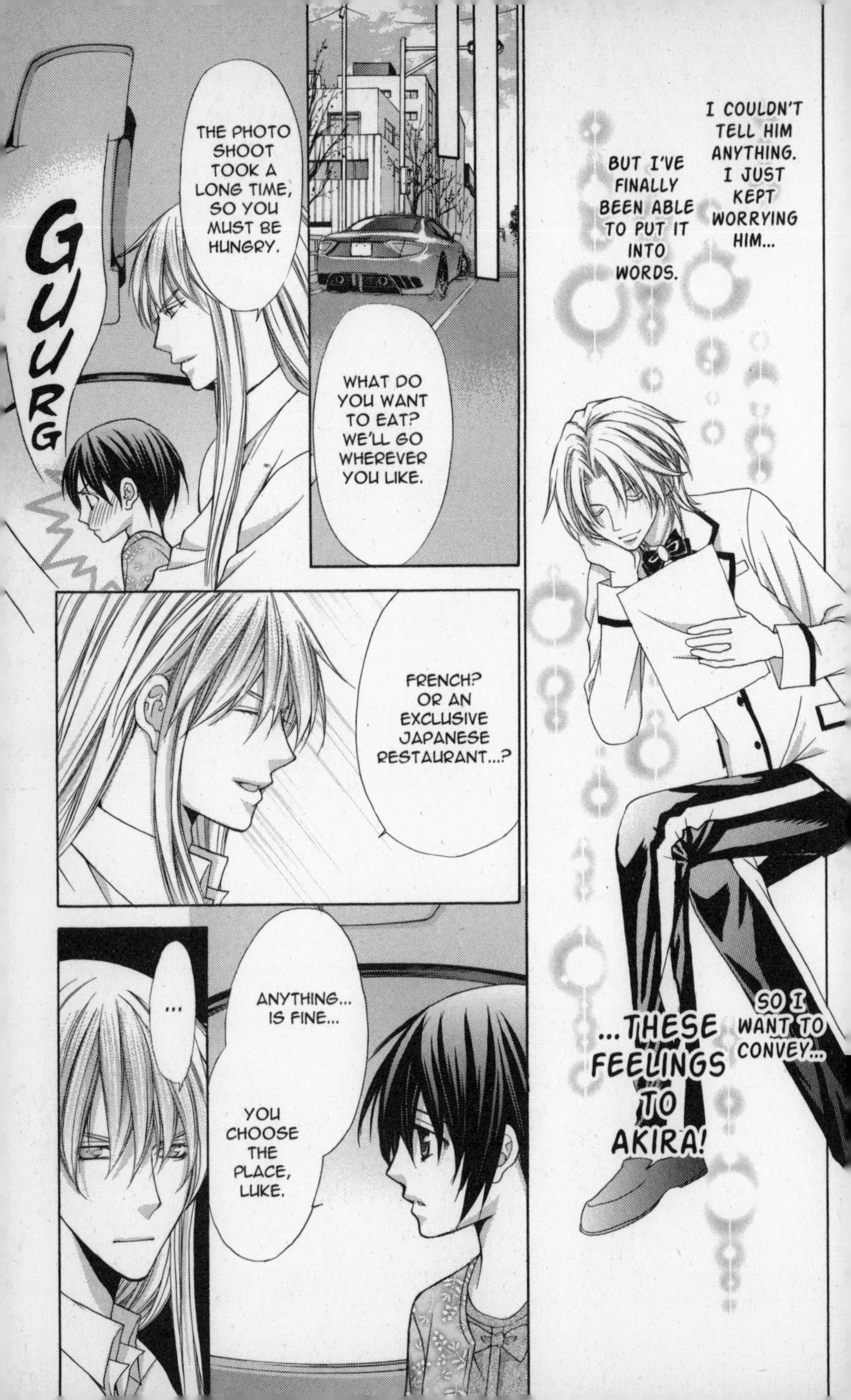
I COULDN'T TELL HIM ANYTHING. I JUST KEPT WORRYING HIM...
BUT I'VE FINALLY BEEN ABLE TO PUT IT INTO WORDS.
SO I WANT TO CONVEY...
...THESE FEELINGS TO AKIRA!
WHAT DO YOU WANT TO EAT? WE'LL GO WHEREVER YOU LIKE.
THE PHOTO SHOOT TOOK A LONG TIME, SO YOU MUST BE HUNGRY.
GUURG
FRENCH? OR AN EXCLUSIVE JAPANESE RESTAURANT...?
ANYTHING... IS FINE...
YOU CHOOSE THE PLACE, LUKE.
...

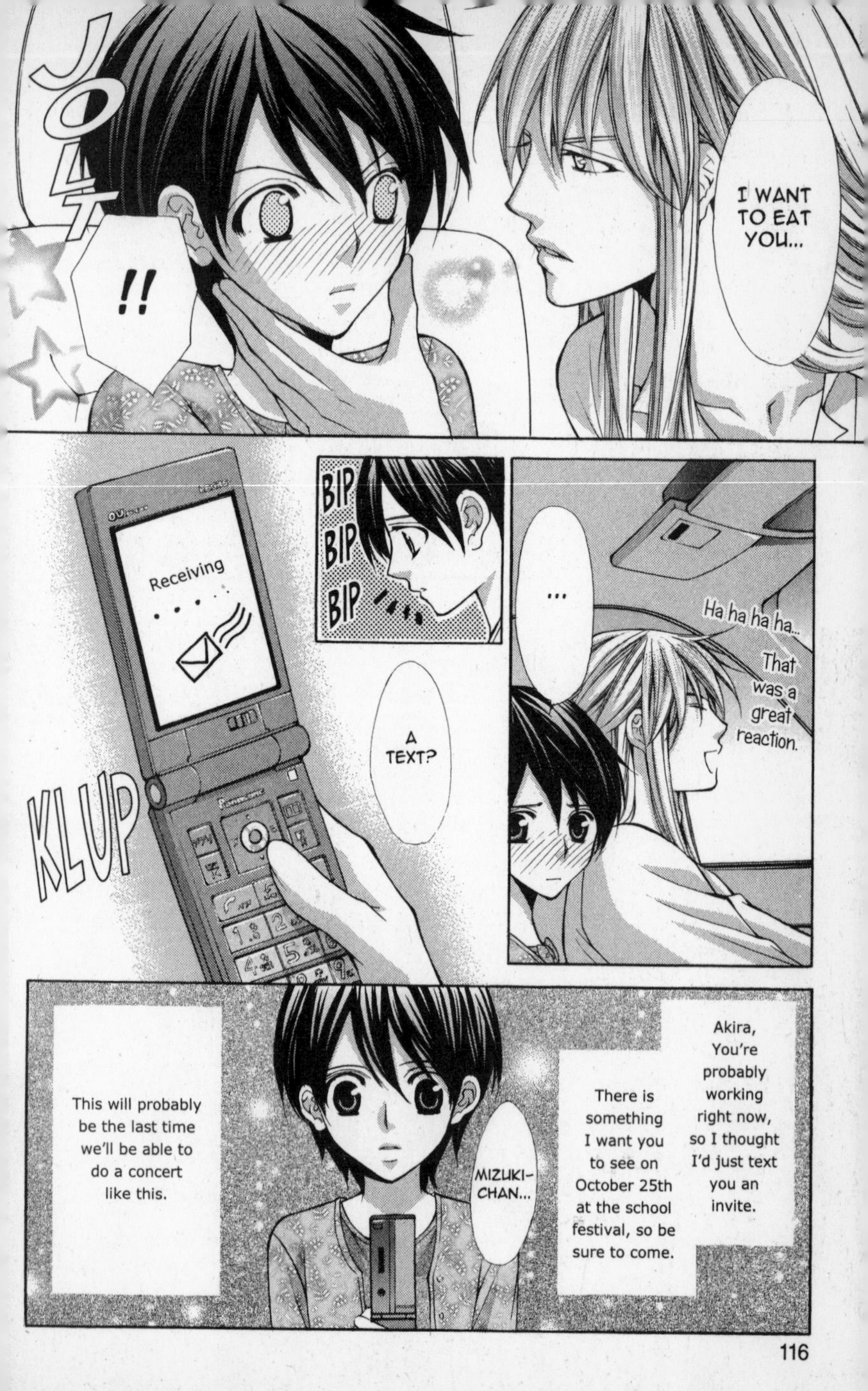
I WANT TO EAT YOU...
JOLT
!!
...
Ha ha ha ha...
That was a great reaction.
BIP BIP BIP
A TEXT?
Receiving
KLUP
Akira, You're probably working right now, so I thought I'd just text you an invite.
There is something I want you to see on October 25th at the school festival, so be sure to come.
MIZUKI-CHAN...
This will probably be the last time we'll be able to do a concert like this.

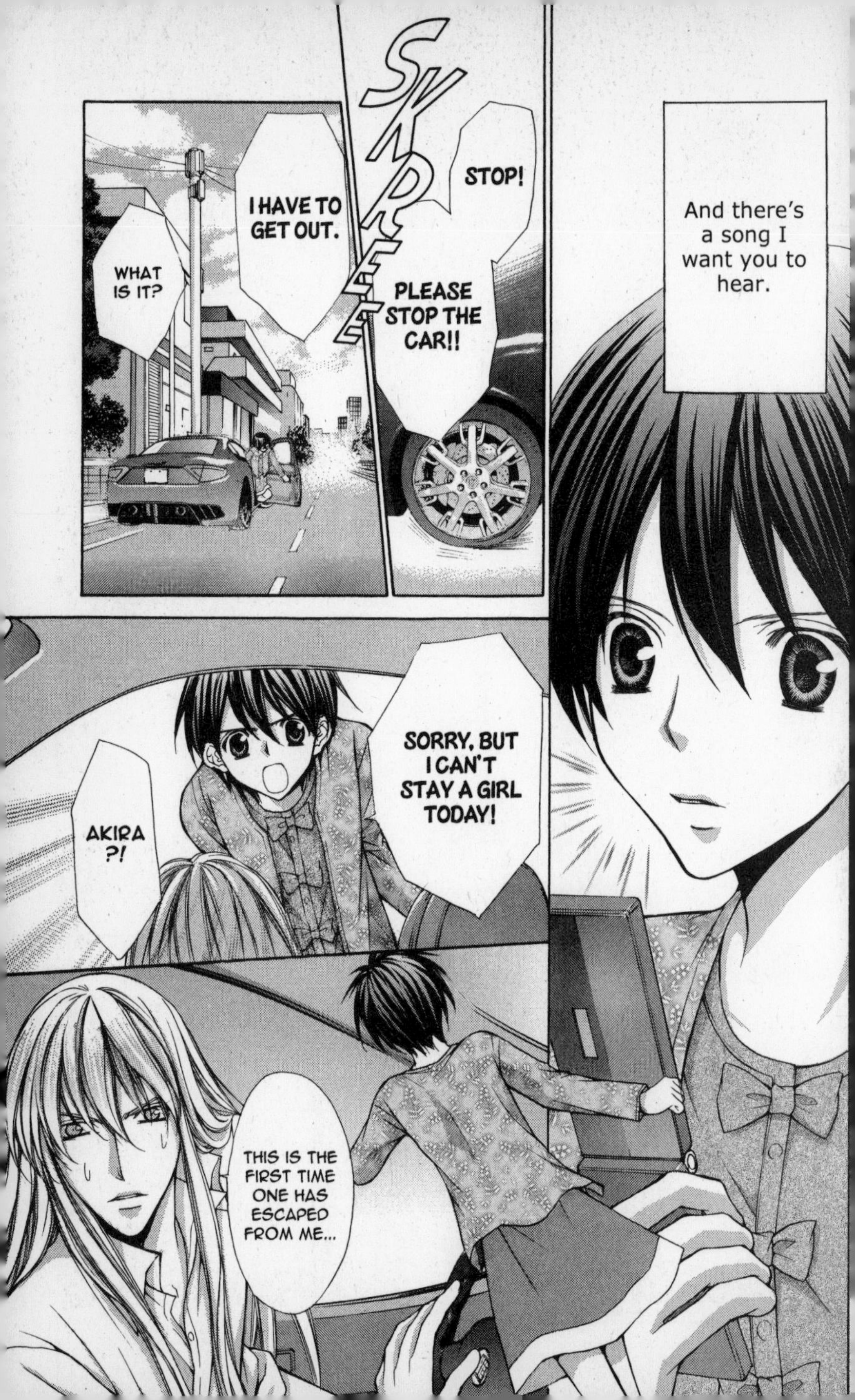
And there's a song I want you to hear.
STOP!
PLEASE STOP THE CAR!!
SKREEE
I HAVE TO GET OUT.
WHAT IS IT?
SORRY, BUT I CAN'T STAY A GIRL TODAY!
AKIRA ?!
THIS IS THE FIRST TIME ONE HAS ESCAPED FROM ME...

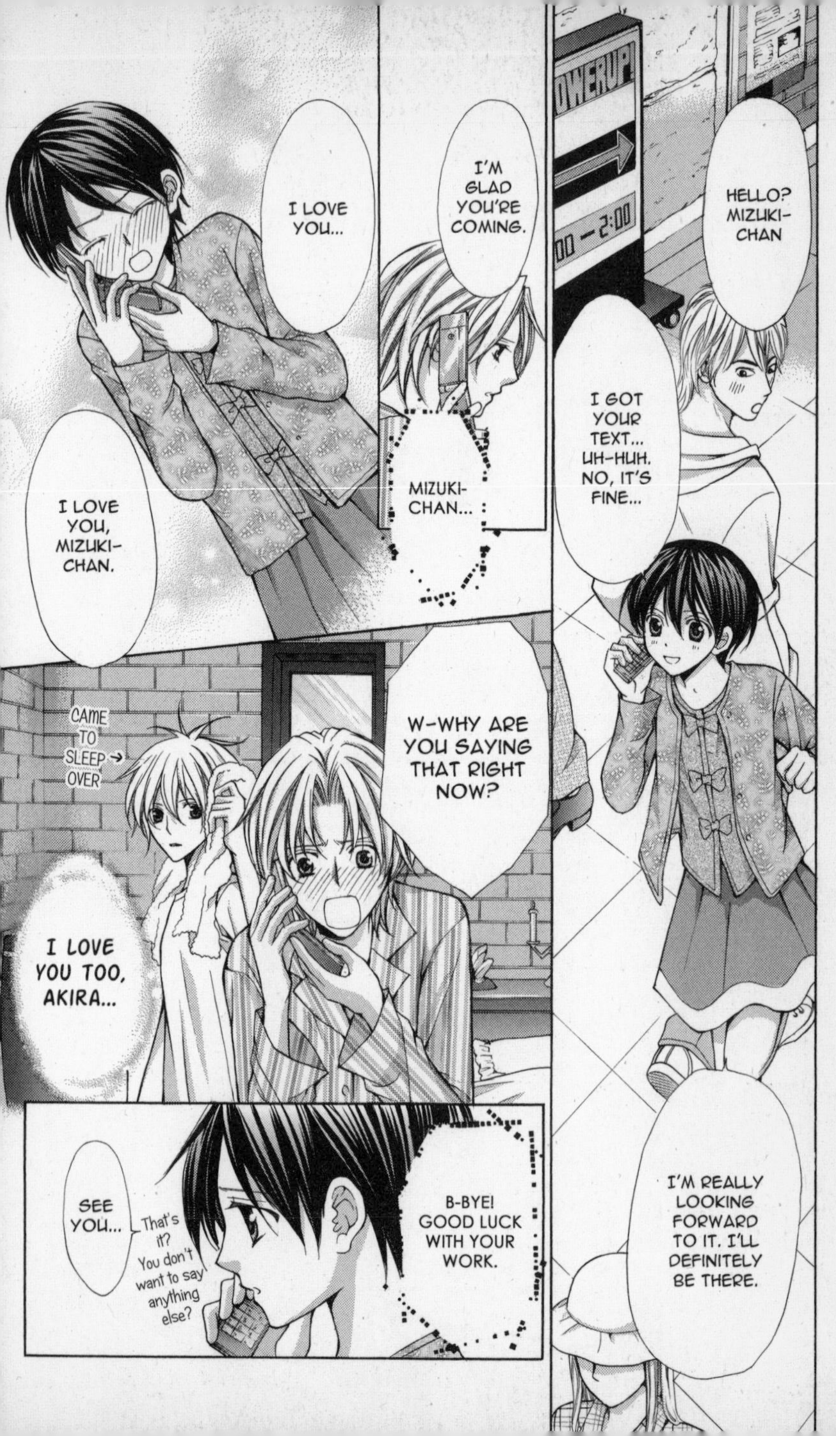
HELLO? MIZUKI-CHAN
I GOT YOUR TEXT... UH-HUH. NO, IT'S FINE...
I'M REALLY LOOKING FORWARD TO IT. I'LL DEFINITELY BE THERE.
I'M GLAD YOU'RE COMING.
MIZUKI-CHAN...
I LOVE YOU...
I LOVE YOU, MIZUKI-CHAN.
W-WHY ARE YOU SAYING THAT RIGHT NOW?
CAME TO SLEEP OVER →
I LOVE YOU TOO, AKIRA...
B-BYE! GOOD LUCK WITH YOUR WORK.
SEE YOU...
That's it? You don't want to say anything else?

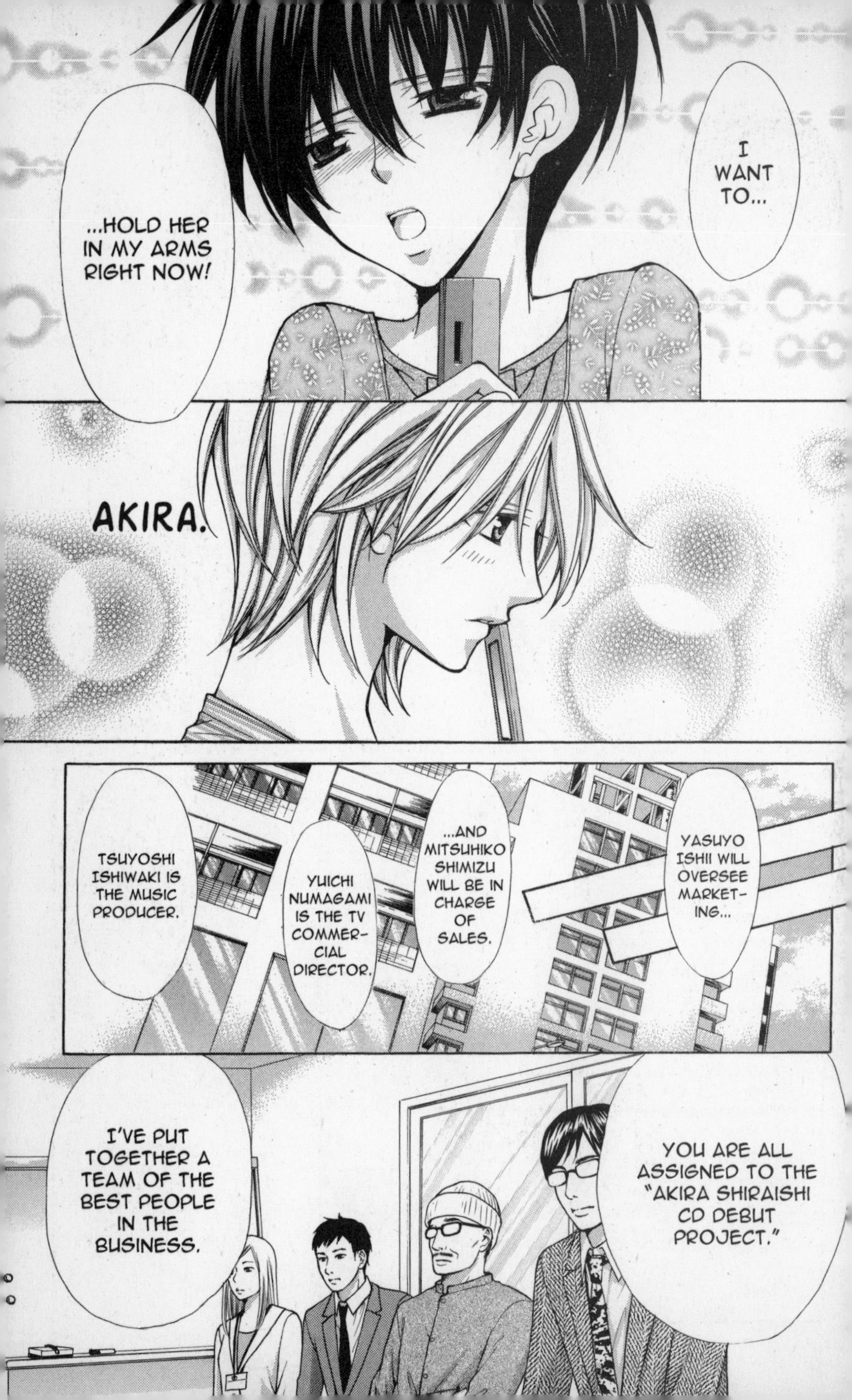
I WANT TO...
...HOLD HER IN MY ARMS RIGHT NOW!
AKIRA.
YASUYO ISHII WILL OVERSEE MARKET-ING...
...AND MITSUHIKO SHIMIZU WILL BE IN CHARGE OF SALES.
YUICHI NUMAGAMI IS THE TV COMMER-CIAL DIRECTOR.
TSUYOSHI ISHIWAKI IS THE MUSIC PRODUCER.
YOU ARE ALL ASSIGNED TO THE "AKIRA SHIRAISHI CD DEBUT PROJECT."
I'VE PUT TOGETHER A TEAM OF THE BEST PEOPLE IN THE BUSINESS.

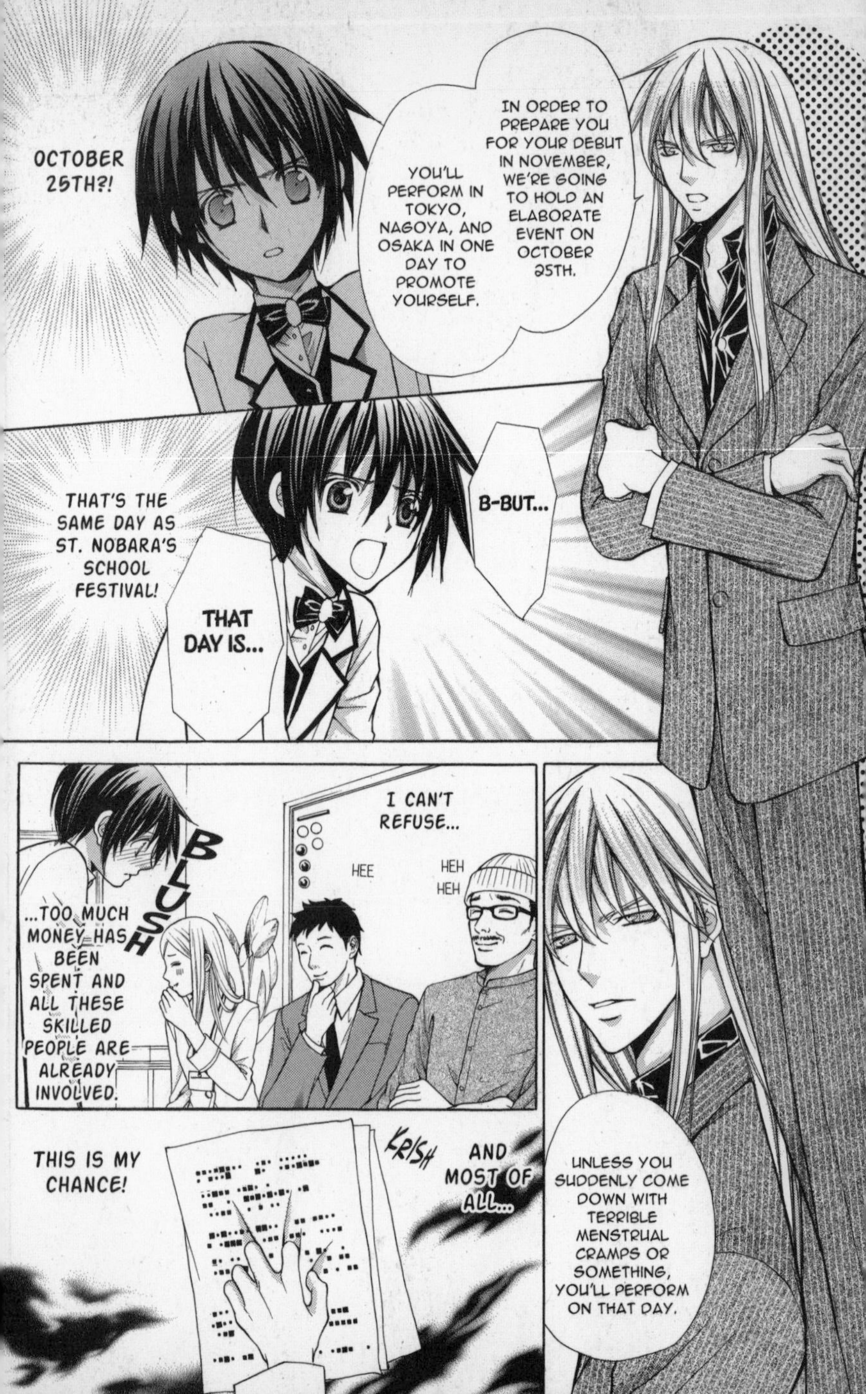

IN ORDER TO PREPARE YOU FOR YOUR DEBUT IN NOVEMBER, WE'RE GOING TO HOLD AN ELABORATE EVENT ON OCTOBER 25TH.
YOU'LL PERFORM IN TOKYO, NAGOYA, AND OSAKA IN ONE DAY TO PROMOTE YOURSELF.
OCTOBER 25TH?!
B-BUT...
THAT DAY IS...
THAT'S THE SAME DAY AS ST. NOBARA'S SCHOOL FESTIVAL!
UNLESS YOU SUDDENLY COME DOWN WITH TERRIBLE MENSTRUAL CRAMPS OR SOMETHING, YOU'LL PERFORM ON THAT DAY.
I CAN'T REFUSE...
HEH HEH
HEE
BLUSH
...TOO MUCH MONEY HAS BEEN SPENT AND ALL THESE SKILLED PEOPLE ARE ALREADY INVOLVED.
AND MOST OF ALL...
KRISH
THIS IS MY CHANCE!

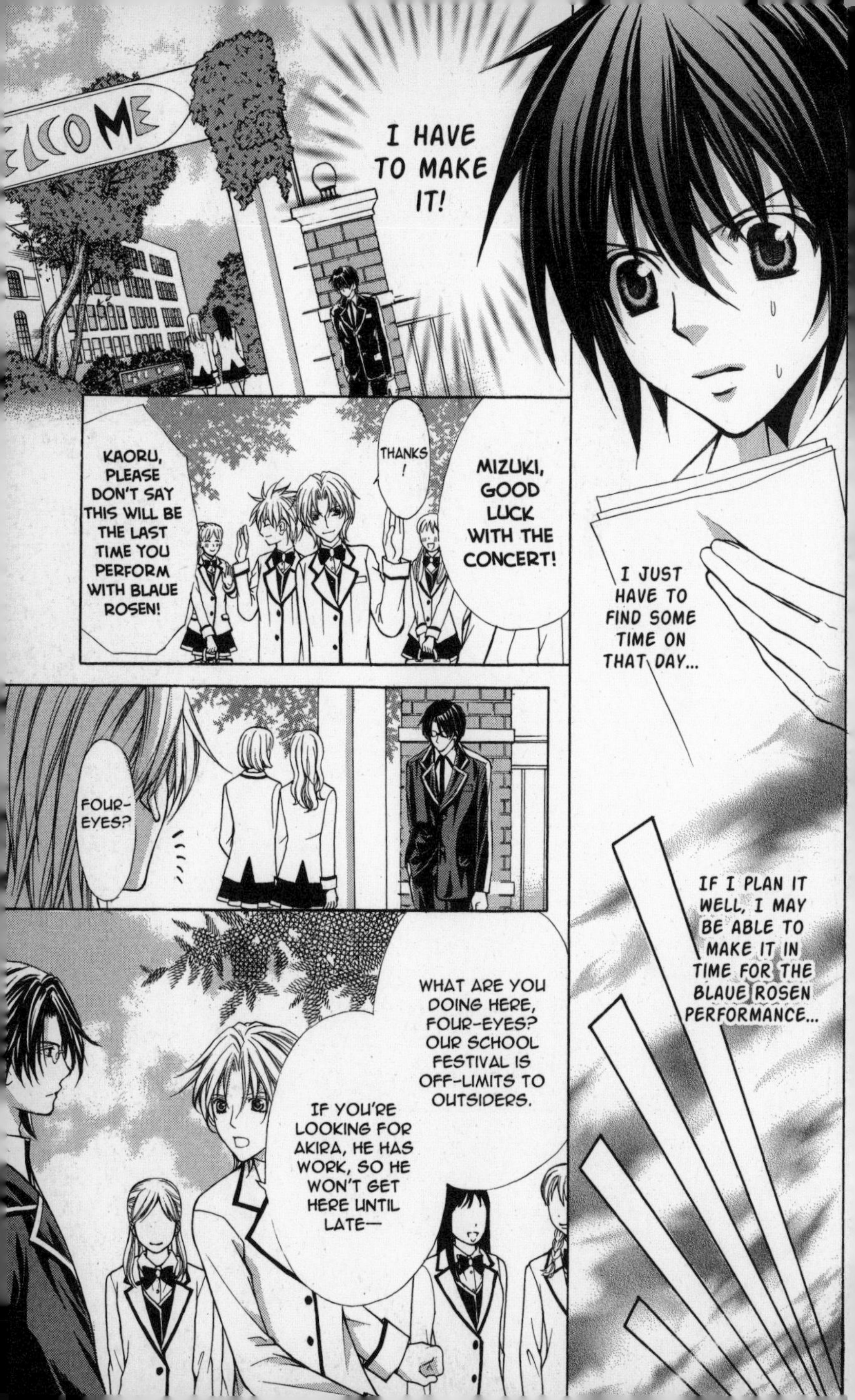
I JUST HAVE TO FIND SOME TIME ON THAT DAY...
IF I PLAN IT WELL, I MAY BE ABLE TO MAKE IT IN TIME FOR THE BLAUE ROSEN PERFORMANCE...
I HAVE TO MAKE IT!
MIZUKI, GOOD LUCK WITH THE CONCERT!
THANKS!
KAORU, PLEASE DON'T SAY THIS WILL BE THE LAST TIME YOU PERFORM WITH BLAUE ROSEN!
FOUR-EYES?
WHAT ARE YOU DOING HERE, FOUR-EYES? OUR SCHOOL FESTIVAL IS OFF-LIMITS TO OUTSIDERS.
IF YOU'RE LOOKING FOR AKIRA, HE HAS WORK, SO HE WON'T GET HERE UNTIL LATE—

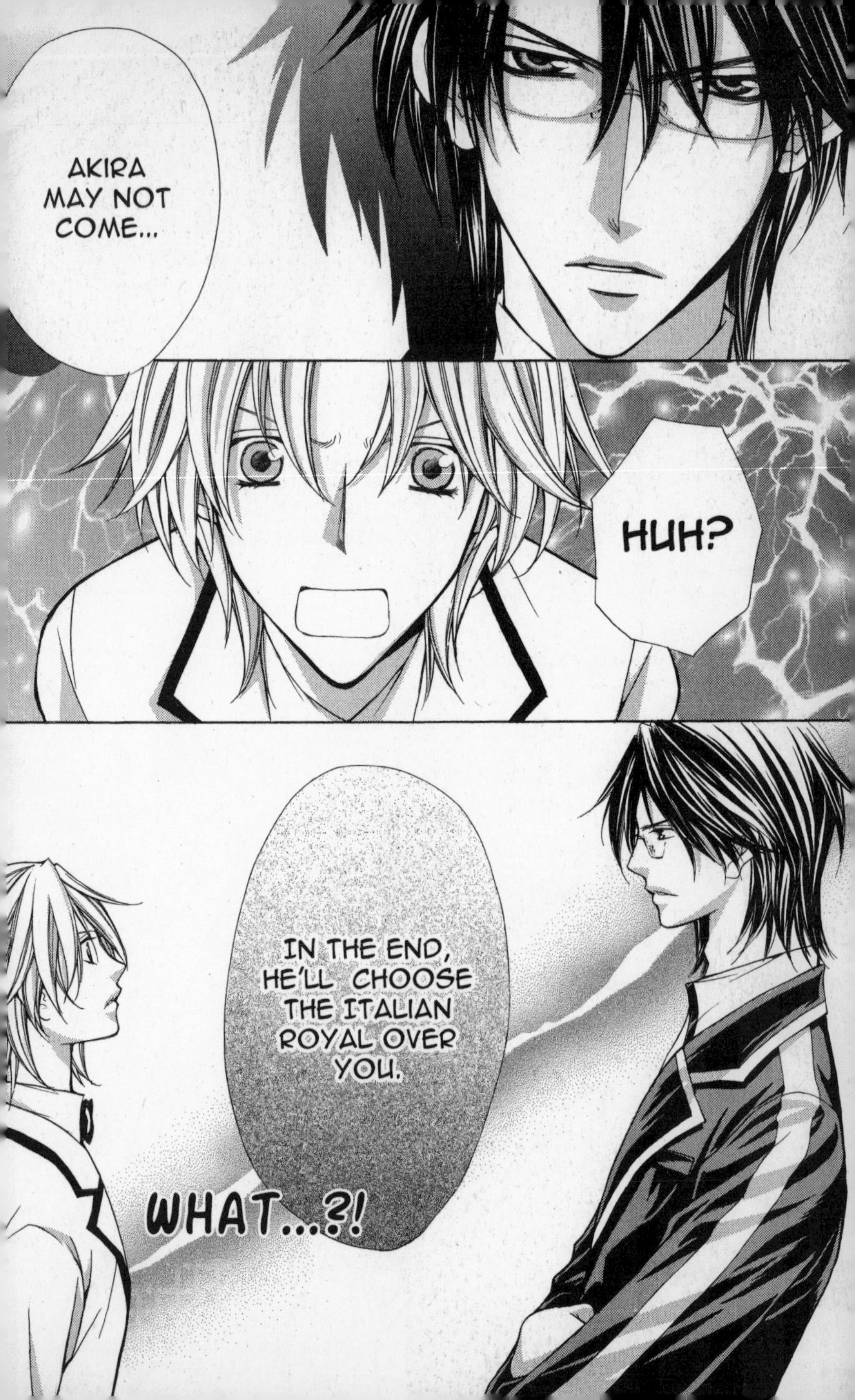
AKIRA MAY NOT COME...
HUH?
IN THE END, HE'LL CHOOSE THE ITALIAN ROYAL OVER YOU.
WHAT...?!

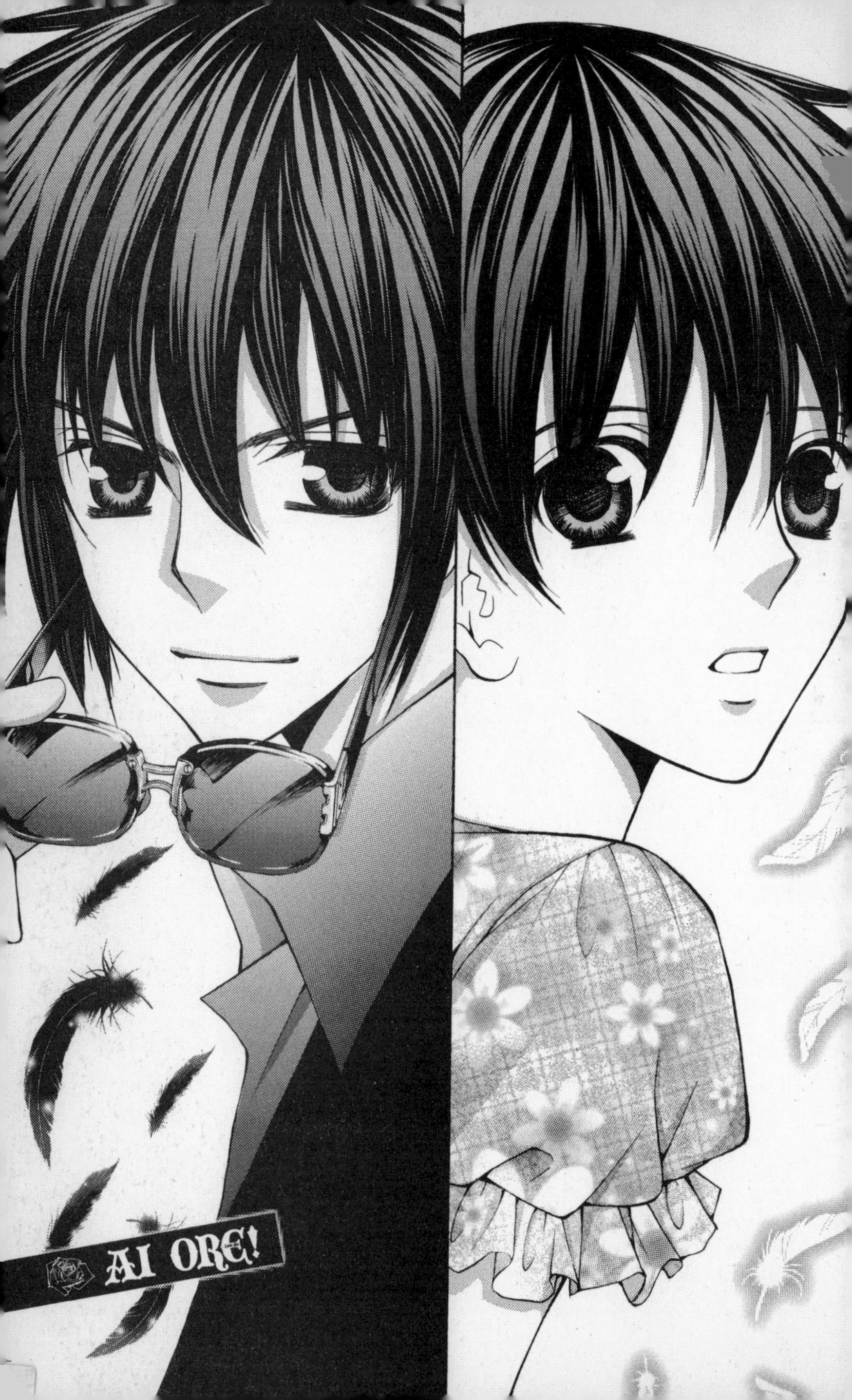
AI ORE!

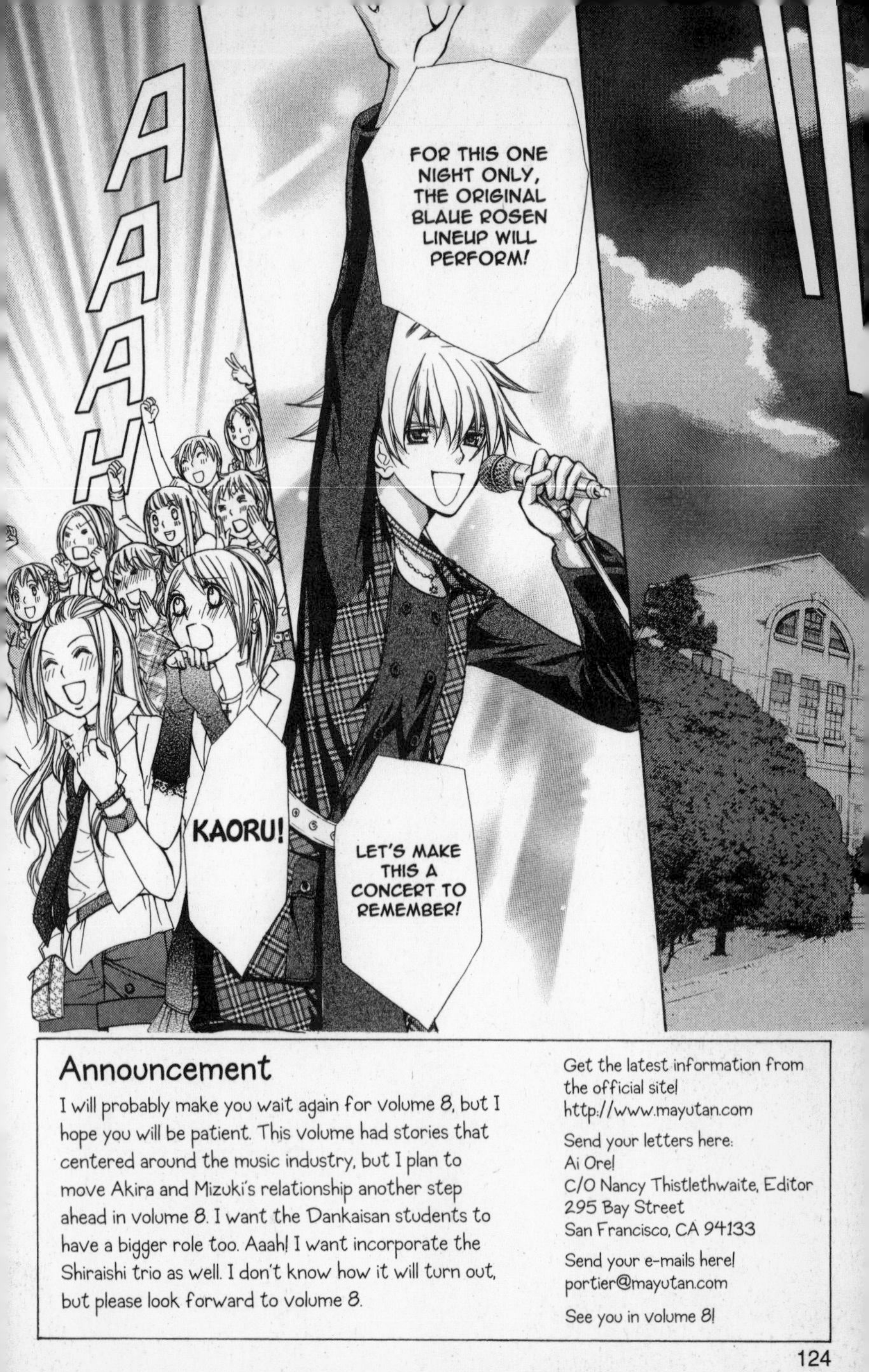
FOR THIS ONE NIGHT ONLY, THE ORIGINAL BLAUE ROSEN LINEUP WILL PERFORM!
LET'S MAKE THIS A CONCERT TO REMEMBER!
AAAAH
KAORU!

Announcement

I will probably make you wait again for volume 8, but I hope you will be patient. This volume had stories that centered around the music industry, but I plan to move Akira and Mizuki's relationship another step ahead in volume 8. I want the Dankaisan students to have a bigger role too. Aaah! I want incorporate the Shiraishi trio as well. I don't know how it will turn out, but please look forward to volume 8.

Get the latest information from the official site!
http://www.mayutan.com

Send your letters here:
Ai Ore!
C/O Nancy Thistlethwaite, Editor
295 Bay Street
San Francisco, CA 94133

Send your e-mails here!
portier@mayutan.com

See you in volume 8!

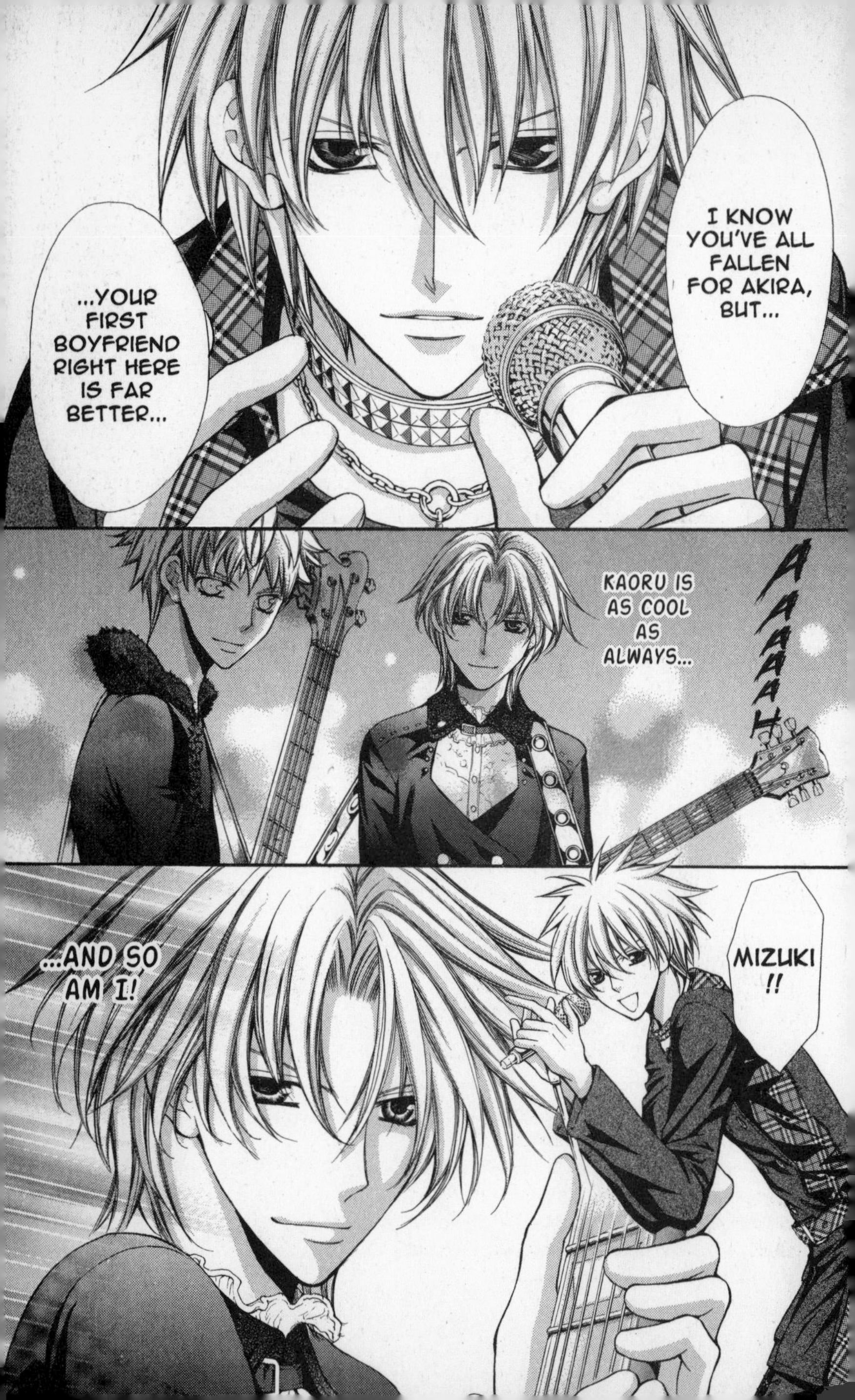
I KNOW YOU'VE ALL FALLEN FOR AKIRA, BUT...
...YOUR FIRST BOYFRIEND RIGHT HERE IS FAR BETTER...
AAAAAH
KAORU IS AS COOL AS ALWAYS...
MIZUKI !!
...AND SO AM I!

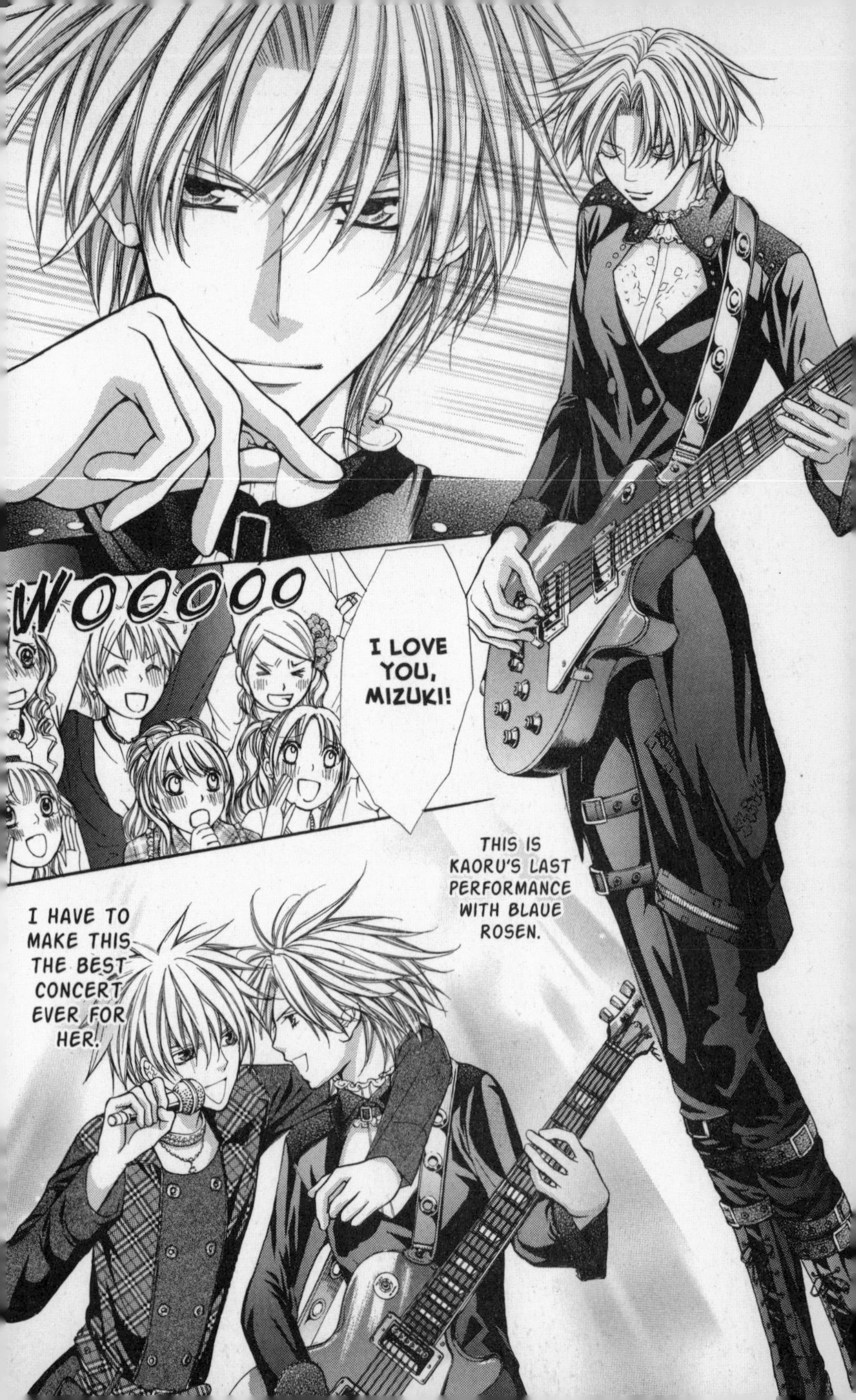
I LOVE YOU, MIZUKI!
WOOOOO
THIS IS KAORU'S LAST PERFORMANCE WITH BLAUE ROSEN.
I HAVE TO MAKE THIS THE BEST CONCERT EVER FOR HER.

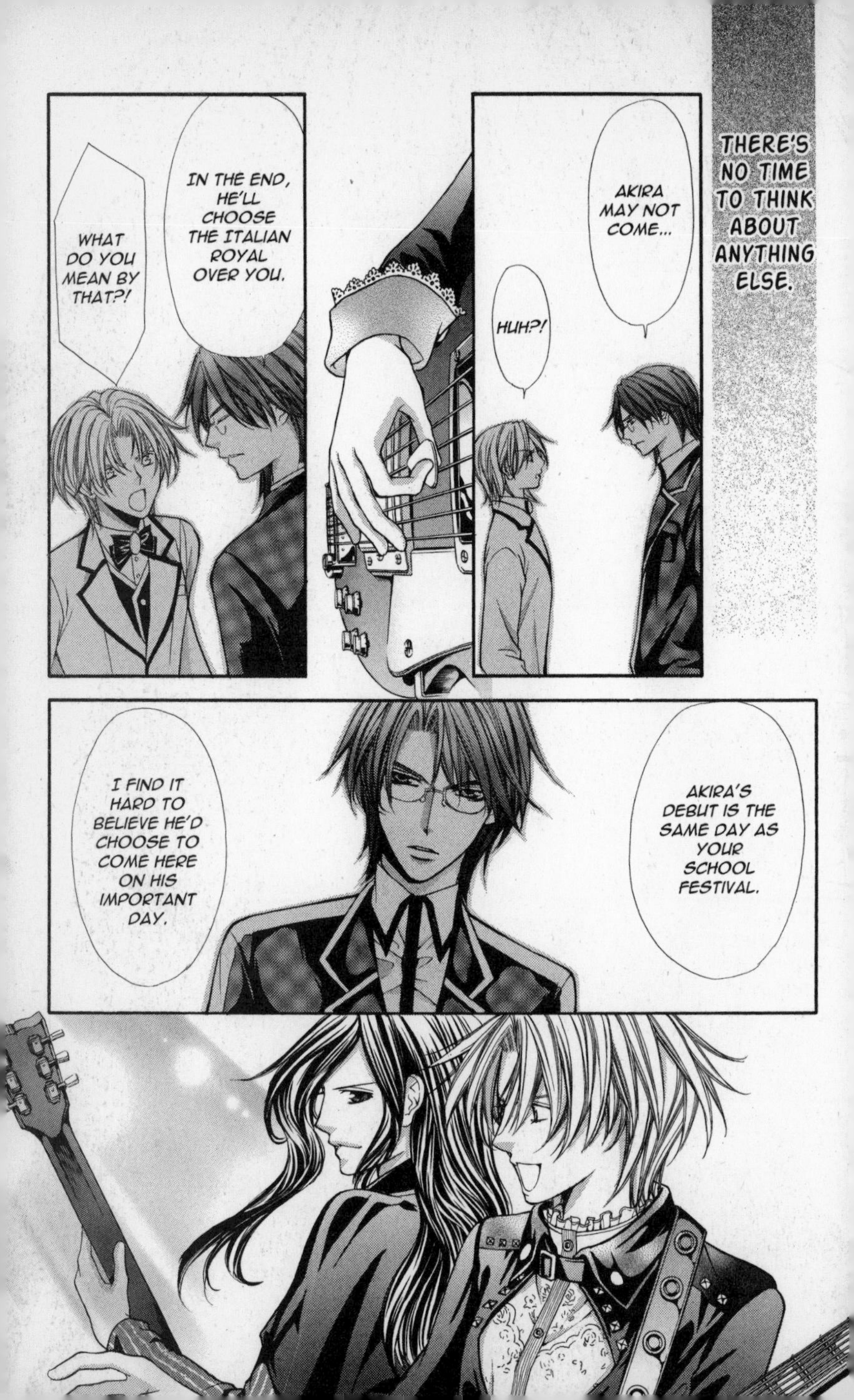
THERE'S NO TIME TO THINK ABOUT ANYTHING ELSE.
AKIRA MAY NOT COME...
HUH?!
IN THE END, HE'LL CHOOSE THE ITALIAN ROYAL OVER YOU.
WHAT DO YOU MEAN BY THAT?!
AKIRA'S DEBUT IS THE SAME DAY AS YOUR SCHOOL FESTIVAL.
I FIND IT HARD TO BELIEVE HE'D CHOOSE TO COME HERE ON HIS IMPORTANT DAY.

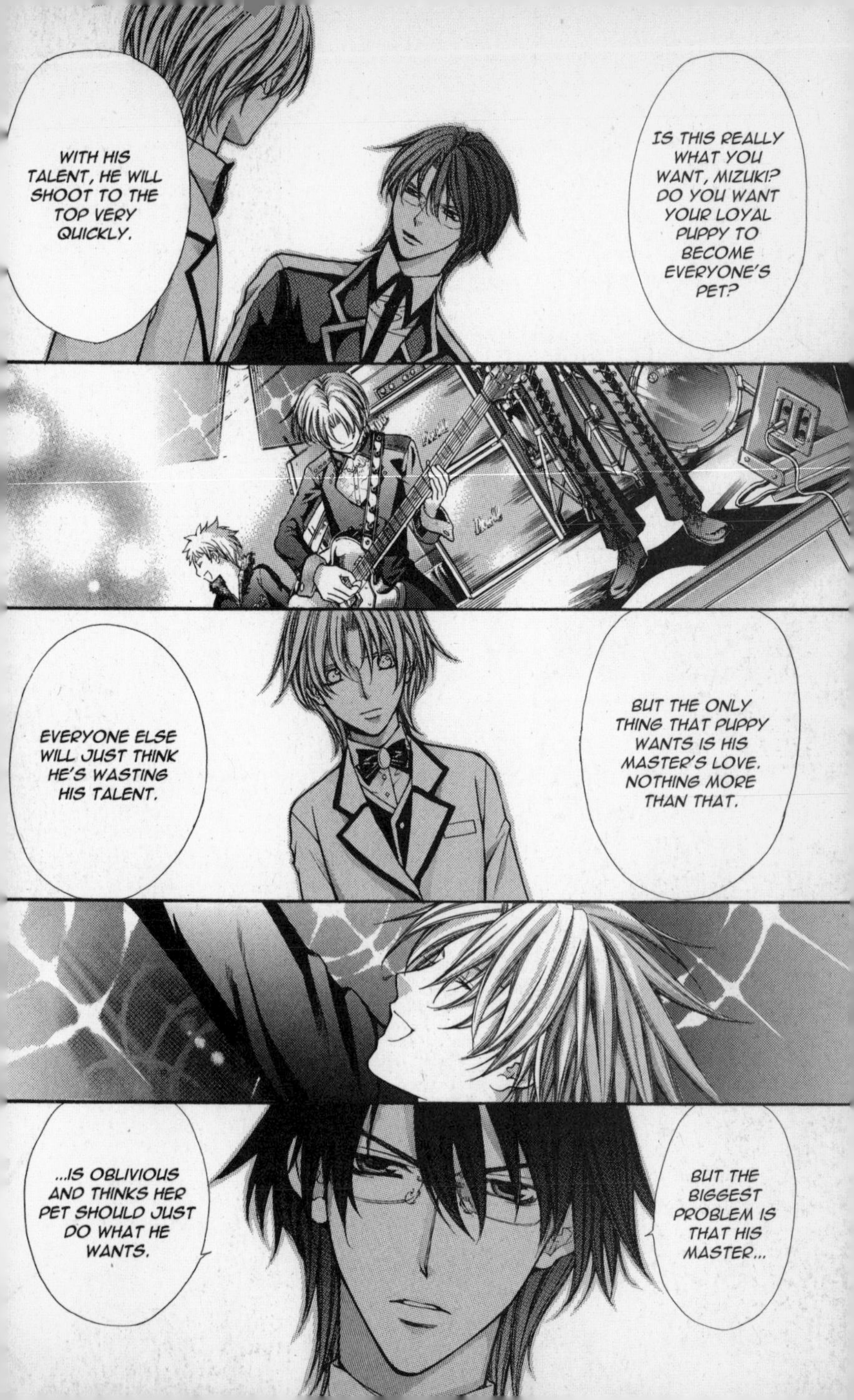
IS THIS REALLY WHAT YOU WANT, MIZUKI? DO YOU WANT YOUR LOYAL PUPPY TO BECOME EVERYONE'S PET?
WITH HIS TALENT, HE WILL SHOOT TO THE TOP VERY QUICKLY.
BUT THE ONLY THING THAT PUPPY WANTS IS HIS MASTER'S LOVE. NOTHING MORE THAN THAT.
EVERYONE ELSE WILL JUST THINK HE'S WASTING HIS TALENT.
BUT THE BIGGEST PROBLEM IS THAT HIS MASTER...
...IS OBLIVIOUS AND THINKS HER PET SHOULD JUST DO WHAT HE WANTS.

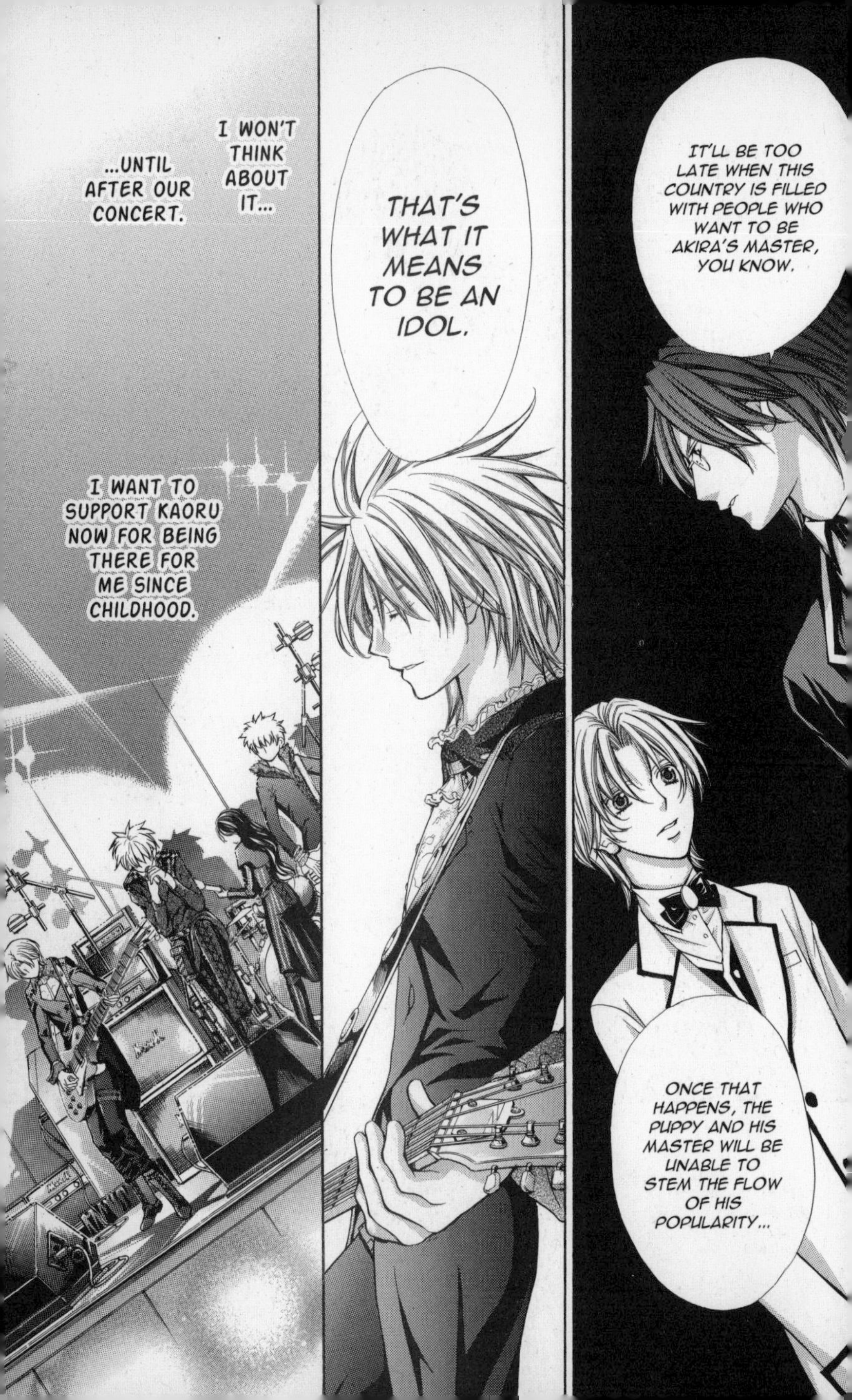
IT'LL BE TOO LATE WHEN THIS COUNTRY IS FILLED WITH PEOPLE WHO WANT TO BE AKIRA'S MASTER, YOU KNOW.
ONCE THAT HAPPENS, THE PUPPY AND HIS MASTER WILL BE UNABLE TO STEM THE FLOW OF HIS POPULARITY...
THAT'S WHAT IT MEANS TO BE AN IDOL.
I WON'T THINK ABOUT IT...
...UNTIL AFTER OUR CONCERT.
I WANT TO SUPPORT KAORU NOW FOR BEING THERE FOR ME SINCE CHILDHOOD.

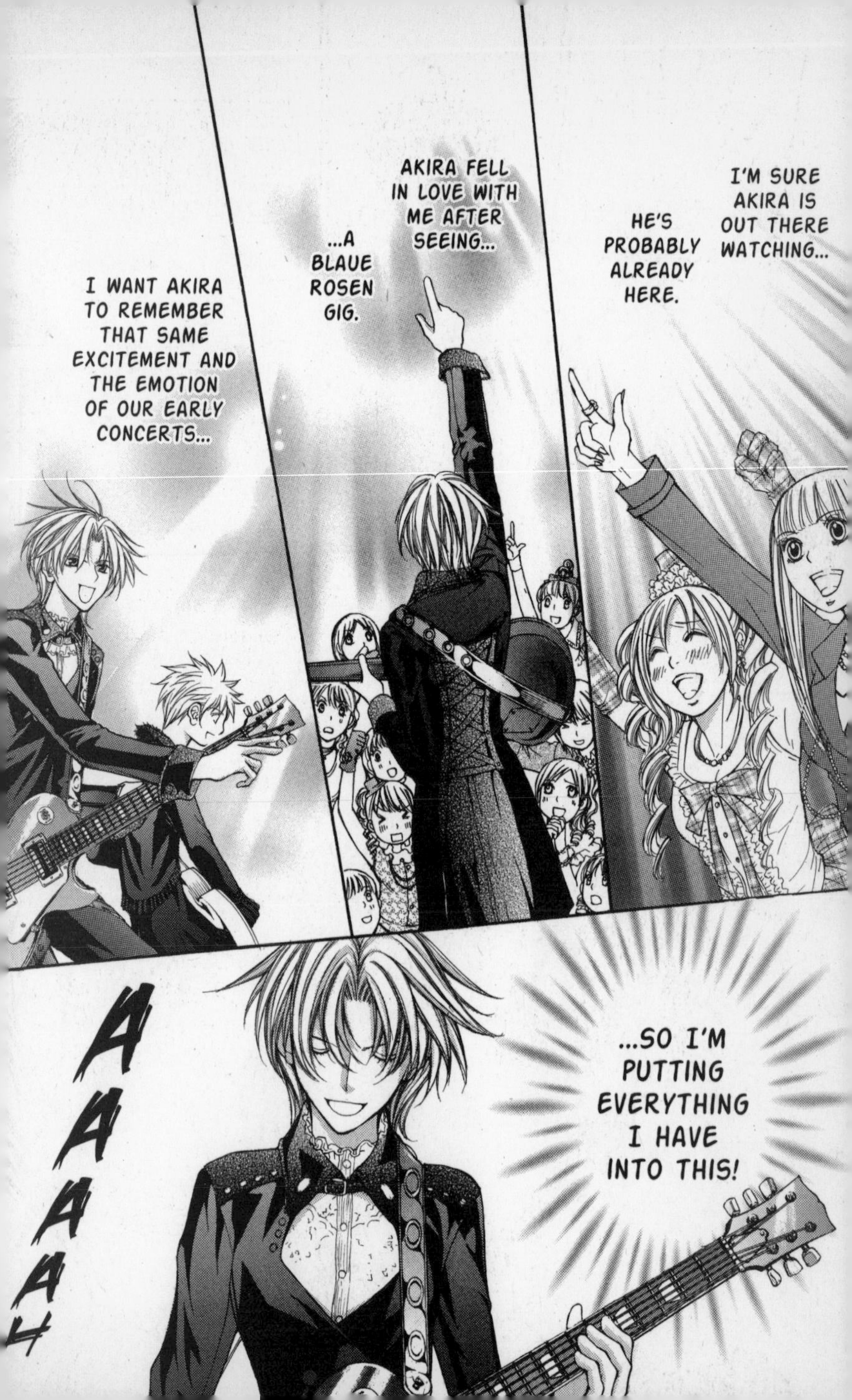
I'M SURE AKIRA IS OUT THERE WATCHING...
HE'S PROBABLY ALREADY HERE.
AKIRA FELL IN LOVE WITH ME AFTER SEEING...
...A BLAUE ROSEN GIG.
I WANT AKIRA TO REMEMBER THAT SAME EXCITEMENT AND THE EMOTION OF OUR EARLY CONCERTS...
...SO I'M PUTTING EVERYTHING I HAVE INTO THIS!
AAAAH

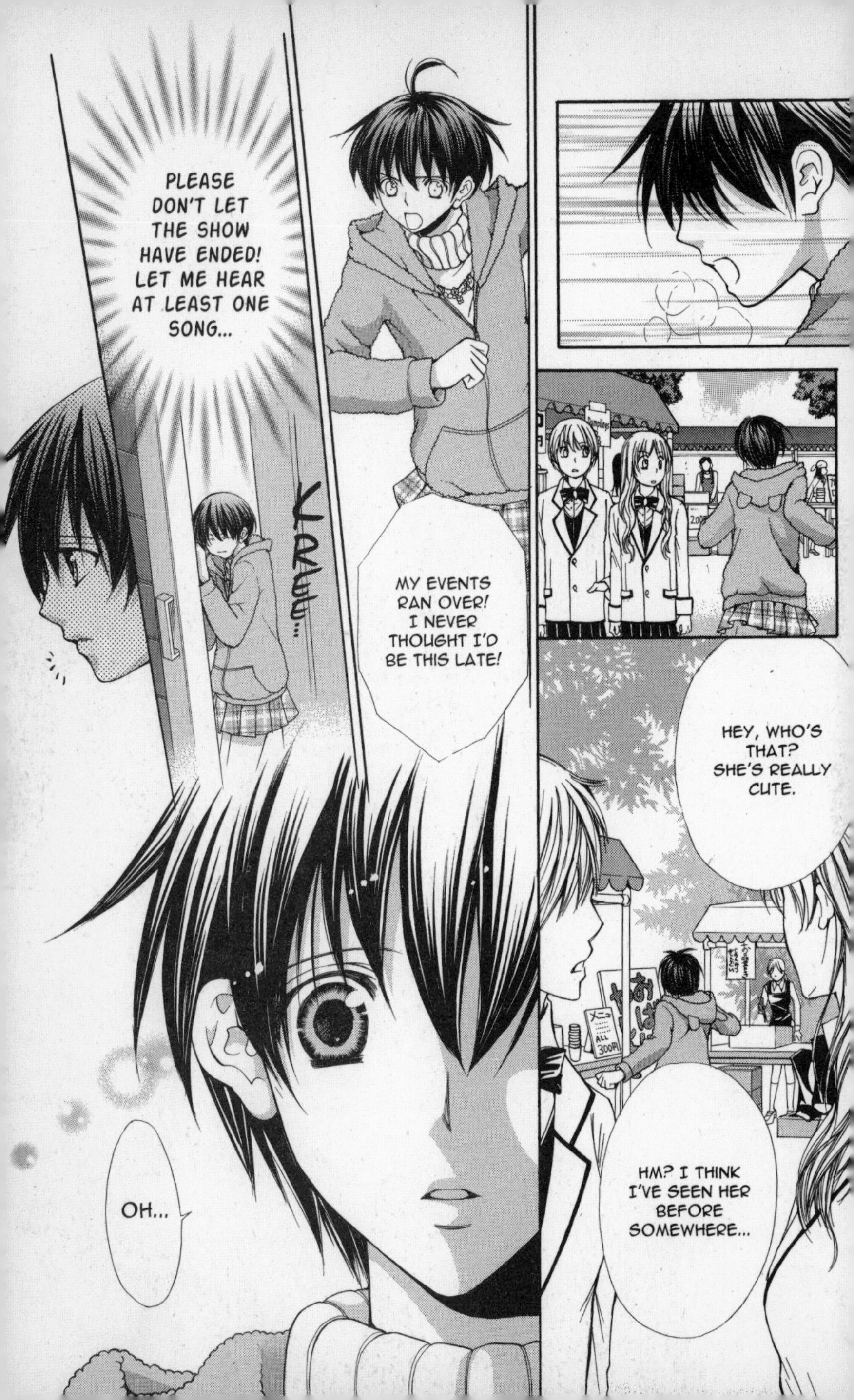
HEY, WHO'S THAT? SHE'S REALLY CUTE.
HM? I THINK I'VE SEEN HER BEFORE SOMEWHERE...
MY EVENTS RAN OVER! I NEVER THOUGHT I'D BE THIS LATE!
PLEASE DON'T LET THE SHOW HAVE ENDED! LET ME HEAR AT LEAST ONE SONG...
OH...

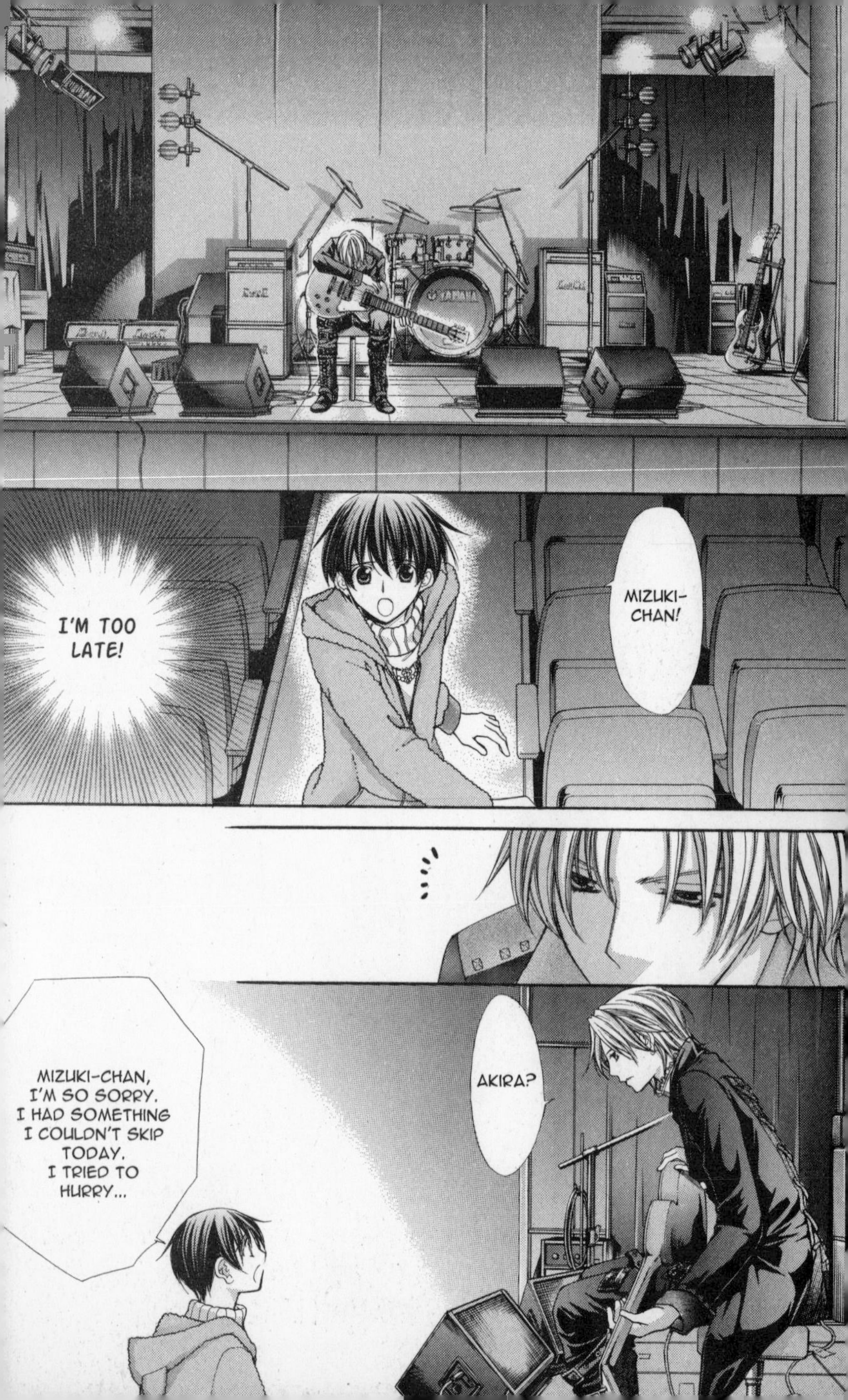
MIZUKI-CHAN!
I'M TOO LATE!
AKIRA?
MIZUKI-CHAN, I'M SO SORRY. I HAD SOMETHING I COULDN'T SKIP TODAY. I TRIED TO HURRY...

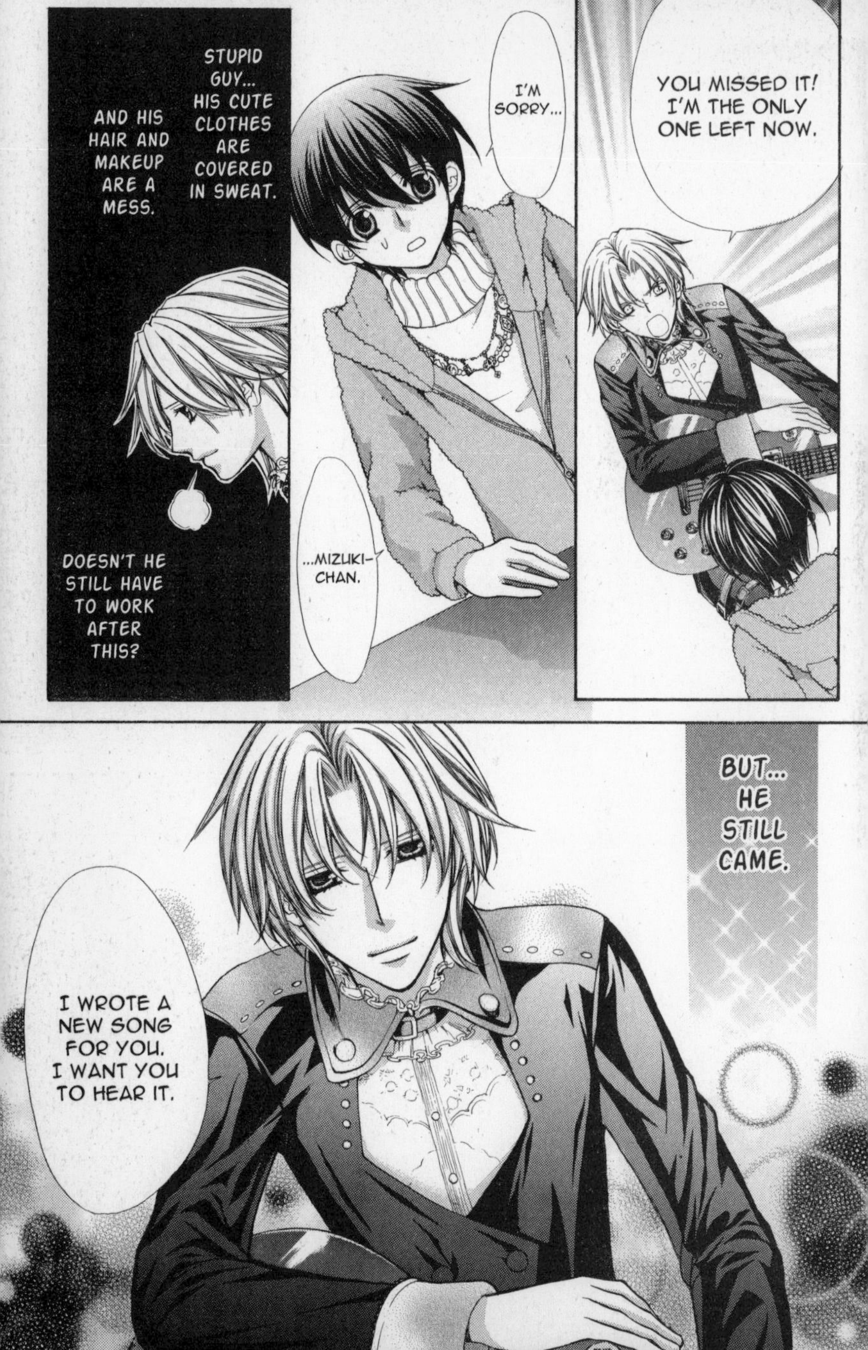
YOU MISSED IT! I'M THE ONLY ONE LEFT NOW.
I'M SORRY...
...MIZUKI-CHAN.
STUPID GUY... HIS CUTE CLOTHES ARE COVERED IN SWEAT.
AND HIS HAIR AND MAKEUP ARE A MESS.
DOESN'T HE STILL HAVE TO WORK AFTER THIS?
BUT... HE STILL CAME.
I WROTE A NEW SONG FOR YOU. I WANT YOU TO HEAR IT.

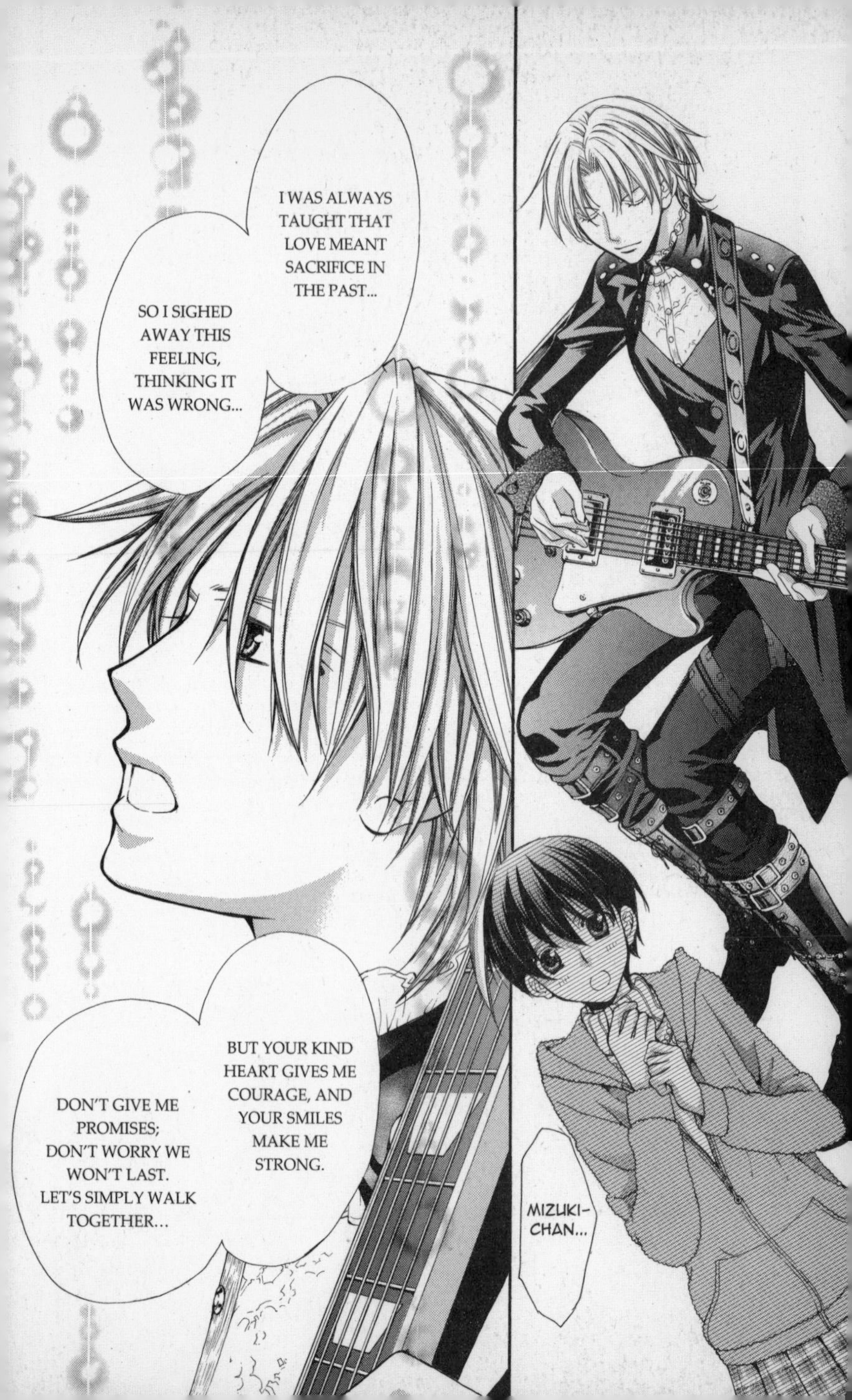
MIZUKI-CHAN...
I WAS ALWAYS TAUGHT THAT LOVE MEANT SACRIFICE IN THE PAST...
SO I SIGHED AWAY THIS FEELING, THINKING IT WAS WRONG...
BUT YOUR KIND HEART GIVES ME COURAGE, AND YOUR SMILES MAKE ME STRONG.
DON'T GIVE ME PROMISES; DON'T WORRY WE WON'T LAST. LET'S SIMPLY WALK TOGETHER...

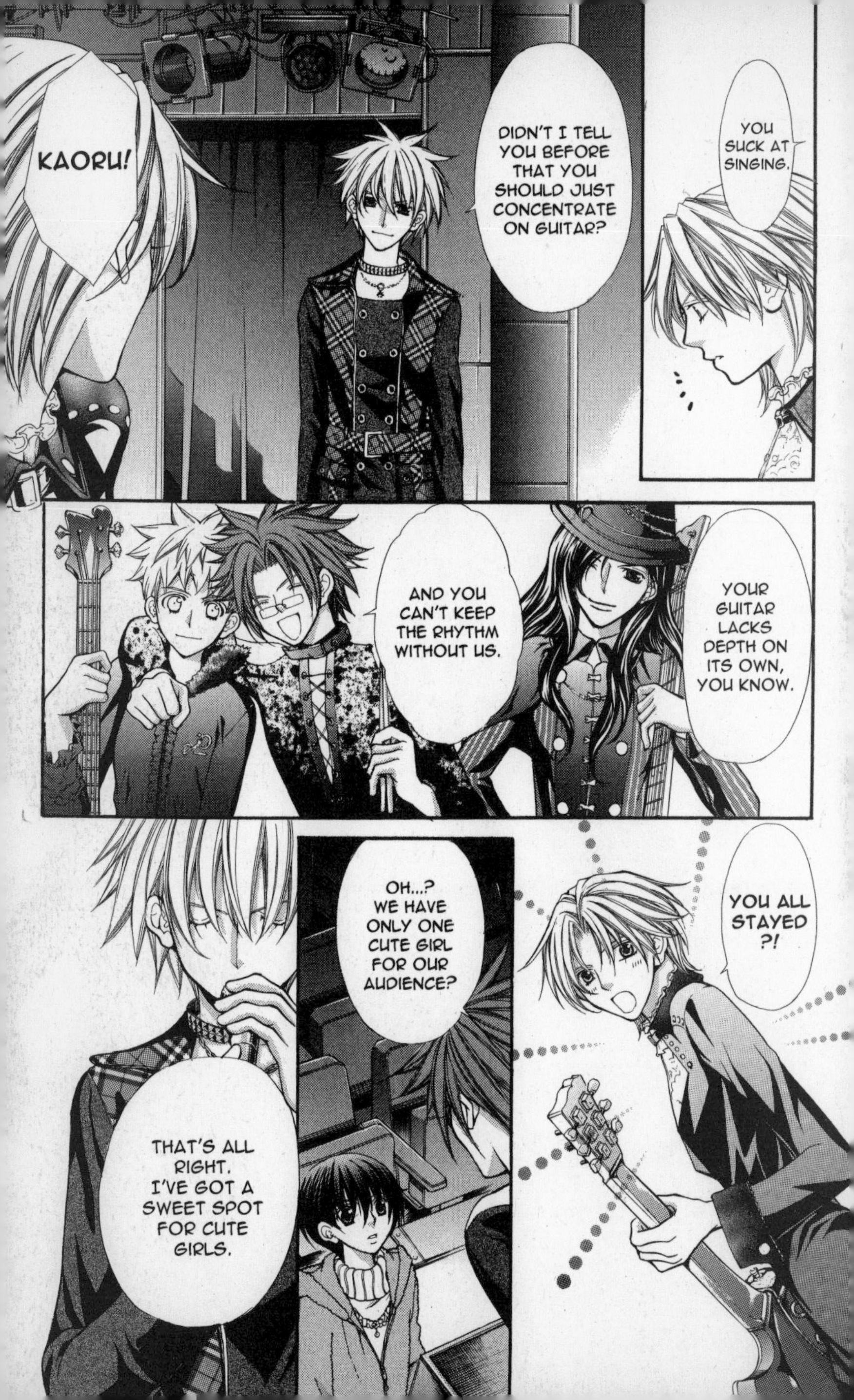
YOU SUCK AT SINGING.
DIDN'T I TELL YOU BEFORE THAT YOU SHOULD JUST CONCENTRATE ON GUITAR?
KAORU!
YOUR GUITAR LACKS DEPTH ON ITS OWN, YOU KNOW.
AND YOU CAN'T KEEP THE RHYTHM WITHOUT US.
YOU ALL STAYED ?!
OH...? WE HAVE ONLY ONE CUTE GIRL FOR OUR AUDIENCE?
THAT'S ALL RIGHT. I'VE GOT A SWEET SPOT FOR CUTE GIRLS.

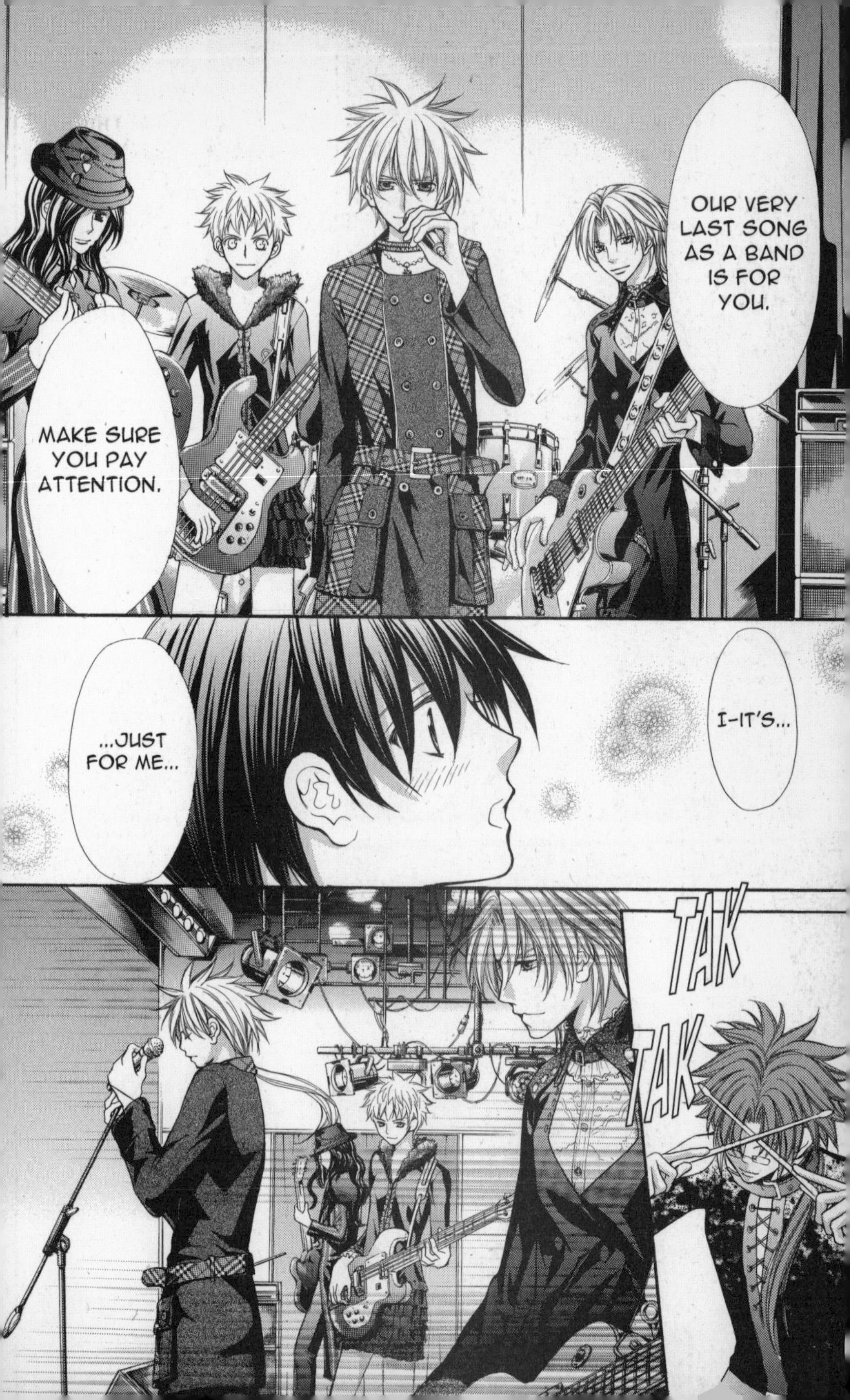
OUR VERY LAST SONG AS A BAND IS FOR YOU.
MAKE SURE YOU PAY ATTENTION.
I-IT'S...
...JUST FOR ME...
TAK
TAK

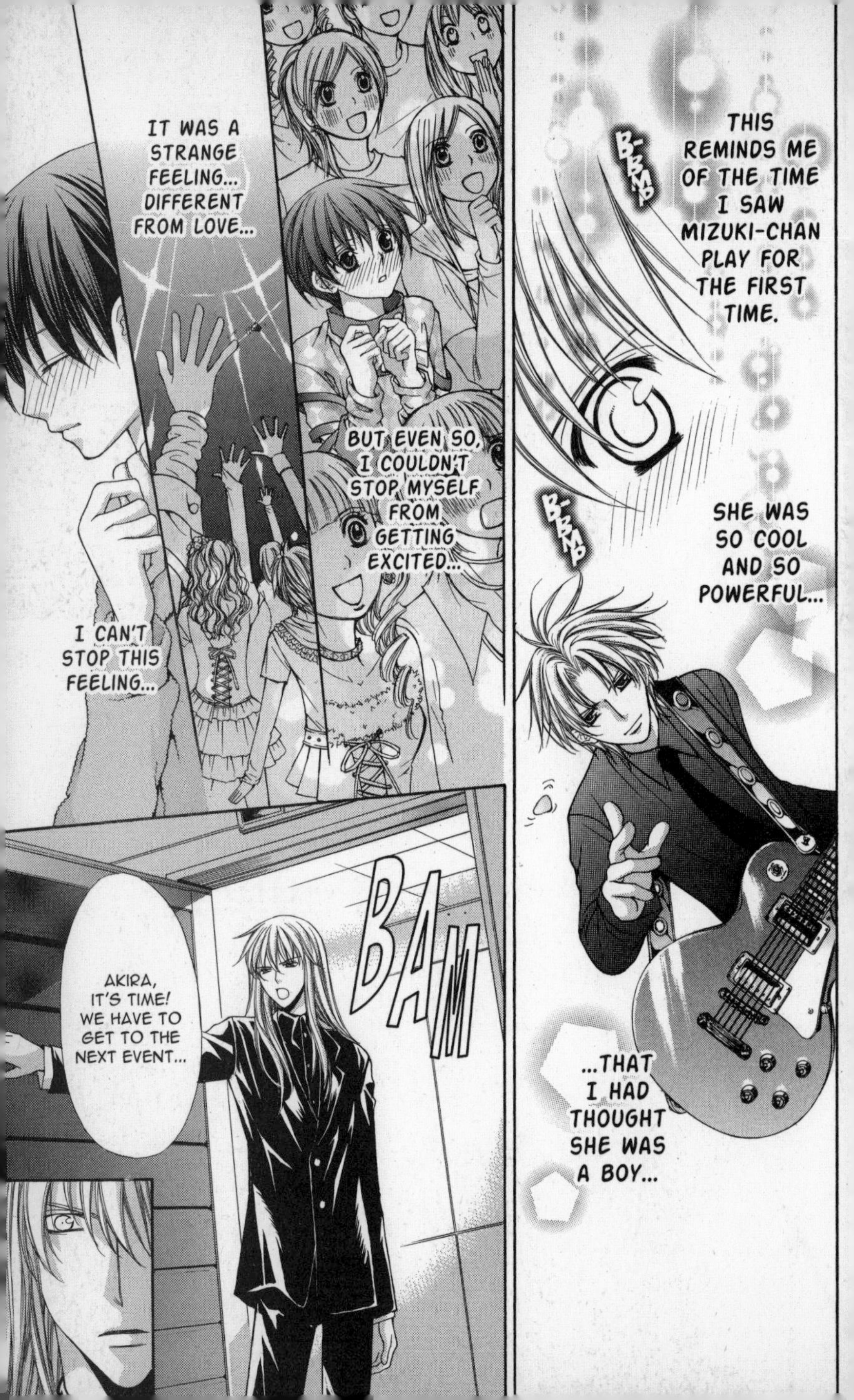
THIS REMINDS ME OF THE TIME I SAW MIZUKI-CHAN PLAY FOR THE FIRST TIME.
B-BMP
B-BMP
SHE WAS SO COOL AND SO POWERFUL...
...THAT I HAD THOUGHT SHE WAS A BOY...
IT WAS A STRANGE FEELING... DIFFERENT FROM LOVE...
BUT EVEN SO, I COULDN'T STOP MYSELF FROM GETTING EXCITED...
I CAN'T STOP THIS FEELING...
BAM
AKIRA, IT'S TIME! WE HAVE TO GET TO THE NEXT EVENT...

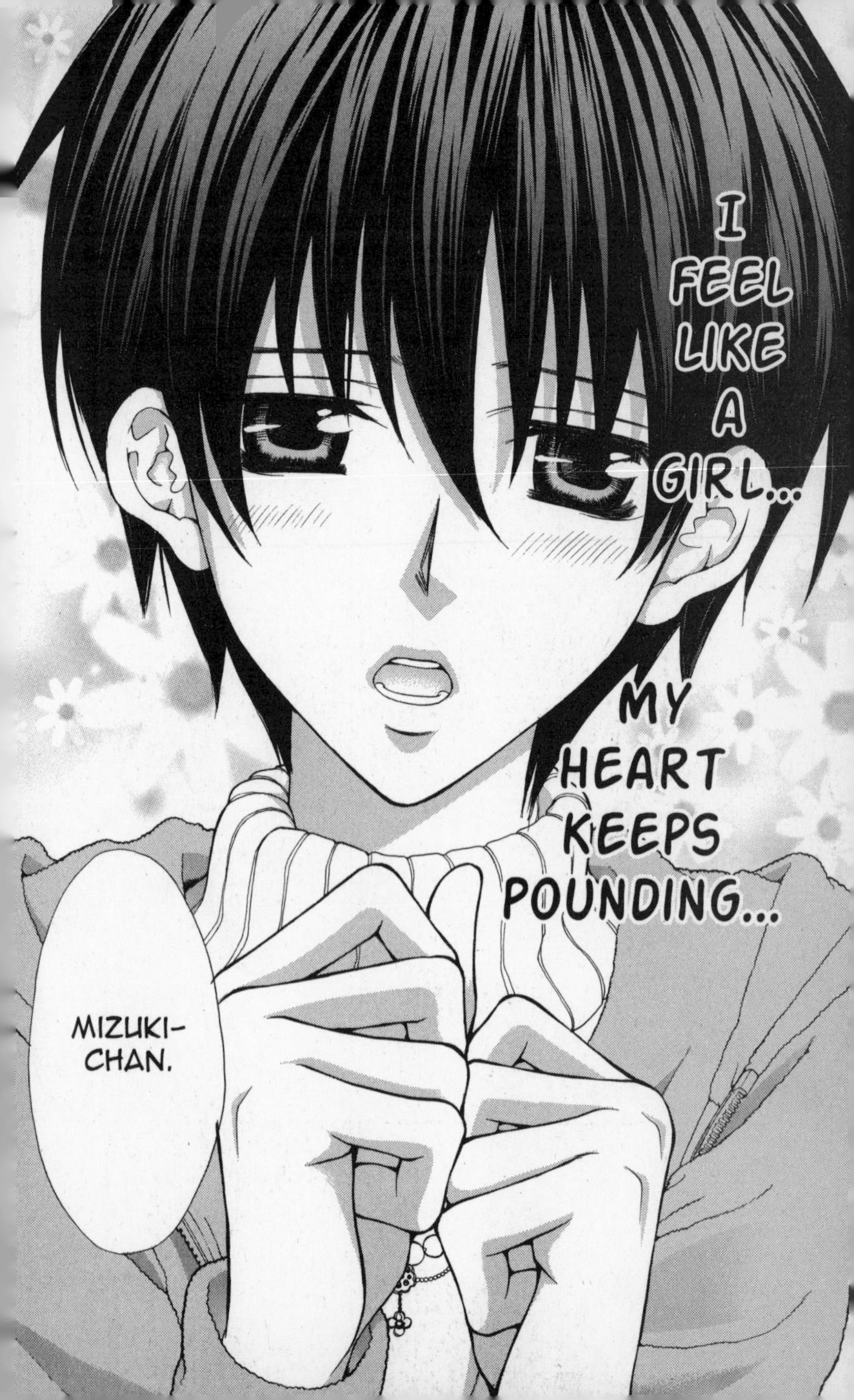
I FEEL LIKE A GIRL...
MY HEART KEEPS POUNDING...
MIZUKI-CHAN.

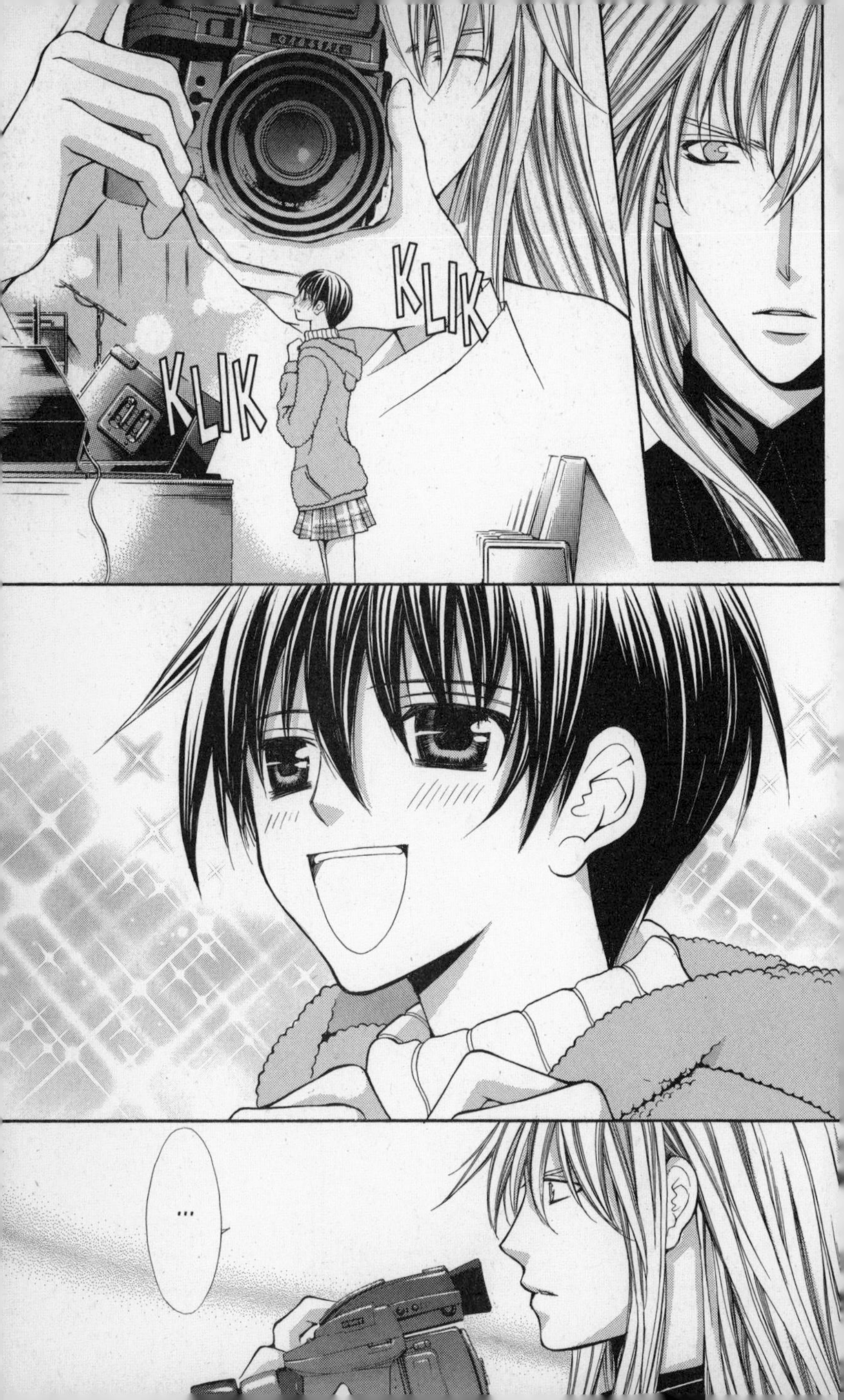
KLIK
KLIK
...

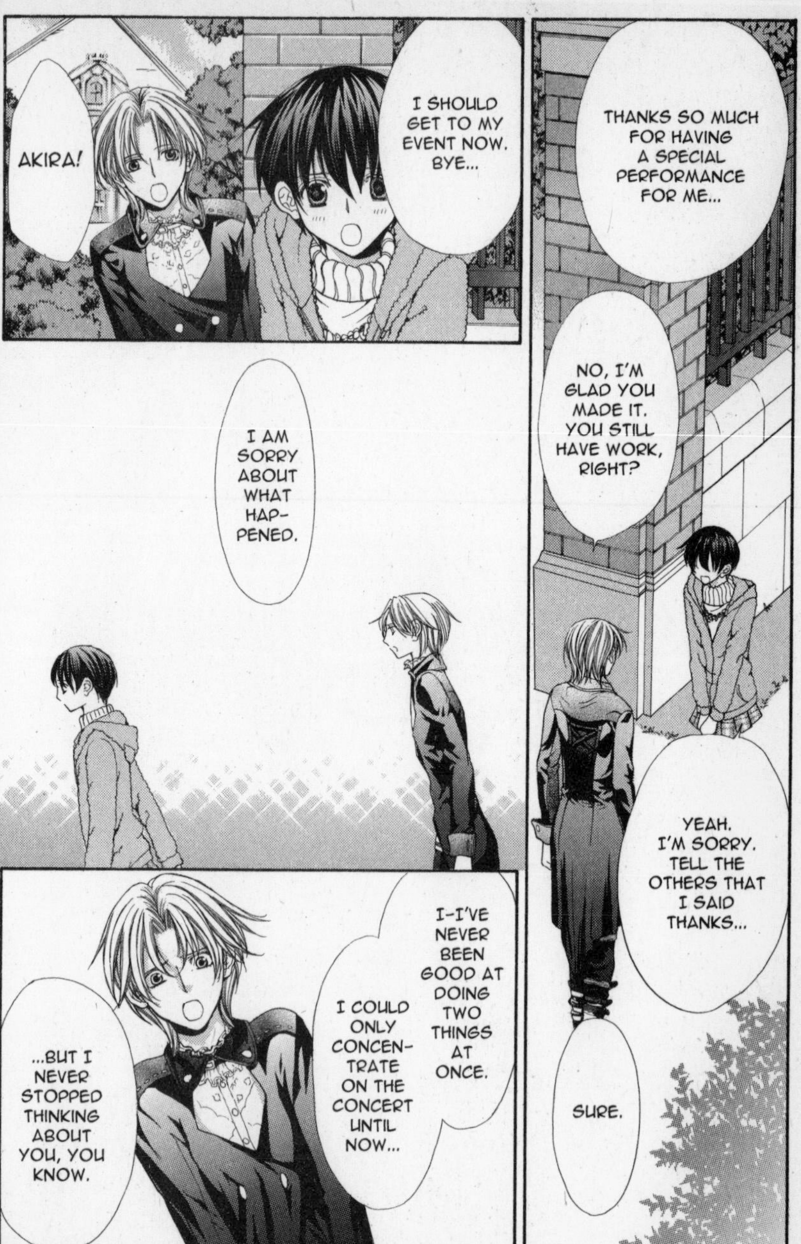
THANKS SO MUCH FOR HAVING A SPECIAL PERFORMANCE FOR ME...
NO, I'M GLAD YOU MADE IT. YOU STILL HAVE WORK, RIGHT?
YEAH. I'M SORRY. TELL THE OTHERS THAT I SAID THANKS...
SURE.
I SHOULD GET TO MY EVENT NOW. BYE...
AKIRA!
I AM SORRY ABOUT WHAT HAP-PENED.
I-I'VE NEVER BEEN GOOD AT DOING TWO THINGS AT ONCE.
I COULD ONLY CONCEN-TRATE ON THE CONCERT UNTIL NOW...
...BUT I NEVER STOPPED THINKING ABOUT YOU, YOU KNOW.

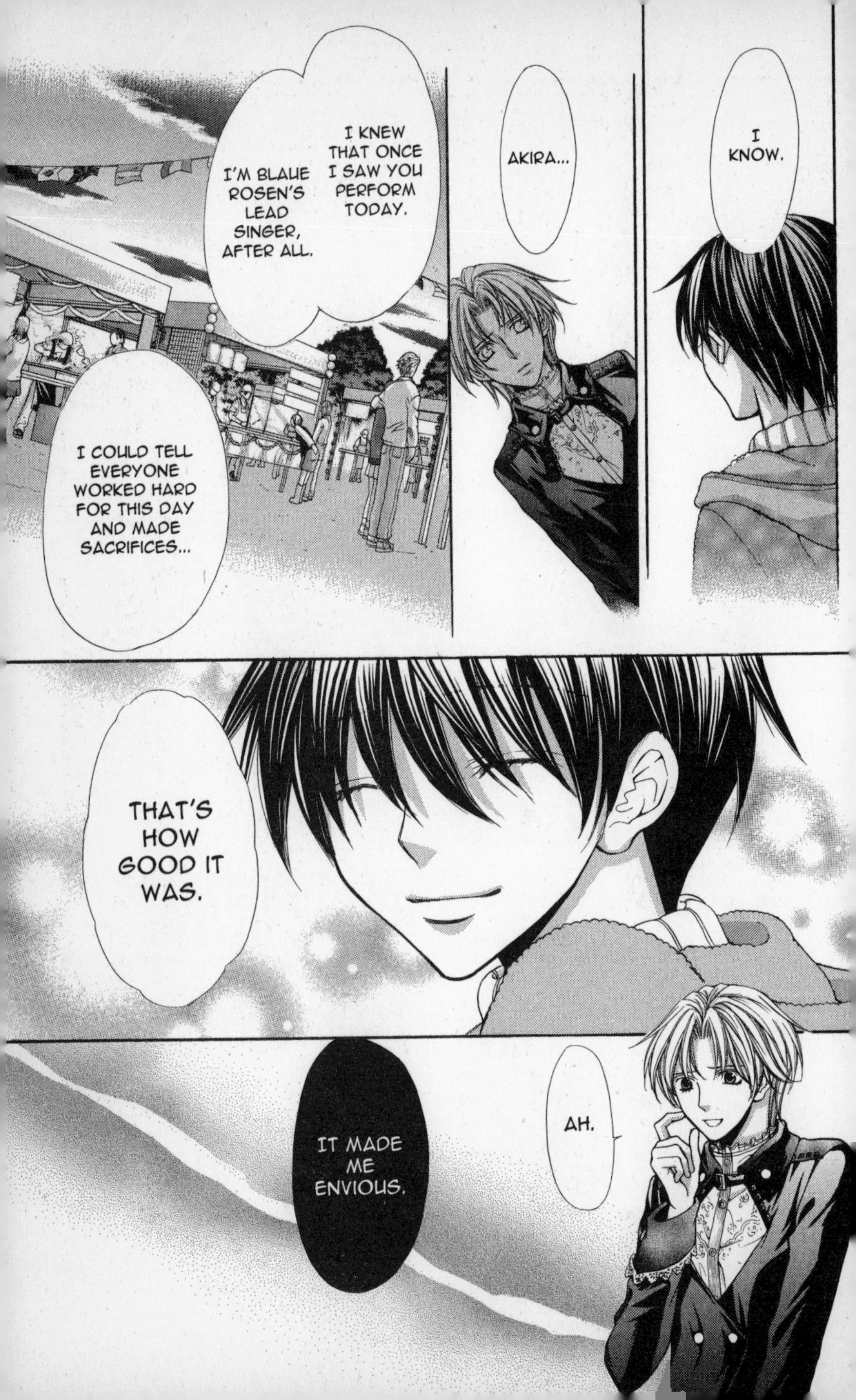
I KNOW.
AKIRA...
I KNEW THAT ONCE I SAW YOU PERFORM TODAY.
I'M BLAUE ROSEN'S LEAD SINGER, AFTER ALL.
I COULD TELL EVERYONE WORKED HARD FOR THIS DAY AND MADE SACRIFICES...
THAT'S HOW GOOD IT WAS.
AH.
IT MADE ME ENVIOUS.

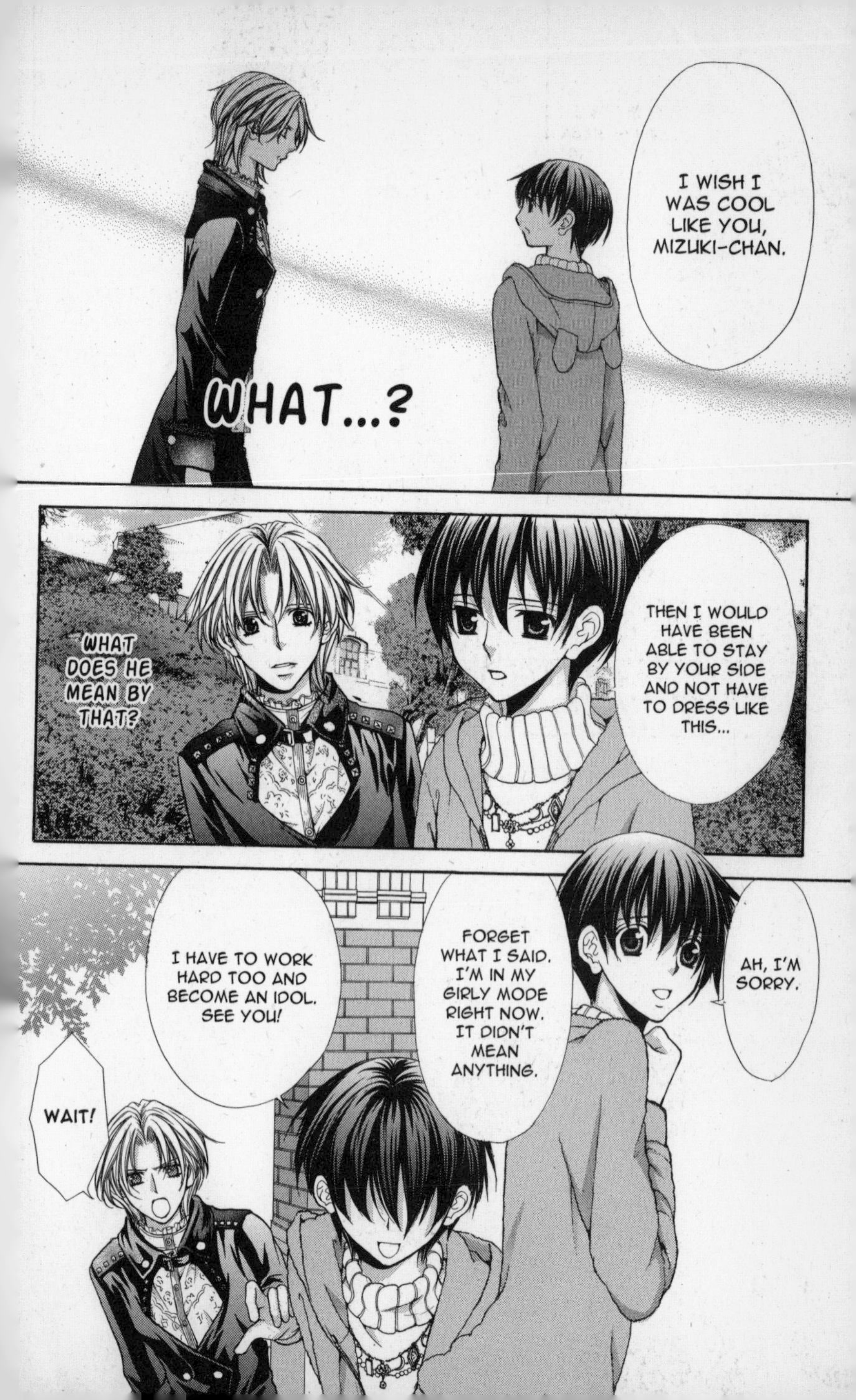
I WISH I WAS COOL LIKE YOU, MIZUKI-CHAN.
WHAT...?
THEN I WOULD HAVE BEEN ABLE TO STAY BY YOUR SIDE AND NOT HAVE TO DRESS LIKE THIS...
WHAT DOES HE MEAN BY THAT?
AH, I'M SORRY.
FORGET WHAT I SAID. I'M IN MY GIRLY MODE RIGHT NOW. IT DIDN'T MEAN ANYTHING.
I HAVE TO WORK HARD TOO AND BECOME AN IDOL. SEE YOU!
WAIT!

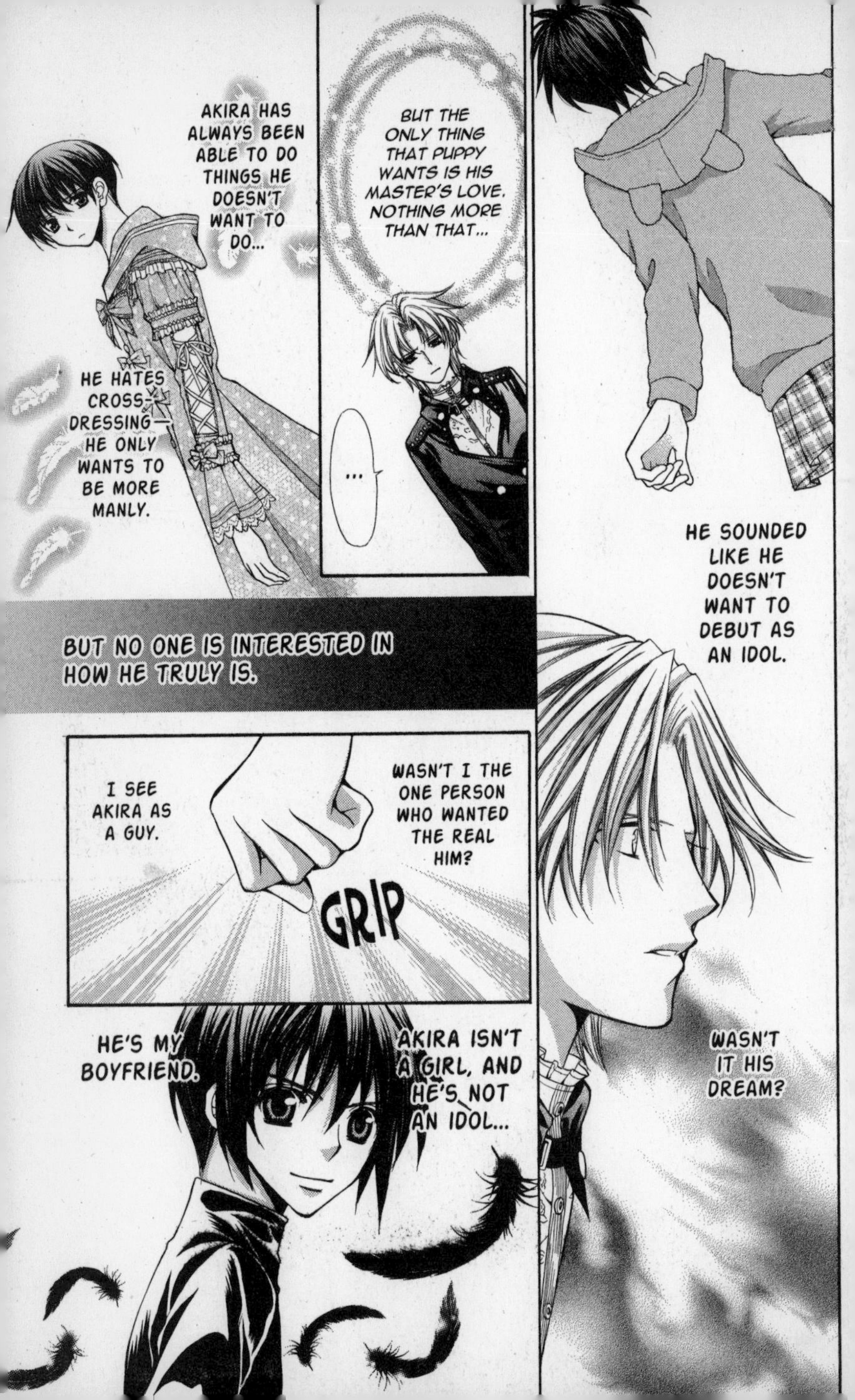
HE SOUNDED LIKE HE DOESN'T WANT TO DEBUT AS AN IDOL.
WASN'T IT HIS DREAM?
BUT THE ONLY THING THAT PUPPY WANTS IS HIS MASTER'S LOVE. NOTHING MORE THAN THAT...
...
AKIRA HAS ALWAYS BEEN ABLE TO DO THINGS HE DOESN'T WANT TO DO...
HE HATES CROSS-DRESSING—HE ONLY WANTS TO BE MORE MANLY.
BUT NO ONE IS INTERESTED IN HOW HE TRULY IS.
WASN'T I THE ONE PERSON WHO WANTED THE REAL HIM?
I SEE AKIRA AS A GUY.
GRIP
AKIRA ISN'T A GIRL, AND HE'S NOT AN IDOL...
HE'S MY BOYFRIEND.

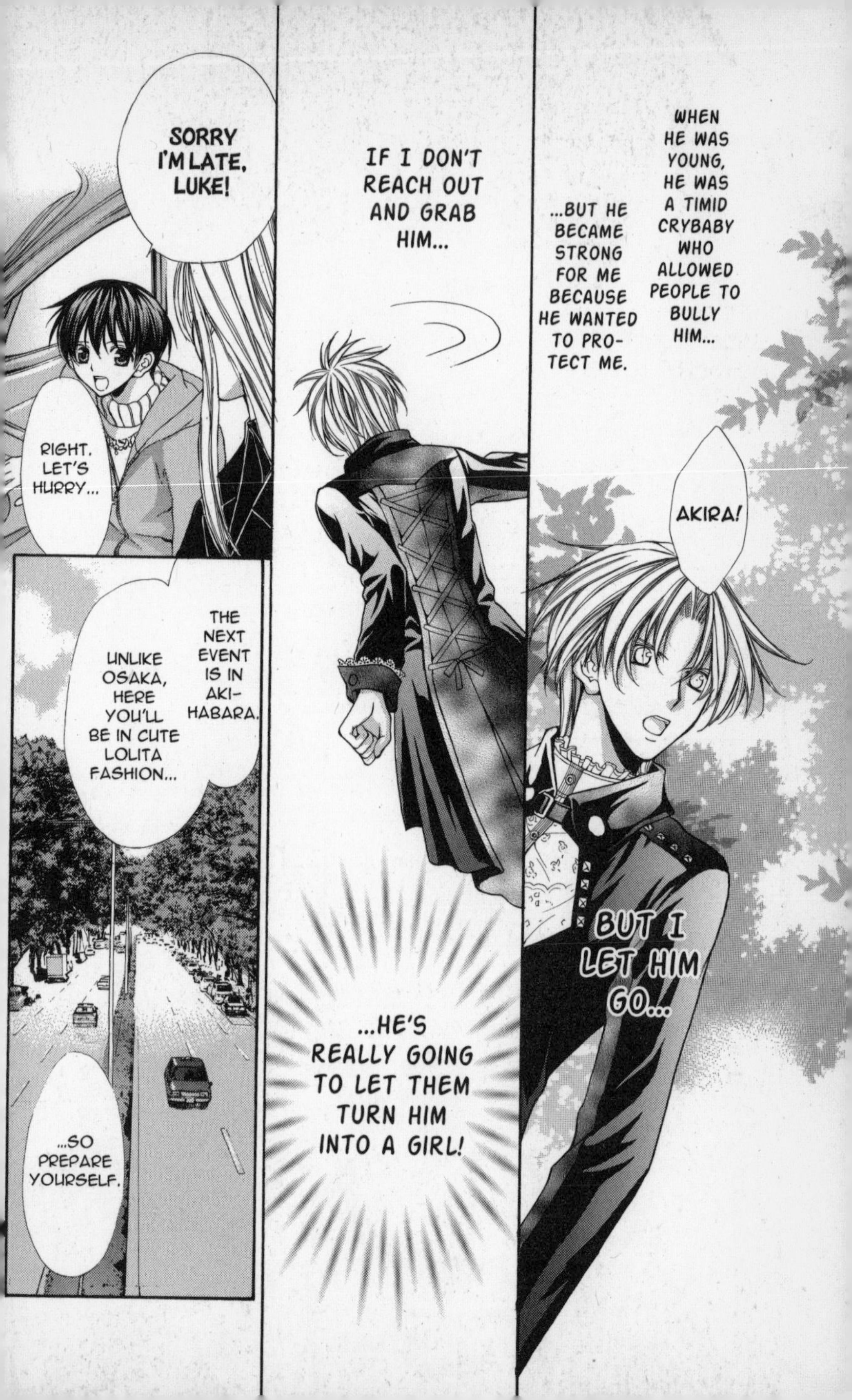
WHEN HE WAS YOUNG, HE WAS A TIMID CRYBABY WHO ALLOWED PEOPLE TO BULLY HIM...
...BUT HE BECAME STRONG FOR ME BECAUSE HE WANTED TO PROTECT ME.
AKIRA!
BUT I LET HIM GO...
IF I DON'T REACH OUT AND GRAB HIM...
...HE'S REALLY GOING TO LET THEM TURN HIM INTO A GIRL!
SORRY I'M LATE, LUKE!
RIGHT. LET'S HURRY...
THE NEXT EVENT IS IN AKI-HABARA.
UNLIKE OSAKA, HERE YOU'LL BE IN CUTE LOLITA FASHION...
...SO PREPARE YOURSELF.

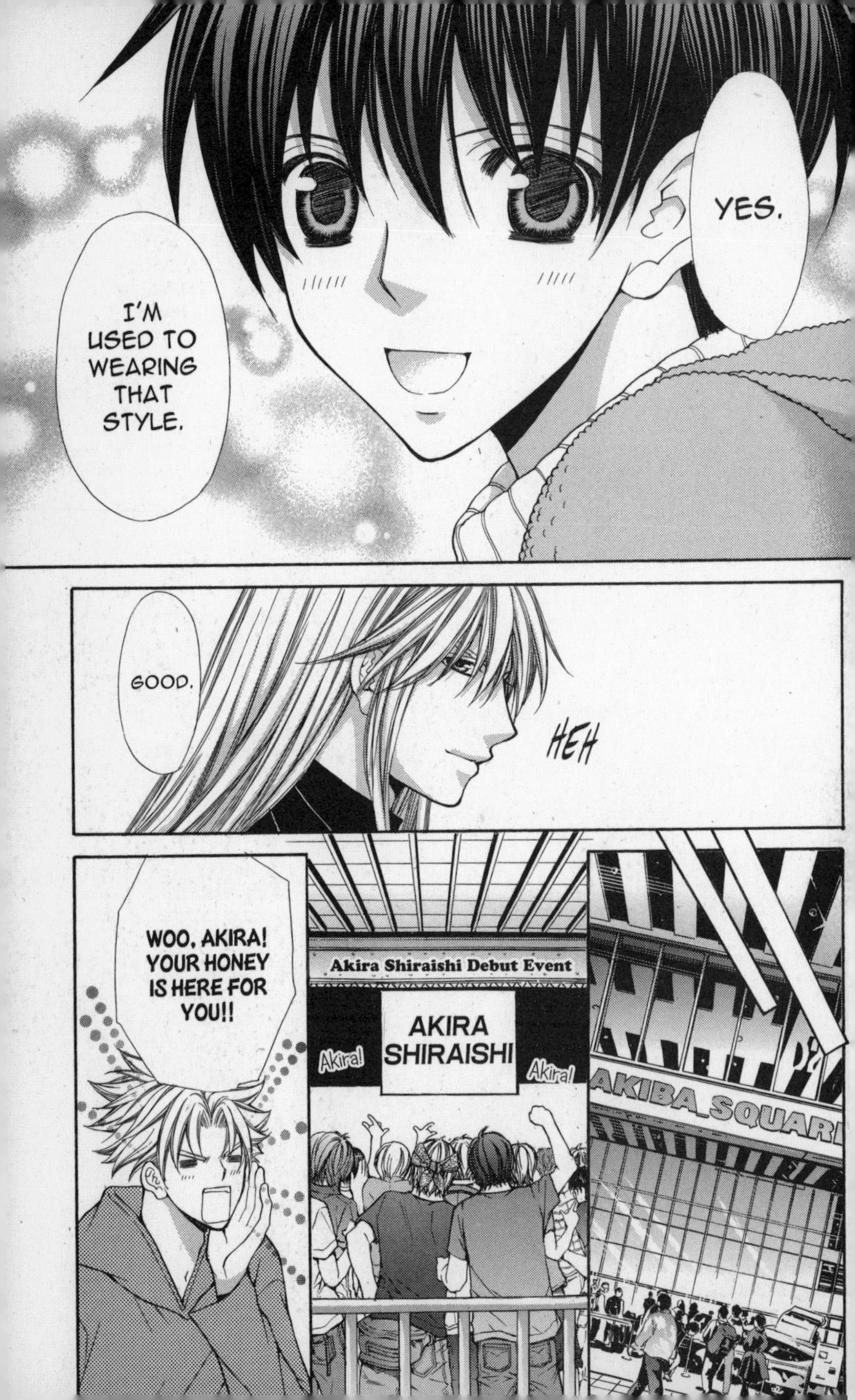
YES.
I'M USED TO WEARING THAT STYLE.
GOOD.
HEH
AKIBA_SQUAR
Akira Shiraishi Debut Event
AKIRA SHIRAISHI
Akira!
Akira!
WOO, AKIRA! YOUR HONEY IS HERE FOR YOU!!

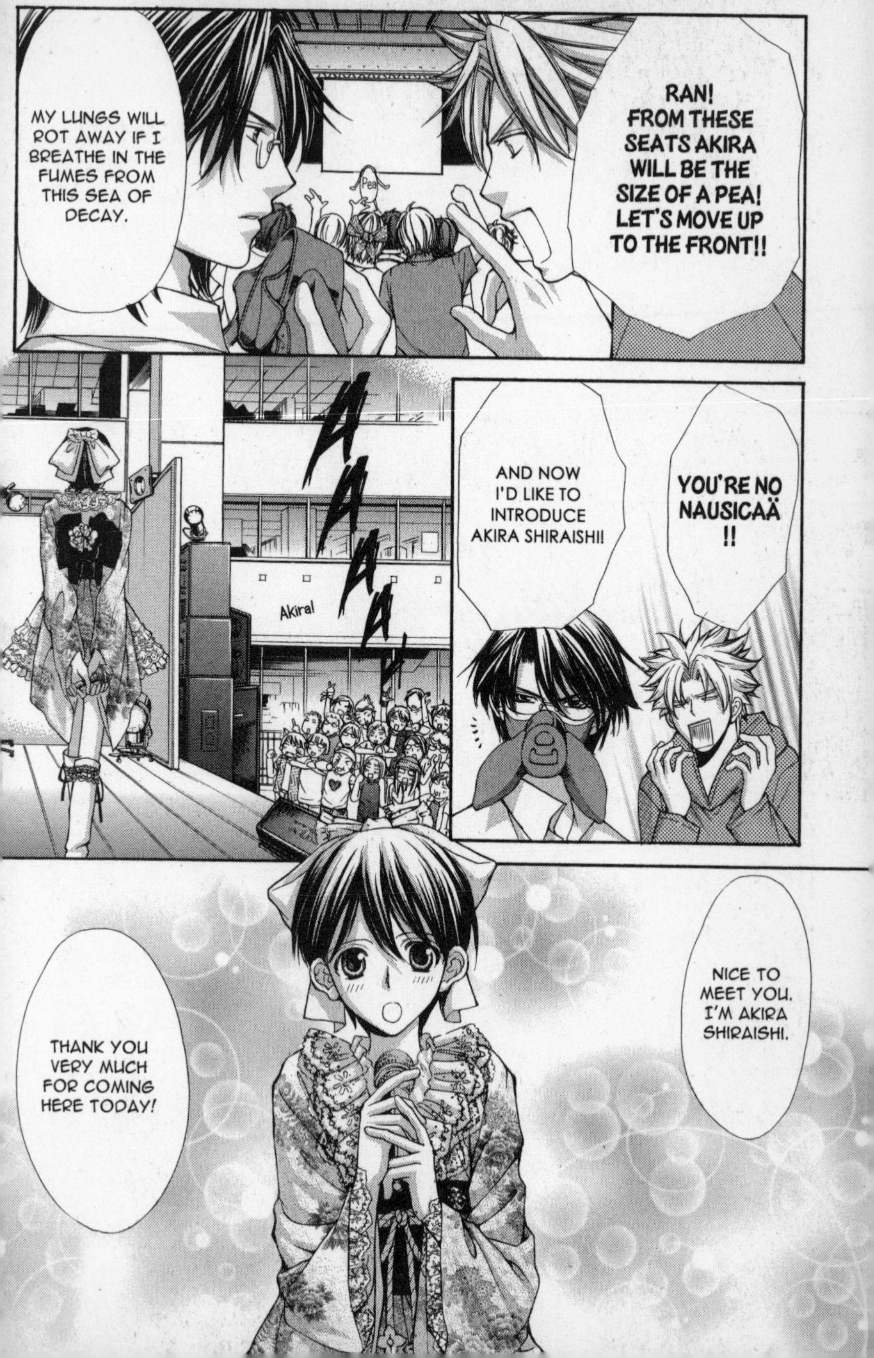
RAN! FROM THESE SEATS AKIRA WILL BE THE SIZE OF A PEA! LET'S MOVE UP TO THE FRONT!!
Pea
MY LUNGS WILL ROT AWAY IF I BREATHE IN THE FUMES FROM THIS SEA OF DECAY.
YOU'RE NO NAUSICAÄ !!
AND NOW I'D LIKE TO INTRODUCE AKIRA SHIRAISHI!
Akira!
NICE TO MEET YOU. I'M AKIRA SHIRAISHI.
THANK YOU VERY MUCH FOR COMING HERE TODAY!

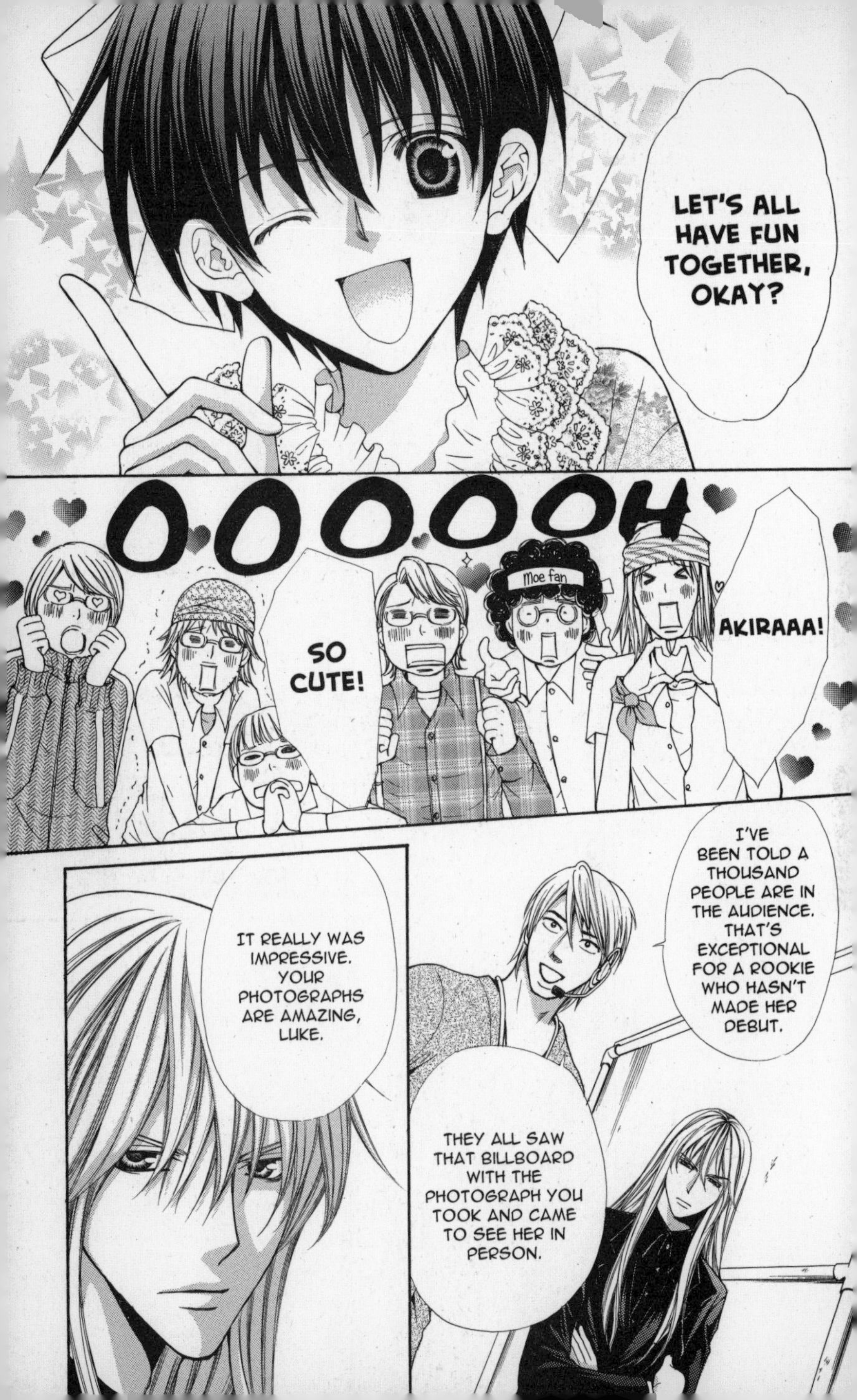
LET'S ALL HAVE FUN TOGETHER, OKAY?
O.O.O.O.OH
AKIRAAA!
Moe fan
SO CUTE!
I'VE BEEN TOLD A THOUSAND PEOPLE ARE IN THE AUDIENCE. THAT'S EXCEPTIONAL FOR A ROOKIE WHO HASN'T MADE HER DEBUT.
THEY ALL SAW THAT BILLBOARD WITH THE PHOTOGRAPH YOU TOOK AND CAME TO SEE HER IN PERSON.
IT REALLY WAS IMPRESSIVE. YOUR PHOTOGRAPHS ARE AMAZING, LUKE.

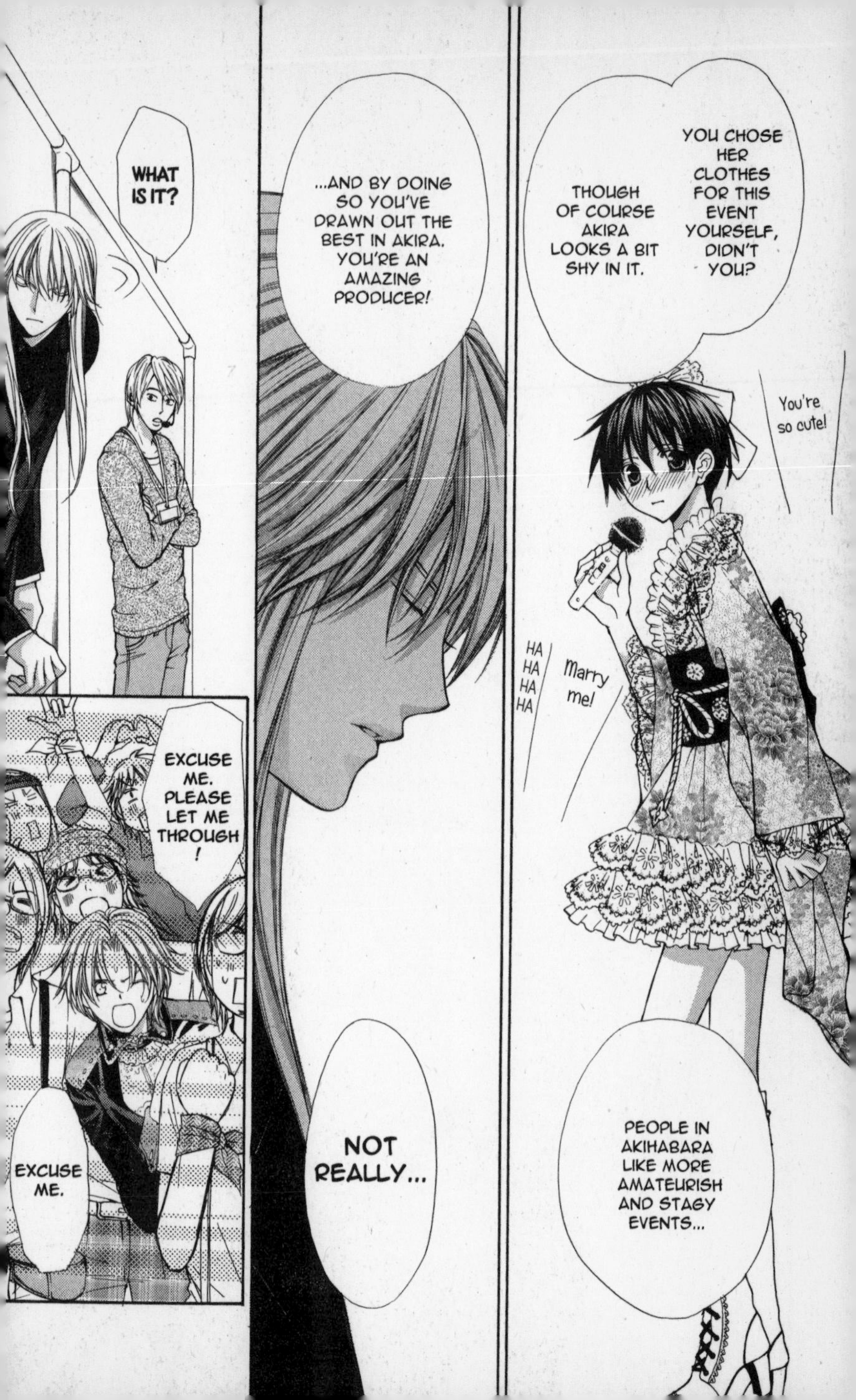
YOU CHOSE HER CLOTHES FOR THIS EVENT YOURSELF, DIDN'T YOU?
THOUGH OF COURSE AKIRA LOOKS A BIT SHY IN IT.
You're so cute!
Marry me!
HA HA HA HA
PEOPLE IN AKIHABARA LIKE MORE AMATEURISH AND STAGY EVENTS...
...AND BY DOING SO YOU'VE DRAWN OUT THE BEST IN AKIRA. YOU'RE AN AMAZING PRODUCER!
NOT REALLY...
WHAT IS IT?
EXCUSE ME. PLEASE LET ME THROUGH!
EXCUSE ME.

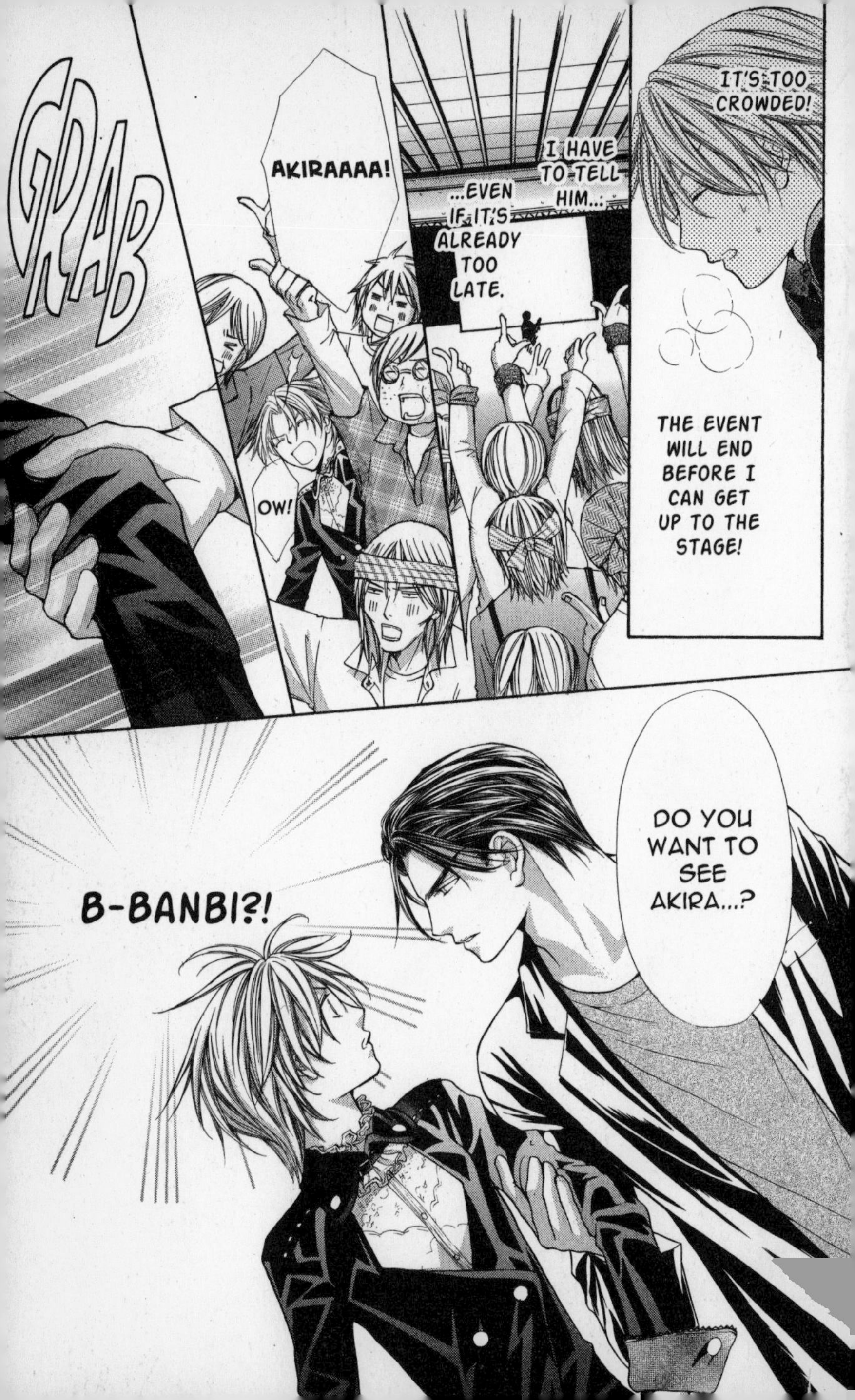
IT'S TOO CROWDED!
THE EVENT WILL END BEFORE I CAN GET UP TO THE STAGE!
I HAVE TO TELL HIM...
...EVEN IF IT'S ALREADY TOO LATE.
AKIRAAAA!
OW!
GRAB
DO YOU WANT TO SEE AKIRA...?
B-BANBI?!

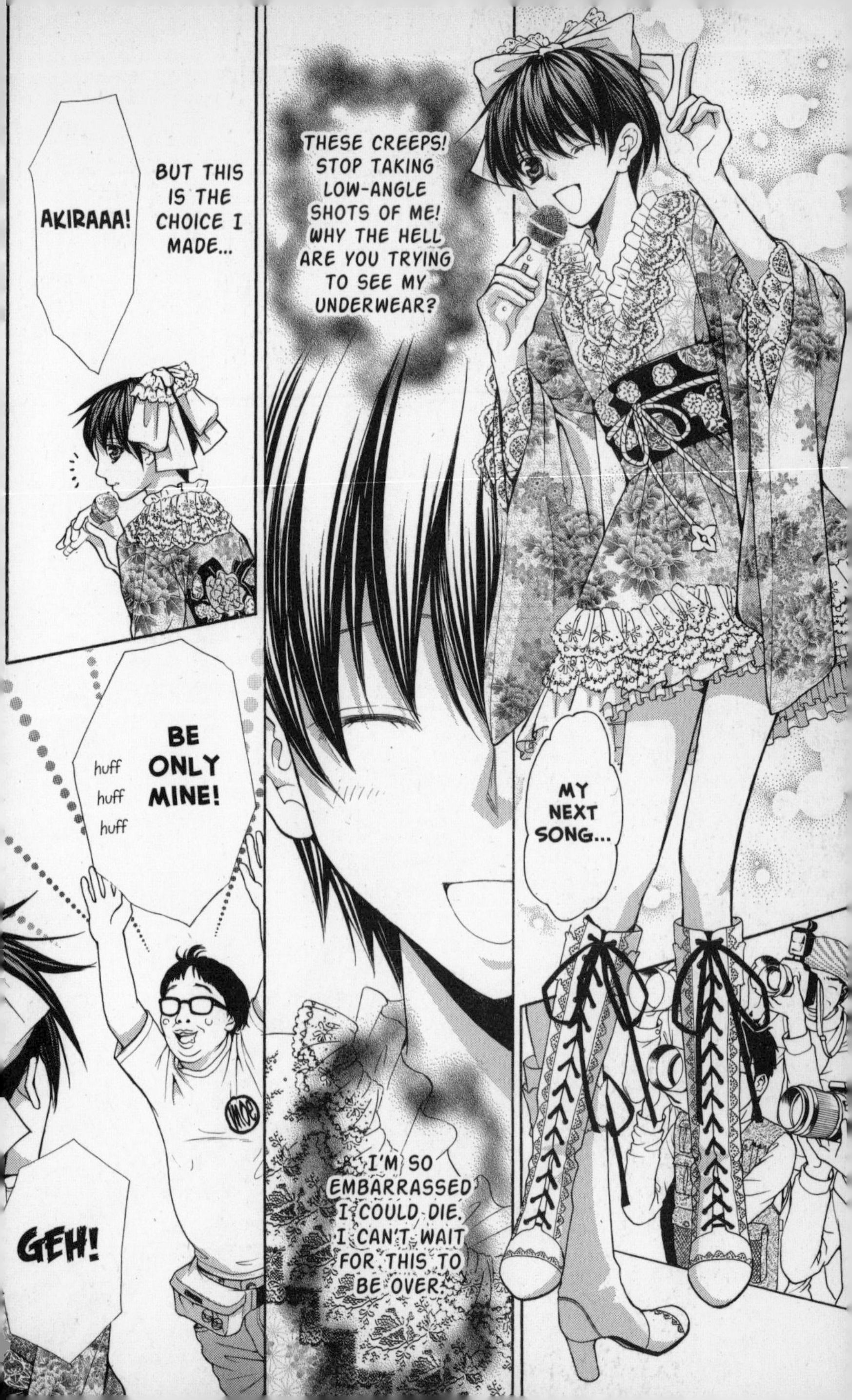
MY NEXT SONG...
THESE CREEPS! STOP TAKING LOW-ANGLE SHOTS OF ME! WHY THE HELL ARE YOU TRYING TO SEE MY UNDERWEAR?
I'M SO EMBARRASSED I COULD DIE. I CAN'T WAIT FOR THIS TO BE OVER.
BUT THIS IS THE CHOICE I MADE...
AKIRAAA!
BE ONLY MINE!
huff huff huff
GEH!

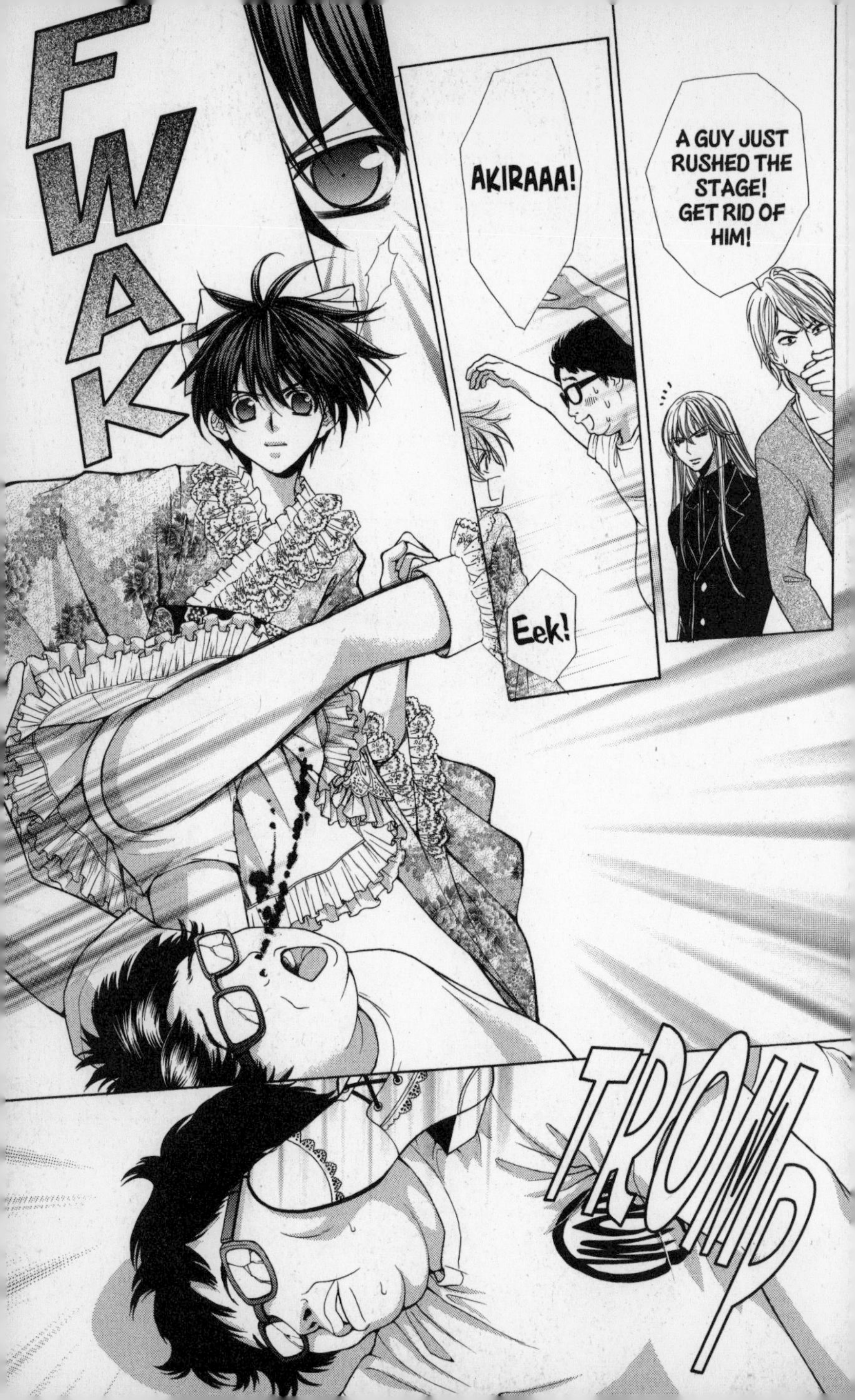
A GUY JUST RUSHED THE STAGE! GET RID OF HIM!
AKIRAAA!
Eek!
FWAK
TROMP

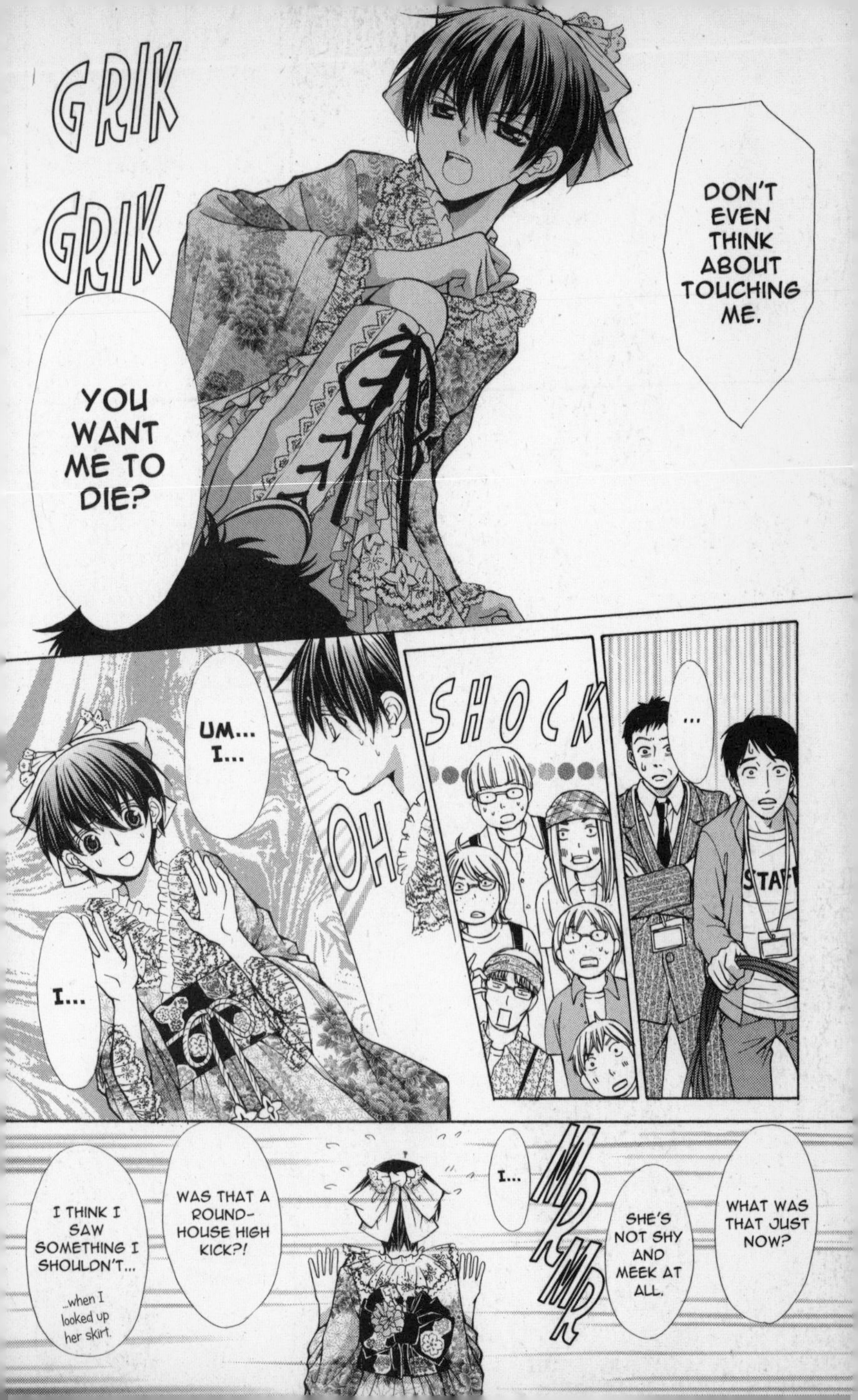
DON'T EVEN THINK ABOUT TOUCHING ME.
GRIK GRIK
YOU WANT ME TO DIE?
...
SHOCK
OH
UM... I...
I...
WHAT WAS THAT JUST NOW?
SHE'S NOT SHY AND MEEK AT ALL.
MRMR
I...
WAS THAT A ROUND-HOUSE HIGH KICK?!
I THINK I SAW SOMETHING I SHOULDN'T...
...when I looked up her skirt.

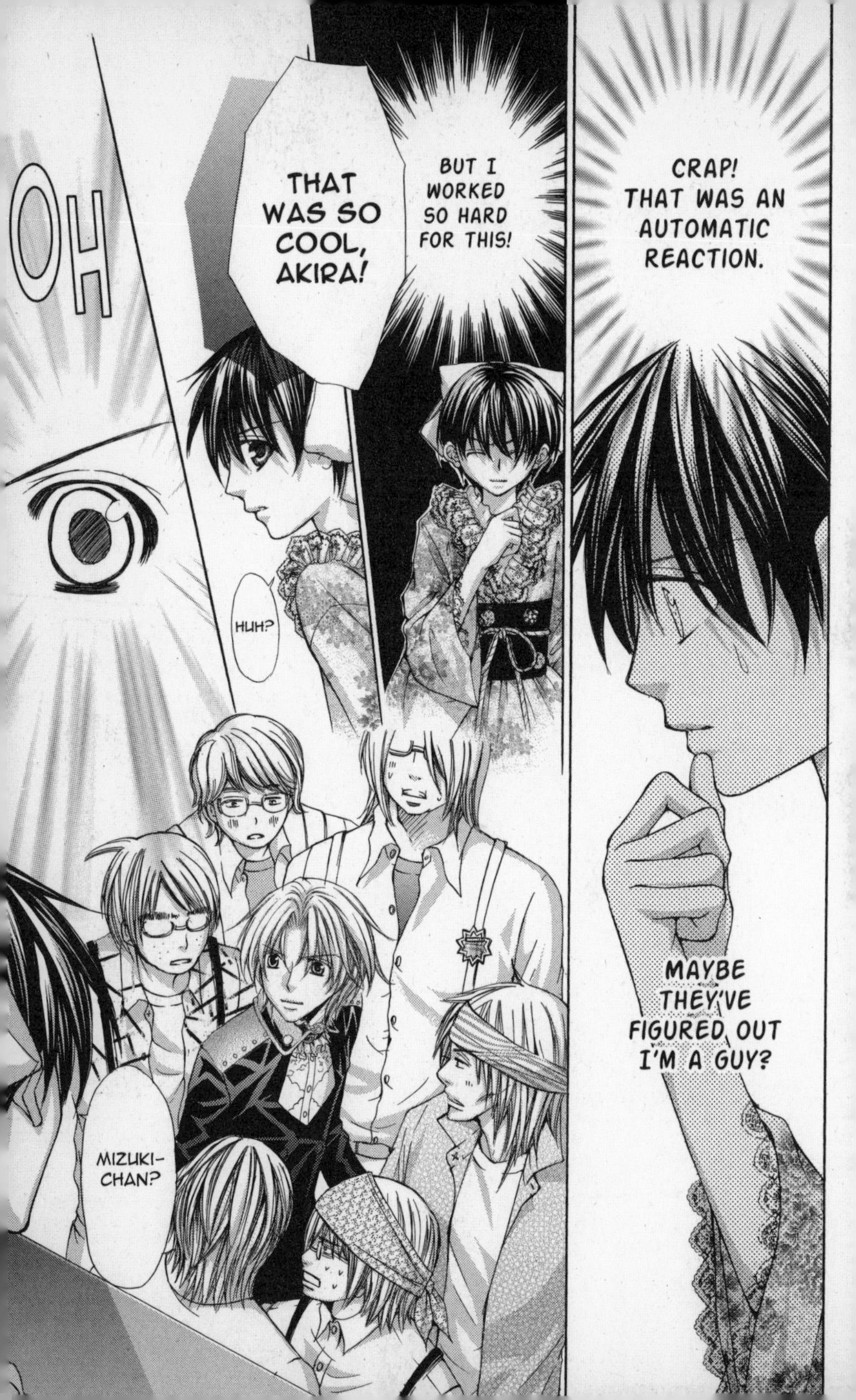
CRAP! THAT WAS AN AUTOMATIC REACTION.
MAYBE THEY'VE FIGURED OUT I'M A GUY?
BUT I WORKED SO HARD FOR THIS!
THAT WAS SO COOL, AKIRA!
HUH?
OH
MIZUKI-CHAN?

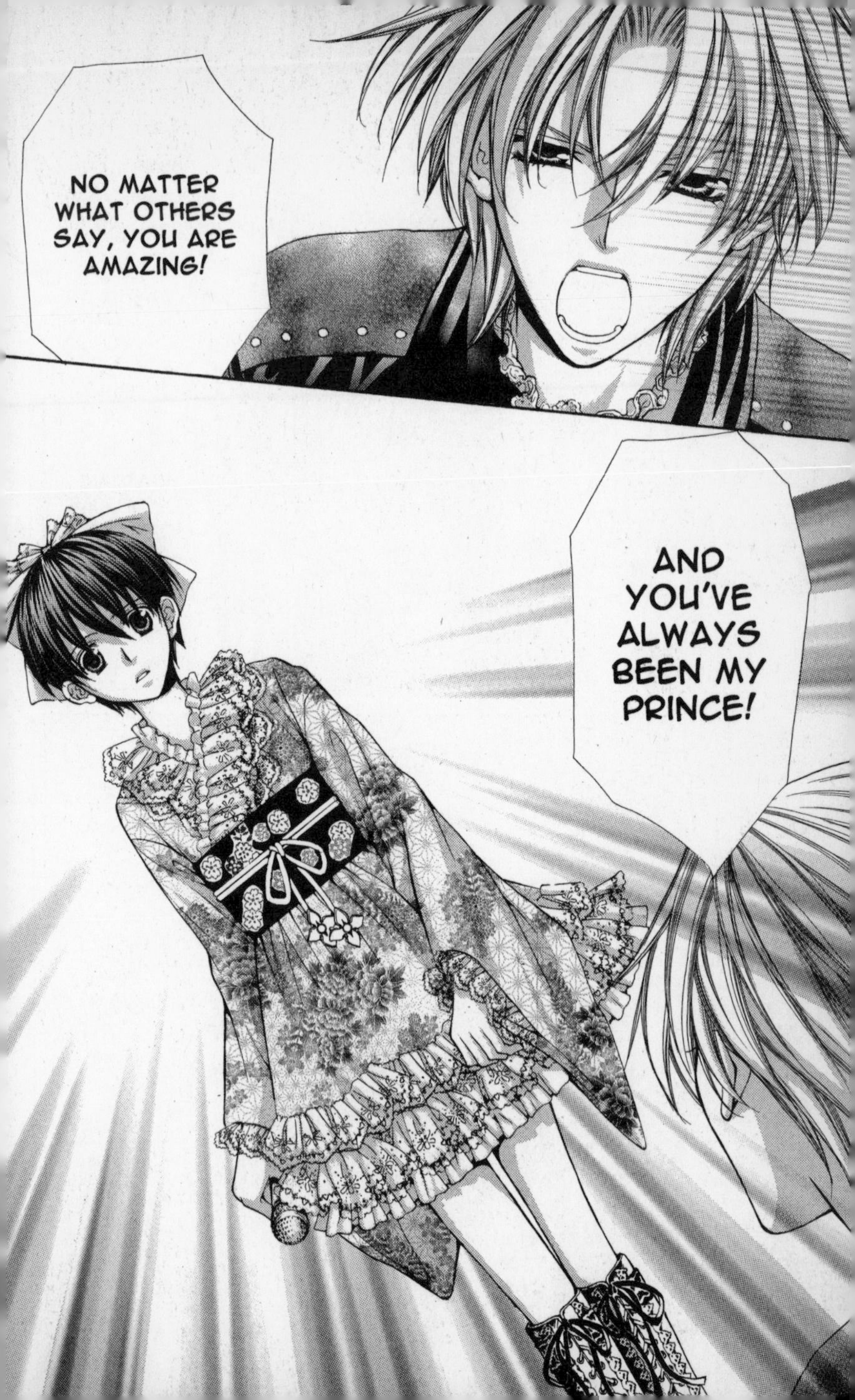
NO MATTER WHAT OTHERS SAY, YOU ARE AMAZING!
AND YOU'VE ALWAYS BEEN MY PRINCE!

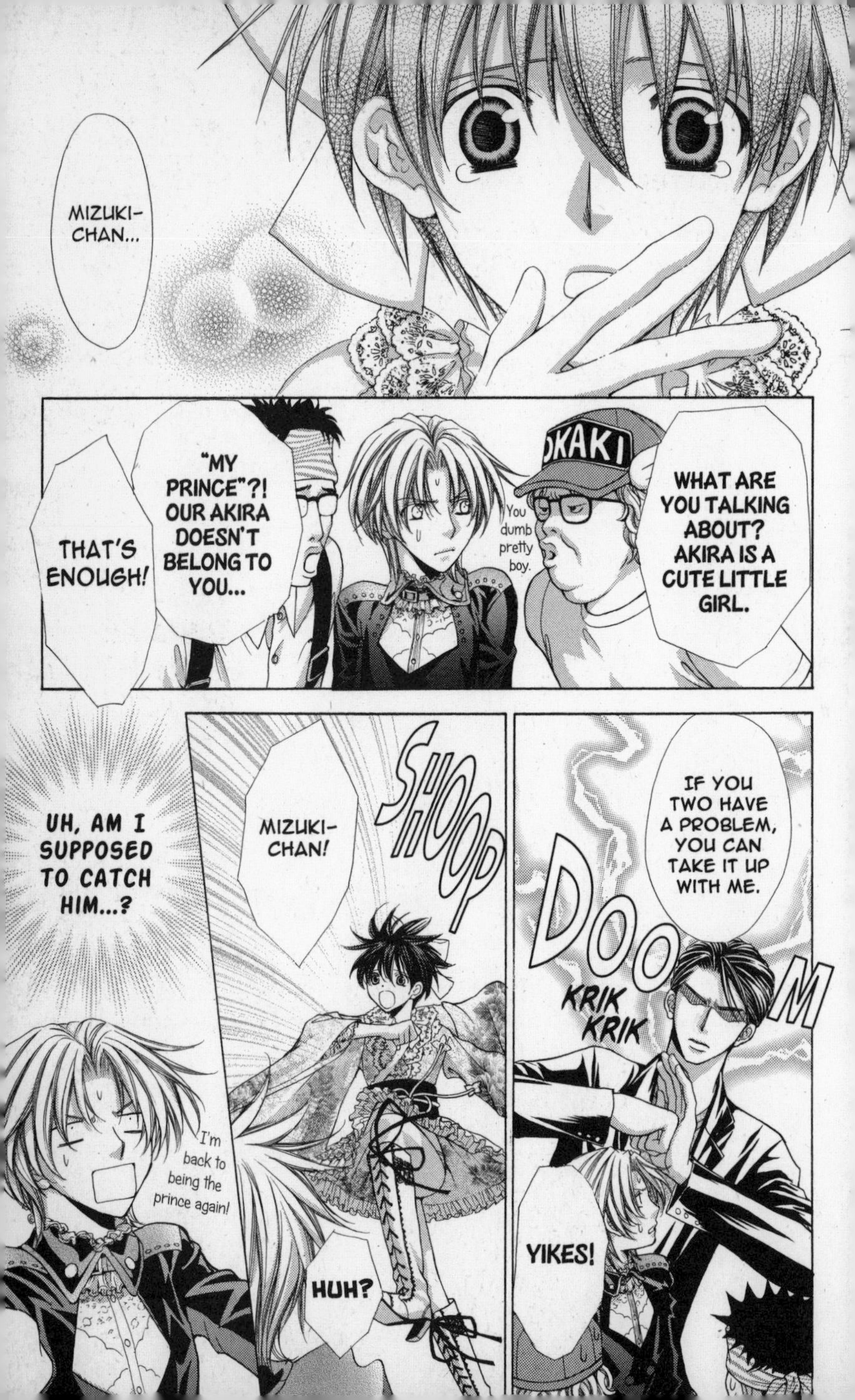
MIZUKI-CHAN...
WHAT ARE YOU TALKING ABOUT? AKIRA IS A CUTE LITTLE GIRL.
You dumb pretty boy.
"MY PRINCE"?! OUR AKIRA DOESN'T BELONG TO YOU...
THAT'S ENOUGH!
IF YOU TWO HAVE A PROBLEM, YOU CAN TAKE IT UP WITH ME.
DOOOM
KRIK KRIK
YIKES!
SHOOP
MIZUKI-CHAN!
HUH?
UH, AM I SUPPOSED TO CATCH HIM...?
I'm back to being the prince again!

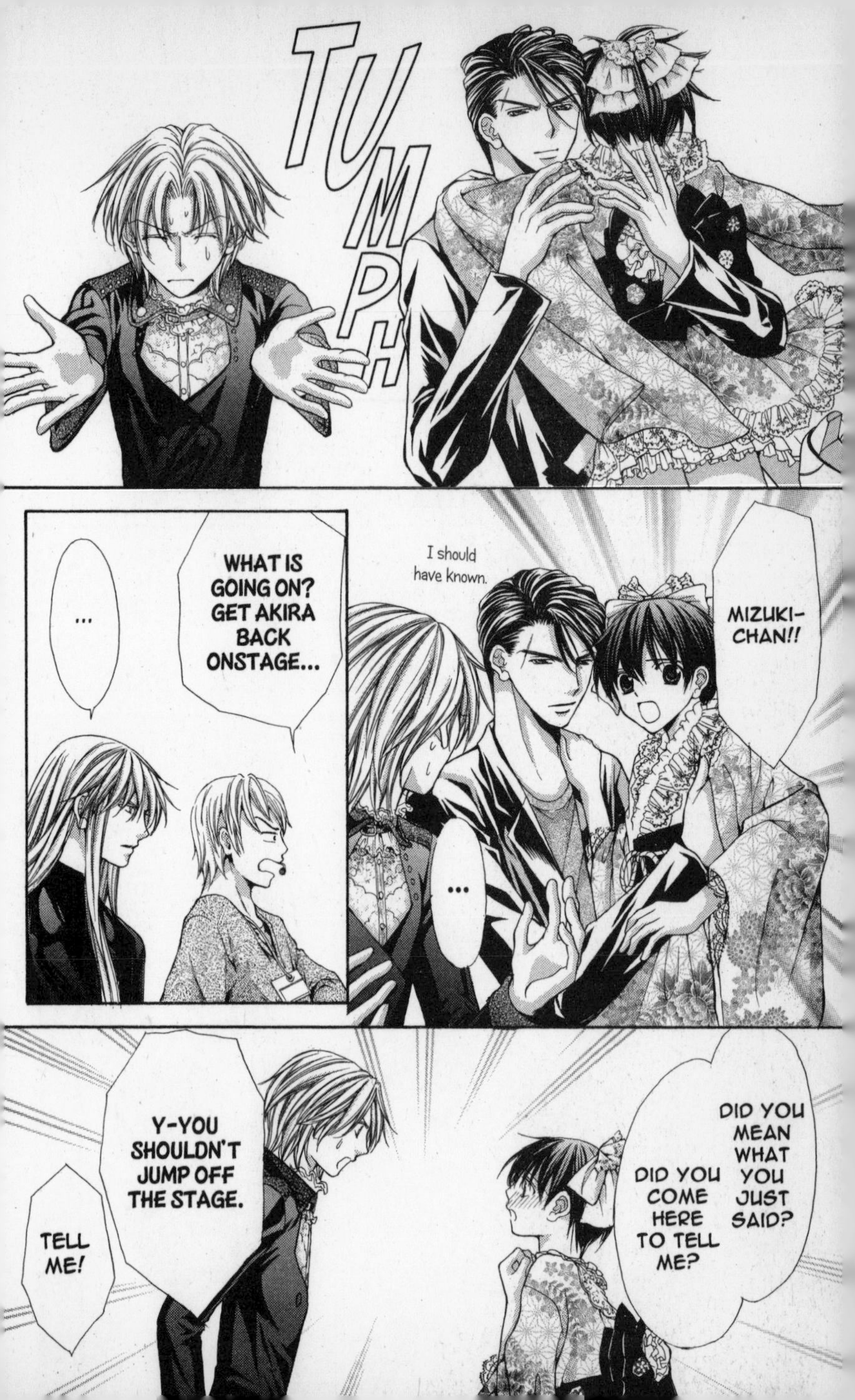
TUMPH
MIZUKI-CHAN!!
I should have known.
...
WHAT IS GOING ON? GET AKIRA BACK ONSTAGE...
...
DID YOU MEAN WHAT YOU JUST SAID?
DID YOU COME HERE TO TELL ME?
Y-YOU SHOULDN'T JUMP OFF THE STAGE.
TELL ME!

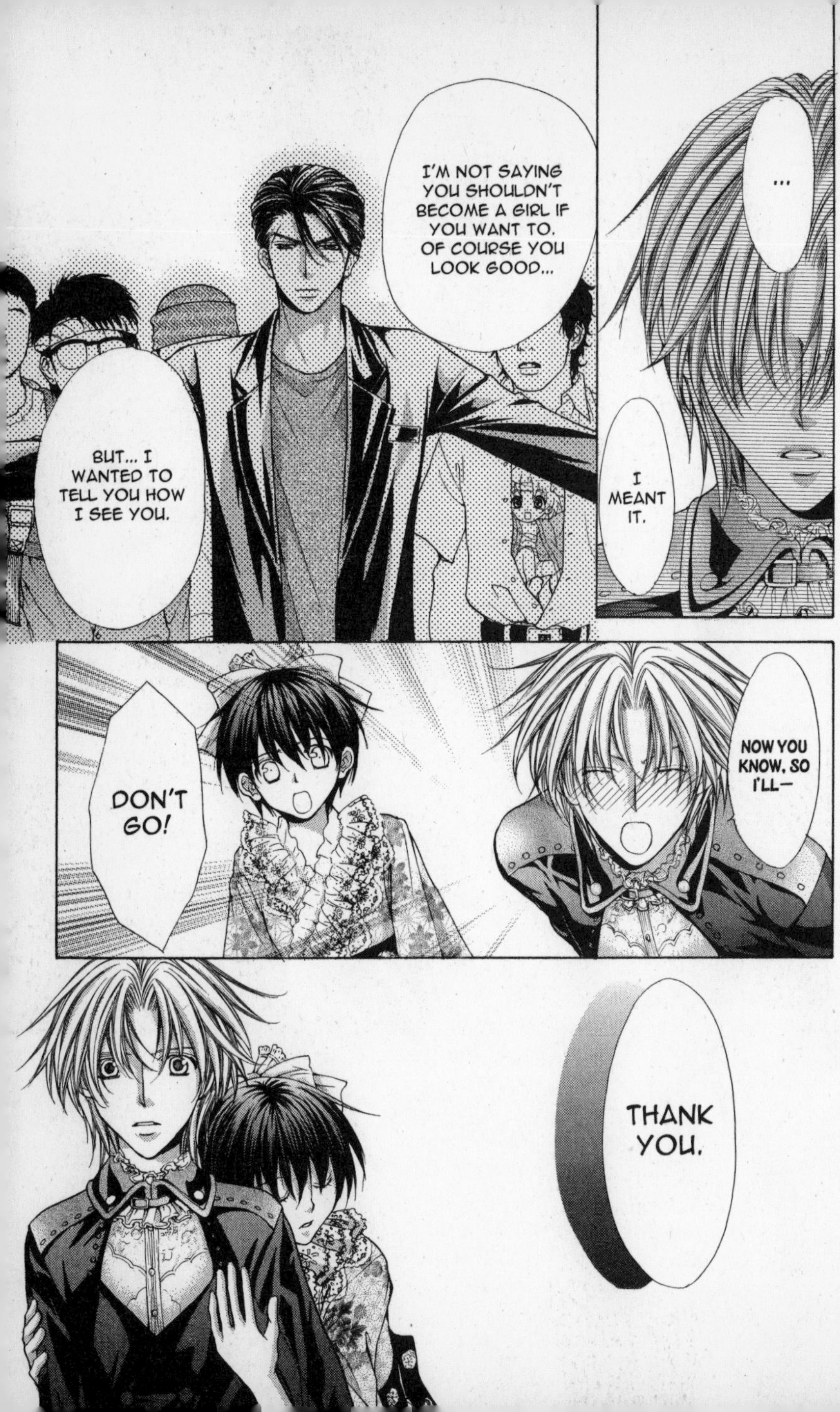
...
I MEANT IT.
I'M NOT SAYING YOU SHOULDN'T BECOME A GIRL IF YOU WANT TO. OF COURSE YOU LOOK GOOD...
BUT... I WANTED TO TELL YOU HOW I SEE YOU.
NOW YOU KNOW, SO I'LL—
DON'T GO!
THANK YOU.

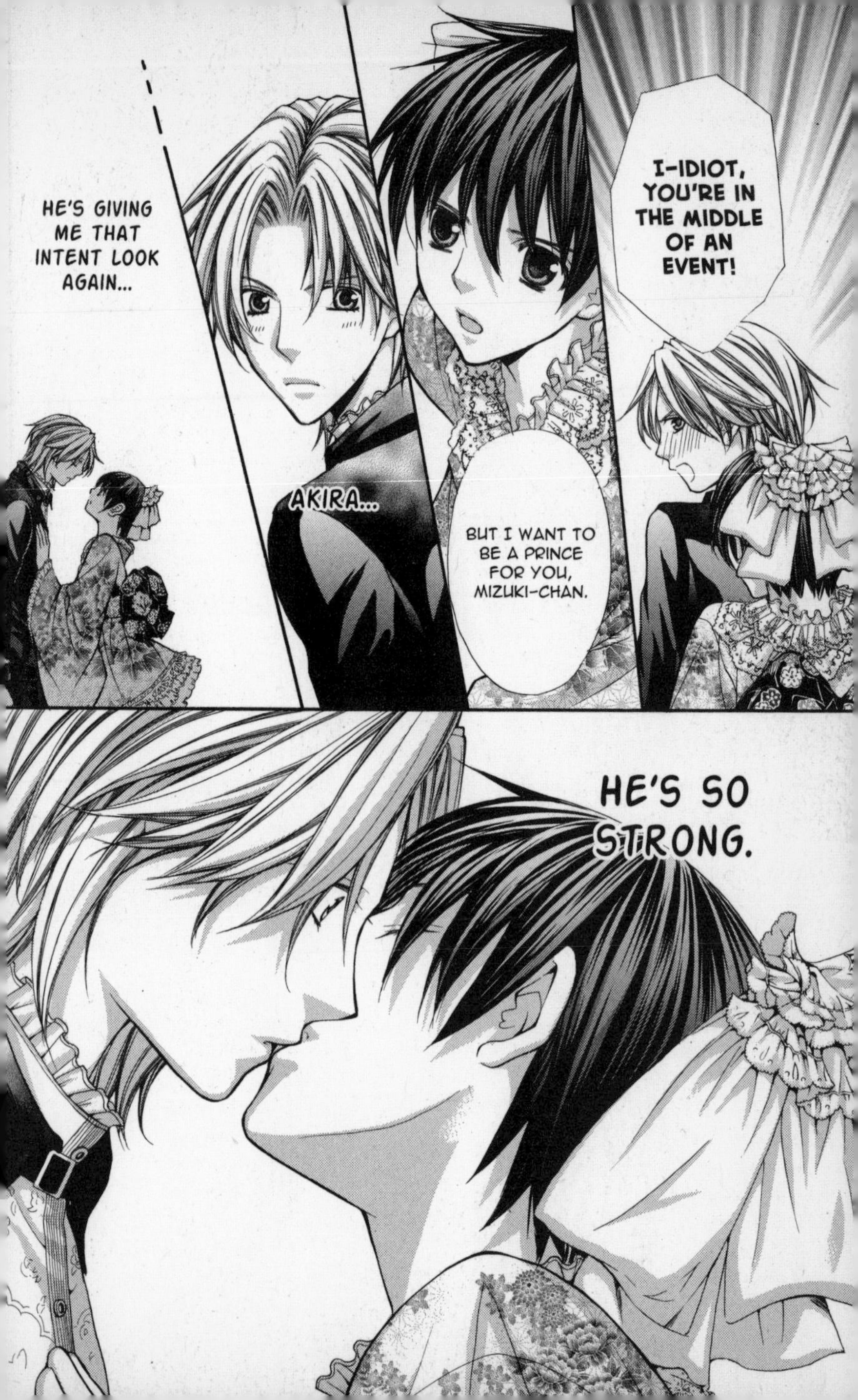

I-IDIOT, YOU'RE IN THE MIDDLE OF AN EVENT!
BUT I WANT TO BE A PRINCE FOR YOU, MIZUKI-CHAN.
HE'S GIVING ME THAT INTENT LOOK AGAIN...
AKIRA...
HE'S SO STRONG.

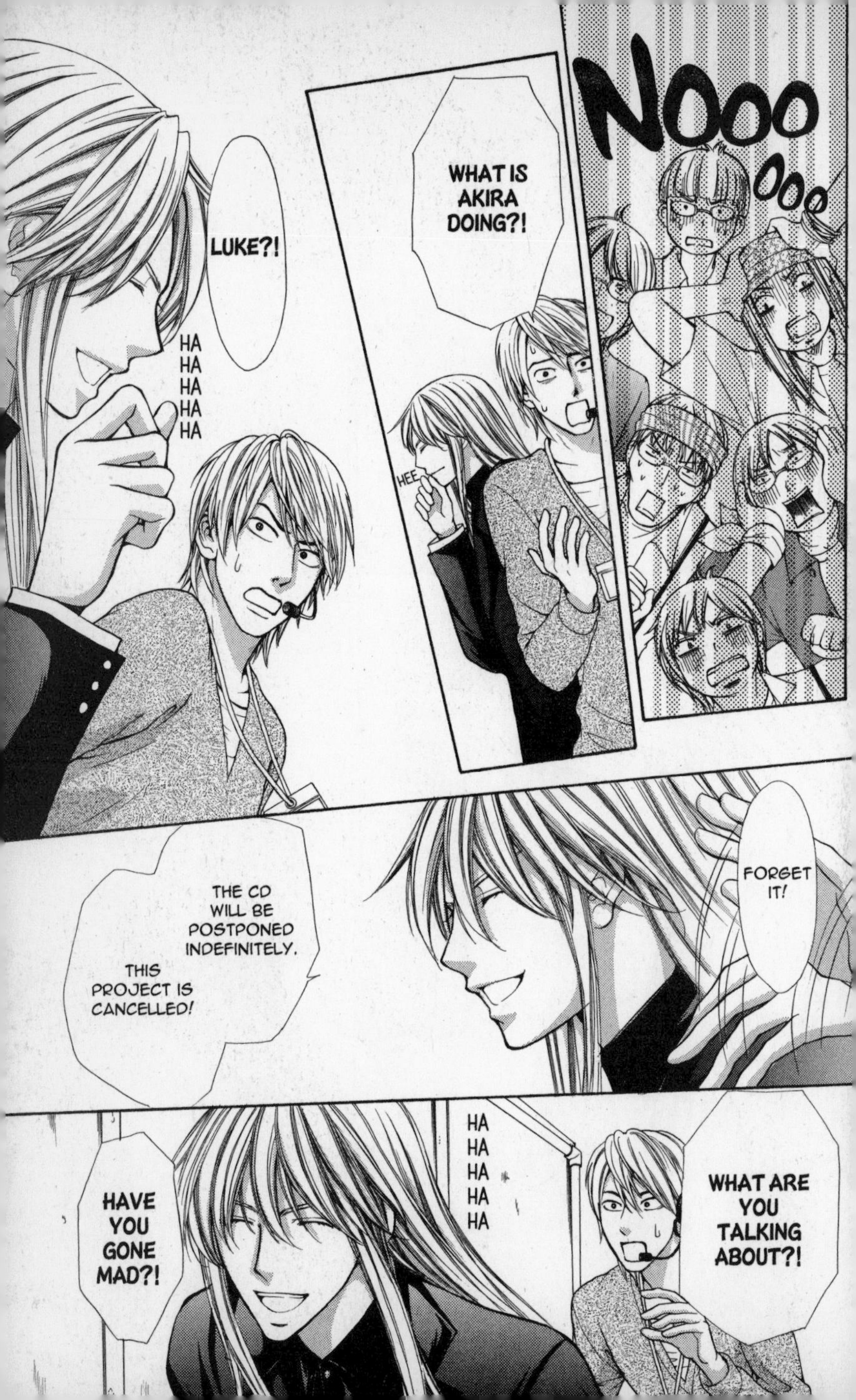
NOOO
OOO
WHAT IS AKIRA DOING?!
HEE
LUKE?!
HA HA HA HA HA
FORGET IT!
THE CD WILL BE POSTPONED INDEFINITELY.
THIS PROJECT IS CANCELLED!
WHAT ARE YOU TALKING ABOUT?!
HA HA HA HA HA
HAVE YOU GONE MAD?!

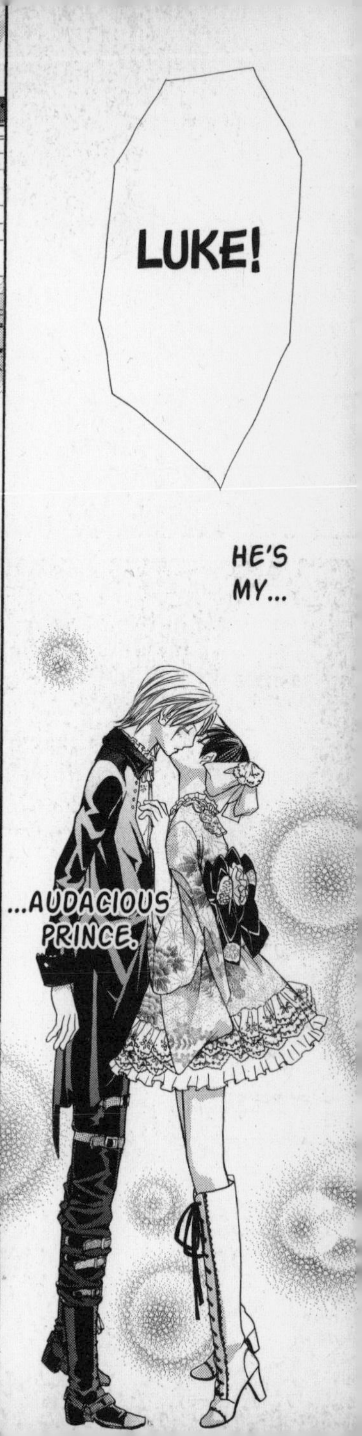
LUKE!
HE'S MY...
...AUDACIOUS PRINCE.

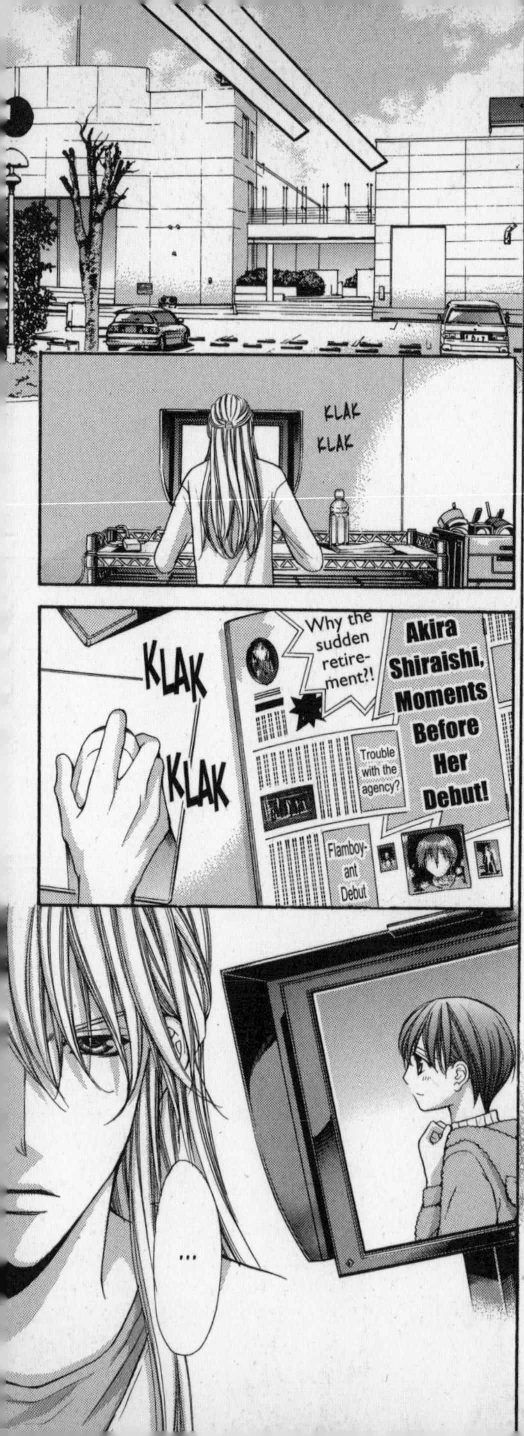
KLAK KLAK
KLAK KLAK
Akira Shiraishi, Moments Before Her Debut!
Why the sudden retirement?!
Trouble with the agency?
Flamboyant Debut
...

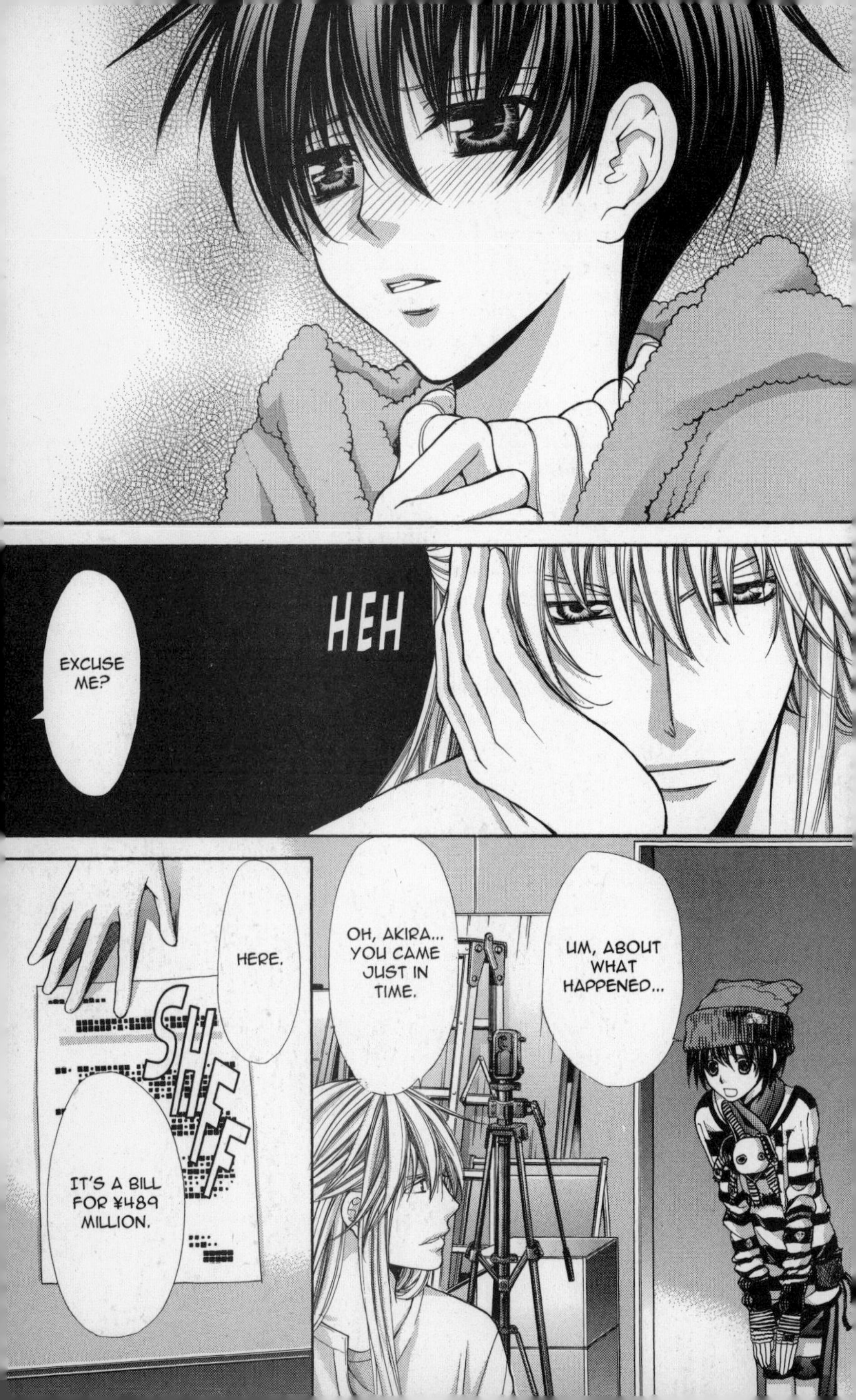
HEH
EXCUSE ME?
UM, ABOUT WHAT HAPPENED...
OH, AKIRA... YOU CAME JUST IN TIME.
HERE.
SHFF
IT'S A BILL FOR ¥489 MILLION.

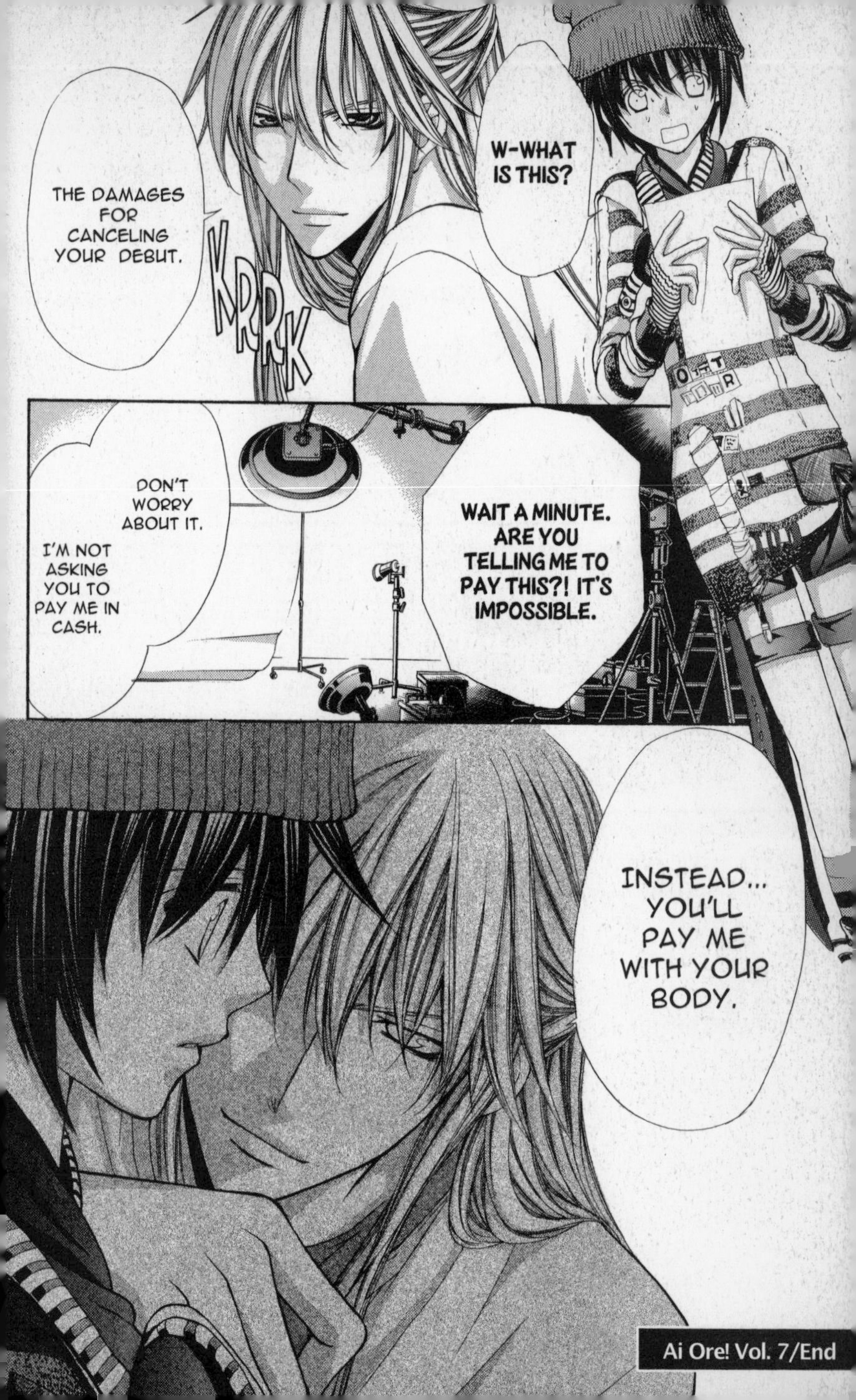
W-WHAT IS THIS?
THE DAMAGES FOR CANCELING YOUR DEBUT.
KRRK
WAIT A MINUTE. ARE YOU TELLING ME TO PAY THIS?! IT'S IMPOSSIBLE.
DON'T WORRY ABOUT IT.
I'M NOT ASKING YOU TO PAY ME IN CASH.
INSTEAD... YOU'LL PAY ME WITH YOUR BODY.

Ai Ore! Vol. 7/End

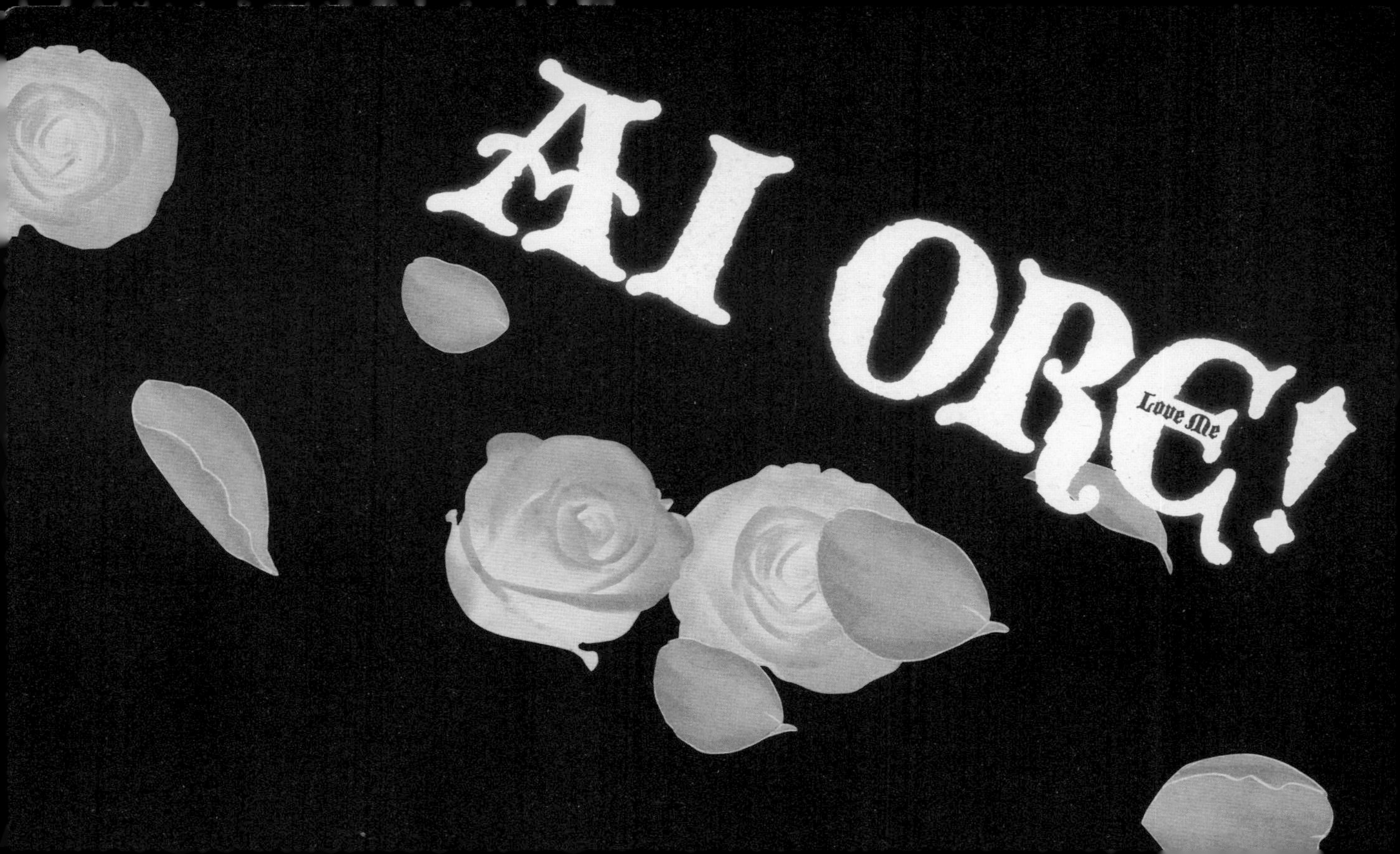
AI ORE!
Love Me

The showbiz arc is now entering the best part. Akira does all sorts of cross-dressing this time! I had a lot of fun doing it. Drawing Akira's clothes took a lot of time, so please pay attention to those as well.

-Mayu Shinjo

Mayu Shinjo was born on January 26. She is a prolific writer of shojo manga, including the series *Sensual Phrase*. Her current series include *Ai Ore!* and *Demon Love Spell*. Her hobbies are cars, shopping and taking baths. Shinjo likes The Prodigy, Nirvana, U2 and Glay.

Ai Ore!

Volume 7
Shojo Beat Edition

STORY AND ART BY
MAYU SHINJO

Translation/Tetsuichiro Miyaki
Touch-up Art & Lettering/Inori Fukuda Trant
Design/Yukiko Whitley
Editor/Nancy Thistlethwaite

Ai Ore! ~Danshikou no Hime to Joshikou no Ouji~
Volume 4
© Mayu SHINJO 2010
First published in Japan in 2010 by KADOKAWA
SHOTEN Co., Ltd., Tokyo.
English translation rights arranged with
KADOKAWA SHOTEN Co., Ltd., Tokyo.

Printed in the U.S.A.

Published by VIZ Media, LLC
P.O. Box 77010
San Francisco, CA 94107

10 9 8 7 6 5 4 3 2 1
First printing, November 2012

www.viz.com

www.shojobeat.com

⊔IZMAИGA

Read manga anytime, anywhere!

From our newest hit series to the classics you know and love, the best manga in the world is now available digitally. Buy a volume* of digital manga for your:

- iOS device (**iPad®**, **iPhone®**, **iPod® touch**) through the **VIZ Manga app**

- Android-powered device (**phone or tablet**) with a browser by visiting VIZManga.com

- **Mac or PC computer** by visiting VIZManga.com

VIZ Digital has loads to offer:

- 500+ ready-to-read volumes
- New volumes each week
- FREE previews
- Access on multiple devices! Create a log-in through the app so you buy a book once, and read it on your device of choice!*

To learn more, visit www.viz.com/apps

* Some series may not be available for multiple devices.
Check the app on your device to find out what's available.

viz.com/apps

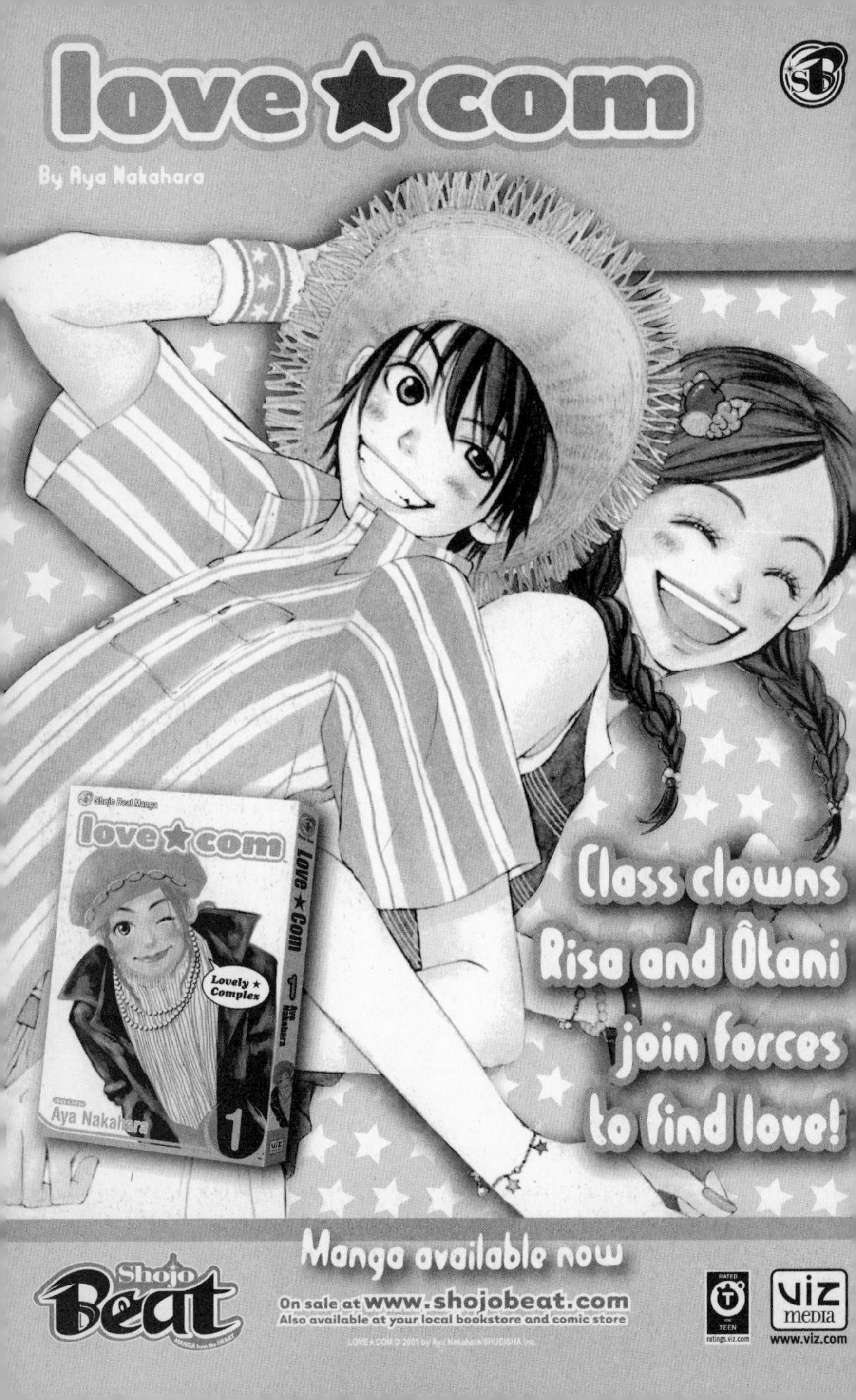
love★com
By Aya Nakahara
Shojo Beat Manga
love★com
Lovely★Complex
Love★Com
1
Aya Nakahara
Class clowns Risa and Ôtani join forces to find love!
Manga available now
Shojo Beat
On sale at www.shojobeat.com
Also available at your local bookstore and comic store
LOVE★COM © 2001 by Aya Nakahara/SHUEISHA Inc.
RATED T TEEN
ratings.viz.com
VIZ MEDIA
www.viz.com

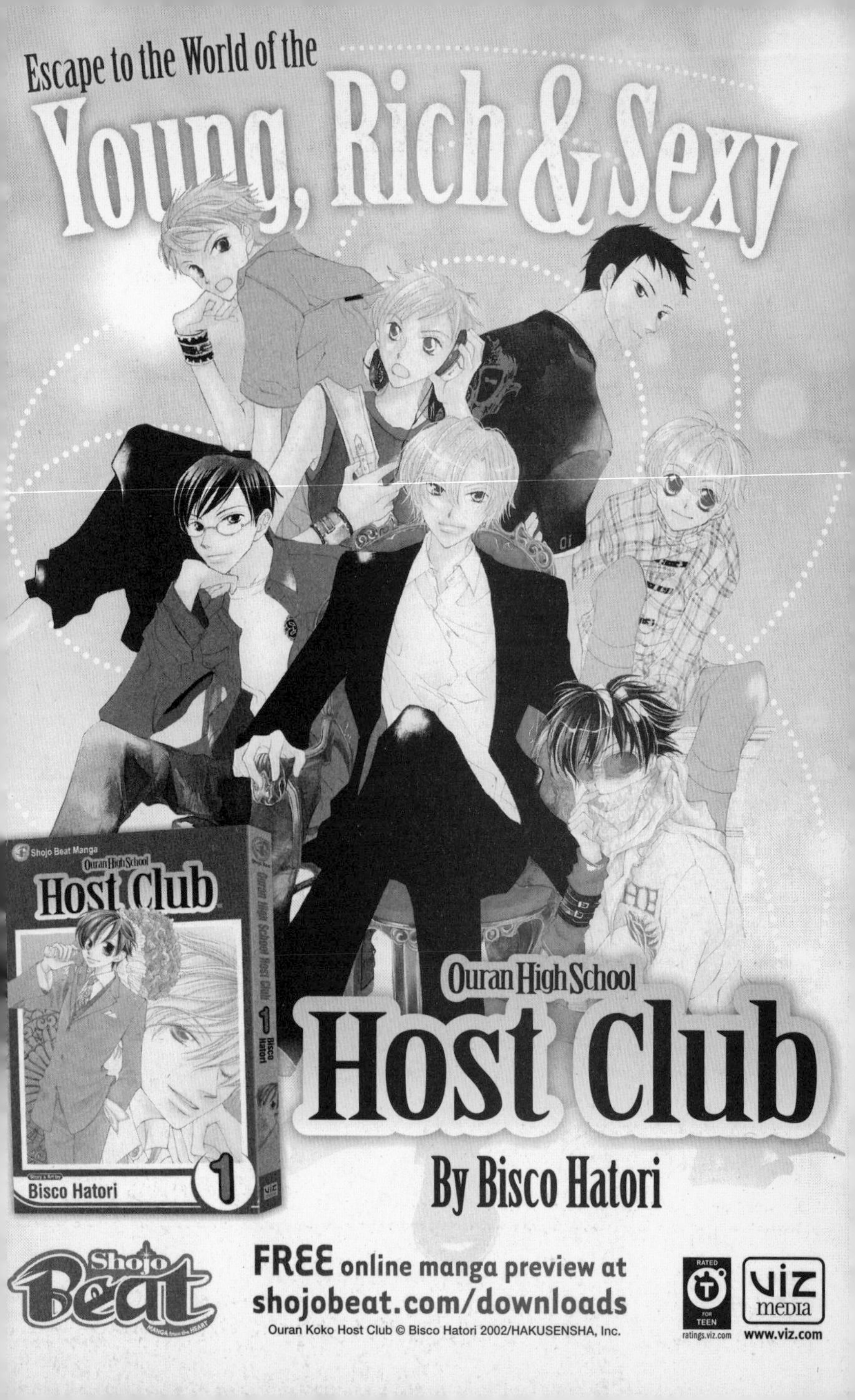
Escape to the World of the
Young, Rich & Sexy
Shojo Beat Manga
Ouran High School
Host Club
Bisco Hatori
1
Ouran High School
Host Club
By Bisco Hatori
Shojo Beat
FREE online manga preview at
shojobeat.com/downloads
Ouran Koko Host Club © Bisco Hatori 2002/HAKUSENSHA, Inc.
RATED T FOR TEEN
ratings.viz.com
VIZ media
www.viz.com

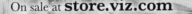

Surprise!

You may be reading the wrong way!

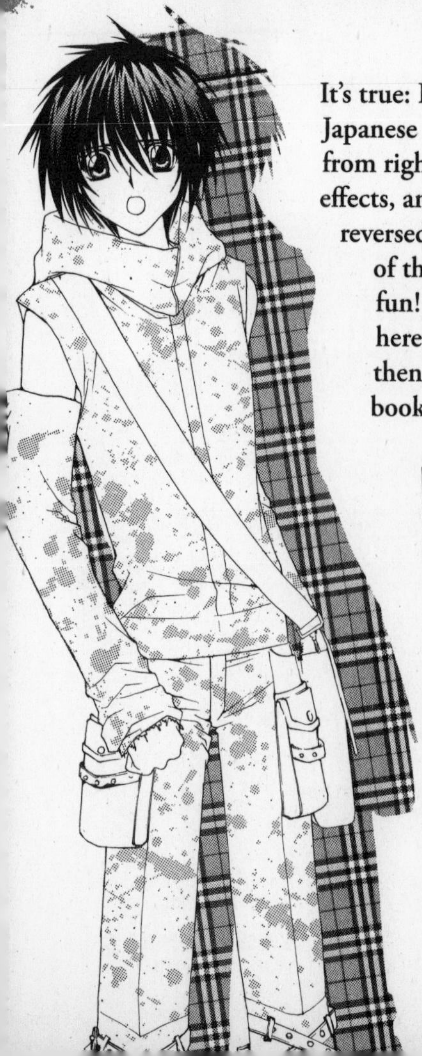

It's true: In keeping with the original Japanese comic format, this book reads from right to left—so action, sound effects, and word balloons are completely reversed. This preserves the orientation of the original artwork—plus, it's fun! Check out the diagram shown here to get the hang of things, and then turn to the other side of the book to get started!

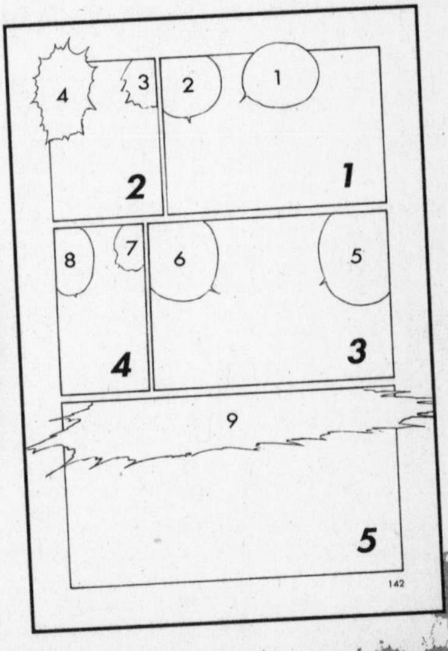
1
2
1
3
4
2
5
6
3
7
8
4
9
5
142